T0321854

Edge Computing and Computational Intelligence Paradigms for the IoT

G. Nagarajan
Sathyabama Institute of Science and Technology, India

R.I. Minu
SRM Institute of Science and Technology, India

A volume in the Advances in
Computational Intelligence and
Robotics (ACIR) Book Series

Published in the United States of America by
IGI Global
Engineering Science Reference (an imprint of IGI Global)
701 E. Chocolate Avenue
Hershey PA, USA 17033
Tel: 717-533-8845
Fax: 717-533-8661
E-mail: cust@igi-global.com
Web site: http://www.igi-global.com

Library of Congress Cataloging-in-Publication Data

Names: Nagarajan, G., 1977- editor.
Title: Edge computing and computational intelligence paradigms for the IoT /
   G. Nagarajan and R.I. Minu, editors.
Description: Hershey, PA : Engineering Science Reference, [2020] | Includes
   bibliographical references.
Identifiers: LCCN 2018055426| ISBN 9781522585558 (hardcover) | ISBN
   9781522585565 (softcover) | ISBN 9781522585572 (ebook)
Subjects: LCSH: Internet of things. | Cloud computing. | Electronic data
   processing--Distributed processing.
Classification: LCC TK5105.8857 .E34 2020 | DDC 004.67/8--dc23 LC record available at https://
lccn.loc.gov/2018055426

This book is published in the IGI Global book series Advances in Computational Intelligence and
Robotics (ACIR) (ISSN: 2327-0411; eISSN: 2327-042X)

British Cataloguing in Publication Data
A Cataloguing in Publication record for this book is available from the British Library.

All work contributed to this book is new, previously-unpublished material.
The views expressed in this book are those of the authors, but not necessarily of the publisher.

For electronic access to this publication, please contact: eresources@igi-global.com.

Advances in Computational Intelligence and Robotics (ACIR) Book Series

ISSN:2327-0411
EISSN:2327-042X

Editor-in-Chief: Ivan Giannoccaro, University of Salento, Italy

MISSION

While intelligence is traditionally a term applied to humans and human cognition, technology has progressed in such a way to allow for the development of intelligent systems able to simulate many human traits. With this new era of simulated and artificial intelligence, much research is needed in order to continue to advance the field and also to evaluate the ethical and societal concerns of the existence of artificial life and machine learning.

The **Advances in Computational Intelligence and Robotics (ACIR) Book Series** encourages scholarly discourse on all topics pertaining to evolutionary computing, artificial life, computational intelligence, machine learning, and robotics. ACIR presents the latest research being conducted on diverse topics in intelligence technologies with the goal of advancing knowledge and applications in this rapidly evolving field.

COVERAGE

- Intelligent control
- Adaptive and Complex Systems
- Artificial Intelligence
- Brain Simulation
- Synthetic Emotions
- Agent technologies
- Fuzzy Systems
- Neural Networks
- Heuristics
- Artificial Life

IGI Global is currently accepting manuscripts for publication within this series. To submit a proposal for a volume in this series, please contact our Acquisition Editors at Acquisitions@igi-global.com or visit: http://www.igi-global.com/publish/.

Titles in this Series

For a list of additional titles in this series, please visit:
http://www.igi-global.com/book-series/advances-computational-intelligence-robotics/73674

For an entire list of titles in this series, please visit:
http://www.igi-global.com/book-series/advances-computational-intelligence-robotics/73674

701 East Chocolate Avenue, Hershey, PA 17033, USA
Tel: 717-533-8845 x100 • Fax: 717-533-8661
E-Mail: cust@igi-global.com • www.igi-global.com

Editorial Advisory Board

Table of Contents

Detailed Table of Contents

R. I. Minu, SRM Institute of Science and Technology, India

G. Nagarajan, Sathyabama Institute of Science and Technology, India

In the present-day scenario, computing is migrating from the on-premises server to the cloud server and now, progressively from the cloud to Edge server where the data is gathered from the origin point. So, the clear objective is to support the execution and unwavering quality of applications and benefits, and decrease the cost of running them, by shortening the separation information needs to travel, subsequently alleviating transmission capacity and inactivity issues. This chapter provides an insight of how the internet of things (IoT) connects with edge computing.

Fabio Diniz Rossi, IFFar, Brazil

Bruno Morais Neves de Castro, IFB, Brazil

Matheus Breno Batista dos Santos, IFB, Brazil

In infrastructure as a service (IaaS), the edge computing paradigm proposes the network node distribution of storage and computing resources to ensure swift access throughout a fog environment. The edge platform landscape fragmentation requires flexible and scalable approaches. Based on the above, the most recent works highlight lightweight virtualization, the process of making any hardware shares its resources with other applications without impacting on performance issues. In this sense, this chapter conveys current concepts, techniques and open challenges of lightweight virtualization for edge computing.

Chapter 3

Pravin A., Sathyabama Institute of Science and Technology, India
Prem Jacob, Sathyabama Institute of Science and Technology, India
G. Nagarajan, Sathyabama Institute of Science and Technology, India

The IoT concept is used in various applications and it uses different devices for collecting data and processing the data. Various sets of devices such as sensors generate a large amount of data and the data will be forwarded to the appropriate devices for processing. The devices used will range from small devices to larger devices. The edge computing becomes the major role in overcoming the difficulties in cloud computing, the nearby devices are used as servers for providing better services. Most of the issues such as power consumption, data security, and response time will be addressed. The IoT plays a major role in many real-world applications. In this chapter, the basics and the use of the Edge computing concept in different applications are discussed. Edge computing can be used to increase the overall performance of the IoT. The performance of various applications in terms of edge computing and other methodologies are analyzed.

Chapter 4

V. J. K. Kishor Sonti, Sathyabama Institute of Science and Technology, India
Sundari G., Sathyabama Institute of Science and Technology, India

The emergence of a novel technology always has had a greater influence on the environmental and social conditions of an individual or society. Technology has taken social living to leaps and bounds in the past few decades. Any advancement in the technology has certainly has healthy and adverse implications on the growth engine of the society. The standard of living of the people often gets perturbed by the richness of scientific innovation in the form of technological products. In this context, the emerging innovation that is slowly conquering the social lifestyle in the recent past is internet of things (IoT). IoT offers the advantage of anytime from anywhere, helps in predicting the outcome with accuracy, the transfer of data and in the implementation of flexible electronics. The concept of smart cities to wearable electronics, high-end computing systems applications would not have been possible without IoT. There is another aspect of IoT that has greater influence on the society. The ethical and legal implications are complex to understand, and this book chapter addresses all these issues.

Chapter 5

G. Geetha, Jerusalem College of Engineering, India

The internet of things is a prime technology that promises to improve human lives. The revolution of the internet of things (IoT), along with the rapid growing of robots in many applications of everyday life, makes embedded IoT with robotics applications impact the future social growth. IoT technology aims at improving the quality of following social things similar to urban life by collecting personal data, tracking human movements, mapping them with various sources of information. The objective of the internet of things is to connect billions of things like sensors, actuators, RFID devices, and others make this technology an important aspect in our everyday life and work. The IoT could emphasize the social values as privacy, equality, trust, and individual choice and their implementation and management.

Chapter 6

Baghavathi Priya S., Rajalakshmi Engineering College, India
Vinothini Arumugam, Rajalakshmi Engineering College, India

The new conceivable rule of the future is going to be anything can be connected and will be connected over the internet. Technically, internet of things, is defined as the computing concept of connecting the devices over the internet. This adds a level of digital intelligence to the devices, enabling them to communicate without the human being involved. This chapter will discuss about the business aspects, models, and opportunities involved in IoT. The internet of things or IoT is basically about the interconnection of uniquely identifiable and programmable embedded devices within its infrastructure with the help of the internet.

Chapter 7

Nilamadhab Mishra, Debre Berhan University, Ethiopia

The progressive data science and knowledge analytic tasks are gaining popularity across various intellectual applications. The main research challenge is to obtain insight from large-scale IoE data that can be used to produce cognitive actuations for the applications. The time to insight is very slow, quality of insight is poor, and cost of insight is high; on the other hand, the intellectual applications require low cost, high quality, and real-time frameworks and algorithms to massively transform their data into cognitive values. In this chapter, the author would like to discuss the overall data science and knowledge analytic contexts on IoE data that are generated from smart edge computing devices. In an IoE-driven e-BI application, the e-consumers are using the smart edge computing devices from which a huge volume of IoE data are generated, and this creates research challenges to traditional data science and knowledge analytic mechanisms. The consumer-end IoE data are considered the potential sources to massively turn into the e-business goldmines.

Chapter 8

Vaios Koumaras, INFOLYSIS P.C., Greece
Marianna Kapari, INFOLYSIS P.C., Greece
Angeliki Papaioannou, INFOLYSIS P.C., Greece
George Theodoropoulos, INFOLYSIS P.C., Greece
Ioannis Stergiou, INFOLYSIS P.C., Greece
Christos Sakkas, INFOLYSIS P.C., Greece
Harilaos Koumaras, NCSR "Demokritos", Greece

The ubiquity of the internet led to a diverse number of devices referred to as the "things" to have online access. The internet of things (IoT) framework's infrastructure is formed by sensors, actuators, computer servers, and the communication network. Within this framework, the chapter focuses on IoT interoperability challenges through virtualization agility. The use of SDN/NFVs aims to face the 5G interoperability challenge by allowing the automatic deployment and programming of network services. Consequently, virtual gateways need to be used so that interoperability is ensured between various objects and technologies. As a result, experiments will be performed on various IoT platforms which consist of physical and virtual parts. In specific, the process will be on top of a testbed so that MQTT, CoAP, and UDP protocols will be instantiated and set up in order to provide an interoperable layer using a virtual gateway.

Chapter 9

Pradheep Kumar K., BITS Pilani, India
Srinivasan N., Sathyabama Institute of Science and Technology, India

In this chapter, an automated planning algorithm has been proposed for IoT-based applications. A plan is a sequence of activities that leads to a goal or sub-goals. The sequence of sub-goals leads to a particular goal. The plans can be formulated using forward chaining where actions lead to goals or by backward chaining where goals lead to actions. Another method of planning is called partial order planning where all actions and sub-goals are not illustrated in the plan and left incomplete. When many IoT devices are interconnected, based on the tasks and activities involved resource allocation has to be optimized. An optimal plan is one where the total plan length is minimum, and all actions consume similar quantum of resources to achieve a goal. The scheduling cost incurred by way of resource allocation would be minimum. Compared to the existing algorithms L2-Plan (Learn to Plan) and API, the algorithm developed in this work improves optimality of resources by 14% and 36%, respectively.

Chapter 10

Linoy A. Tharakan, Mar Thoma Institute of IT, India
Dhanasekaran R., Syed Ammal Engineering College, India
Suresh A., Syed Ammal Engineering College, India

The possibility of internet of things (IoT) was produced in parallel to WSNs. The term IoT was formulated by Kevin Ashton in 1999 and alludes to remarkably identifies items and their virtual portrayals in a "internet like" structure. While IoT does not accept a specific communication approach, wireless data transfer will assume a noteworthy part, and specifically, WSNs will multiply numerous applications. The small, cheap, and low-powered WSN sensors will bring the IoT to even the smallest items introduced in any sort of condition at sensible expenses. There are several methods and tactics for distributed IoT systems to prevent security attacks or contain the extent of damage of such attacks. Many of these deserve significant computational, communication, and storage requirements, which often cannot be contented by resource-constrained sensor nodes. This chapter proposes a WSN architecture with energy-efficient communication with secure data packets with a proposed LDS (Lino-Dhanasekaran, Suresh) algorithm which is useful in IoT applications.

Chapter 11

Kavitha V., SRM Institute of Science and Technology, India
Vimaladevi M., Erode Sengunthar Engineering College, India
Manavalasundaram V. K., Velalar College of Engineering and Technology, India

Agriculture is one particular sector that is prone to different problems. In India the situation of farmers is even worse. They face a lot of issues ranging from inadequate rainfall, temperature-related issues, crop diseases, animal issues, etc. It is quite a complex job for a farmer to analyze and ascertain climatic, soil, and other vital conditions for the growth of the crop every day. Also, for a farmer to predict the oncoming rainfall and its pattern and to judge suitable soil and ambient environment for crop growth requires historical records of the crop growth data of that particular region of cultivation. This chapter addresses the issues in handling big data related to agri-sector issues. Finally, a prototype model for collecting information from the IoT devices that will be placed in fields to alert the farmers about plant disease infection risk is presented.

Chapter 12

Internet of things (IoT) plays an imperative role in making the shop floor greener, safer, and more efficient. Enhancement in security and personal satisfaction can be accomplished by interfacing gadgets, vehicles, and infrastructure all around the shop floor. Best technical solutions can be attained in shop floor by assembling different stakeholders to work together. This chapter provides intelligence to garbage bins, using an IoT model with sensors that represent waste gathering management solution. It can peruse, gather, and transmit gigantic volume of information. This information is used to vigorously handle waste collection mechanism and the notification is sent to UDS department. Simulations for some cases are agreed out to examine the profits of such system over a conventional system.

With the development of promising technology, industrial, and instructive enhancement, there are greater changes in the lifestyles of people in smart cities, and also there is more chance of health problems in urban areas. The way of life of individuals in metro-urban areas with expansive volume of populace is similarly influenced by different application and administration frameworks. In this way, the majority of the urban communities are transforming into smart urban areas by receiving mechanized frameworks in every conceivable segment. Therefore, there are more health-related issues, and health hazard issues can be identified in urban areas. This chapter carries out a detailed survey of health issues and improved solutions in automated systems using big data analytics, IoT, and smart applications.

Chapter 14

In an IoT environment, smart object, an ultimate building block, enables the thing-to-thing communication in a smooth way. Huge numbers of heterogeneous objects are connected with each other for sharing data and resources with less human intervention. Sensor data can be used to provide different features by automation, which causes less manpower and less disturbances to human life. Integrating IoT technologies into healthcare domain is major research area, which provides continuous monitoring of human health condition without any interruption and provides optimal services in emergency cases. The proposed system is embedded with enhanced innovative method to predict future events based on its observations. In this chapter, a new framework for smart healthcare systems is introduced by adding intelligent decision making, data fusion, and prediction algorithms using machine learning concepts.

Chapter 15

In today's world, the quality of the crops is of utmost importance. Crops need to be effectively cared for, and steps are needed to ensure their healthy growth. Smart Irrigation is a major topic that has been implemented in certain regions, but the accumulation of various sensors is the key to the effective safety of crops. In the chapter, various sensors are being deployed and used in synchronization. The primary ones included in the system are the water level and moisture sensor, which works in correspondence with the water motor; the proximity (PIR) sensor, which works in accordance with the buzzer and the webcam; and finally, the light-dependent resistor (LDR), which works in relation with the artificial light. The analog data received from the sensors are transmitted to the raspberry-pi and then sent over the network using a Wi-Fi module to Ubidots, where the data will be analyzed, and necessary actions will be taken. The components to be used in the system will guarantee overall prolific, scalable, and ardent implementation.

Preface

The Internet of Things (IoT) creates opportunities for innovation, value chain enhancement and transformation. Identifying IoT use cases across a range of industries and measuring strategic value helps to identify what to pursue and avoid wasting resources on deployments with limited value. The Edge computing is focused on devices and technologies that are attached to the things in the Internet of Things. By Gartner by 2020, the amount spend on edge infrastructure will reach up to 18% of the total IoT infrastructure cost. The Edge computing requires prefect computational intelligence for processing power and communication capabilities on edge gateway for complete automation. Both by adding of intelligence to IoT devices and to IoT networks, sensors, actuators and everything at the edge, as well as the analysis and processing of IoT data, are moving closer to the edge.

OBJECTIVE

The main objective of this book is to provide a complete insight on the recent advancement in IoT through intelligence. In this evolving era the IoT is converting the scale and range of data from BigData to Huge data and almost to full data. IoT would be the key enabler for our digital innovation. This research book "Handbook of Research on Edge Computing and Computational Intelligence Paradigms for the IoT." will emphasize the innovation research idea of integrating intelligence in Internet of Things.

INSIDE THIS BOOK

Edge Computing and Computational Intelligence Paradigms for the IoT consist of 15 chapters. The first five chapters give an elaborative view of the general concept and critical review of Edge computing. The next five chapters gives the computational aspect of Edge computing in Internet of Things. The rest of the chapters gives the brief idea of advanced application and future trends in Edge computing. The abstract view of each 15 chapters are given below:

Chapter 1: Bridging the IoT Gap Through Edge Computing

In present day scenario the computing is migrating fast from the on-premises server to the cloud server and now, progressively from the cloud to Edge server where the data are gather from the origin point. So the clear objective is to support the execution and unwavering quality of applications and benefits, and decrease cost of running them, by shortening the separation information needs to travel, subsequently alleviating transmission capacity and inactivity issues. This chapter provides an insight of how the Internet of Things (IoT) connects with Edge computing.

Chapter 2: Lightweight Virtualization for Edge Computing

In perspective to Infrastructure as a Service (IaaS), Edge Computing paradigm proposes network node distribution of storage and computing resources to ensure swift access throughout Fog environment. Edge platform landscape fragmentation requires flexible and scalable approaches. Based on the above, the most recent works highlight Lightweight Virtualization, the process of making any hardware shares its resources with other applications without impact on performance issues. In this sense, this chapter conveys current concepts, techniques and open challenges of Lightweight Virtualization for Edge Computing.

Chapter 3: A Comprehensive Survey on Edge Computing for the IoT

The Internet of Things concept is used in various applications and it uses different devices for collecting the data and processing the data. Various set of devices such as sensors are generating a large amount of data and the data will be forwarded to the appropriate devices for processing. The devices used will be ranging from small devices to larger devices. The Edge computing becomes the major role in overcoming the difficulties in Cloud Computing, The nearby devices are used as servers for providing a better services. Most of the issues such as power consumption, data security and response time will be addressed. The Internet of Things plays a major role in many real world application. In this paper the basics and the use of Edge computing concept in different applications are discussed. The Edge Computing can be used to increase the overall performance of the Internet of Things. The performance of various applications in terms of Edge Computing and other methodology are analyzed.

Chapter 4: Need for Internet of Things

Emergence of a novel technology always had a greater influence on the environmental and social conditions of an individual or society. Technology has taken the social living to the leaps and bounds in the past few decades. Any advancement in the technology has certainly has healthy and adverse implications on the growth engine of the society. The standard of living of the people often gets perturbed by the richness of scientific innovation in the form of technological products. In this context, the emerging innovation that is slowly conquering the social life style in the recent past is Internet of Things (IoT). Internet of Things offers advantage of anytime from anywhere, helps in predicting the outcome with accuracy, transfer of data and in the implementation of flexible electronics. The concept of Smart cities to wearable electronics, high end computing systems applications would not have been possible without Internet of Things. There is another aspect of Internet of Things that has greater influence on the society. The ethical and legal implications are complex to understand and this book chapter address all these issues.

Chapter 5: Internet of Things – Impact of IoT on Human Life

The Internet of Things is a prime technology that promises to improve human lives. The revolution of the Internet of Things (IoT), along with the rapid growing of robots in many applications of everyday life, makes embedded Internet of Things with robotics applications impacts the future social growth. Internet of Things technology aims at improving the quality of following social things similar to urban life by collecting personal data, tracking human movements, mapping them with various sources of information. The objective of the Internet of Things is to connect billions of things like sensors, actuators, RFID devices and others make this technology an important aspect in our everyday life and work. The Internet of Things could emphasize the social values as privacy, equality, trust and individual choice and their implementations and managements

Chapter 6: Business Aspects, Models, and Opportunities of IoT

The new conceivable rule of the future is going to be "Anything can be connected and will be connected over the Internet. Technically, Internet of Things, is defined as, the computing concept of connecting the devices over the internet. This adds a level of digital intelligence to the devices, enabling them to communicate without the human being involved. This chapter will discuss about the business aspects, models and opportunities involved in Internet of Things. The Internet of Things or IoT is basically about the interconnection of uniquely identifiable and programmable embedded devices with in its infrastructure with the help of internet.

Chapter 7: Data Science and Knowledge Analytic Contexts on IoE Data for E-BI Application Case

The progressive data science and knowledge analytic tasks are gaining popularities across various Intellectual applications. The main research challenge is to obtain insights from large scale Internet of Things data that can be used to produce cognitive actuations for the applications. The time to insight is very slow, quality of insight is poor, and cost of insight is high, on the other hand, the Intellectual applications require low cost, high quality, and real time frameworks and algorithms to massively transform their data into cognitive values. In this chapter, the author would like to discuss the overall data science and knowledge analytic contexts on Internet of Things data that are generated from smart edge computing devices. In an Internet of Things driven e-BI application, the e-consumers are using the smart edge computing devices from where huge volume of Internet of Things data are generated and create research challenges to traditional data science and knowledge analytic mechanisms. The consumer-end Internet of Things data are considered as the potential sources to massively turn into the e-business goldmines.

Chapter 8: IoT Interoperability on Top of SDN/NFV-Enabled Networks

Nowadays, the ubiquity of the Internet led to a diverse number of devices referred to as the "things" to have online access. The Internet of Things (IoT) framework's infrastructure is formed by sensors, actuators, compute servers and the communication network. Within this framework, the chapter focuses on Internet of Things interoperability challenges through virtualization agility. The use of SDN/NFVs aims to face the 5G interoperability challenge by allowing the automatic deployment and programming of network services. Consequently, virtual gateways need to be used so that interoperability is ensured between various objects and technologies. As a result, experiments will be performed on various Internet of Things platforms which consist of physical and virtual parts. In specific, the process will be on top of a testbed so that MQTT, CoAP and UDP protocols will be instantiated and set up in order to provide an interoperable layer using a virtual gateway.

Chapter 9: Modified Backward Chaining Algorithm Using Artificial Intelligence Planning IoT Applications – AI Planning for IoT Applications

In this work, an automated planning algorithm has been proposed for Internet of Things based applications. A plan is a sequence of activities, which leads to a goal or sub-goals. The sequence of sub-goals leads to a particular goal. The plans can be formulated using forward chaining where actions lead to goals or by backward chaining where goals lead to actions. Another method of planning is called partial order planning where all actions and sub-goals are not illustrated in the plan and left incomplete. When many Internet of Things devices are interconnected, based on the tasks and activities involved resource allocation has to be optimized. An optimal plan is one where the total plan length is minimum and all actions consume similar quantum of resources to achieve a goal.

The scheduling cost incurred by way of resource allocation would be minimum. Compared to the existing algorithms L2-Plan (Learn To Plan) and API, the algorithm developed in this work improves optimality of resources by 14% and 36% respectively.

Chapter 10: Data Security in WSN-Based Internet of Things Architecture Using LDS Algorithm – WSN Architecture With Energy Efficient Communication

The possibility of internet of things (IoT) was produced in parallel to WSNs. The term Internet of Things was formulated by Kevin Ashton in 1999 and alludes to remarkably identifies items and their virtual portrayals in a "internet like" structure. While Internet of Things does not accept a specific communication approach, Wireless data transfer will assume a noteworthy part, and specifically, WSNs will multiply numerous applications. The small, cheap and low powered WSN sensors will bring the Internet of Things to even the smallest items introduced in any sort of condition, at sensible expenses. There are several methods and tactics for distributed Internet of Things systems to prevent security attacks or contain the extent of damage of such attacks. Many of these deserve significant computational, communication, and storage requirements, which often cannot be contented by resource-constrained sensor nodes. This chapter proposes a WSN architecture with energy efficient communication with secure data packets with a proposed LDS (Lino-Dhanasekaran, Suresh) algorithm which is useful in Internet of Things applications

Chapter 11: Intelligent Pest Control Using Internet of Things Design and Future Directions

Agriculture is one particular sector which is prone to different problems, In India the situation of farmers are even worse, they face a lot of issues ranging from inadequate rainfall, temperature related issues, crop diseases, animal issues etc. it is quite a complex job for a farmer to analyze and ascertain climatic, soil and other vital conditions for the growth of the crop every day. Also for a farmer to predict the oncoming rainfall and its pattern and to judge suitable soil and ambient environment for crop growth require historical records of the crop growth data of that particular region of cultivation. This chapter addresses the issues in handling big data related to agri-sector issues. Finally, a prototype model for collecting information from the Internet of Things devices which will be placed in fields and it alerts the farmers about plant disease infection risk.

Chapter 12: Self-Alerting Garbage Bins Using Internet of Things

Internet of Things (IoT) plays an imperative role in making the shop floor greener, safer, and more efficient. Enhancement in security and personal satisfaction can be accomplished by interfacing gadgets, vehicles and infra structure all around the shop floor. Best technical solutions can be attained in shop floor by assembling different stakeholders to work together. This paper provides intelligence to garbage bins, using an Internet of Things model with sensors that represent waste gathering management solution. It can peruse, gather, and transmit gigantic volume of information. This information is used to vigorously handle waste collection mechanism and the notification is send to uds department. Simulations for some cases are agreed out to examine the profits of such system over a conventional system.

Chapter 13: Resolution of Issues and Health Improvement Using Big Data and IoT

With the development of promising technology, industrial and instructive enhancement there are greater change in life style of people in smart city and also there is more chance of various health problem in urban areas. The way of life of individuals in metro urban areas with expansive volume of populace is similarly influenced by different application and administration frameworks. In this way presently the majority of the urban communities are transforming into smart urban areas by receiving mechanized frameworks in every conceivable segment. Therefore there is more number of health related issues and health hazard issues can be identified in urban areas. This article carries out a detailed survey of health issues and improved solutions in automated systems using Big Data Analytics, Internet of Things and Smart Applications.

Chapter 14: Enhancement of IoT Smart Hospital System Survey Paper – Smart Hospital Survey Work

In an Internet of Things environment, smart object an ultimate building block enables the thing to thing communication in smooth way. Huge numbers of Heterogeneous objects are connected with each other for sharing data and resources with less human intervention. These sensor data can be used to provide different features by automation which causes less man power and less disturbances to human life. Nowadays integrating Internet of Things technologies into Healthcare Domain is major research area, which provides continues Monitoring of Human Health Condition without any interruption and provide optimal services in emergency cases also. The proposed System is embedded with enhanced innovative method to predict future events based on its observations. In this work a new framework for Smart Healthcare Systems is introduced by adding Intelligent Decision Making, Data Fusion and Prediction algorithms using Machine Learning Concepts.

Chapter 15: Autonomous Crop Care System Using Internet of Things

In today's world, the quality of the crops is of utmost importance which is a major source of food for billions of people. Crops need to be effectively cared and steps are needed to ensure their healthy growth. Smart Irrigation is a major topic which has been implemented in certain regions but the accumulation of various sensors is the key to the effective safety of crops. In the proposed work various sensors are being deployed and used in synchronization .The primary ones included in the system are the water level and moisture sensor which works in correspondence with the water motor, the proximity (PIR) sensor which works in accordance with the buzzer and the webcam, and finally, the Light Dependent Resistor (LDR) which works in relation with the artificial light. The analog data received from the sensors are transmitted to the raspberry-pi and then sent over the network using a Wi-Fi module to Ubidots, where the data will be analyzed and necessary actions will be taken. The components to be used in the system will guarantee overall prolific, scalable and ardent implementation.

Overall this book provides a complete insight regarding the budding technology Edge Computing and its application.

TARGET AUDIENCE

The book would serve broad audience including researchers, academics, advanced students, and working professionals who are interested in exploring the limits in the field of Internet of Things, Edge computing, computational intelligence, healthcare, Irrigation, environmental, governmental, defense and network companies.

Acknowledgment

We cannot express enough thanks to my review committee for their continued support and encouragement. We offer my sincere appreciation for the learning opportunities provided by my committee.

Our completion of this project could not have been accomplished without the support of Ms. Jordan Tepper, Development Coordinator, IGI Global and her team.

At the outset, we express my deepest sense of gratitude and reverence to our parent and son, N. Hariharan and N. Sreeharan. Thank you for allowing me time away from you to research and write.

Chapter 1
Bridging the IoT Gap Through Edge Computing

R. I. Minu
SRM Institute of Science and Technology, India

G. Nagarajan
Sathyabama Institute of Science and Technology, India

ABSTRACT

In the present-day scenario, computing is migrating from the on-premises server to the cloud server and now, progressively from the cloud to Edge server where the data is gathered from the origin point. So, the clear objective is to support the execution and unwavering quality of applications and benefits, and decrease the cost of running them, by shortening the separation information needs to travel, subsequently alleviating transmission capacity and inactivity issues. This chapter provides an insight of how the internet of things (IoT) connects with edge computing.

DOI: 10.4018/978-1-5225-8555-8.ch001

INTRODUCTION

Electronic gadgets connected to one another and doing the magic is the key concept of Internet of Things (IOT). Mark Hung (2018), VP of Gartner sited that the magic word (IoT) had reached beyond the hype and started to operate in many phases. They insist all the major leaders to practice and provide complete insight about it. This technology was first introduced in the year 1999 as cited by Shi, Cao, Zhang, Li, and Xu (2016). At present this technology is used to many domain such as smart agriculture, smart city, smart Government, smart healthcare and the list goes on. According to the Cisco datasheet (Cisco Knowledge Network, 2014) and Evans (2011) that by 2019, more than 45% of data created, processed, analyzed would be from IoT devices. They had given a figure of 500 zettabytes of data will be generated by the IoT devices. So this much data is needed to be stored and analyzed in the Cloud.

BASIC STRUCTURE OF INTERNET OF THINGS

Processing of this much amount of data is one of the challenging parts. In IoT the cloud computing is one of the major backbones, but due to uncontrolled data flow it requires some intelligent service. One of the evolving technologies to speed-up the procedure is the Edge Computing. The basic differences between cloud and Edge computing is that, in cloud the processing of data done in a centralized manner. As shown in the Figure 1 the device generated data are taken directly in cloud and processed and the output is sent back to the actuator. Where is Edge computing as shown in Figure 2, the data are pushed, collected and analyzed near the IoT devices.

WHY WE NEED EDGE COMPUTING?

To answer the question of why we need again a new Edge computing is listed in Figure 3. The three main reasons of why we prefer Edge computing.

Edge figuring is ideal for IoT for three reasons. Immediately, in light of the way that the data is taken care of nearer the motivation behind root,

Figure 1. IoT basic schematic without edge

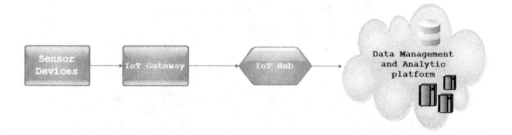

Figure 2. IoT basic schematic with edge

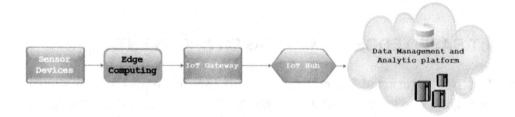

you diminish the inactivity among devices and data getting ready layer, along these lines engaging speedier response and fundamental authority. This in like manner suggests the costs related to ingesting a considerable measure of data in the cloud are broadly lower and framework limit is opened up for various exceptional weights.

Furthermore, as edge enrolling suggests the data is limited, should any individual contraption breakdown, it doesn't have a pound on effect on others as needs be. Holding the data locally similarly gives a lift to consistence and security as there are fewer open entryways for software engineers to get to all data immediately.

Finally, by circling and securing your data into humbler data vaults, you can even more adequately section creating examination into specific sorts of gathering and geographic locale as you don't have to pull data removes from a bound together corporate database. This makes data accumulation stunningly less complex and empowers you to give progressing examination explicitly to overseers specifically locale.

Figure 3. Need for edge computing

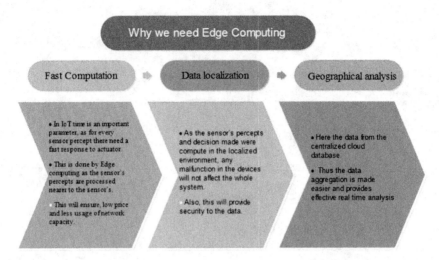

IoT BASED EDGE COMPUTING ENVIRONMENT

The list of Internet of Thing based Edge computing environment is shown in Figure 4. The considered parameters are networking technologies, computing paradigms Attributes, Computing nodes and Application. The networking technologies used by an IoT devices would be mainly

Figure 4. IoT based edge computing environment

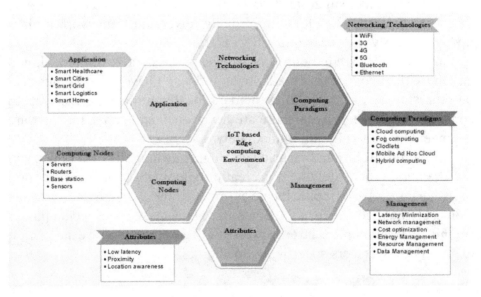

Table 1. Summary of existing technology

Model	Author	Contributions
Cloudlet	• Satyanarayanan, Bahl, Caceres, & Davies (2009) • Satyanarayanan, Schuster, Ebling, Fettweis, Flinck, Joshi, & Sabnani (2015)	• A new cloudlet-based architecture for overcoming the technical obstacles in mobile computing. • An open ecosystem based on the concept of cloudlets supporting many exciting mobile applications.
Mobile edge computing	• Mobile-edge Computing Industry Initiative-ETSI (2015) • Mao, You, Zhang, Huang, & Letaief (2017) • Mach, & Becvar (2017)	• An overview of MEC definition, architectural blueprint, requirements, and challenges of MEC as well as the objectives of the MEC initiative. • A comprehensive survey of the state-of-the-art MEC research focusing on joint radio and computational resource management. • A comprehensive survey of major use cases and reference scenarios, current advancement in standardization of MEC, and research on computation offloading.
Fog computing	• Chiang, & Zhang (2016) • OpenFog Consortium (2016)	• A summary of the opportunities and challenges of fog computing focusing primarily on the networking context of IoT. • An overview of Fog computing definition, reference architecture, use cases and challenges for fog computing as well as the future research and work.
Comprehensive Surveys	• Satyanarayanan (2017) • Klas (2015) • Hassan, Gillani, Ahmed, Yaqoob, & Imran (2018)	• An overview of edge computing definition, origin and background, challenges, and applications. Discussions of the future research directions of edge computing. • A comprehensive comparison of three approaches: fog computing, MEC and Cloudlet. Discussions of further work and research in order to get concepts like Fog, MEC and Cloudlets adopted by industry. • A comprehensive tutorial of three state-of-threat edge computing technologies, namely MEC, cloudlets, and fog computing. A comparison of standardization efforts, principles, architectures, and applications for these three technologies. The difference between mobile edge computing and fog computing from the • View point of RANs.

wireless communication as most of the sensors would be deployed in remote areas were wired connection is impossible to connected. So the general technologies used to get connected are Bluetooth, Wi-Fi, ZigBee, 3G, 4G, 5G, and so on. Various paradigms were used in IoT to provide all kind of services. Cloud computing is used to store and retrieve data generated by an IoT devices. To reduce the latency, the Fog computing is used to provide data for the instant decision making. The other kind of computing is used to provide better computing. At different service level, different kind of management strategy were used to maintain the flow of process. The first management to be deal with latency management, with respect to IoT, the signals diverted to the actuator should be less. If the processing time is more that kind of system never help the Smart World.

Table 2. Comparison of different computing technique

Features	FOG computing	Edge computing	Cloud computing
Availability of server nodes	Availability high range of servers	Less scalable than fog computing	Availability of few servers
Type of services	Distributed and localized limited and special for specific domain	Mostly uses in cellular mobile networks	Worldwide and global services
Location identification	Yes	Yes	NO
Mobility features	Provided and fully supported	Provided and partially supported	Limited
Node devices	Routers, Switches, Access Points, Gateways	Servers running in base stations	Data Center in a box
Node location	Varying between End Devices and Cloud	Radio Network Controller/Macro Base Station	Local/Outdoor installation
Software Architecture	Fog Abstraction Layer based	Mobile Orchestrator based	Cloudlet Agent based
Context awareness	Medium	High	Low
Proximity	One or Multiple Hops	One Hops	One Hops
Access Mechanisms	Bluetooth, Wi-Fi, Mobile Networks	Mobile	Wi-Fi
Internode Communication	Supported	Partial	Partial
Real-time interaction	Supported	Supported	Supported
Real-time response	Highest	Highest	Lower
Big data storage & duration	Short duration and targeted to specific area	Depends on the scenario of services and applications	Life time duration as its managing for big data
Big data analytic capacity and computation quality	Life time duration as its managing for big data	Short time capacity for prioritized computing facilities	Long-time capacity only with categorization computing facilities
Working environment & positions	Streets, roadside, home, malls, field tracks (e.g., every Internet existing areas)	Deployed by the specific services provider in specific indoor areas	Indoors with massive components at cloud service provider owned place
Architectural design	Distributed	Distributed	Centralized
Number of users facilitated	Locally related fields (e.g., IIoT, STL devices)	Specific related fields (e.g., mobile users)	General Internet connected users
Major service provided	Cisco IOx, Intel	Cellular network companies	Google, Amazon, IBM, and Microsoft Azure

As in IoT, the sensors would flourish with enormous amount of data, it requires data management, network management, resource management and cost optimization management. Next comes the attributes, for different project environment various set of attributes is required, in the figure few of them are listed. For effective data transfer, it required several kinds of nodes. The major computing nodes are server, router, wireless sensor nodes, and so on. Then comes the major component application. Smart Healthcare, in this application there are various product are now available such as Fitbit, smart syringe, smart pill, smart BP controller and so on. Smart cities, this is one of the Global projects of all developed and developing countries. Under Smart cities comes the Smart Hospital, Smart Government, Smart Road management, Smart School, Smart Agriculture, and so on. Nagarajan and Minu (2018) had explained the usage of Smart IoT devices in agriculture. Smart grids are one of the answers for today's Energy management crises.

SUMMARY

The Edge computing is one of the budding technology which will enrich the Internet of Things. The overall summary of all the technology used in Edge computing with respect to IoT is briefed in Table 1 and Table 2.

REFERENCES

Chiang, M., & Zhang, T. (2016). Fog and IoT: An overview of research opportunities. *IEEE Internet Things J.*, *3*(6), 854–864. doi:10.1109/JIOT.2016.2584538

Cisco Knowledge Network. (2014). Cisco global cloud index: Forecast and methodology 2014–2019 [Data file]. Retrieved from https://www.cisco.com/Cisco_GCI_Deck_2014-2019_for_CKN__10NOV2015_.pdf

Evans, D. (2011). The Internet of Things: How the next evolution of the Internet is changing everything. CISCO.

Hassan, N., Gillani, S., Ahmed, E., Yaqoob, I., & Imran, M. (2018). The Role of Edge Computing in Internet of Things. *IEEE Communications Magazine*, (99), 1–6.

Hung, M. (2018). Control your IoT Destiny: Insights of IoT. *Gartner*. Retrieved from https://www.gartner.com/en/information-technology/insights/internet-of-things

Mach, P., & Becvar, Z. (2017). Mobile edge computing: A survey on architecture and computation offloading. *IEEE Communications Surveys and Tutorials*, *19*(3), 1628–1656. doi:10.1109/COMST.2017.2682318

Mao, Y., You, C., Zhang, J., Huang, K., & Letaief, K. B. (2017). A survey on mobile edge computing: The communication perspective. *IEEE Communications Surveys and Tutorials*, *19*(4), 2322–2358. doi:10.1109/COMST.2017.2745201

Mobile-edge Computing Industry Initiative-ETSI. (2015),Mobile-edge Computing Introductory Technical White Paper [Data Sheet]. Retrieved from, https://portal.etsi.org/

Nagarajan, G., & Minu, R. I. (2018). Wireless soil monitoring sensor for sprinkler irrigation automation system. *Wireless Personal Communications*, *98*(2), 1835–1851. doi:10.100711277-017-4948-y

OpenFog Consortium. (2016). OpenFog Reference Architecture for Fog Computing [Data Sheet]. Retrieved from https://www.openfogconsortium.org

Satyanarayanan, M. (2017). The emergence of edge computing. *Computer*, *50*(1), 30–39. doi:10.1109/MC.2017.9

Satyanarayanan, M., Bahl, P., Caceres, R., & Davies, N. (2009). The case for VM-base cloudlets in mobile computing. *Pervasive Comput.*, *8*(4), 14–23. doi:10.1109/MPRV.2009.82

Satyanarayanan, M., Schuster, R., Ebling, M., Fettweis, G., Flinck, H., Joshi, K., & Sabnani, K. (2015). An open ecosystem for mobile-cloud convergence. *IEEE Communications Magazine*, *53*(3), 63–70. doi:10.1109/MCOM.2015.7060484

Shi, W., Cao, J., Zhang, Q., Li, Y., & Xu, L. (2016). Edge computing: Vision and challenges. *IEEE Internet of Things Journal*, *3*(5), 637–646. doi:10.1109/JIOT.2016.2579198

Chapter 2
Lightweight Virtualization for Edge Computing

Fabio Diniz Rossi

iD https://orcid.org/0000-0002-2450-1024
IFFar, Brazil

Bruno Morais Neves de Castro
IFB, Brazil

Matheus Breno Batista dos Santos
IFB, Brazil

ABSTRACT

In infrastructure as a service (IaaS), the edge computing paradigm proposes the network node distribution of storage and computing resources to ensure swift access throughout a fog environment. The edge platform landscape fragmentation requires flexible and scalable approaches. Based on the above, the most recent works highlight lightweight virtualization, the process of making any hardware shares its resources with other applications without impacting on performance issues. In this sense, this chapter conveys current concepts, techniques and open challenges of lightweight virtualization for edge computing.

DOI: 10.4018/978-1-5225-8555-8.ch002

INTRODUCTION

Internet of Things (IoT) development technologies surrounds the world promoting massive impact on numerous industries and fields of humanity (Vaquero & Rodero-Merino, 2014). Strictly linked to sensor networks, IoT huge capacity of data collection brought new insights into the world, from connecting ordinary objects to build a vast network of sensors.

Based on the market, IoT brings meaning to the concept of ubiquitous connectivity for businesses, governments, and customers with its innate management, monitoring, and analytics. This IoT distinct, innovative potential swiftly embraced Cloud computing comprehensive services exponential growth, suddenly proving its utility on automating ordinary tasks (Galante & Bona, 2012) and, consequently, generating tons of data to be interpreted in an online environment.

The exponential requisition of the cloud-based centralized gateway infrastructure prompted inefficiency to the real-time services supply chain, where delay barrier constraints the development of self-driven cars and other low-latency IoT initiatives. This new obstacle promoted scientific approaches around edge computing concept of network node distributed resources intermediate layer, where the servers reversely dispatch data processing to constrained devices deployed at the network edge, providing low-latency domain to data generators (Shi, Cao, Zhang, Li, & Xu, 2016).

Figure 1 demonstrates the entire Fog computing architecture, where we have multiple sensors distributed geographically, searching data from various sources, and sending such data in real time to be processed. On the other hand, a set of servers running cloud services must receive such a massive amount of data and turn it into information. In order to bring cloud services closer to customers (in this case represented by IoT sensors), parts of the cloud services can pre-process on intermediate network devices, known as edge devices (Shi & Dustdar, 2016).

Supported by these concepts, many past works highlight the use of virtualization on top of edge devices due to its potential elasticity. Despite traditional hardware and software configuration for a dedicated server, virtualization allows running multiple OS and applications over same hardware. Being Lightweight Virtualization more adaptable and versatile than traditional Hypervisors techniques, it has the independence of OS base and works without virtualization of hardware. This somewhat disruptive

Figure 1. Fog architecture

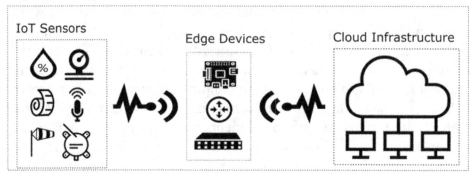

technology can lead to faster initialization, lower system overhead and, lastly, excellent energy efficiency to the nodes (Xavier, Neves, Rossi, Ferreto, Lange, & De Rose, 2013).

Over the last decade, the proposal of Lightweight Virtualization implementation to edge-driven IoT has become popular as a feature to fulfill network scalability, multi-tenancy, and privacy. A direct benefit that emerges from employing Lightweight Virtualization in the IoT edge domain is avoiding the strict dependency on any given technology or use case (Morabito et al., 2018), which, in IoT heterogeneous environment can provide the flexibility to connect to any device and distribute computational and database services around the edge network seamlessly.

Virtualization support enables the possibility of Network Function Virtualization (NFV) over such devices. Based on this, the service provider can deploy various types of network and computing services in the form of micro clouds. Virtualization on edge devices minimizes investment as there is no need for a massive centralized infrastructure. Services are instantiated depending on consumer demand. Also, the core infrastructure does not need significant modifications to accommodate any service (Chiosi, Clarke, Willis, Reid, Feger, Bugenhagen, & Benitez, 2012; Morabito et al., 2018; Vaquero & Rodero-Merino, 2014; Chiosi, Clarke, Willis, Reid, Feger, Bugenhagen, & Benitez, 2012).

NFV over edge devices can directly offer network failover, security in the form of channel encryption with the consumer, WAN optimization where there are low link speed channels, and analysis and diagnosis based on network traffic for troubleshooting purposes or package prioritization. In the sense of micro clouds, the computing node is migrated from a centralized infrastructure to the edge device, facilitating the delivery of the service to the consumer, regarding the quality of service (Chiosi et al., 2012; Vaquero & Rodero-Merino, 2014; Chiosi et al., 2012) .

This chapter presents the following contributions:

- The integration of lightweight virtualization within edge computing.
- The importance of edge computing devices regarding the flexibility of running lightweight virtualization and sharing of physical resources.
- A discussion of the challenges, opportunities, and trends for lightweight virtualization and edge computing.

From the above, lightweight virtualization is an approach to implement applications in a very different scenario, in which a system run on top of hardware sharing processing power and storage with the operational system base and other applications in virtualization, requiring fewer devices dedicated to one specific task. Edge computing best use relies on lightweight virtualization, transforming intermediary server in a more useful machine without upgrades or top of the line hardware.

This chapter discusses the advantages offered by the many kinds of lightweight virtualization, besides the importance and simultaneously of edge computing in a Fog environment. Afterward, the authors will summarize the work, making it possible to view challenges, trends, and future research directions.

VIRTUALIZATION LANDSCAPE

First, this section introduces the virtualization and a quick history of its evolution. Virtualization consists of providing a platform that supports concurrent execution of multiple operating systems or applications in a parallel and isolated manner. Due to the speed of deploying a large number of virtual machines (VMs), this is the base technology for several other computational paradigms. The elasticity and fault tolerance of virtualized environments allow the fulfillment of customer requests in order to maintain the agreed quality of service. Therefore, virtualization is presented as a fundamental component to cloud infrastructures, offering such features.

However, more traditional virtualization technologies cause overhead on application performance (Morabito, 2017). It is mainly caused by (1) virtualization layer, which must translate all application-level instructions to the host operating system, and (2) a ring-blocking system, which controls all input and output data to be interpreted by virtualization layer. Although there is a loss of performance in this virtualization model, there are some features that still hold them as an ideal choice, such as resource isolation.

These are essential requirements when it comes to embedded platforms such as edge devices. Such devices have limited hardware regarding design, which limits them in resources as well. Also, their applications are usually time-based, which characterizes them as real-time designed equipment, operating systems, and applications.

Thus, in order to reduce the performance overhead caused by the more traditional virtualization proposals, the containers technology was proposed. Container-based virtualization runs at the operating system level, and all VMs share a single kernel, which reduces the overhead commonly caused by traditional virtualization technologies (Xavier et al., 2013). Therefore, containers offer almost native performance to the supported applications. However, there is a loss of resource isolation, since the kernel can not limit the use of slices of distributed resources between VMs. Also, since containers run on the same Kernel, that is, the entire environment must run on the same operating system.

To address environments that must maintain heterogeneous operating systems, a new virtualization proposal emerges, called microservice architecture (unikernels). This paradigm consists of small operating systems compiled for specific purposes that are staggered and managed as processes by the host operating system (Morabito, Cozzolino, Ding, & Beijar, 2018). As a result, VMs can be delivered faster due to reduced system image size, resulting in scalability improvements, ease of maintenance of applications, and reduced instantiation time of VMs.

All previous virtualization proposals allow charging based on the number of resources used versus the time. Thus, until then, the service providers had their costs tied to the number of resources required to meet the requests of customers.

A new virtualization proposal called serverless (also called Function as a Service - FaaS) allows billing only based on the code running in the cloud environment. Serverless has been widely adopted due to the recent shift from enterprise application architectures to containers and microservices. This new paradigm provides developers with a simplified programming model for creating cloud applications that abstracts most operational concerns. This way, when Serverless is adopted, the service customer has no control over the resources where part of the application is running, nor does it need to create VMs or network configurations.

Through this new paradigm, a computing model is envisaged in which all resources are effectively grouped, including hardware, operating systems, and runtime environments. Also, Serverless enables developers to deploy large applications in a variety of small roles, allowing application components to be scaled individually.

Besides, when this paradigm is adopted, collections are only performed based on the number of requests and the execution time of the functions. Therefore, this characteristic can generate significant cost reduction when compared to the traditional model of service deployment through VMs.

Several papers in the literature present serverless computing emphasize that the Serverless paradigm was presented as a means to (1) introduce more cost efficiencies, (2) reduce configuration overhead, and (3) rapidly increase an application's ability to scale over the resources of the cloud. Based on this, the authors provide an overview and feature analysis of various serverless computing platforms from multiple providers, such as AWS Lambda and Google Cloud functions (Villamizar, Garcés, Ochoa, Castro, Salamanca, Verano, & Lang, 2017).

All of these virtualization models can and do apply to fog and edge computing environments. This chapter will present each type of virtualization and its applicability on fog environments and edge computing devices individually, discussing, in the end, some open challenges.

LIGHTWEIGHT VIRTUALIZATION CONCEPTS

The idea of virtualization is not new. The IBM System 360 of the 1960s already offered to partition between operating systems. However, virtualization is a technology that has remained dormant due to the need for powerful computational resources for the satisfactory execution of several VMs (Barham, Dragovic, Fraser, Hand, Harris, Ho, & Warfield, 2003).

The increase in the potential of computing resources, especially regarding processor speed, provides an environment conducive to the emergence of Xen in 2004. It is a proposal that allows the execution of multiple guests operating systems on a para-virtualized base system, and which offers the execution of virtualized applications, although it presents a small loss of performance (Barham et al., 2003). Several other proposals followed the same path of Xen, only with modifications between virtualization or paravirtualization, as in the case of VMWare, Bochs, VirtualBox, and so on.

Due to the overhead caused by the virtualization layers of previous paradigms, newer lighter virtualization proposals are beginning to be studied. The LXC (Linux Containers) project starts in 2008, delivering virtualized application performance equal to or very close to its native environment runs. Stable versions of Containers have emerged almost ten years later and currently offer high performance, although they have a direct negative implication on other metrics, especially on the issue of resource isolation (Xavier et al., 2013).

At this point, the embedded systems community focuses their attention on the capabilities that virtualization can deliver for environments that require real-time responses but at the same time would like to run stand-alone applications in parallel or even migrate applications from one device to another.

In the same period, new proposals for virtualization arise, such as unikernels and serverless computing. The first consists of a kernel only recompiled with the minimum necessary for the application to execute correctly. It creates a small operating system and application image, which can instantiate how many replicas are needed to meet customer demand. Serverless allows part of the application code - the most massive part - to run outside the embedded device, usually having the workload sent to a function that is located in an external cloud environment.

Typically a Telco company offers services directed to its customer, as a firewall, DNS, VPN, and other services. It usually has dedicated hardware to each service spread along its network. This approach turned out to be painful to set up and to maintain considering how heterogeneous and diverse can be the devices, systems, and integration between them. Network Function Virtualization (NFV) is born as an alternative to the traditional model, suggesting generic network devices, but management over which service (and where and when it) should be deployed using lightweight virtualization (Vaquero & Rodero-Merino, 2014).

In partnership with NFV, the idea of software defined networks is really useful for NFV considering its capabilities of separate planes of control and data forwarding. Software defined networks are based on the separation of the data planes and control of the network, which refers to the set of functions, logically centralized in network controllers, which influences how the packets are routed to destinations in the network by elements that it defines to accomplish such task through a well-defined communication interface. In this way, the intelligence of the network concentrates mostly in the control plane, which can potentially harbor any network application that allows the implementation of better strategies for routing traffic by many actuators in different granularities (Chiosi et al., 2012). Consequently, software defined networks can establish efficient algorithms in the data plane to act in the load balancing in links, having as political criteria that contain any requirements that are useful to this task.

It is needed to clarify that Software Defined Networks isn't dependent on NFV and vice versa, although, approaches relying on both can have fuller exploitation of resources available and better execution. NFV benefits include, but aren't limited to:

- Reducing equipment cost and power consumption.
- Increased speed of time-to-market, reducing the innovation cycle.
- Multiple environments are running simultaneously, allowing production, testing, and reference development workspace running on the same conditions.
- An offer of services and adjustments based on geography and consumer profile.
- Open the market for new players and more innovative takes on software development.
- Multi-tenancy for secure separation of administrative domains.
- Maximize the efficiency of the network.

Building NFV applications on the hypervisor model allow orchestration software (e.g., vSphere, OpenStack, CloudStack) to select, configure, and initialize VMs and hosts according to high-level service operations for specifying application profiles with specific settings depending on your location and network service. In this way, the tasks of orchestration and management become flexible to the point of forming chains of services easily by programming elements at the edges of the network.

The major premise of NFV is the high-volume support of low-cost servers playing a variety of roles to make efficient resource allocation dynamic to different VNFs. Addressing the efficient use of virtualized resources requires that they are scalable to the dimensions of the services offered by VNFs as well as that they, defined in an extensive heterogeneity (e.g., firewall, DPI, BRAS), can use data plan applications depending on the need (Bremler-Barr, Harchol, Hay, & Koral, 2014; Technical Report, 2004).

At different geographic scales, from data centers to WANs, the capacity to adapt to current virtualization technologies, especially concerning network equipment, may have different peculiarities. For example, currently routers in large Internet domains, around thousands worldwide, have significant buffers, make use of large amounts of memory for storing their BGP tables, and thus differ from centralized data network about 100,000 in a single data center, where it prizes for small rows and routing tables due to the nature of the traffic in this environment.

In performance requirements for NFs virtualization technologies, the following parameters stand out: a VNF instance must have its performance specifications well-defined to operate according to the available resources of the shared and isolated infrastructure in which it is instantiated; and forms of collecting information on storage, network, and processing of VNFs must be well defined and consequently carried out at different levels of infrastructure (eg, hypervisors, servers, VMs). These requirements will significantly influence the continuity of NFs and the very concept of NFV. In this case, virtualization technologies will possibly have, initially, not as good behaviors as dedicated middleboxes, but will bring the flexibility needed to provide elasticity to network functions. In this case, they are much better established and guaranteed if they can be scalably monitored at various levels of operation and granularity, thus providing consistent states of NFs and their respective environments.

LIGHTWEIGHT VIRTUALIZATION PARADIGMS

Virtualization is a reasonably widespread concept for large servers, but it is a relatively new technology for embedded systems. However, it is a technology mature enough to address some of the challenges of the area, such as the increase in software complexity given new market demands. In particular, embedded systems can benefit from virtualization's ability to deal with heterogeneous and competing systems. Also, the virtualization layer makes the underlying application transparent to the application, allowing the same application to run over multi-core to migrate to single-core overhead without requiring any modification to the application code.

In the context of fog and edge computing, elasticity capabilities allow new features to be added at runtime depending on demand and released when there is no longer such a need, saving resources. Besides, the ability to migrate VMs between devices over the network makes infrastructure management more flexible. Finally, the security provided by virtualization between the base system running at the superuser level is separate from the applications, ensuring that codes in userspace will not access resources outside of their quota system.

A few years ago, virtualization began to move into the embedded systems field. At that time, virtualization was managed by hypervisors. Although some popular hypervisors used for server computing have been adapted for embedded systems, currently with the advancement of semiconductor technology and the reduction of its costs, hardware support for virtualization can be created and new hypervisors for embedded environments have been developed from scratch (Mitake, 2011).

Traditional Virtualization

One of the most used virtualization proposals on servers is Xen. Xen is an open-source hypervisor that supports the largest current cloud environments, but although it was developed for servers, it was modified for embedded environments, especially for running on ARM processors.

Xen is responsible for manipulating the CPU, memory, stopping, and scheduling the VMs. Xen is a type 1 hypervisor, so it interacts directly with the hardware and the VMs that run on it. An instance running in a VM on Xen is called the domain or guest. There is a particular domain, called Domain 0 (dom0), which is responsible for I/O.

Figure 2 shows the Xen framework, which is a traditional virtualization paradigm. On the hardware, there is a modified operating system where the hypervisor is inserted to perform the translation of the system calls

Figure 2. Xen, a traditional model of virtualization

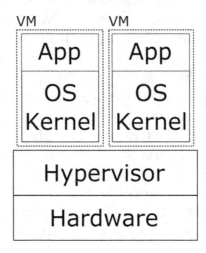

coming from the VMs (dom0). On the hypervisor, each VM contains a new operating system that supports one or more applications. This operating system does not have to be the same as the underlying system and does not require any modification. For the VM, there is the impression that the slice of hardware resources destined for each VM is the real underlying hardware. This slice of resources can be reallocated between VMs when needed.

The Xen I/O system is based on a ring structure for reading and writing between the application and the underlying operating system. Therefore, there is a loss of performance of virtualized applications due to overhead in the interpretation of the signals by the hypervisor.

For its execution on embedded environments, where time happens to be a decisive factor, changes were made on the scheduler, implemented real-time concepts for specific VMs. It enabled applications to keep running over the traditional scheduler (Credit Scheduler) while an RT-Xen managed other VMs.

Containers

A container is a set of processes that are isolated from the rest of the system and managed directly by the kernel. These processes are run from a distinct image that provides all the files needed for its execution. By

Figure 3. Containers structure and organization

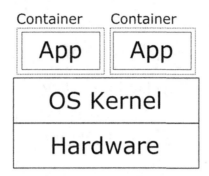

providing an image that contains all the dependencies of an application, the container is portable and consistent during all stages from development, testing, and ultimately production.

Figure 3 shows the layer structure of the Containers. Unlike traditional virtualization, Containers do not maintain a hypervisor. Process management is performed directly by the operating system kernel, very similar to Jails. The non-existence of a hypervisor enables Containers to provide applications with performance identical to a native environment.

On the other hand, the new design of management of the VMs in Containers enabled improvement in performance, but it impacted another fundamental metric: the isolation of resources. While in traditional virtualization resource management is relatively rigid in a sense and maintain the number of resources intended for each virtual machine, regardless of the need for resources of such VMs, Containers cannot preserve such limits (Xavier et al., 2013).

Because the Kernel manages containers, applications running on this paradigm must run on the same operating system. It is a fascinating proposal for embedded devices when competing applications do not compete for the same resources. In edge computing environments, Containers allow applications to migrate dynamically between devices, bringing some of the processing to the customer.

Unikernel

Unikernel is a library operating system. Although not a new idea, it was not implemented due to the inability to deal with numerous different

Figure 4. Unikernel structure and organization

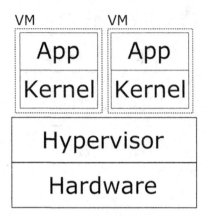

hardware. With the advent of hypervisors, this concern to deal directly with the hardware has been overcome making it possible for an operating system with these characteristics to be executed in any computational environment.

As can be seen in Figure 4, when we use Unikernel, there is no division between user space and kernel space. There is only one program running, and it contains everything from the high-level code of the application to the low-level device I/O routines, being a unique and self-contained image that does not require anything additional to be initialized.

Unikernel can be considered a sort of light virtualization, but implemented in a way different from the shared vision in the same operating system as in other paradigms of virtualization. Therefore, it is an operating system that uses a genuinely minimalist concept to create the software stack, that is, it is only concerned with the specific needs for each application. In operating system design, the libraries used to build it are the ones strictly required to run the application, thereby making it lighter than traditional VMs.

One of the advantages of Unikernel over other paradigms is that it improves security by being a tiny and specific operating system with no applications/ports that are not used by the standard application. Also, its performance is high due to its lightness, the inexistence of multiple processes with the need for management and the exclusion of changes in user contexts in its implementation (Kuenzer, Ivanov, Manco, Mendes, Volchkov, Schmidt, & Huici, 2017).

Fog and edge computing environments can benefit from this type of virtualization because the VMs created are minimalist, allowing you to put full applications in a few kilobytes. Also, since they are small, a large number of these can be instantiated on the same device, serving a large number of requests with little hardware design space.

Serverless Computing

Serverless has emerged as a new paradigm aimed at deployment of fog applications and has been boosted due to the migration of enterprise applications to new architectures through the adoption of Containers and Microservices. The term Serverless computing was defined by the industry to describe a programming model and a design in which small snippets of code run in the cloud as a function. It is important to emphasize that the Serverless paradigm uses servers, but resource management such as resource provisioning, monitoring, maintenance, scalability, and fault tolerance is the responsibility of the cloud service provider.

Serverless computing is defined as a paradigm where the customer provides the code, and the cloud provider manages the environmental life cycle of running that code. Serverless can be defined as the partial realization of an event-oriented ideal, in which applications are determined by the actions and events that trigger them (Baldini, Castro, Chang, Cheng, Fink,, Ishakian, & Suter, 2017).

Event-based systems are two entities called publisher and subscriber. This paradigm, called Publish / Subscribe, is suitable for the development of several new applications that are developed for collaborative environments or high-performance code compositions. Besides, this model is also ideal for a controlled environment which requires the immediate notification of any changes in the data to the customer. For this, the customer only needs to subscribe to a specific service and the server will register the subscriber for that service.

In serverless computing, similar to general-purpose event-based systems, users register their roles in the cloud provider that offers the option of deploying applications through the use of Serverless, and in turn, such functions are driven on a basis in events. Events can trigger functions in a variety of ways, such as through a Hypertext Transfer Protocol route, or even based on a timer or object added or removed from a database.

Serverless computing is a paradigm that must be exploited by IoT embeds, edge and fog computing, since part of the code (usually the heaviest) can be processor outside the embedded intermediate device. Therefore, the local code makes an Hypertext Transfer Protocol request to an external cloud environment, and this external function processes data directly and returns only the responses to the edge device.

Summary

Figure 5 summarizes this section on the different virtualization paradigms that can be applied to the fog computing environments. In Figure 5 we can see the difference between the paradigms regarding the responsibility of administration of part of the computational environment between the provider of the service and the customer.

Based on the previously discussed, we can see that choosing the virtualization paradigm appropriate to each context of fog computing depends necessarily on the metrics that must be addressed. If the main issue is to maintain the isolation of resources, the ideal is still more traditional virtualization. Containers can deliver performance when that is the most critical issue. Unikernel enables high scalability to meet growing demands. Serverless can provide a response when the matter consists of resource saving or battery.

Figure 5. Virtualization paradigm administration layers

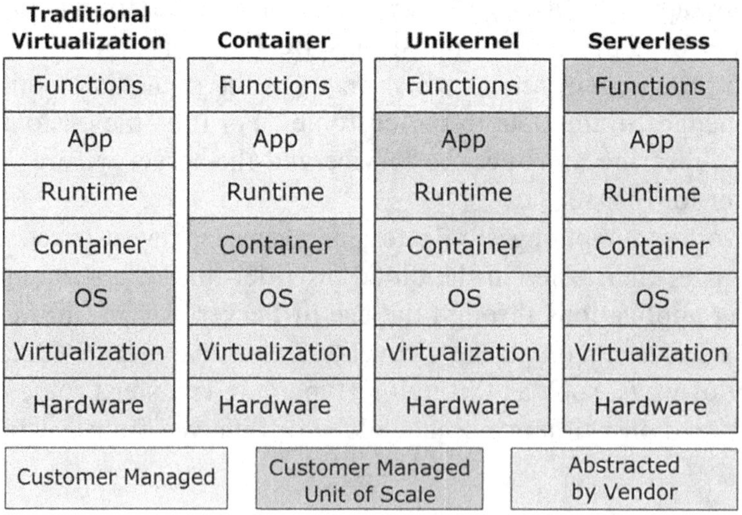

Traditional Virtualization	Container	Unikernel	Serverless
Functions	Functions	Functions	Functions
App	App	App	App
Runtime	Runtime	Runtime	Runtime
Container	Container	Container	Container
OS	OS	OS	OS
Virtualization	Virtualization	Virtualization	Virtualization
Hardware	Hardware	Hardware	Hardware

Customer Managed	Customer Managed Unit of Scale	Abstracted by Vendor

In addition to the above proposals, there are some isolated implementations of virtualizers for embedded systems that can be implemented on edge devices.

SPUMONE (Multiplexing one into two) consists of a lightweight virtualization layer that provides a hybrid operating system environment that is composed of a Real-Time Operating System that runs on a General Purpose Operating System. SPUMONE was designed with three primary goals: to enable minimal modification in the guest operating system through paravirtualization; the hypervisor should be as light as possible; operating systems should be able to reboot without interfering with the others. This proposal supports SH-4 architecture and virtualizes only the processor (Kanda, Yumura, Kinebuchi, Makijima, & Nakajima, 2008).

XtratuM was developed for RISC and ARM architectures and consists of a hypervisor specially designed for mission-critical real-time embedded systems. XtratuM was developed based on the following requirements: data structures are stationary to allow better control of the resources used; the code is not preemptive to make the system fast and straightforward; the VMs manage the peripherals.

EDGE COMPUTING INTEGRATION

Cloud computing paradigm for years provisioned effective computational power supply-chain to the market. However, due to its centralized gateway design (Fig. 6), the increasing network traffic and IoT exponential data production growth in edge side defined the need for cloud alternative solutions. In order to support this new and volatile market, the industry made an effort to find efficient ways to provide services with reduced latency and data access barriers.

Figure 6. Cloud Computing paradigm

The statement defined Edge Computing paradigm, which proposes data storage and processing in distributed servers through the network edge. This intermediate layer aims to make possible preparation, analysis and, in specific cases, the process of data generated from edge devices before its transmission to the cloud. Besides, Edge Computing is not intended to substitute the actual Cloud Computing paradigm, but complement it by offloading its heavy single gateway design and allowing the execution of real-time IoT applications, once the model mitigates the significant demand for faster communication and processing (Bonomi, Milito, Natarajan, & Zhu, 2014; Morabito, Petrolo, Loscri, & Mitton, 2018).

Therefore, Edge Computing implementation benefits include (1) privacy enhancement by the possibility of preprocessing and filter data locally (2) cloud outage mask (3) highly responsive cloud services (Satyanarayanan, Lewis, Morris, Simanta, Boleng, & Ha, 2013) . However, in IoT heterogeneous environment not only the privilege of upload and request in fast speed is needed, but also interoperability, scalability, hardware abstraction and elasticity. For those reasons, the proposal of Lightweight Virtualization application in edge-driven IoT has been discussed.

Before entering Edge Computing demands of Lightweight Virtualization, we have to comprehend its implementation challenges:

- **Programmability:** Edge Computing platform heterogeneity characterizes different runtime power along the network (Bonomi, Milito, Natarajan, & Zhu, 2014; Awadam, 2018). It raises questions about what method could resolve deployment for Edge Computing paradigm, considering the requirement of applications capable of conducting real-time requisitions by defining on what nodes in area computation should occur.
- **Standardization of Communication Protocols:** Having multiples systems and devices working together is hard to establish a network pattern between them. Some ecosystems have their protocols, difficulting integration among other devices. At the same time, how they would identify each device beyond MAC address and IP address still to be defined.
- **Data Abstraction:** Cloud current environment embeds information composition and treatment strategy, providing relevant functionalities to data analytics. However, at the same time, it turns the entire solution

gamma, to a certain degree, addicted to its resources. In the Edge Computing approach, data abstraction issues comprise innovative ways to grant equivalent or higher-level analytics delivery with active data edge filtering.

- **Service Management:** It should have four fundamental features: differentiation, extensibility, isolation, and reliability. The distinction means that every device is unique and for that should be treated differently. Extensibility is the capacity to absorbing new devices under the same network and devices be replaced by others. Isolation means that located failures should not affect the whole system, as also every device on the network should be integrated with others but the private info is protected. Reliability of the system, managing as many devices as possible, for devices, presenting alerts when close to a failure, and, for data, being constant and trustable.

- **Optimization Metrics:** Due to the Edge Computing diverse computation capability, metrics have to be defined when it means management of workload distribution. The primary objective is the optimal allocation rules achievement, where latency and energy efficiency are the most relevant metrics. Latency consists of performance evaluation, considering computation time, bandwidth availability and, in a macro view, WAN delays. Energy efficiency defines the tradeoff around computation and transmission relative costs. Finally, this parameter measurement target resource usage information, which results in better cost-benefit to clients and service providers.

Edge Computing constraints observation alert to two elected Lightweight Virtualization models: unikernels and container-based virtualization. Both fulfill scalability by reducing storage and power consumption with its independence of hardware virtualization and heavy OS dependencies (Plauth, Feinbube, & Polze, 2017). However, the most significant advantage of Lightweight Virtualization for Edge Computing implementation is the defined interoperability by avoiding strict dependence on any given technology (Vashi, Ram, Modi, Verma, & Prakash, 2017).

Lightweight Virtualization comes as an Edge Computing boosting. Therefore, Edge Computing use cases are also put in higher-level. For example, Edge Computing papers often mention smart home applicability, while Lightweight Virtualization for Edge Computing impact brings to the table intelligent city discussions. Furthermore, the debate incorporates autonomous cars, augmented reality, and other higher proportion stuff.

In smart city solutions, Lightweight Virtualization for Edge Computing expands possibilities in data collected computation management domain. In particular, the proposal of a sensorial network with implemented Edge Computing and other edge elements around the city could improve real-time search for valuable data easiness, like suspects of a recent crime. The contemporary ubiquitous computing concept of interconnected processing devices is compelled as well. For example, a traditional computing architecture outage mask could concede reliability reduction to the smart traffic light scenario, once edge elements could support in case of signal unavailability or pedestrian vacancy.

The field of research and development established many concepts and directives. Those initiatives include: Internet of Vehicles - idea of a network of cars which can communicate with each other, Vehicular Cloud computing - the architectural model for Internet of Vehicles, vehicular edge computing – edge computing designed for vehicles and devices related to it, car's on-board units - hardware inside of vehicles for processing and exchange info with networks, and Vehicle-to-everything – systems for connecting with any device or node in the network that can interfere in the car, comprehends other kinds of systems as Vehicle to Vehicle.

This area can be expanded and improved by lightweight virtualization in the edge elements, allowing Vehicular Edge Computing to add functionality to vehicle to vehicle. Instead of only receive and sending info between cars, a lightweight virtualization enabled on-board unit can execute a functioning delivery by another vehicle or other edge element and vice versa. Another use of Lightweight Virtualization in Internet of Vehicles is the always perform the most recent version of an application and systems delivered over the air in the time of execution of a specific task, overcoming the complex updating process. Better management of resources can provide better autonomy for electric cars and keep some hardware dedicated to critic situations thanks to Lightweight Virtualization.

In augmented and virtual reality, high-resolution graphics help to immerse in the virtual world generated. Although, devices used for it usually don't bear the requirements to achieve the developer's desired experience. To workaround this problem, some applications use cloud computing for most heavy processing (Yu et al., 2018). The problem with cloud computing is an unwanted delay.

Therefore, the use of edge computing and lightweight virtualization can remove the need for cloud computing solutions and keep end-user hardware more simple. Not only image processing would take advantage of Lightweight Virtualization, but other elements could use the features of lightweight virtualization as multi-tenancy for multiplayer or container isolated execution for privacy.

DISCUSSION AND OPEN CHALLENGES

Edge orchestration of services is enhanced by virtualization. Services can be instantiated or released on demand, or even migrated from one device to another at runtime. It means that in times of high demand, services can maintain the quality of service agreed between provider and consumers, and in times of low demand, the services released save costs to the provider. However, there is still a research area to be explored that consists of deploying the virtualized infrastructure on the physical substrate. No specific platform allows the provider manager to instantiate a whole fog architecture from a controller.

Monitoring virtualized services is another issue that deserves attention. There are several Application Programming Interfaces that allow the management of virtualized environments that meet the requirements of edge devices. However, this heterogeneity of environments causes the provider to opt for a minimum number of solutions since most monitoring environments are designed for specific virtualizers. Also, edge devices, in general, are equipped with more limited processing and memory components than larger servers. It means that the impact of monitoring tools on such devices should be extensively studied. The most common is to define a set of few metrics to be monitored, with acceptable measurement intervals, so as not to cause device purpose overhead. It is not a trivial operation, so such monitoring characteristics should be studied and configured on a case-by-case basis.

From the point where services are moved to an environment outside the core infrastructure, such services become vulnerable to security issues such as integrity. Well-known techniques in traditional networks that culminate in a redirection of packet flow from real devices to fake devices can capture data can affect the environment of fog computing. Therefore, authentication methods between consumer and edge devices must be implemented. Also, data traffic between edge devices and the cloud is proposed to be performed through encrypted networks. These two mechanisms try to ensure reliable and fast communication between consumer and edge devices, and seamless integration between edge devices and cloud environments. However, the fog computing environment is diverse and heterogeneous, which makes it difficult to propose a single model of security and privacy.

A significant issue to be further developed when it comes to virtualization over edge devices falls on standards and regulations. Not every edge device supports any paradigm or virtualization proposal. Many processors that power devices do not offer a virtualization instruction set architecture capable of enabling and maintaining virtualizers running. While this is an architectural option for some device vendors, perhaps this is a deciding factor in choosing these devices in the coming years. For these devices, some hardware emulation tools have been developed and can be a way to keep older devices running virtualized applications.

Being a recent field in IT makes in the last years, containers technologies have emerged and become more popular because of full support by open source communities. Unikernels need mature more to competing with containers regarding development effort for portability. Containers can be adapted to carry any application, but unikernels are limited by the programming language and libraries inside of minimalistic operational system.

For its characteristics, edge devices must not store relevant data. With data stored in edge devices, you increase insecurity for them be more physical close to nodes. But dealing with a massive amount of data not stored locally can increase the time of response and consumption over broadband, and for that making it less worthwhile. Distributed data among edge devices can be impossible to reunite in one unit to process info. To solve partially, it can use volatile date locally and save reduced data centrally.

Faced with the growth prospects of the current plans for implementing NFV fundamentals in proofs of concept, some questions arise and raise resolution requirements are still not observed by telecom companies. For example, virtual customer premises equipment, where network equipment sits at the frontier between users and service providers, brings with it the properties of portability and elasticity, which will suppress costs of telecommunication companies' operational services. Network Function

Virtualization comes as an alternative to that, providing the ability to dynamically deploying on-demand network services or user-services where and when needed. At the first moment it can pretend to cause an adverse impact for the telco in opening the market for more experienced players, but in the long run, it will bring them closer to users. Unikernels are more comfortable to be used than containers in this scenario for their characteristic of running on the same hypervisor as VMs with a slight impact on the infrastructure. Although, security and reliability remain as the main topic for technology questions.

When dealing with network function virtualization for edge architecture, the customization of network functions, as well as their programming in the data plane, need attention concerning the permissiveness of agents, whether these end users or network operators. Therefore, according to Network Function Virtualization portability requirements, such agents may require the installation of applications and network functions in generic devices similar to what exists in computing, in operating systems. Thus, the standardization of northbound and southbound interfaces for software defined networking need to be defined either by hardware or software in different low or high-level languages for orchestration and network management to define NFs in programming paths in wireless network cores.

Security is still a trend for embedded edge virtualization. IoT devices are going to be used in large scale in industrial and household applications. Such devices are more susceptible to hacker attacks than any other connected devices in the network. Therefore, methods to improve security must be utilized for the embedded hypervisors. For example, a secure boot process must be implemented to ensure the authenticity of the hypervisor and VMs.

When we work on server virtualization, VMs on the same host can perform various services for different users without any association among them. On the contrary, embedded systems are customized devices with a defined purpose. Consequently, VMs on an embedded hypervisor would play different services to achieve a common aim. As a result, the VMs must interact using the hypervisor interface mechanism. Consequently, more effective and secure communication services must be introduced.

Multicore processors are broadly utilized for embedded devices. Therefore, the hypervisor must be designed to work on a multicore platform. However, multicore support adds parallel execution at the hypervisor's kernel, which requires synchronization primitives. It increases the hypervisor's kernel complexity significantly, and it can impact on performance issues. Therefore, the port to multicore processors must be prudently designed (Morabito et al., 2018).

FUTURE RESEARCH DIRECTIONS

Virtualized edge computing is a deployed computing resource on the margins of the business, a recent trend of decentralization that promises many changes in how IoT will interact with the cloud, especially remote facilities away from data centers, as is the case officer, retail stores, factories, and others. Several works argue that edge computing would not be an innovation, but it would be a departure from the cloud the return of traditional models of computing distribution. However, most of them overlook the fact that with the Internet of Things and extensive device connectivity, this departure from the cloud does not mean a setback in digital transformation, but a new one. This computational model is already widely used in monitoring network security and detecting threats. When failures are detected at marginal points on the network, these network streams or devices can be quarantined, which ensures that internal systems are not compromised.

Virtualization on edge computing presents a series of critical future directions and open challenges for the IT area, including:

- Proper operation and maintenance for sensors and other mobile devices deployed at remote sites.
- Need for structured security and able to ensure that remote devices are not compromised.
- The requirement by companies that IT professionals and operators be trained to work with virtualization on IoT and edge devices.
- The importance of constant revisions in business processes that use virtualization on edge and IoT.
- Indispensability to establish adequate bandwidth so that data of concern to the business, collected by edge devices, reach the areas where they are needed.

Understanding these characteristics is essential to understanding the importance that virtualization on edge computing has for the IT market and the changes that this concept may pose to IT professionals. When we look at the growth of mobile device usage, it is impossible not to take into account that the large volume of data produced is far away from corporate headquarters at points considered to be of organizational advantage outside the core servers.

Therefore, the movement of organizations towards lightweight virtualized edge computing is a shift towards the devices that produce the most significant volume of information, ensuring faster data processing than would be possible if data were to be transported to data centers. In this way, lightweight virtualization provides the scalable and secure environment required to process such a large volume of data in real time.

The importance of IoT to the operational area is another important reason for the relevance of the virtualization on edge devices, which allow the strategic application of these platforms, turning to the automation of machines and alerts in the management of problems with the network, equipment, and infrastructure.

REFERENCES

Awada, U. (2018). CMS: Container Orchestration Across Multi-region Clouds.

Baldini, I., Castro, P., Chang, K., Cheng, P., Fink, S., Ishakian, V., & Suter, P. (2017). Serverless computing: Current trends and open problems. *Research Advances in Cloud Computing,* 1-20.

Barham, P., Dragovic, B., Fraser, K., Hand, S., Harris, T., Ho, A., & Warfield, A. (2003). Xen and the art of virtualization. *Operating Systems Review, 37*(5), 164–177. doi:10.1145/1165389.945462

Bonomi, F., Milito, R., Natarajan, P., & Zhu, J. (2014). Fog Computing: A Platform for Internet of Things and Analytics. In *Big Data and Internet of Things: A Roadmap for Smart Environments* (pp. 169-186).

Bremler-Barr, A., Harchol, Y., Hay, D., & Koral, Y. (2014). Deep packet inspection as a service. In *Proceedings of the 10th ACM International on Conference on emerging Networking Experiments and Technologies* (pp. 271-282). New York: ACM.

Broido, A. (2001). Analysis of RouteViews BGP data: Policy atoms.

Chiosi, M., Clarke, D., Willis, P., Reid, A., Feger, J., Bugenhagen, M., & Benitez, J. (2012). Network functions virtualisation: An introduction, benefits, enablers, challenges and call for action. In *SDN and OpenFlow World Congress*.

Galante, G., & Bona, L. C. E. D. (2012). A survey on cloud computing elasticity. In *Proceedings of the 2012 IEEE/ACM Fifth International Conference on Utility and Cloud Computing* (pp. 263-270). 10.1109/UCC.2012.30

Kanda, W., Yumura, Y., Kinebuchi, Y., Makijima, K., & Nakajima, T. (2008). Spumone: Lightweight cpu virtualization layer for embedded systems. In *Proceedings of the IEEE/IFIP International Conference on Embedded and Ubiquitous Computing* (Vol. 1, pp. 144-151). IEEE. 10.1109/EUC.2008.157

Kuenzer, S., Ivanov, A., Manco, F., Mendes, J., Volchkov, Y., Schmidt, F., & Huici, F. (2017). Unikernels Everywhere: The Case for Elastic CDNs. *ACM SIGPLAN Notices, 52*(7), 15–29. doi:10.1145/3140607.3050757

Masmano, M., Ripoll, I., Crespo, A., & Metge, J. (2009). Xtratum: a hypervisor for safety critical embedded systems. In *Proceedings of the 11th Real-Time Linux Workshop* (pp. 263-272).

Mitake, H., Kinebuchi, Y., Courbot, A., & Nakajima, T. (2011). Coexisting real-time OS and general purpose OS on an embedded virtualization layer for a multicore processor. In *Proceedings of the 2011 ACM Symposium on Applied Computing* (pp. 629-630). New York: ACM. 10.1145/1982185.1982322

Morabito, R. (2017). Virtualization on internet of things edge devices with container technologies: A performance evaluation. *IEEE Access*, *5*, 8835–8850. doi:10.1109/ACCESS.2017.2704444

Morabito, R., Cozzolino, V., Ding, A. Y., Beijar, N., & Ott, J. (2018). Consolidate IoT edge computing with lightweight virtualization. *IEEE Network*, *32*(1), 102–111. doi:10.1109/MNET.2018.1700175

Morabito, R., Petrolo, R., Loscrì, V., & Mitton, N. (2018). LEGIoT: A Lightweight Edge Gateway for the Internet of Things. *Future Generation Computer Systems*, *81*, 1–15. doi:10.1016/j.future.2017.10.011

Plauth, M., Feinbube, L., & Polze, A. (2017, September). A performance survey of lightweight virtualization techniques. In *Proceedings of the European Conference on Service-Oriented and Cloud Computing* (pp. 34-48). Cham: Springer.

Satyanarayanan, M. (2017). The emergence of edge computing. *Computer*, *50*(1), 30–39. doi:10.1109/MC.2017.9

Satyanarayanan, M., Lewis, G., Morris, E., Simanta, S., Boleng, J., & Ha, K. (2013). The Role of Cloudlets in Hostile Environments. *IEEE Pervasive Computing*, *12*(4), 40–49. doi:10.1109/MPRV.2013.77

Server., B.R.A. (2004). Technical Report DSL Forum TR-092.

Shi, W., Cao, J., Zhang, Q., Li, Y., & Xu, L. (2016). Edge computing: Vision and challenges. *IEEE Internet of Things Journal*, *3*(5), 637–646. doi:10.1109/JIOT.2016.2579198

Shi, W., & Dustdar, S. (2016). The Promise of Edge Computing. *Computer*, *49*(5), 78–81. doi:10.1109/MC.2016.145

Vaquero, L. M., & Rodero-Merino, L. (2014). Finding your way in the fog: Towards a comprehensive definition of fog computing. *Computer Communication Review*, *44*(5), 27–32. doi:10.1145/2677046.2677052

Vashi, S., Ram, J., Modi, J., Verma, S., & Prakash, C. (2017). Internet of Things (IoT): A vision, architectural elements, and security issues. In *Proceedings of the International Conference on I-SMAC (IoT in Social, Mobile, Analytics and Cloud)*. 10.1109/I-SMAC.2017.8058399

Villamizar, M., Garcés, O., Ochoa, L., Castro, H., Salamanca, L., Verano, M., ... Lang, M. (2017). Cost comparison of running web applications in the cloud using monolithic, microservice, and aws lambda architectures. *Service Oriented Computing and Applications*, *11*(2), 233–247. doi:10.100711761-017-0208-y

Xavier, M. G., Neves, M. V., Rossi, F. D., Ferreto, T. C., Lange, T., & De Rose, C. A. (2013). Performance evaluation of container-based virtualization for high performance computing environments. In *Proceedings of the 21st Euromicro International Conference* on *Parallel, Distributed and Network-Based Processing (PDP)* (pp. 233-240). 10.1109/PDP.2013.41

Xavier, M. G., Neves, M. V., Rossi, F. D., Ferreto, T. C., Lange, T., & De Rose, C. A. (2013). Performance evaluation of container-based virtualization for high performance computing environments. In *Proceedings of the 21st Euromicro International Conference* on *Parallel, Distributed and Network-Based Processing (PDP)* (pp. 233-240). 10.1109/PDP.2013.41

Yu, W., Liang, F., He, X., Hatcher, W., Lu, C., Lin, J., & Yang, X. (2018). A Survey on the Edge Computing for the Internet of Things. *IEEE Access*, *6*, 6900–6919. doi:10.1109/ACCESS.2017.2778504

Chapter 3
A Comprehensive Survey on Edge Computing for the IoT

Pravin A.
Sathyabama Institute of Science and Technology, India

Prem Jacob
Sathyabama Institute of Science and Technology, India

G. Nagarajan
Sathyabama Institute of Science and Technology, India

ABSTRACT

The IoT concept is used in various applications and it uses different devices for collecting data and processing the data. Various sets of devices such as sensors generate a large amount of data and the data will be forwarded to the appropriate devices for processing. The devices used will range from small devices to larger devices. The edge computing becomes the major role in overcoming the difficulties in cloud computing, the nearby devices are used as servers for providing better services. Most of the issues such as power consumption, data security, and response time will be addressed. The IoT plays a major role in many real-world applications. In this chapter, the basics and the use of the Edge computing concept in different applications are discussed. Edge computing can be used to increase the overall performance of the IoT. The performance of various applications in terms of edge computing and other methodologies are analyzed.

DOI: 10.4018/978-1-5225-8555-8.ch003

INTRODUCTION

IoT Plays a major part in the real world due to the increase in the use of the IoT devices. In recent many IoT devices are used which will be gathering large amount of data and the data will be send to the appropriate devices for processing. The IoT devices such as sensors and other devices which will be interconnected through the network for the proper flow of data. The amount of data generated by these devices will be a huge one due to the increase in the use of these devices. In many real world application such as electricity grid, Agriculture, Vehicle monitoring, Smart city and other applications are using these IoT devices. The IoT applications which will be using the Cloud concept cannot able to meet the upcoming demands. There are some difficulties which are faced by applications and that drawback can be overcome by using some new technology. The difficulties such as the delay in the transmission of the data through the network, power consumption, data security and the response time. The Edge computing plays a major role in the IoT applications. The edge computing will have multiple nodes and the user will be very near to that. Due to the Edge computing concept the performance of the IoT applications will be improved. The Edge technology will provide mechanisms for reducing the network traffic, the reducing the response time and other problems that exists in the network. The other factors are increase in the lifetime of the nodes. The major things to be focused is about the advantages of the Edge computing and comparing it with the existing technology. The major focus is towards the Integration of the IoT and the Edge computing concept.

INTERNET OF THINGS

There are many IoT applications such as smart grids, smart homes, smart city, Agriculture, smart health etc. Every application will be using the sensors for gathering information and other devices for processing. The IoT Devices which can be able to communicate with each other through Internet and can be controlled Remotely.

Figure 1. Different types of sensors

Sensors

The application uses large amounts of sensors for collecting the information, the sensors are used to sense the temperature, humidity, sound and other information. The information that is sensed by the sensor will depends up on the type of the sensors that will be used.

Figure 1 specifies different types of sensors such as the passive infrared sensor (PIR), the soil humidity sensor, the touch sensor, the ultrasonic sensor, the temperature sensor and the light sensor is represented in the Figure 1, There are many other sensors which will be used for sensing different types of data. For example, the soil humidity sensor which will be used to measure the humidity level in the soil.

IoT Applications

The Figure 2 specifies different IoT application such as health care, agriculture, industry, transportation and smart home, other than the listed areas IoT is used in many others such as wearables, retail, automation, security, etc. The applications use IoT devices for collecting and processing the information, for example the sensors will continuously gather the information. The information collected by the sensors will be transferred

Figure 2. Different IoT applications

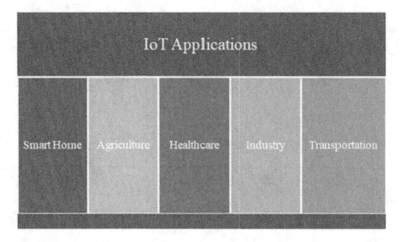

to the cloud environment and further the information will be accessed by the application and processed. If the Healthcare is considered various information from the patient will be gathered by the sensors that are attached. There are certain IoT devices we are using in our daily life such as Laptops, smartphone, television, smart meters, Setupbox, printers, connected cars and other set of devices that are connected. The usage of these devices is increasing and in future the usage of connected devices will be keep on increasing. In future most of the devices that are used in our day to day life will be connected and these devices will be generating a large amount of data. The data generated by these devices will be processed and depends upon the outcome further action will be taken.

The IoT devices that are used in our day to day life is given in the Figure 3, It is not at all limited to the devices that are given in the figure.

The entire process flow of an IoT application is given in the Figure 4, where the data gathered by the IoT devices is transferred through the network to the cloud environment and further it will be given to the particular application. The data gathered by the IoT devices will be stored in the cloud environment. The IoT gateway which will perform some set of data processing task by collecting the information from the sensors and the data will be forwarded to the cloud environment. The data will be further send to the application for further process.

Figure 3. IoT devices used in our day to day life

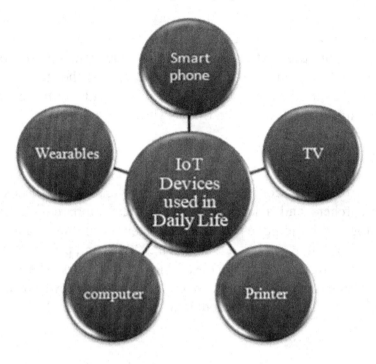

Figure 4. General process flow of IoT Application

EDGE COMPUTING

In the Edge computing concept, the servers will be very close to the users compared to the cloud environment. It will provide a better service and latency will also be low compared to the cloud. There will be an increase in the performance in terms of less computing power.

Architecture

At the bottom of the architecture the end devices such as sensors and other devices and the next level is the Edge nodes which will provide a better service to the end users, the computation and the storage of data is limited. The cloud environment which will provide unlimited storage and processing and the response time is slow.

Survey

The Edge computing concept for the IoT applications is discussed by many researchers and also, they have further compared the existing methodology with the Edge computing concept. The impact and the use of Edge computing is analysed (Zhao et al., 2018) and proposed a three-phase methodology for analysing the traffic in the network. The concept of the Edge computing is discussed (Shi et al., 2016) and they have analysed different case studies and provided detail about different challenges that

Figure 5. Architecture of Edge computing Network

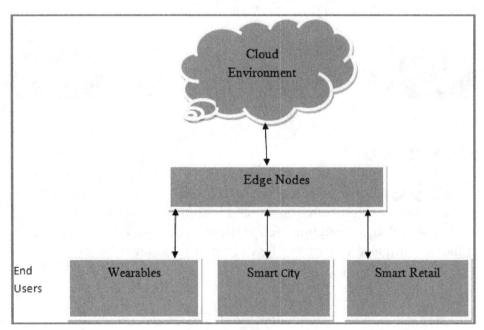

are faced. The Social IoT and the Edge computing concept is combined by means of an Agent approach and the effectiveness is analysed by using certain use cases (Circielli et al., 2018). The use of MEC (Multi-Access Edge Computing) in different application and various technical aspects related to that is discussed (Mach et al., 2017). Discussed about major use cases and reference categories and how the existing methods integrated with the concept (Mach et la, 2017). The comparison in terms of Edge computing and the Fog computing is performed and the Radio Access network in terms of Fog computing are also discussed (Ai et al., 2018a). The set of survey about Integrating the IoT with the cloud environment is discussed and clear clarification is given (Atlam et al., 2018). The entire concept of the Fog computing and how it can be used to improve the performance of the new set of IoT application. Fog computing related papers are discussed (Dasgupta et al., 2017) by analysing various set of research papers and also suggested what are the further advancement that can be done. Different set of use case for Fog computing is discussed and comparison is done with the existing research (Perera et al., 2017). Discussed about the steps to increase the performance of the IoT and also the Edge computing is categorized based on various factors (Yu et al., 2018). The impact of the Edge computing technologies with the IoT applications is discussed and also compared the performance by performing certain experimental analysis. Discussed about certain amount of security issues and privacy in terms of Fog computing (Premsankar et al., 2018). The overview and future work in terms of the multi access Edge computing concept is discussed (Yi et al., 2015) and comparison is performed. Main focus is on Fog computing and several surveys are made related to the security issues (Shahzadi et al., 2017).

REFERENCES

Ai, Y., Peng, M., & Zhang, K. (2018). Edge computing technologies for Internet of Things: A primer. *Digital Communications and Networks*, *4*(2), 77–86. doi:10.1016/j.dcan.2017.07.001

Atlam, H., Walters, R., & Wills, G. (2018). Fog Computing and the Internet of Things: A Review. *Big Data and Cognitive Computing*, *2*(2), 10.

Bhanu Sravanthi, D., & Rekha, G. (2017). Fog Computing a Survey of Integrating Cloud and IOT. *International Journal of Innovative Research in Computer and Communication Engineering*, *5*(3).

Cicirelli, F., Guerrieri, A., Spezzano, G., Vinci, A., Briante, O., Iera, A., & Ruggeri, G. (2018). Edge computing and social internet of things for large-scale smart environments development. *IEEE Internet of Things Journal*, *5*(4), 2557–2571.

Dasgupta, A., & Gill, A. Q. (2017). Fog Computing Challenges: A Systematic Review. In Proceedings of the *Australasian Conference on Information Systems*.

Mach, P., & Becvar, Z. (2017). Mobile Edge Computing: A Survey on Architecture and Computation Offloading. IEEE Communications Surveys & Tutorials, 19(3), 1628-1656.

Perera, C., Qin, Y., Estrella, J. C., Reiff-Marganiec, S., & Vasilakos, A. V. (2017). Fog computing for sustainable smart cities: A survey. *ACM Computing Surveys*, *50*(3), 32.

Porambage, P., Okwuibe, J., Liyanage, M., Ylianttila, M., & Taleb, T. (2018). Survey on Multi-Access Edge Computing for Internet of Things Realization. IEEE Communications Surveys & Tutorials, 20(4), 2961-2991. doi:10.1109/COMST.2018.2849509

Premsankar, G., Di Francesco, M., & Taleb, T. (2018). Edge computing for the Internet of Things: A case study. *IEEE Internet of Things Journal*, *5*(2), 1275–1284. doi:10.1109/JIOT.2018.2805263

Shahzadi, S., Iqbal, M., Dagiuklas, T., & Qayyum, Z. U. (2017). Multi-access edge computing: Open issues, challenges and future perspectives. *Journal of Cloud Computing*, *6*(1), 30.

Shi, W., Cao, J., Zhang, Q., Li, Y., & Xu, L. (2016). Edge computing: Vision and challenges. *IEEE Internet of Things Journal, 3*(5), 637–646.

Yi, S., Qin, Z., & Li, Q. (2015). Security and privacy issues of fog computing: A survey. In *Proceedings of the International conference on wireless algorithms, systems, and applications*. Cham: Springer. 10.1007/978-3-319-21837-3_67

Yu, W., Liang, F., He, X., Hatcher, W. G., Lu, C., Lin, J., & Yang, X. (2018). A Survey on the Edge Computing for the Internet of Things. *IEEE Access, 6*, 6900–6919. doi:10.1109/ACCESS.2017.2778504

Zhao, Z., Min, G., Gao, W., Wu, Y., Duan, H., & Ni, Q. (2018). Deploying edge computing nodes for large-scale IoT: A diversity aware approach. *IEEE Internet of Things Journal, 5*(5), 3606–3614.

Chapter 4
Need for Internet of Things

V. J. K. Kishor Sonti
Sathyabama Institute of Science and Technology, India

Sundari G.
Sathyabama Institute of Science and Technology, India

ABSTRACT

The emergence of a novel technology always has had a greater influence on the environmental and social conditions of an individual or society. Technology has taken social living to leaps and bounds in the past few decades. Any advancement in the technology has certainly has healthy and adverse implications on the growth engine of the society. The standard of living of the people often gets perturbed by the richness of scientific innovation in the form of technological products. In this context, the emerging innovation that is slowly conquering the social lifestyle in the recent past is internet of things (IoT). IoT offers the advantage of anytime from anywhere, helps in predicting the outcome with accuracy, the transfer of data and in the implementation of flexible electronics. The concept of smart cities to wearable electronics, high-end computing systems applications would not have been possible without IoT. There is another aspect of IoT that has greater influence on the society. The ethical and legal implications are complex to understand, and this book chapter addresses all these issues.

DOI: 10.4018/978-1-5225-8555-8.ch004

INTRODUCTION

Emergence of a novel technology always had a greater influence on the environmental and social conditions of an individual or society. Technology has taken the social living to undergo the leaps and bounds in the past few decades. Any advancement in the technology has certainly has healthy and adverse implications on the growth engine of the society. Right from Industrial revolution to Information era, the world has seen the advancements in technology and their societal implications. Today cyber physical systems are taking the major share in the growth market of industry and their implications are certainly the most needed topic alongside of their practice in the society.

The standard of living of the people often gets altered by the richness of scientific innovation in the form of technological products (Kowatsch et al., 2012). In this context, the emerging innovation that is conquering the social life style in the recent past is Internet of Things (IoT).

IoT offers advantage of "anytime from anywhere," helps in predicting the outcome with accuracy, feasible transfer of data and ease in the implementation of flexible electronics. The concept of Smart city to Wearable electronics, high end computing systems applications would not have been a reality without IoT.

Another dimension is the use of IoT applications incautiously. Sometimes, the ethical and legal implications are complex to perceive, where security of the personal information is at stake. The algorithms used for anytime anywhere computing may be foolproof, but in the implementation stages less care would lead to malicious attack on the systems. This may lead to the trepidation among the end user that "Simpler is the concept, Complex is the implementation" (Haroon et al., 2016).

Even though IoT belongs to the smartest class of technological evolution, researchers, engineers and students practicing IoT should be very cautious in weighing the social implications.

Internet of Things

The typical definition of IoT states "as a network of items embedded with sensors, which are connected to the internet." The term IoT was coined by Kevin Ashton, Proctor and Gamble in 1999 (Kevin, 1999).

Technology convergence was the prime principle behind all the innovations in the recent past. IoT is one such convergence arrived at, where machine learning, sensor networks, automation and embedded systems are contributed.

Smart devices, Smart systems and Smart cities are the generic sequence of evolution for IoT based products, (Elmangoush et al., 2013). In this category, the first smart machine was reported in 1982 at Carnegie Mellon University, where a modified coke machine was able to send the information stating that the recently loaded drinks were chill, when compared with previously stored drinks.

Architecture of IoT

This is basically a three-tier architecture, which comprises three main stages namely Sensing, Networking and Applications. Sensing is performed using primary receptors or sensors of temperature, humidity, pressure and other related entities. Networking of sensors is done using wireless technology or any other suitable communication network. End user will be offered with variety of applications involving health care to home appliances management.

The applications are related to hospitals, consumer appliances, ICT infrastructure, logistic companies, industries involved in manufacturing, Utilities, Insurance companies and Application developers. This framework generally includes smart homes and cities, logistics, health care, media, manufacturing and energy.

Figure 1. Internet of things – diversity in applications

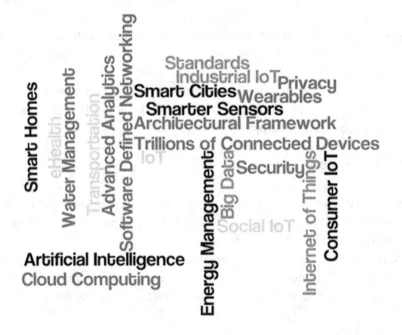

The revolution brought by this system is Machine to Machine interaction, where the human intervention is minimal, (Atzori et al., 2010). The exhaustive nature of these applications ranges from consumer to industry. There is a prediction that by 2019, devices connected using IoT will account for 9.1 billion (Business Insider, 2015).

Impact of IoT

IoT had made greater impact in commercial, public sector and thereby on consumers. The eco balance, intelligent services, divergent value chains and providing novel feasible solutions are the takeaways of this technology. These aspects are more elaborately discussed in the subsequent sections.

A prediction about IoT usage devices connected using IoT pertinent to wind and solar installations may increase at a compound annual growth rate (CAGR) of 21% during 2014 -2020, the total number of connections growing up to 50 billion in 2020 according to tech-giants like Intel.

Challenges of IoT

Besides providing numerous opportunities in exploring different paths to ease human life, IoT also possess challenges in implementation with respect to

Figure 2. IoT – A roadmap

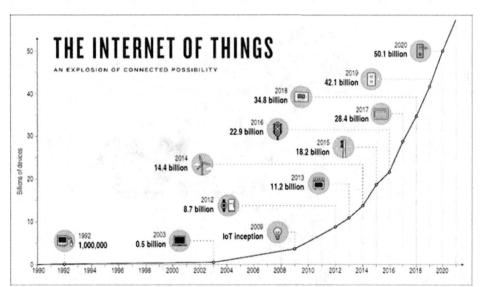

Figure 3. Challenges of IoT

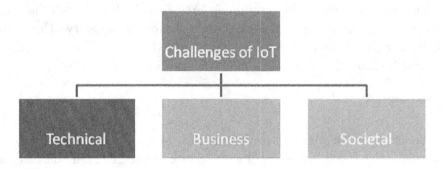

technical, business and societal aspects (Brous & Janssen, 2015; Haller et al., 2009). This book chapter is intended to explore the societal aspects or challenges from social perspective of IoT implementation.

Before emphasizing on the social implications, let us also look into the positive aspects of the implementation of Internet of Things.

IoT in Smart Computing

The ubiquitous computing is often regarded as anytime anywhere computing. This is very useful in making thinks simple and encouraging machine to machine

Figure 4. Smart city

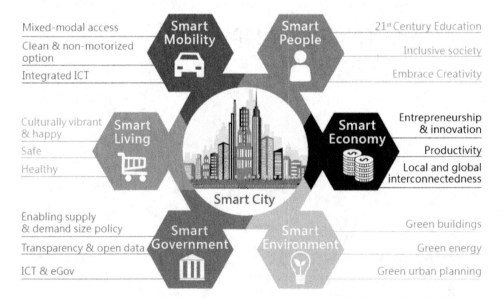

interaction with less or no human intervention. The mere extension of this idea resulted in an application called 'SMART CITY". The smart city includes transportation, economy, governance, environment and smart homes (Ali & Awad, 2018; Shen & Carug, 2014). This multidisciplinary conjunction has been wonderful in making living so simple. A typical smart city environment is depicted in the Figure 4.

Sensing, networking, analyzing and controlling are the basic foundation principles upon which the concept of Smart City evolved. The seamless connectivity of the devices, data analyzers, sensors and other assisting communication networks are helping the end-user in making intelligent decisions. Tracking became so easy which in other way increased the security and safety in transportation. Inclusion of Machine learning along with this setup of Internet of Things certainly enhanced the effectiveness that resulted in the reduction of road accidents. All these advantages made this technology in other way popular as Internet of People (IoP).

IoT in Health Care

Internet of Things for medical and health related aspects is also known as Internet of Health Things. Digitized healthcare system has already penetrated into our day to day lives in the form of health gadgets such as Fitbit.

Health data analysis has increasingly become important nowadays. Managing health of chronic patients became quite easy with IoT. Monitoring health, analyzing

Figure 5. IoT in Health care

the vital parameters, ensuring necessary medical help to patient became so fast and flexible while offering health care services to hospitals and doctors. With the evolution of IoT based applications in health industry, today our mobile is playing the role of a personal physician.

IoT in Automation

Industry 4.0 is the current trend in automation. The basic principles of Industry 4.0 includes Interconnection, Transparency of data, Decentralization in decision making and Providing able and fast technical assistance. The interconnectivity of the machines and people to communicate each other using Internet of Things has boosted the trends in automation to the next level. The evolution of automation leading to Industry 4.0 is depicted in Figure 6.

Huge amount of data collection is possible that is being generated during manufacturing process. This data is effectively processed and analyzed using IoT based systems. These cyber physical systems allows the users to make prompt

Figure 6 . Evolution of industry automation (Greg Cline, 2017)

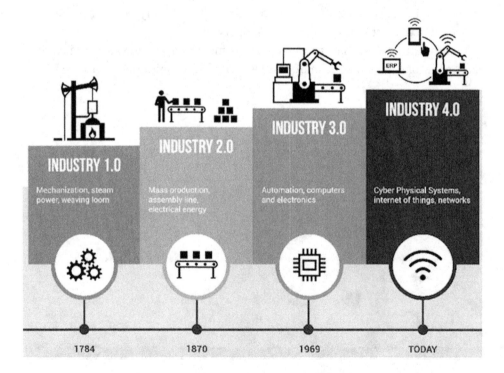

decisions, sometimes decisions are taken autonomously by the machine, which reduces any further delay in control and processing of the machines. The visual information, key parameters variation during the working state of a machine, problem solving using IoT providing necessary technical inputs and assistance to workers and managers in the industry workspace (Hermann, Pentek, & Otto, 2016; Marr, 2018; Bonner, 2018).

IoT to IIIoT

The intrusion of internet in our lives has made a lot of difference in the way we think, we do things and we conduct our life. Internet of Things (IoT) is the next stage, where the automation and application were hand in hand. Industrial internet of things (IIoT) is another version, where the use of internet of things is mainly in factories and energy sector. Now, Industrial Infrastructure Internet of Things (IIIOT) is fast in making inroads in terms of enabling infrastructure more suitable to IoT applications. For example, digital street-lighting, digital air conditioning in public transportation places, optical cables in smart homes makes IIIoT massive in creating needed physical modules.

Societal Implications

Already world advanced in the utilization aspect of this technology, this is a junction where enough analysis and discussion are needed to explore the social implications of this technology. Virtual access to information, outsourcing and unauthenticated sharing of information are some of the complicated areas to be addressed in the backdrop of understanding the possible extension of this novel concept. Data privacy is the major concern to discuss elaborately besides understanding the principles on which the implementation of this technology is based.

Our transit is from "Information Processing age" to "Intelligence Processing Age", evolution of such technologies based on fast and flexible computing methodologies should be carefully weighed before infusing into the complex systems that are already developed from years. The social implications of this technology mostly shall be understood from a specific context rather than in a generic manner. For example, the issues in health care are distinct from the adverse effects in automation or environmental aspects. But, still in this chapter the attempt has been made to address few major issues pertinent to the social implications of this technology.

Data Privacy

Information transparency is a key issue in using IoT based systems. This must be carefully addressed in the advanced design system concepts such as Industry 4.0. Huge amount of data is produced with heavy machinery and corresponding control systems working for relentless hours. The intervention of Internet of Things in this scenario may create issues pertinent to data privacy. Proper regulation in flooding of information is much needed step towards ensuring data privacy. Sometimes the encryption of data from end to end may incur more expenses, when compared to the data acquisition and processing in conventional methods.

Any open ports make the IoT device prone to attacks, becomes highly vulnerable as security in data transfer is missing, (Siponen, & Willison, 2009). Authentication of communication parties should be the prime aspect for any data transmission, particularly in applications related to personal health, research and defense requirements. Data sharing to unauthorized individuals or organizations is unwarranted and unsafe. This may be a very common phenomenon, if the IoT based systems are not properly managed in terms of authentication or authorization in transferring sensitive data. Hackers' accessing the database is a common possibility. The systems should be consistently monitored and effectively addressed without disturbing the regular work environment is a challenging task.

Reduction in Employment Opportunities

Too much technical presence sometimes become unpleasant for humans as it cut down the employment opportunities. The autonomy of the machine intervention in manufacturing certainly hampers the employment of people. In the scenario of breakdown of the system involving IoT at every level of processing, there is a natural scarcity of trained or qualified manpower. This leads to the situation where economically potential losses are invited by the industry. The situation will be worsened if such incident happens in health care services. For example, an ICU system controlled by IoT stops functioning due to random causes or technical glitches, un-availability of qualified nursing or medical staff leads to the loss of life.

Reliability and Stability issues

Reliability and Stability are two aspects those are majorly concerned, when it comes to healthcare and automation. A machine-to-machine communication becomes critical in establishing reliability and stability. Maintaining the integrity of the huge productivity systems is always a herculean task. Replacing partly or fully trained technical manpower with rich set of ethics and moral standard is always becomes a point of discussion.

The decision making by devices or machines connected through Internet of Things may become obsolete as they are naturally pre-programmed or pre-defined solutions. In industry hierarchy, the role of top management may be reduced due to too much machine to machine communication. This is not a healthy trend for the industry. The aspect of accountability remains questionable with this kind of intervention. Inner tuning, transformation over a period of time in par with dynamic changes of work space, living conditions is common for humans. This needs a deliberate up- gradation of the technology, which was setup with high investments, may not be always feasible for the industry. We can train a skilled worker to the updated requirements but to train or un-train a system developed for a specific purpose, which is also involved in networking with other systems, the effort and money will be definitely demanding.

Legal and Ethical Issues

A lapse in ensuring data privacy and security always leads to legal complications. Reduced accountability due to too much machine interference definitely affects the value chain. Logistics, human resource management, marketing, sales and services, infrastructure development are some of the segments of the value chain in any industry, where accountability remains vital; whatever may be the advancement in the procedures. All these areas are highly sensitive inviting legal and ethical issues anytime during establishment or operation. Intellectual property rights and criminal usage of information is possible and leads to legal issues, (Weber, 2010).

Ethics is a subject mostly associated with humans. Training machines to develop integrity still remains as a distant reality. Exploration of humanoids, robots and other artificial intelligence products always had the limitations in terms of Emotional Intelligence. Remote operation of these systems by unauthorized individuals or social extremists will pose serious questions to our method of implanting technology overshadowing the security versus development.

Less Vigilant Workforce

Too much automation or technology intervention naturally encourages existing workforce as less proactive to any situation. The best scenario to understand this fact is malfunctioning of a traffic signal near a busy junction. Even though the traffic regulating person exist in the junction, not often the situation arises where human intervention is must, due to increased smart traffic management systems. The traffic regulatory person remains obsolete for most of the time and will have a less chance to react smartly for the much-needed scenario that arises due to collapse of the machine-to-machine regulatory environment.

Possible Methods of Using Technology

A Collision free road map for the effective implementation with less intense adverse social implications is the need of the hour. The usage of Internet of Things shall be restricted to the level of controlling systems rather than in other manpower related operational zones. Adhering to standardized systems, assuring utmost security as well as privacy, and reducing inter-operability issues are must. Public attitudes, opinions are most crucial before deploying this technology in any specific domain that is directly influencing the social life. Addressing social vulnerability is a major concern when replacing the manpower with machine. Sensors shall be placed only in the data collections point where the transparency and privacy in data acquisition is not at stake. Developing the systems in line with the policies and practices of the regional and national regulations is another must look into consideration. Involving multi-disciplined people in designing procedures for the effective implementation of this technology is another prime factor towards reaching uncomfortable junctions.

CONCLUSION AND FUTURE SCOPE

Machine replacing man is advancement, but it should not be at the cost of questioning mere livelihood of effective manpower in various sectors. As always said, an efficient teacher in a classroom cannot be replaced effectively by a robot. The decision making by machines using IoT need not be at the scale of replacing humans. This will certainly question the natural intelligence as artificial intelligence still not procured the ideal state in human presence replacement.

IoT is still in the early stages of development, which means still the road is left free to redesign the policies and principles involving more stakeholders. These policies should mitigate the negative impact of the implementation of this technology. In future, there should be more debates and discussions, awareness campaign about the positives and challenges of using this technology among general public. The policy framing is the major concern when the induction of new technology takes place, which should carefully weigh the implications on society.

REFERENCES

Ali, B., & Awad, A. (2018). Bako Ali 1 ID and Ali Ismail Awad(2018)."Cyber and Physical Security Vulnerability Assessment for IoT-Based Smart Homes. *Sensors (Basel)*, *18*(3), 817. doi:10.339018030817

Atzori, L., Iera, A., & Morabito, G. (2010). The Internet of Things: A survey. *Computer Networks*, *54*(15), 2787–2805. doi:10.1016/j.comnet.2010.05.010

Bonner, M. (2018). What is Industry 4.0 and What Does it Mean for My Manufacturing?

Brous, P. & Janssen, M. (2015). Effects of The Internet of Things (Iot): A Systematic Review of The Benefits and Risks. In *Proceedings of the 2015 International Conference on Electronic Business*, Taipei.

Elmangoush, A., Coskun, H., Wahle, S., & Magedanz, T. (2013, March). Design aspects for a reference M2M communication platform for Smart Cities. In *Proceedings of the 2013 9th International Conference on Innovations in Information Technology (IIT)* (pp. 204-209). IEEE.

Haller, S., Karnouskos, S., & Schroth, C. (2008, September). The internet of things in an enterprise context. In Future Internet Symposium (pp. 14-28). Springer. doi:10.1007/978-3-642-00985-3_2

Haroon, A., Shah, M. A., Asim, Y., Naeem, W., Kamran, M., & Javaid, Q. (2016). Constraints in the IoT: The world in 2020 and beyond. *Constraints*, *7*(11), 252–271.

Hermann, M., Pentek, T., & Otto, B. (2016, January). Design principles for industrie 4.0 scenarios. In *Proceedings of the 2016 49th Hawaii international conference on system sciences (HICSS)* (pp. 3928-3937). IEEE.

Kowatsch, T., & Maass, W. (2012). [Social Acceptance and Impact Evaluation.]. *IoT-I Deliverable*, *D2*, 4.

Marr, B. (2018). Why Everyone Must Get Ready For The 4th Industrial Revolution.

Shen, S., & Carug, M. (2014). An Evolutionary Way to Standardize the Internet of Things. *J. ICT Stand.*, *2*(2), 87–108. doi:10.13052/jicts2245-800X.222

Siponen, M. T., & Willison, R. (2009). Information Security Management Standards: Problems and Solutions. *Information & Management*, *46*(5), 267–270. doi:10.1016/j.im.2008.12.007

Weber, R. (2010). Internet of Things - New security and privacy challenges. *Computer Law & Security Review*, *26*(1), 23–30. doi:10.1016/j.clsr.2009.11.008

ADDITIONAL READING

Crump, J. & Brown, I. (2013). Chairs of BCS. A report of a workshop on the Internet of Things - The Societal Impact of the Internet of Things organized by BCS.

Greenough, J. (2014). The Corporate 'Internet Of Things' Will Encompass More Devices. BusinessInsider. Retrieved from www.businessinsider.in/ The-Corporate-Internet-Of-Things-Will-Encompass-More-Devices-Than-The-Smartphone-And-Tablet-Markets-Combined/articleshow/45483725.cms

Liffler, M. & Tschiesner, A. (2013). The Internet of Things and the future of manufacturing | McKinsey & Company. Mckinsey.com.

Chapter 5
Internet of Things:
Impact of IoT on Human Life

G. Geetha

https://orcid.org/0000-0003-4572-0258
Jerusalem College of Engineering, India

ABSTRACT

The internet of things is a prime technology that promises to improve human lives. The revolution of the internet of things (IoT), along with the rapid growing of robots in many applications of everyday life, makes embedded IoT with robotics applications impact the future social growth. IoT technology aims at improving the quality of following social things similar to urban life by collecting personal data, tracking human movements, mapping them with various sources of information. The objective of the internet of things is to connect billions of things like sensors, actuators, RFID devices, and others make this technology an important aspect in our everyday life and work. The IoT could emphasize the social values as privacy, equality, trust, and individual choice and their implementation and management.

DOI: 10.4018/978-1-5225-8555-8.ch005

INTRODUCTION

The Internet of Things is a prime technology that promises to improve human lives. The revolution of the Internet of Things (IoT), along with the rapid growing of robots in many applications of everyday life, makes embedded IoT with robotics applications impacts the future social growth. IoT technology aims at improving the quality of following social things similar to urban life by collecting personal data, tracking human movements, mapping them with various sources of information. The objective of the Internet of Things is to connect billions of things like sensors, actuators, RFID devices and others make this technology an important aspect in our everyday life and work. The IoT could emphasize the social values as privacy, equality, trust and individual choice and their implementations and managements.

The Internet of Things (IoT) technology is an important aspect of city life in the next ten years. In the IoT domain, various information and communication technologies (ICTs) have been used to reduce various urban problems. Smart cities and various IoT applications will adopt ICTs for urban development process. The cities with IoT frame work allow urban residents and ``things'' to be connected to the Internet by virtue of the extension of the Internet Protocol from IPv4 to IPv6 and sensor technology. The privacy and security related challenges of IoT technologies may affect urben people. Furthermore, disparities in the spread of IoT systems across different countries may allow some countries to subvert the privacy of other countries' citizens.

Literature Survey:

Wigmore (2014) defined the IoT as, "It is a scenario in which objects, animals and people have been provided with unique identifiers or address and the ability to transfer data over a network without necessarily requiring human-to-human or human-to-computer interaction". Systems designed for the purposes of persuasion (Singh et al, 2014) can use IoT for enhanced feedback of the outcomes of actions with disguisers and virtual robots (Bettencourt, 2014). Bettencourt's (2014) proposed paper presents an analysis of the impact of connectivity in advanced informational networks similar to cities, the Internet, and Wikipedia, and the importance of the cost-benefit trade-off of connectivity for the success of the network.

In recent years, smart cities with IoT, have become an aspiration for various decision makers and individuals and have been considered a solution to various urban problems (Hassan et al, 2015). It has been estimated that 100 billion devices related to the Internet of Things (IoT) could enter service in the coming years. So that, people and the things surrounding them will be linked through the internet and facilitating many services and processes (Medaglia et al, 2010). The IoT technology involves a network of physical entities that contain embedded technology for collecting, communicating, sensing, interacting and monitoring with their internal states and the states of the external environment using either wireless or wired connections; these objects also include unique addressing schemes to enable new applications or services and to achieve common goals. The IoT technology is regarded as a means of connecting every physical things in our lives (Vermesan et al, 2013). The IoT technology is oriented around three concepts, those are the Internet or network, things or objects, and semantics (Atzori et al, 2010). Technically, the IoT architecture has been divided into three layers, the perception layer, the network layer, and the application layer. The perception layer has the function of recognizing objects and gathering data. Thus, it works with sensors, smartphones, and radio frequency identification (RFID) tags and various technologies. The network layer consists of a wireless or wired network used for data transmission. The application layer is the end-user layer, in which different IoT applications could be deployed (Domingo et al, 2012).

Impact of IoT on Human Life

Internet of Things is the interconnection of various types of devices, which may be wearable or non-wearable. The impact of technology on human life is prominent. With a big change in the technological world, society has to adapt to new technologies to stay ahead. In fact the IoT technology has filled the gap between digital and physical world. An important aspect of IoT is that it provides interaction between machines and computers, which are so far, in real time. According to some survey, the IoT market value will be approximately *$9 trillion* by 2020. This says that, the pace at which this technology is growing.

As a common user, the general idea about the Internet of things is that it belongs to the IT (Information Technology) domain precisely. However, IoT is a broader term pertaining to everything or all domains. That is IoT applications are belong to small business to big data analysis.

The following are the some ways of affecting social lives with IoT technology:

Anywhere Access

The definition of IoT defines that, the things have been connected over a network, virtually, for instance smart lock, here the IoT user has to access the smart lock through the technology and this makes it easy for the humans. Any user with access to this technology, who wants to control this lock easily by connecting that lock with the personal electronic device, either it be a mobile phone or any embedded device . This makes user to access a device remotely also.

Monitoring the Process

Another advantage of IoT technology is, which is more beneficial for businesses in manufacturing and production of various products by monitoring the respective processes. In manufacturing process that follows assembly lines must be monitored and this can be easily done with the addition of IoT technology. For production department the quality of the product must be tested before delivery, this can also be done with better QoS using IoT technology. A lot of sensed data that are recorded through the wireless sensor network, can be analyzed to improve processes, this makes manufacturing and production process more efficient and also reduce costs.

Accurate Value Prediction

By using advanced technology like environmental sensors and IoT, helps to predict real time natural disasters and can be analyzed, what can occur in the future, one of them being the IOT. For instance the real-time applications of this is smart sensors in the countries like Dublin, Ireland, already creating a real-time prediction of what is going to happen because of natural disasters and also helps the respective governments to take necessary precautions. The importance of accurate value prediction would also come into the picture for the smart health application. With the wearable sensors and IoT technology the doctor can predict the health condition of the patient and give the appropriate treatment.

Secure Data Transfer

In IoT technology devices are connected virtually and physically. In this technology the transfer of data packets is a simple process. This is an advantage for both businesses and people living in this society. With the IoT, various things connected to the internet can access, receive and communicate with each other through the communication protocols like IPv6, RFID, WiFi etc. For each communication protocol, the protocols like IPSec, TLS,SSL, DTLS provides the necessary security and privacy. To improve the efficiency, to simplify the processes and best QoS, IoT is an prominent technology.

Similar to other technologies, IoT technology also has some pros and cons pertaining to social lives. The following IoT implications are instances of the pros for social lives.

Smart Cities

- Smart Traffic or Smart Roads: Intelligent parking system: Monitoring the parking places available in the city.
- Smart lighting
- Garbage management system
- Monitoring energy and water use
- Smart security: Monitoring the security and privacy systems using sensors and surveillance cameras mounted.
- Smart animal farming
- Building automation and smart grids

Smart Business and Industires

- Online shopping
- Secure online payments
- Smart product shipment
- Machine-to-Machine applications
- Smart Healthcare systems
- Smart and mobile medicine systems

Smart Agriculture

- Smart Compost
- Smart plantation
- Smart drip irrigation system

The following are the some disadvantages of IoT technology over the social lives Figure 1.

Job Automation (Unemployemnet)

The IoT technology makes connected machines or things as smarter. So that various applications will become automated for instance, agricultural process or industries. Here the human efforts need not be required as a result, millions of people may lose the work or jobs. From a societal point of view, it could be devastating.

Smart Driving Systems (Driverless)

This technology also creates problems for humans, who is working as drivers. For every driverless car, taxi, truck, train or planes there is a person or human being who is no longer required. Moreover, if any system failure occurs, then it is very difficult to imagine the consequences.

Personal Data will be Under Threat

In IoT technology, data would be stored in the "cloud." The data might be related to family photos to personal financial information and that

Figure 1. Effects of IoT technology in human life

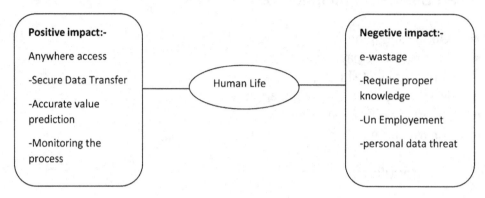

will be maintained somewhere on remote servers it creates. So it is a big challenge to maintain the privacy regarding personal data.

E-Wastage

Billions of electronic devices would be connected with IoT technology and those devices would be replaced if the respective device has failed. So proportional to the growing IoT network, the e-wastage will also be increased

Technical Knowledge Should Require

For any IoT application, to maintain and access the services the respective beneficiary should have basic knowledge regarding IoT technology. And it is a challenge to educate the village illiterate people pertaining to IoT .

With the rapid growth of the IoT, many devices have been connected through sensors for various IoT applications like smart residence and smart cities. In smart home application, there have been significant benefits derived from the IoT to enhance the features like energy, increase security and make life easier. In smart city application, which empower citizens at the individual and organizational level to participate and assist in designing cities more effective, productive, secure and healthy. The new technological innovations and advancements have a positive impact on everyday social lives, these implications enhance the explosive growth of data in the IoT. This huge amount of data must be managed in an effective manner. The traffic on the networks must also be addressed for better social implications. The cloud computing technology can be used to handle the unpredictable workloads for various IoT applications. Another implication has to be considered for proper security measures and policies, since the data and devices becoming more exposed in IoT applications. With these unprecedented data, there are obvious challenges with data governance and the impact of this data on networks, and how to maintain the necessary security. The developments of IoT will move faster than their policies and protocols, It is a big challenge to manage the protocols.

Future Impact of IoT on Social Lives

Based on the Gartener's prediction 8 billion of connected devices were present upto 2017 for 2020 it may become 50 billion. To handle the sensor data the technology like big data analytics comes into the picture and the augmentation of artificial intelligence with IoT creates wonders in for various social implications. Chatbots are another important future IoT implication with IoT and machine learning. Wearable sensors and body devices are intelligent enough to understand the status and monitor our physiology this makes humans to achieve specific health-related goals and warns the patients about specific problems In future, human lives will fully depends on IoT and sensors, that is, various sensors will be seamlessly incorporated into all aspects of everyone's lives, for instance the sensors will be embedded in the mattresses or in their car steering to monitor the human's physical and mental state reports for precautions.

REFERENCES

Atzori, Iera, & Morabito. (2010). The Internet of Things: A survey. *Comput. Netw., 54*(15), 2787-2805.

Bettencourt, L. (2014). Impact of changing technology on the evolution of complex informational networks. *Proceedings of the IEEE, 102*(12), 1878–1891. doi:10.1109/JPROC.2014.2367132

Domingo. (2012). An overview of the Internet of Things for people with disabilities. *J. Netw. Comput. Appl., 35*(2), 584-596.

Hassan & Lee. (2015). The paradox of the sustainable city: De_nitions and examples. *Environ. Develop. Sustainability, 17*(6), 1267-1285.

Medaglia, C. M., & Serbanati, A. (2010). An overview of privacy and security issues in the Internet of Things. In The Internet of Things. New York, NY: Springer. doi:10.1007/978-1-4419-1674-7_38

Quilici-Gonzalez, J. A., Broens, M. A., Gonzalez, M. E. Q., & Kobayashi, G. (2014). Complexity and information technologies: an ethical inquiry into human autonomous action. Scientiae Studia, 12.

Singh, V., Mani, A., & Pentland, A. (2014). Social persuasion in online and physical networks. *Proceedings of the IEEE, 102*(12), 1903–1910. doi:10.1109/JPROC.2014.2363986

Vermesan, O. (2013). Internet of Things strategic research and innovation agenda. In Internet of Things: Converging Technologies for Smart Environments and Integrated Ecosystems. River Publishers.

Wigmore, I. (2014). Internet of Things (IoT). *TechTarget.* Available: http://whatis.techtarget.comldefinition/Internet-of-Things

Chapter 6
Business Aspects, Models, and Opportunities of IoT

Baghavathi Priya S.
Rajalakshmi Engineering College, India

Vinothini Arumugam
Rajalakshmi Engineering College, India

ABSTRACT

The new conceivable rule of the future is going to be anything can be connected and will be connected over the internet. Technically, internet of things, is defined as the computing concept of connecting the devices over the internet. This adds a level of digital intelligence to the devices, enabling them to communicate without the human being involved. This chapter will discuss about the business aspects, models, and opportunities involved in IoT. The internet of things or IoT is basically about the interconnection of uniquely identifiable and programmable embedded devices within its infrastructure with the help of the internet.

DOI: 10.4018/978-1-5225-8555-8.ch006

INTRODUCTION

The Internet of Things or IoT is basically about the interconnection of uniquely identifiable and programmable embedded devices with in its infrastructure with the help of internet (Minerva.R.,2015). The IoT can transform any business of an industry starting from manufacturing to even save the endangered species of the world. The IoT is trendy because of the combination of increased global internet access and also by the growing number of devices designed to connect and this in return is creating endless opportunities. The statistics say that it is expected that more than 20 billion people, systems and physical objects will be connecting and sharing data seamlessly over the internet by 2020.

What Is the Scope of IoT?

The IoT essentially makes things 'smart' and brings major changes in delivery of products, goods and services. IoT connect devices that are embedded in various devices through the internet. When these devices/ objects are represented digitally, then can easily be controlled from anywhere. This type of digital connectivity helps us to collect more data from places and thereby ensuring efficiency, improved safety and IoT security. Companies prefer IoT technology as a transformational force that can help them to improve their performance through IoT analytics and IoT security to deliver better results (Hota.J et al.,2015). This IoT is an advanced automation and analytics system which comes with a combination of networking, sensing, big data and artificial intelligence technology to deliver a complete framework for a product or service. The IoT framework facilitates greater transparency, control and performance when applied to any industry or system. The IoT framework has applications across many industries through their unique flexibility and ability to be suitable for any environment. As a result of this, it enhances data collection, automation, operations and much more other functionalities through smart devices and powerful enabling technology.

How IoT Can Help the Business?

IoT platform is the future and it helps the large/small scale organizations to reduce cost through their improved performance and efficiency, infrastructure utilization, and increased productivity. With its improved tracking of devices and objects using the sensors and connectivity, they can capture the real-time data and this insights & analytics would help the organizations to make smarter decisions to increase the performance across all business units (Hui, G., 2014). The major strength of IoT is data, the growth and convergence of the data, processes and things on the internet that would make those such connections to be more relevant and important and hence creates more opportunities for peoples, businesses and industries and increases sales. According to a research by Business Insider, global manufacturers will invest $70 billion in IoT solutions in 2020.IoT is mainly about the inter-connection of devices to fetch real-time data. With this amplification in connectivity, it brings innovation in the way we use and relate to those devices. Hence in this emerging IoT marketplace, the concept of the services related to those connected devices help to bring more value for the business. As a result of this, the IT pioneers are implementing new ideas of connecting both the things and devices to deliver new services to the market. IoT is considered as the biggest frontier which can improve our lives in many aspects. Those devices which have never been networked can get connected and respond just like the smart devices do, for e.g. your car, refrigerator, and home speakers. IoT is set to transform our world completely (Zanella.A.et al.,2014).

Some of the benefits of using IoT include (Ustundag.A.,et al 2018)

Increased Business Opportunity: IoT has certainly opened the door for more new business opportunities and helps companies to increase their revenue using the advanced business models and services. IoT has the ability to transform the way the businesses and customers approach the world by leveraging the scope of IoT beyond connectivity. Also, IoT helps to build strong business cases at a reduced time to market and improves the scales.

Infrastructure Modernization: Using IoT, the organizations can track the infrastructure assets such as software, equipment, machinery and tools using the sensors and connectivity and brings down real-time insights for the business. With the help of tracking system, the organizations can easily identify the issues and do the preventive maintenance to improve the asset utilization.

Connectivity to Many Devices Process: As IoT helps to connect maximum number of devices to the internet, it facilitates the businesses to be smarter with the tracking of real-time operational insights thereby reducing the operational cost. This data collected from logistics network, supply chain etc. helps to reduce the inventory, mitigates cost, reduces time to market and improves maintenance by reducing the downtime.

Increased Productivity: technology is easy to understand with just-in-time training for employees. It improves the labor efficiency and predominantly reduces the mismatch of skills and helps in increased organizational productivity.

Reduced Cost: Organization's operational cost reduces with the help of IoT since the infrastructure is utilized efficiently and improved productivity. The data captured helps in predictive analytics and real-time diagnostics and this reduces the maintenance cost.

BACKGROUND

IoT- internet of things, is a term that is defined as, the interconnection through internet with the physical devices, vehicles, home appliances and other items embedded with sensors, software's and enabling them to send and receive data. The idea of adding sensors and intelligence to the devices or the basic objects was discussed in the early 1990s, but the process was slow because the technology was not advanced to support this initiative during that time period. The first phrase on 'internet of things' was coined in 1999 by kevin ashton, the co-founder of mit's(massachusetts institute of technology) auto-id center, but it almost took a decade for the digital technology to catch up with the vision. This has been made possible with the availability of the broadband internet and the advancement in the wireless networking services. Initially IoT was concentrated on the business and manufacturing sector. But now, it has been extended to household and offices with the help of smart devices. For any business or service, the key business aspects have to be properly designed to achieve it. The major business aspects to be taken into consideration are 1. Technology, IoT works on a huge global technological platform and companies have to open for adopting the new standards. 2.Business Innovation, the combination of the people and the smart devices will lead to innovation in the business(Zanella.A.et al.,2014). 3.Competencies, the ability to link the business ideas with the technology and the software services with deep domain knowledge and creativity enhances the business. 4. Market, IoT has the potential to combine many separate businesses into a group and meet in the market to increase the overall sales. 5.Cost, IoT will transform business operations by helping to reduce business costs and boost profits. One of the toughest challenges the companies developing IoT products face lies in choosing the right business model and there is no single canonical business model for IoT and implementers of IoT solutions will have to consider carefully, where their product, service, or solution sits within the IoT value-chain that is based on the right business model. The IoT sector is moving fast and the key to long term survival lays in the ability of IoT solution providers to create and maintain differentiation. IoT technologies prove economically feasible only when they can deliver recurring and continuous value for the customer. The core potential business models that can be applied to an IoT product or services are 1. Value added feature, 2. Simple purchase, 3. Pay per use, 4. Ecosystem play, 5. Secondary revenue stream, 6. A platform for co-sharing, 7. A platform for cross-selling and 8. Benefit share with the provider(Hubert C. Y. Chan.,2015). Based on the business needs and the service demand, the associated business model has to be selected. India's IoT market is In order to build an IoT product, certain business aspects have to be followed to achieve it because the IoT is built on a complex ecosystem with a host of different technologies. expected to grow exponentially over the next couple of years with new projects on hand. The recent survey states that the maximum IoT business opportunity comes from the following sectors namely 1. Medical/Healthcare, 2. Energy, 3. Industrial, 4. Education. The key drive for this opportunity is mainly because of the government initiatives, development of smart applications and increasing internet penetration across the country. The other opportunities will include smart homes, water and traffic management system, fitness trackers, smart transportation, smart grids, surveillance and security with the help of smart sensors and clustered systems(Zanella.A.et al.,2014). The threats of IoT falls under three categories namely 1. Privacy, 2. Security and 3. Safety. The personal information that will potentially reside on the network are prone to cybercriminal attacks and therefore every aspect of the system must be secure and provides the necessary control to the users. The security and privacy challenges can be addressed by following the Secure System Development Life Cycle(SDLC) practices, secure coding practices and periodic penetration testing activities. Introducing security in the early life cycle will result in the successive implementation of the IoT product.

BUSINESS ASPECTS

Technology

The Internet of Things will demand an extensive range of new technologies and skills that many companies haven't yet mastered, says Nick Jones, vice president and distinguished analyst at Gartner.

IoT Security: Security technologies will be required to protect IoT devices and platforms from both information attacks and physical tampering, to encrypt their communications, and to address new challenges such as impersonating "things" or denial-of-sleep attacks that drain batteries. IoT security will be complicated by the fact that many "things" use simple processors and operating systems that may not support sophisticated security approaches.

IoT Analytics: IoT business models will exploit the information collected by "things" in many ways, which will demand new analytic tools and algorithms. As data volumes increase over the next five years, the needs of the IoT may diverge further from traditional analytics.

IoT Device (Thing) Management: Long-lived nontrivial "things" will require management and monitoring, including device monitoring, firmware and software updates, diagnostics, crash analysis and reporting, physical management, and security management. Tools must be capable of managing and monitoring thousands and perhaps even millions of devices.

Low-Power, Short-Range IoT Networks: Low-power, short-range networks will dominate wireless IoT connectivity through 2025, far outnumbering connections using wide-area IoT networks. However, commercial and technical trade-offs mean that many solutions will coexist, with no single dominant winner.

Business Innovation

The Internet of Things such as smart cities, connected vending machines, connected cars and smart homes are beginning to change the way we live our lives today (Khorov. E et al.,2015). New business scenarios are opening across industries like Utilities, Retail, Automotive, Public Sector and Healthcare. Large and small technology firms are helping enterprises uncover wisdom from the mountains of data in the connected world. With this new frontier of highly fragmented technologies and standards, who will be the winners? Corporate venturing and innovation teams must find a pragmatic and systematic approach to evaluating this gold rush of opportunities.

Smart Lighting Solutions: Lighting Control and Energy Optimization

The Nokia IoT Smart Lighting solution provides energy monitoring and dynamic control capabilities. Integration with the Nokia IMPACT IoT Platform provides data collection and management, integration into existing wireless networks, and device management for light sensors (secure provisioning and communication). This interconnected and ubiquitous smart lighting solution enables municipalities to optimize electricity use and reduce costs through real-time inventory management; while automatically detecting lighting issues and failures to help ensure maximum uptime. A management dashboard to monitor individual street lights, showing the location of each light on a map, as well as each light's status (on/off). Configuration settings, allowing for remote control of each light's operation, luminosity level (for LED lights) and the name of each light point. Analytics functionality, with details on the energy consumption of each street light (Chiang.M.,et al 2016). Integration with the Nokia IMPACT IoT Platform, which provides data collection and management, integration into existing wireless networks, and device management for light sensors (secure provisioning and communication).

Smart Parking Solutions: Reduced time spent finding parking, resulting in reduced traffic congestion, lower fuel consumption and fewer emissions Improved parking space utilization; Increased revenue for law enforcement; Enhanced analytics capabilities, providing details on revenue, current versus historic occupancy rates, total number of spaces available and more; Track parking meter status and violations, in real time.

How Scene Analytics Provides Real-Time Monitoring and Analytics?

The Nokia Scene Analytics solution works by turning cameras into IoT sensors. It derives abstract information such as motion, direction, density, and velocity vectors from each video feed, then uses machine learning technology – developed by Nokia's Bell Labs – to analyze these vectors in real time. The software establishes patterns, identifies anomalies, and generates alerts. Nokia Scene Analytics enhances situational awareness and prioritizes streams for their anticipated relevance, automatically allocating network resources based on dynamic application needs. The least relevant streams are cut off at the source, ensuring network availability for the most critical ones. The Nokia Scene Analytics solution, in parallel with the Nokia IMPACT IoT Platform, works with any video monitoring solution. The software is agnostic to video resolutions, camera brands, and networking options, so you can quickly implement it with the equipment you already have.

Medical and Fitness Spheres: Fitness wearables are not new to us and it seems that they are connected to the Internet as they communicate with our smartphones. But IoT goes further. A fit bracelet connected with the IoT system can do much more. The easiest and the most obvious ability of such devices is to pass data about your heartbeat to a medical establishment or to a doctor in an emergency occasion.

Solar Roads: They are reusable and removable panels made of cheap materials. The panels use solar energy and have lots of advantages. For instance, they can warn drivers about obstacles and animals on the road. They have led lights that improve the visibility, can be used as a carriageway marking and help control traffic.

Traffic Controllers: Various sensors could be used to predict dangerous situations on the road. They can track the number of cars and redirect upcoming vehicles to different roads.

Smart Bus Stops: They can not only show the information about traffic but also be interactive, turn heating\air conditioning on and off when there are people on the bus stop and when it's empty.

IoT Toys: Toymail is a company that already produces toys with talkies inside. What a user has to do is to download a special app, buy a toy and leave it with a child. Talkies allow a user to send messages to a child and get replies. This is a great way always to be near your child even if you are at work.

Cars: Security when a driver is in a car and when he or she isn't. Multiple built-in sensors can easily identify a driver defining such parameters as weight, height and arm length. If these parameters don't match the IoT car locks itself immediately. As well as that, sensors can also improve security on the road, when a driver is in a car. Simple distance measurements between cars can save lots of lives.

Territory IoT Monitoring: In farming, IoT devices can do lots of tasks. They can measure the soil humidity and control the water supply. They can control how ripe fruit and vegetable are and inform the farmer about harvesting time and so on. Smart approaches reduce costs and advances forecasts, planning and harvesting processes.

Competencies

Information Management: IoT data is distributed, voluminous and continuous, so double-down to efficiently capture, organize and govern it all.

Analytics: Improved operational intelligence (to improve business outcomes) is the whole point of IoT projects, and you may need a mix of localized, aggregated and deep analytics (Westerlund..M.,et al.,2014).

Integration: Whether IT (e.g., ERP, SCM) or OT (e.g., MES, BMS) Apps, complex IoT projects typically embrace and extend core business Apps, data and processes.

Security: IoT significantly expands your security threat surface so assess your risks and invest to sufficiently protect your IoT networks, platforms, Apps and data.

Five practices that Build Organizational IoT Competence: Benson highlighted five main practices successful companies adopt that build organization competence including: Having a baseline current in IoT competence in the areas of digital innovation, technology maturity, and businesses clarity and market readiness; Developing and communicating a clear, compelling actionable IoT strategy across the organization that includes executive support, funding from the top and a mandate for cross-department collaboration; Starting small with early wins targeted at reducing business risk while addressing pressing questions early; Looking for opportunities to standardize and reuse common components across divisions and projects; Closing the knowledge gap by building the organization from the outside in. Starting with external help and simultaneously, developing and growing core IoT competencies over time.

Market

The Internet of Things enables marketers to create totally different experiences in bridging the digital and physical world. 'connected consumer' who is becoming hyper-connected once you start adding devices as happens in the Internet of Things, is a great source of data for marketing. Internet of Things in marketing also enables marketers to provide highly contextual and tailored messages to consumers, for instance in connection with digital signage in physical situations such as in stores or via mobile or other devices in digital interactions. In the shopping environment of retail, marketers are increasingly looking at IoT. Research shows that the customer is often key in retail IoT business case. Some projections say there will be 23.3 billion IoT devices by 2019, which is twice as many tablets, smartphones and PCs today combined. According to the infographic 51% of the world's top global marketers expect that IoT will revolutionize the marketing landscape by 2020. After looking at some consumer evolutions Market resumes the ways marketers will use IoT (mainly in a data-driven marketing view) as follows:

- Analyzing customer buying habit across the platform's customers use.
- More and previously unobtainable data regarding the way's consumers interact with devices and products (the "connected devices" themselves).
- Getting a better insight into the buying journey and in which stage of it the customer is.
- Real-time interactions, POS notifications and of course targeted ads.

Cost: "The Internet of Things is going to be a big thing for small business," says Tim Reid, a network system engineer and consultant for private industry and government. Referring to the concept of billions of objects being connected to the Internet, Reid points out that smaller firms will be able to cut costs and become more competitive. A study by logistics service provider DHL and IT firm Cisco predicts that the IOT will save businesses $1.2 trillion in productivity costs alone.

Inventory Management: You can keep track of costly inventory – even with it being in a remote location such as a warehouse. With inventory sensors on small items or large products, businesses can reorder stock as it runs low.

Safety Compliance: "There are many local, state and federal regulations, but small businesses often don't have the funds to hire compliance teams internally," says Reid. IOT allows small businesses to use sensors to measure air quality, temperature, and other conditions that may be governed.

Potential Revenue Stream: "The big thing about the Internet of Things is that it can be a model for recurring revenue every month," says Reid. For example, a small business can put sensors on a product that it installs and "offer to monitor it for customers for a monthly fee."

Security: For years, video surveillance has utilized physical tape that could be removed or damaged. With the IOT, videos are connected to the Internet and can be viewed remotely. "Business owners can track access to their building based on fingerprints and badges. This is inexpensive and easy to implement," says Reid.

Wages and Labor Savings: If your business monitors or repairs products for customers, the IOT can be revolutionary. Traditionally, companies send out a person to repair a product or resolve an issue on site, which can be costly. With the IOT, data can be sent from the product directly to your company's computer. You can troubleshoot, rule out problems and make decisions without leaving your office.

Energy Management: Gone are the days of the maintenance staff going from room to room and building to building to adjust the thermostat. "It is now connected to sensors that can be controlled remotely," says Reid. Businesses can save on energy costs by powering down when parts of their facilities are not being used.

Business Models

Value Added Services in IoT

We can enhance a basic voice or video call enough that a subscriber would be willing to spend more on it? For example, call recording or conferencing or prepaid charging or even getting a daily joke are examples of that. Most IoT network traffic is related to data from sensors. However, there will be cases when value-added real time communications will be required, such as when someone may need to talk to you through the SIM card in your car(Guo L.,et al, 2017). Or when this happens, there will likely be a need to record this voice and/or video call. Or maybe closer to home, if someone is ringing your doorbell, then a live video feed can go to either your smartphone or your desktop or your tablet, whichever you choose, so you can see if you want to actually get up and go to the door. There have also been many healthcare examples written about where voice and/or video would be required. In these cases, the value-add is real-time communications via voice or video. It's an add-on to the normal IoT traffic routine, one that for specific use cases makes sense. Dialogic has been participating in value added services for real-time communications since its inception almost 35 years ago.

Value Added Features in Mobile Communication: The majority of revenue is derived from the provision of value-added services (Guo L.,et al, 2017) and operators are building new capabilities to address these new service areas. While connectivity will underpin the development of the Internet of Things, to avoid becoming commoditized, mobile operators need to leverage their networks' potential to provide value added services and build what could become a US$422.6 billion industry. The majority of these revenues are to be derived from the 'Service Wrap' 11. The 'Service Wrap' comprises the service that the end customer pays for that relies on the underlying connectivity, and operators are investing in building new capabilities that improve their offering to IoT service propositions.

Smart Buildings

Creating Value Through Efficiency: With BMS already firmly established in the CRE sector, it is perhaps no surprise that many of the initial uses of IoT technology help CRE companies by increasing efficiency through enhanced building performance and better portfolio and liquidity management.

Enhanced Building Performance: IoT-enabled BMS can be used to reduce energy use, repair and maintenance, and administrative costs. For instance, property owners can use the data collected by motion and occupancy sensors at a building level to regulate air-conditioning and lighting in real time, thereby reducing energy costs and optimizing the internal environment for its data intended purpose. CRE companies can also offer clear value to tenants, since the system could lead to lower energy bills. According to Bettina Tratz-Ryan, research vice president at Gartner Inc., "Especially in large sites, such as industrial zones, office parks, shopping malls, airports or seaports, IoT can help reduce the cost of energy, spatial management and building maintenance by up to 30 percent. "The continuous monitoring and predictive capability of IoT-enabled buildings can also preempt a repair or maintenance issue by enabling a building manager to take appropriate corrective action before tenants even notice a problem. According to a Johnson Controls survey of the company's Building Efficiency Panel, 70 percent of respondents believe that the ability to predict and diagnose problems and provide or propose solutions will be a "game changer."

Creating Value Through Differentiation: With the amount of connectivity and data generated by IoT-enabled buildings, CRE owners have an opportunity to differentiate themselves by using the information to identify unmet consumer demands, provide more sophisticated services to their tenants and transform tenant and user experience, and contribute to the broader ecosystem. By offering services their competitors as yet lack, CRE companies using IoT applications in this way could charge premium prices and improve margins. In fact, tenants will likely soon come to expect IoT features, meaning that a building lacking them may trade at a discount.

Creating Value Through New Revenue Sources: While creating value through new revenue sources is likely a longer-term prospect, CRE companies can perhaps offer analytics-as-a-service (Guo L.,et al, 2017). This essentially means that companies can combine, analyze, and present insights from the large sets of data in a manner that tenants or other stakeholders can purchase and augment their actions and behavior.

As an example, data on people moving within a building can potentially be sold to advertisers or urban planners to help them in their decision making. In another example, retail real estate owners can capture and analyze end-customer demography, purchase, and movement data and sell it to their tenants. CRE companies can likely sell building performance information to institutional investors to allow them to make informed investment decisions.

Turning Value Into Revenue: Feature-based packaging refers to companies' ability to provide flexible offerings by allowing customers to configure their products, enabling or disabling features as desired. With IoT applications, this becomes particularly important because companies are no longer locked into selling a single product but, rather, can sell that same product in several different ways based on the combination of features offered to the customer. In fact, those product features can even change over time through over-the-air updates or purchases. By offering many different versions of a product at different price points, a company can capture a greater share of the market—and therefore increase its revenues.While feature-based packaging has traditionally been highly popular in the virtual goods market, it has started gaining traction among industrial machinery and durable goods companies as well. For example, one manufacturer of electric vehicles is now able to send over-the-air software updates that add new features and functionality to its cars, and allows customers to purchase software-based upgrades to unlock some of the functionalities that are already available in their cars. For $8,500 above the purchase price, customers can choose an upgraded version, which can travel about 40 more miles per charge without the need of changing hardware or even taking the car to the service center. The manufacturer can simply flip the software switch remotely.

IoT Case Study: How Nexia Implements Feature-Based Packaging?

Nexia focuses on home automation systems, offering solutions for controlling smart-home devices such as locks, sensors, lights, thermostats, and video cameras(Odusote.A.,2016).

Issue: Home automation has been a fragmented industry, with multiple standards and frameworks competing to augment manufacturers' proprietary ecosystems. The lack of integration across technologies and devices has necessitated workarounds, complicating home automation and limiting industry growth.

Solution: Nexia employs an open architecture that supports more than 230 different types of devices across manufacturers. The company designed an interface that focuses on user behavior and features so that homeowners do not have to deal with the complexity of integrating different devices. In doing so, Nexia implemented feature-based packaging by providing a huge selection of compatible products across manufacturers as components that can be integrated like building blocks. Consumers need purchase only those blocks that they want to use; they can upgrade to add more blocks anytime, increasing both the value to the customer and the revenue opportunities for the company.

Monetization strategy: The initial cost is a start-up kit that includes the Nexia Hub and a dimmer module. From here, consumers can customize their experience with an à la carte selection of add-ons across various categories such as security, climate, lighting, energy, garage, and water. These add-ons can be bought together or separately and can be further packaged into combinations of features and manufacturers.

What Can a Toothbrush Teach Us About IoT Business Models?

(Vakulenko.M.,2016) A toothbrush example, as simple as it may sound, helps demonstrate that technology (software, connectivity or data), when viewed as a feature of a product, is hardly a game-changer for the product maker; opening the product to external innovation by developers can create a competitive advantage that is difficult to replicate; and, e-commerce companies see devices not as a source of profits, but as a part of the customer acquisition costs, serving as a vehicle for customer acquisition and engagement (Amazon Echo or Xiaomi phones are not much different, in this respect).Broadly speaking, a business model describes the rationale of how an organization creates, delivers and captures value. We add to that the question of how an organization creates a sustainable competitive advantage (a barrier to entry that is difficult to replicate by competitors).

Simple Purchase Model

Microsemi Collaborates with HMS Industrial Networks AB to Introduce Highly Secure Anybus CompactCom 40 Industrial Protocol Solutions. Anybus CompactCom 40-series products benefit from the flexibility of using SmartFusion2 technology when designing the NP40 that is the core in the Anybus CompactCom, enabling support of multiple industrial Ethernet protocols on a single FPGA platform and accelerating time-to- market while lowering total cost of ownership for our customers," said Christian Bergdahl, product marketing manager at HMS Industrial Networks. "We were able to leverage on SmartFusion2's advantages when designing the NP40 into scalable, reprogrammable, low power and secure industrial Ethernet solutions with a simple purchase model--allowing us to continue bringing our customers the latest industrial connectivity technology for embedded solutions."

According to HMS Industrial Networks' internal analysis, although serial fieldbus protocols still dominate industrial networking today, industrial Ethernet is growing at a rate of 17 percent per annum--more than double the fieldbus growth rate. This growth allows HMS Industrial Networks and Microsemi to continue developing products catering to the specific needs of this expanding market opportunity. HMS Industrial Networks is now offering its Anybus CompactCom 40-series products to its customers.

Steps in Simple Purchase Model: A simple purchase model is basically 3 steps: Create a purchase order (or place a purchase order with your supplier/vendor), receive the goods from your supplier/vendor and lastly, make the payment for the goods received.

Model of a Purchase Protocol: A typical purchase interaction commonly involves a customer, a merchant, and a trusted instance (which, in turn, interacts with one or more banks). Most of the existing commercial protocols in which one customer purchases goods from one merchant are well approximated by the abstract model. In the first step the client provides a description of the goods to be purchased, as well as some data representing a payment information (e.g., e-cash token, credit-card number, or account information). It also incorporates the initiation of the transaction, of the means to contact the participating instances (client, merchant, banks), etc. In the second step (money check) the validity of the payment information specified in the order If electronic cash token is used as means of payment, they will be "marked" after positive validation in order to prevent double-spending. The third step (prepare goods) represents the preparatory phase for goods delivery. This step and its predecessor (money check and prepare goods) are related in that preparation is not executed until subsequent payment is guaranteed by the financial institution.

Again, this step depends on the type of goods (electronic or real) to be delivered. The transfer of goods is closely related to the actions performed in the prepare goods phase where the details of this transfer have been arranged. In the case of electronic goods that have already been shipped in an encrypted way, this step corresponds to the transfer of the keys needed for decryption. Analogously, when encrypted electronic contracts have been transferred previously, the appropriate keys are delivered, and, in the case of non-electronic goods, shipment is initiated subsequently.

Pay Per Use IoT Model

This is a traditional method and they are usually associated with utilities such as electricity. Now, companies from all segments are looking at the opportunity of using this notion for products to transform business models where the consumer pays according to their level *of* use or consumption of the product and create new revenue streams. Software-based services enable IoT producers to bundle product aids, services and feature sets in new and creative ways that generate incremental new revenue streams in the form of subscription or pay-per-use models.

Streamline Billing for Greater Transparency: Furthermore, adopting pay-per-use makes the billing process so much simpler. IoT provides the data for service usage and this information can be directly charged. This format is incredibly clear, increases transparency across the whole billing cycle, and accelerates the process. Likewise, if there is room for improvement in terms of rates or tariffs, businesses have the information to identify this and act accordingly.

Reduce Production and Maintenance Costs with Pay-Per Use Service or machinery(Lai et al.,2018). Used to achieve better quality are also becoming available on a pay-per-use basis in what is known as equipment-as-a-service or EaaS. This means scalable costs which enable businesses to become more profitable by reducing operational costs. The changes in investments to a EaaS model changes the responsibilities and progressions related to maintenances well. Sensor data from the equipment itself enables predictive maintenance scenarios. The opportunity to make the shift from conventional maintenance models to implement a predictive maintenance program maximize uptime and reduce costs for repairs. This directly impacts efficiency and quality in the manufacturing processes. The key to enter this new era is collaboration between operator and supplier. Historical machinery data and sensor data combined with engineering knowledge enables decision makers to implement a predictive maintenance program.

Optimizing Product Quality With IoT-Driven Pay-Per-Use Models

It is not just the customer that benefits from these new business models. The business can also improve its product, create new services, and adopt new business models. A prime example of this is in agriculture. Farmers can now use pay-per-use services supported by IoT for tasks such as oil preparation, harvesting, and post-harvest field management to ensure consistent, high-quality. Gone are the days of trial and error. But there are many other examples in different sectors, such as manufacturing. Organizations that produce IoT enabled products can collect data on customer behavior and adapt products according to increase customer satisfaction or choose a more suitable billing model.

Ecosystem Play

Ecosystem Play is an ecosystem in which multiple separate devices can be linked. The ecosystem may be open (allowing anyone to attach to it) or closed (in which people have to pay to join the ecosystem) Example: Interconnected thermostat to which door sensors, smoke alarms, and CCTV cameras can be connected. The connected cyber physical systems transform and make more connected our life, people and things into overall world. Internet of Things is at a peak of hype and builds its own Ecosystem based on sensors and actuators, which communicate on industry and custom designed platforms through plethora of wireless, cellular and fixed communication networks. The IoT Ecosystem generates enormous amount of data, which is captured, filtered, analyzed and perform through data analytics a fundamental process for making IoT applications smart systems.

Networking via Smart Ecosystems: As smart ecosystems evolve, consumer devices will have to ship with the right networking and automation functions, based on smart ecosystems. The basis for this is cloud computing, dynamic platforms, and intelligent algorithms. They connect networked devices, manage applications, process data, deliver reports and contain advanced analytics functionalities such as cluster analysis and machine learning. An intelligent ecosystem is a combination of an embedded system, a mobile system, and an information system. The device is on the lower level, regardless of whether it is a coffee machine or a system in a factory. An embedded system implements the required functionality and logician the device, turning it into an intelligent device. The mobile system ensures connectivity and the data exchange, for example, with a mobile app as a component. The most common way to connect a device is to use the mobile network, local Wi-Fi, or use another device as a gateway by Bluetooth.

Secondary Revenue Stream Model

Reduced cost of adoption, is funded by a secondary revenue stream, often via the sale of data. Examples include sale of fitness bracelets, where aggregated data is sold to third-parties .By 2025, more than 100 billion Internet of Things connected devices are predicted to be live, generating an overall revenue of close to $10 trillion, writes Neil Hamilton, VP of Business Development at Thingstream.The industry's unprecedented growth to date looks poised to continue globally over the next few years, with the sensors market alone estimated to grow at a CAGR of 26.91% during 2016 to 2020. This has provided businesses with a huge opportunity to utilise IoT applications to reshape their business models, fully optimise their performance and open up new revenue streams through wide-scale, intelligent solutions(Dijkmana,R,M.,et al.,2015). This has contributed to the global implementation of IoT across many sectors, as businesses look for new and innovative methods in which to manage and monetise their services.

Four Revenue Streams Revolutionized by the Internet of Things.

Products-as-a-Service. Products-as-a-service is not an entirely new concept. Leasing a home, paying to use an air pump at a gas station, or even companies having to pay royalties to musicians and authors for their songs and books are all examples of the Product-as-a-Service concept.

Asset Sharing: Similar to Products-as-a-Service, asset sharing is a relatively old concept that recently has been broadened and enhanced with IoT. The idea is that assets owned by either consumers or companies can be rented out, or shared, amongst other consumers or businesses. A basic example of asset sharing would be renting out a car or home.

Automatic Fulfillment: Automatic fulfillment is a newer revenue stream that exploits up-to-the-second inventory data, analytics, and consumer input to replenish goods that customers or other businesses need, when, or even right before, they need it. In retail, automatic fulfillment ensures that supply can meet demand; if one store is out of an item, the IoT network quickly can find the nearest store or warehouse location with that item and work to replenish it as soon as possible. IoT not only speeds up the rate of order fulfillment but also decreases the cost. By setting up automated machines to weigh, package, and label orders as soon as a customer hits a button, companies can set up order fulfillment systems that are somewhat self-sufficient.

Data Monetization: One of the most valuable assets to come out of IoT is data itself. The data economy is older than many might guess. Consumer reports and television ratings are a few examples of data being monetized before the Internet of Things.

A Platform for Co-Sharing Model

Co-selling is an approach to product and service distribution in which channel partners are the primary route to market. If adhered to without exceptions, this approach is beneficial for VARs, integrators and managed service providers because it eliminates the potential for conflict between partners and vendors. The co-selling approach is also useful for identifying opportunities to improve sales and technical support.

C3 IoT: It has announced a strategic partnership with Google Cloud aiming to boost artificial intelligence (AI) and Internet of Things (IoT) development for enterprise digital transformation. Under this partnership, C3 IoT and Google Cloud have developed an integrated solution that looks to smoothly delivers the C3 IoT Platform, a comprehensive platform as a service (PaaS) for rapidly developing and operating big data, predictive analytics, AI, and IoT software applications, on Google Cloud Platform, using the innovative infrastructure and AI services to maximum advantage. In addition, both companies will execute co-marketing, co-selling, and co-training initiatives to rapidly scale distribution globally and accelerate customer success.

Challenges of Reselling: With reselling, the companies recognize the customer problem and sells a partner (often off-the shelf) solution. The partner's role might be in implementation or support, but that's it. There are many challenges with this model. The main one is there can be a disconnect between what the sales rep is selling versus what the partner solution does. This leads to an onslaught of meetings to reset expectations. This model also makes the companies the go-between—which impedes and complicates the sales process. The core of co-selling is connecting sales professionals in the field to allow them to collaborate freely with each other. Sales is personal. Successful partnerships require an investment—learning each other's sales style, accounts, solutions. So, it's critical to build strong relationships—with regular touchpoints, F2F meetings, etc.

Advantages of Co-selling: Co-selling partnerships can reduce sales costs. There is a required investment in sales and marketing to grow a business. The costs of a sales team can be crippling for a new venture or small business. The overhead expenses that enable a sales person to be trained, productive, and armed with the right marketing tools, technology and product support can be onerous in the earlier stages of an organization. Lack of initial investment often produces lack luster results and can actually cost the business even more with unexpected turnover or lengthy sales cycles. Businesses need a specific budget and defined cost of sales to properly staff, train and equip a sales organization to get results.

Time-to-market and time-to-close can be reduced through co-selling partnerships. A new sales hire ramp-up time can be 3-12 months, depending on price of goods to be sold and anticipated sales cycles. Ramp-up requires an "blind faith" investment of time and resources. A business has to invest in sales with nothing more than the anticipation and belief that something is going to be sold. It is a huge price to pay and has great risk. Utilizing a trained and experienced sales team through a co-selling partnership can help you bring revenues in while you invest in building your own sales team.

Co-Selling helps OSIsoft, Achieve Joint Wins.In recent months, the co-selling relationship between operational intelligence provider OSIsoft and Microsoft has become closer than ever. "Working together in the co-sell process with Microsoft, especially on our joint OSIsoft/Microsoft Red Carpet Incubation Program (RCIP), I feel like we are part of one team," said Prabal Acharyya, Worldwide Director of IoT Analytics and One Microsoft at OSIsoft. "Over the past year-and-a-half, there has been a tremendous change in the way we've been able to interact with Microsoft, the field teams, and the new industry resources that have been assigned for the benefit of our customers. The end result is that customers see a single interface with a stronger business value message instead of two or three separate vendors."Martin Otterson, Senior Vice President of Customer Success at OSIsoft, said the results of the collaboration between the two companies have been impressive so far. "By leveraging Microsoft Go-To-Market Services, OSIsoft has been able to create new subscription-based revenue streams and has achieved 12 joint wins with prominent customers including Barrick Gold, Deschutes Brewery, Mitsubishi Hitachi Power Systems, MPWiK S.A. (Wroclaw, Poland) and Toyota Motors Europe," Otterson said.

Co-Selling Activities: OSIsoft, which delivers the PI System, the industry standard in enterprise infrastructure, for management of real-time data and events, has collaborated with Microsoft on a variety of co-sell activities. They have hosted joint webinars for prospective customers, as well as live events in Detroit, Michigan, in San Leandro, California for OSIsoft's sponsored events and OSIsoft User Conference, and in Germany at Hanover Messe, the world's largest industrial technology trade fair."The speed of customer acquisition goes up tremendously because Microsoft is bringing the right technical and customer qualified leads together to the sales process," said Acharyya, who also stressed that the co-sell relationship with Microsoft was about more than the number of leads they receive. "It's important to understand that the co-sell team has a tremendous quality of people. It's not just the headcount, but the skills, knowledge and connections of people we can work together with," he said. "Also, a lot of people think that the co-sell process is a one-stop thing. It's not like you send me the lead and I'll see you in six months. There's actually more of a joint strategy and execution structure to this process."

A Platform for Cross-Selling

Where the product provides a means to cross sell other services. Wind monitoring web-site hosted by a firm that sells a range of weather monitoring equipment is an example of this kind.

IoT-Enabled Up-Selling and Cross-Selling Strategies

Implement A 'Smart Shelf' System: Many brick and mortar stores miss out on sales opportunities simply because there is a gap between what's on the shelf and what's in the back room. For example, a customer may want to purchase an item that isn't on display, but is sitting in the back room. Unless the customer asks an employee to go check the back room, they may wind up leaving the store without purchasing the product. A combination of RFID chips, store shelf sensors, digital price tags, smart displays, and cameras can show managers exactly what is on the store shelf and what is in the back room. By connecting these two sets of data, stores can optimize their inventory process and easily identify what items have the most value to customers.

Maximize Flow Management: How customers move around a store can greatly impact the purchasing decisions they make. Depending on the layout of the store and the location of certain items, customers may not notice an item that they would otherwise purchase. Smart cameras and sensors strategically placed around a store can gather data that managers can use to analyze foot traffic patterns and how they affect consumer purchasing behavior. IoT also can be leveraged to automate digital signage around a store so that customers can have up-to-date insights on what is where, leading to a higher potential for cross-sells.

Benefit Share With The Provider: It is a model where the consumer pays a proportion of revenues/savings to the provider. Examples include energy management solutions where the provider is paid a proportion of the savings in energy bills(Liu, L.,2010).

From Cars and Bikes to Umbrellas: The benefits of IoT and M2M connectivity are plentiful when it comes to the sharing economy. Portable items that can be reused by the community have become very popular over the last few years and have become a key element in the drive towards smart cities(Khorov. E et al.,2015). With bike sharing services appearing in cities all over the world, the success of Citi Bike in New York, Bycyklen in Copenhagen, and Ofo and Mobike in China has shown that there is enough demand to propel sharing services. However, keeping these devices connected, trackable, and secure has proved one of the main challenges that need to be addressed.

Location Tracking: Having a connected device means always knowing where your device is, no matter who is currently renting or borrowing it. This can be especially important for shared cars and bikes, which are, by design, mobile. The ability to pinpoint the location of your devices is twofold. First, it allows the customer to precisely locate it, and, secondly, it allows the owner to know where their customer is taking it or leaving (Gubbi.J., 2013). The Chinese bike share company Mobik has collaborated with Gemalto, in order to provide a wireless connection to their fleet of bikes. This allows their bikes to be tracked directly, without the need to use the customer's smartphone as a tracking device, as their competitor of does(Rebbeck.T.et al 2014).

Theft Prevention: Alongside being able to track the location of a device, there is the obvious benefit of helping to prevent the theft and misuse of your device. By simply knowing the location of your devices, the problem of users 'walking away' is drastically lowered. As previously mentioned, Mobike and Ofo have pursued different methods for tracking their bikes, and by embedding an IoT SIM in their bike. Mobike has made their bike more secure and trackable, whereas Ofo's system actually allows the previous user to simply remember the combination lock code and take the bike without paying.

IOT BUSINESS OPPORTUNITY

IoT in Medical/Healthcare

Wearables, mobile apps, data-based diagnostics and more could revolutionize the way patients access and receive medical services (Catarinucci.L et al,2015).

- The Internet of Things promises the healthcare industry contextual analysis and insights
- By mapping the information from wearable devices to specific threshold levels, physicians and caregivers can adjust the dosage of medicines more accurately
- During clinical trials, wearable and embedded medical devices can help understand the efficacy and risks of specific drugs better.

Predictive Alerts for Prevention(Vippalapalli,V.et al 2017).Key body vitals reported by wearable devices can be combined with local and external parameters (time, weather) to design advanced analytical models. These models can predict and prevent events such as strokes and heart attacks with confidence and accuracy.

Notifications: By mapping the wearable device's information to specific threshold levels, monitoring systems can send alerts regarding medication dosage to users or their caregivers. This can also help doctors and pharma companies make better decisions on adjusting dosages or changing the medication itself (Hognelid P.et al 2015)

Understanding the Efficacy and Risks of Drugs: During clinical trials, wearable and embedded medical devices can help trial administrators understand the efficacy and risks of specific drugs better. They can also have a greater understanding of a subject's response. It enables them to take proactive action when a potential negative outcome is identified or predicted.

IoT in Energy

IoT is aligned with three key trends in energy: digitization, decentralization and disruption (Reilly Dun2018).

Digitization: Unfortunately, the electric grid is pretty inefficient today in many areas. Not all of the electricity that is generated is able to be consumed. Some of that is natural line loss, but other losses are related to underperforming assets and outages that could be prevented. Sensors throughout the system help to predict problems before they occur. In this digitized landscape, data is the new currency.

Decentralization: IoT technology is also helping integrate distributed energy resources, such as solar, wind and battery. In fact, their contribution is made possible because of IoT devices. IoT is quickly becoming the glue of the modern electric grid.

Disruption: IoT devices and data are enabling more players to participate in electricity markets. We are already seeing this with 3rd party solar providers and the trend will continue as electric vehicle infrastructure expands. Utilities are no longer the only provider of energy services. New market entrants may be complimentary or in direct competition with some aspects of the utility portfolio. In the IoT era, knowing your customer is the key to long term engagement and revenue growth(Sun, Y.,et al 2012).

IoT in Industrial

Digital/connected factory.IoT enabled machinery can transmit operational information to the partners like original equipment manufacturers and to field engineers. This will enable operation managers and factory heads to remotely manage the factory units and take advantage of process automation and optimization.(Want.R.,et al,2015).

Facility Management. The use of IoT sensors in manufacturing equipment enables condition-based maintenance alerts. There are many critical machine tools that are designed to function within certain temperature and vibration ranges. IoT Sensors can actively monitor machines and send an alert when the equipment deviates from its prescribed parameters. By ensuring the prescribed working environment for machinery, manufacturers can conserve energy, reduce costs, eliminate machine downtime and increase operational efficiency.

Production Flow Monitoring: IoT in manufacturing (Lai et al.,2018) can enable the monitoring of production lines starting from the refining process down to the packaging of final products. This complete monitoring of the process in (near) real-time provides scope to recommend adjustments in operations for better management of operational cost. Moreover, the close monitoring highlights lags in production thus eliminating wastes and unnecessary work in progress inventory.

Solutions Internet of Things Brings in Education

Communication Network: Teachers and mentors can communicate with their students online using messengers or web cameras to organize education process. But it cannot allow two parties to imitate personal interaction as if they are sitting in class. But with the help of the Internet of Things in university or school, teacher and student can communicate using connected devices like digital pens and interactive boards that display all information in a real-time mode. All text or pictures can be sent to smartphone or tablet of mentor/student and it speeds up the process of new material assimilation and teaching process. Moreover, it simplifies the learning process since it saves a lot of time(Wirtz BW.,et al 2016).

New Generation of Textbooks: Educational books bring a lot of advantages since they give skills and knowledge to the student. But today paper books become the thing of the past since it is much convenient to have a bunch of digital books on your smartphone or tablet. Today modern public schools and universities offer students list of QR codes where each code is referred to a specific book. A student just needs to scan QR code and get a textbook on his or her device(Ustundag.A.,et al 2018).

Data Collection: Not all students attend all lessons regularly and not all of them are excellent students. It is necessary to do a roll call on each lesson to find out who attends a class and who is absent. Also, teachers need to track of learning performance of all students, it is not so easy process. But IoT applications in education are changing it. It makes it possible to use special wristbands with RFID tags that read the information about each user. A teacher can see promptly how many students attend the class today using his or her tablet/smartphone (Leminen.S.,2012). Moreover, using such devices, a teacher can mark the level of performance of each student to understand weak sides of each student.

Advanced Security: Security comes first in all education facilities no matter where they are located and how large they are. As usual, a security guard is on duty at the entrance of each facility. But this security guard simply cannot be present in all blocks of the school to keep order. That is where biometrics system come to the rescue. Facial recognition system at the entrance to detect all strangers, beacons, and wristbands on all students can prevent intrusion and disorders(Peeters.T.,et al 2015). It concerns not only schools and colleges but also campuses where students live and relax. Using special ID cards to enter to campus will also lead to the decrease of possible intruders. So, Internet of Things and education can be mutually beneficial fields. Also, school buses today in many schools are equipped today with GPS trackers and parents as well as school managers can always see where children are right now (Hubert C. Y. Chan., 2015).

FUTURE RESEARCH DIRECTIONS

The new conceivable rule of the future is going to be "anything can be connected and will be connected over the internet.IT pioneers are implementing new ideas of connecting both the things and devices to deliver new services to the market. IoT is considered as the biggest frontier which can improve our lives in many aspects. Those devices which have never been networked can get connected and respond just like the smart devices do, for e.g. Your car, refrigerator, and home speakers. IoT is set to transform our world completely. In future the authors aim to include applications of IoT in wide range of applications including satellite communication, marine and defense.

CONCLUSION

The IoT is changing things and it is real-time and coming together all around us. The Internet of Things promises the industry contextual analysis and insights. In this chapter the authors have discussed about the business aspects, models and opportunities involved in IoT. Companies prefer IoT technology as a transformational force that can help them to improve their performance through IoT analytics and IoT security to deliver better results.

REFERENCES

Catarinucci, L., Donno, D. D., Mainetti, L., Palano, L., Patrono, L., Stefanizzi, M. L., & Tarricone, L. (2015). An IoT-Aware Architecture for Smart Healthcare Systems. *IEEE Internet of Things Journal*, 2(6), 515–526. doi:10.1109/JIOT.2015.2417684

Chan, H. C. Y. (2015). Internet of Things Business Models. *Journal of Service Science and Management*, 8(04), 552–568. doi:10.4236/jssm.2015.84056

Chiang, M., & Zhang, T. (2016). Fog and IoT: An Overview of Research Opportunities. *IEEE Internet of Things Journal*, 3(6), 854–864. doi:10.1109/JIOT.2016.2584538

Dijkmana, R. M., Sprenkels, B., Peeters, T., & Janssenb, A. (2015). Business models for the Internet of Things. *International Journal of Information Management Elsevier*, 35(6), 672–678. doi:10.1016/j.ijinfomgt.2015.07.008

Dunn, R. (2018). *IoT Energy Applications: From Smart Vehicles to Smart Meters*. Retrieved from https://www.iotforall.com/iot-energy-applications/

Gubbi, J., Buyya, R., Marusic, S., & Palaniswam, M. (2013). IoT: A Vision, Architectural elements, and Future Directions. *Future Generation Computer Systems*, 29(7), 1645–1660. doi:10.1016/j.future.2013.01.010

Guo, L., Wei, S.-Y., Sharma, R., & Rong, K. (2017). Investigating e-business models' value retention for start-ups: The moderating role of venture capital investment intensity. *International Journal of Production Economics*, 186, 33–45. doi:10.1016/j.ijpe.2017.01.021

Hognelid, P., & Kalling, T. (2015) Internet of things and business models. *Proceedings of the 9th international conference on standardization and innovation in information technology, IEEE SIIT 2015*, art. no. 7535598. 10.1109/SIIT.2015.7535598

Hota, J., & Sinha, P. K. (2015). Scope and challenges of Internet of Things: An Emerging Technological Innovation. In *International Conference on Futuristic Trends in Computational analysis and Knowledge management*. IEEE.

Hui, G. (2014). How the internet of things changes business models. *Harvard Business Review*.

Khorov, E., Lyakhov, A., Krotov, & Guschin, A (2015). A survey on IEEE 802.11 ah: An enabling networking technology for smart cities. *Computer Communications, 58,* 53–69.

Lai, C. T. A., Jackson, P. R., & Jiang, W. (2018). Designing Service Business Models for the Internet of Things: Aspects from Manufacturing Firms. *American Journal of Management Science and Engineering, 3*(2), 7–22.

Leminen, S. (2012). Towards IOT Ecosystems and Business Models. *Internet of Things, Smart Spaces, and Next Generation Networking,* 15-26.

Liu, L., & Jia, W. (2010). Business model for drug supply chain based on the internet of things. *IEEE International Conference on Network Infrastructure and Digital Content,* 982-986.

Liu, T., & Lu, D. (2012). The application and development of IoT. *Int. Symp. Inf. Technol. Med. Educ. (ITME), 2,* 991–994.

Minerva, R., Biru, A., & Rotondi, D. (2015). Towards a definition of the Internet of Things (IoT). *IEEE Internet of Things Journal, 1*(1).

Morris, M., Schindehutte, M., & Allen, J. (2005). The entrepreneur's business model: Toward a unified perspective. *Journal of Business Research, 58*(6), 726–735. doi:10.1016/j.jbusres.2003.11.001

Odusote, A., Naik, S., Tiwari, A., & Arora, G. (2016). *Turning value into revenue: What IoT players can learn from software monetization.* Academic Press.

Osterwalder, A., & Pigneur, Y. (2010). *Business model generation: a handbook for visionaries, game changers, and challengers.* Hoboken, NJ: John Wiley & Sons.

Peeters, T., & Janssen, A. (2015). Business models for the Internet of Things. *International Journal of Information Management, 35*(6), 672–678. doi:10.1016/j.ijinfomgt.2015.07.008

Rebbeck, T., Mackenzie, M., & Afonso, Z. (2014). *Low-powered wireless solutions have the potential to increase the m2m market by over 3 billion connections.* Academic Press.

Stankovic, J. A. (2014). Research directions for the Internet of Things. *IEEE Internet of Things Journal*, *1*(1), 3–9. doi:10.1109/JIOT.2014.2312291

Sun, Y., Yan, H., Lu, C., Bie, R., & Thomas, P. (2012). A holistic approach to visualizing business models for the internet of things. *Communications in Mobile Computing*, *1*(1), 1–7. doi:10.1186/2192-1121-1-4

Ustundag, A., & Cevikcan, E. (2018). *Industry 4.0: Managing The Digital Transformation*. Springer Series in Advanced Manufacturing; doi:10.1007/978-3-319-57870-5

Vakulenko, M. (2016). *What can a toothbrush teach us about IoT business models?* Academic Press.

Vippalapalli, V., & Ananthula, S. (2017). Internet of things (IoT) based smart health care system. In *International Conference on Signal Processing, Communication, Power and Embedded System (SCOPES)*. IEEE.

Want, R. (2015). The physical web. *Workshop on IoT Challenges in Mobile and Industrial Systems, 1*(1).

Weinberger, M., Bilgeri, D., & Fleisch, E. (2016). IoT business models in an industrial context. *Automatisierungstechnik*, *64*(9), 699–706. doi:10.1515/auto-2016-0054

Westerlund, M., Leminen, S., & Rajahonka, M. (2014). Designing Business Models for the Internet of Things. *Technology Innovation Management Review*, 345-389.

Wirtz, B. W., Pistoia, A., Ullrich, S., & Göttel, V. (2016). Business models: Origin, development and future research perspectives. *Long Range Planning*, *49*(1), 36–54. doi:10.1016/j.lrp.2015.04.001

Zanella, A., Bui, N., Castellani, A., Vangelista, L., & Zorz, M. (2014). Internet of Things for Smart Cities. *IEEE Internet Things J*, *1*(1), 22–32. doi:10.1109/JIOT.2014.2306328

Chapter 7

Data Science and Knowledge Analytic Contexts on IoE Data for E–BI Application Case

Nilamadhab Mishra

(iD) https://orcid.org/0000-0002-1330-4869

Debre Berhan University, Ethiopia

ABSTRACT

The progressive data science and knowledge analytic tasks are gaining popularity across various intellectual applications. The main research challenge is to obtain insight from large-scale IoE data that can be used to produce cognitive actuations for the applications. The time to insight is very slow, quality of insight is poor, and cost of insight is high; on the other hand, the intellectual applications require low cost, high quality, and real-time frameworks and algorithms to massively transform their data into cognitive values. In this chapter, the author would like to discuss the overall data science and knowledge analytic contexts on IoE data that are generated from smart edge computing devices. In an IoE-driven e-BI application, the e-consumers are using the smart edge computing devices from which a huge volume of IoE data are generated, and this creates research challenges to traditional data science and knowledge analytic mechanisms. The consumer-end IoE data are considered the potential sources to massively turn into the e-business goldmines.

DOI: 10.4018/978-1-5225-8555-8.ch007

INTRODUCTION

In the contemporary and forthcoming days, the convergence of data science, knowledge analytics, Internet of Everything (IoE), big-data, statistical learning, and computational machine learning mechanisms are gaining popularities across various Intellectual e-BI applications. The core intention is to extract the cognitive values from large scale network-centric data that can be potentially used to produce intelligence for the applications. The IoE has a most important influence on the Big Data background. The key awareness on IoE data science evolution is that every IoE object has an IP address and connects to each other. Now, bearing in mind the circumstances of trillions of such connections that may be producing massive volumes of data (IoE big data), and the competence of current data science and knowledge analytics mechanisms are going to be challenged. The IoE evolutionary network connects people, processes, places, and things to internet for communication in and around the universe. The IoE objects focus both physical and logical things. The logical things include process, framework, applications, software, and program, and the physical things include people, places, physical entities, and devices. The data of such physical and logical things constitute a comprehensive IoE data base, where the structured, semi-structured, and unstructured data are available (Mishra et al, 2014). In an IoE data base, ERP and CRM data are considered as structured data, XML data are normally considered as semi-structured data, and email documents, social web contents, pdf, ward, rich text documents are considered as un-structured data. The study reveals that in an IoE data base, around 80% data are unstructured with no pre-defined data models. Such un-structured data are textual, graphics, video, and symbols oriented. The spatial-temporal databases having the facts or events with time-stamps are also a part of IoE database. The rapid increasing of IoE big data applications in today's IoE world progressively lead to several problem issues such as, data volume, velocity, varieties, and value. Analyzing and inferencing cognitive values (knowledge) from large scale IoE data base in a real-time basis is more challenging day by day with the extreme growing of volume, and varieties data that are associated with numerous IoE applications. Such IoE knowledge analytics and inference face a number of real-time problems such as, managing heterogeneous knowledge, transforming varieties data into knowledge, transforming knowledge into actions, transforming actions into cognitive decisions, and tuning the cognitive decisions to coordinate the IoE motivated applications (Mishra et al, 2014). The convergences of statistical and computational learning mechanisms have been researched to deal with the data science and knowledge analytic problems. Data science and knowledge analytic implements are also used for analyzing and exploring various operational tasks associated with the IoE big data submissions, such as-data transformation and analysis, data mining, knowledge discovery, semantic knowledge explorations, structural analysis, and many more. The machine learning technics are implemented in many areas of knowledge discovery and semantic knowledge analytics to explore the application intelligence. In almost all IoE big data applications, a huge amount of data is dumped into the storage that are highly redundant and unsuitable for the purpose of data analysis, modelling, information transformation, knowledge production, and the decision generation. A survey conducted by Par Stream shows that 94% of the organizations surveyed are facing challenges in IoE big data elicitations and analytics, and 70% organizations think that, the IoE big data analytics help to make better and more meaningful decisions for organizations (Mishra et al, 2014).

The main purposes of the research are to design and explore data models, frameworks, architectures, and algorithms on network-centric data, mainly IoE data to accomplish the data science and knowledge analytic tasks for Intellectual e-BI applications. The data science aims for knowledge analytic frameworks and algorithms to build and organize knowledge and insights that transform the real world e-BI applications into intellectual e-BI applications.

In the current and upcoming days, the data science and knowledge analytic tasks are gaining popularities across various Intellectual e-BI applications. The main aim is to get the insights from large scale network-centric data, such as IoE data that can be used to produce intelligence for the applications. In the current Intellectual e-BI applications, the network-centric data are highly unstructured and ambiguous, and create research challenges in inferencing the potential knowledge. The survey reveals that time to insight is slow, quality of insight is poor, and cost of insight is high for IoE big data applications, on the other hand, those Intellectual e-BI applications require low cost, high quality, and real time frameworks and algorithms to massively transform their data into cognitive values of goldmines. Such cognitive values are utilized as knowledge and insights for creating worth of the Intellectual e-BI applications.

The research contribution encompass both theoretical and simulated research for various Intellectual e-BI applications, such as industrial, healthcare, and business intelligence e-BI. The different frameworks and algorithms are designed and explored for knowledge discovery, representation, semantic analytic, knowledge re-analytics and inferences. The real world applications are modeled through smart architectures, algorithms, and frameworks to accomplish the data science and knowledge analytics tasks.

Following data science and knowledge analytic tasks and frameworks are planned and succeeded with the expectation of putting into practice of the intellectual e-BI applications. Data-centric knowledge discovery strategy for a safety critical sensor application, sensor data distribution and knowledge inference framework for a cognitive based distributed storage sinks environment, cognitive inference device for activity supervision in the elderly, cognitive adopted framework for IoE big data management and knowledge discovery, IoE knowledge reengineering framework for semantic knowledge analytics for business intelligence services, knowledge granules analytics and cluster framework for IoE big data for a business intelligence application, and a framework for trustful knowledge analytic on cloud centered IoE environment.

BACKGROUND ANALYSIS

Technology Analysis

Science implies the gaining of knowledge from systematic study, so the data science might therefore imply a focus involving data, and by extension, statistics, or the systematic study of the organization, properties, and analysis of data and its role in inference, including our confidence in inference (Mishra et al, 2014). The promise of data science is that if data from a system can be recorded and understood then this understanding (knowledge and inferences) can potentially be utilized to improve the system (Mishra et al, 2015). Data Science is the extraction of knowledge from large volumes of data that are structured or unstructured, which is a continuation of the field data mining and predictive analytics, also known as knowledge discovery and data mining KDD (Chang et al, 2015). In data science, various tasks are associated that can be explored and integrated to design the application for numerous intellectual e-BIs that are associated with the physical world. Statistical computing and visualizations are important tasks of data science, that include data manipulation and cleaning, importing and exporting data, managing missing values, data frames, functions, lists, matrices, writing functions, and the use of packages. Efficient programming practices and methods of summarizing and visualizing data are emphasized throughout the data science environment. Cognitive computing is an important concern of data science, where we build a new computational problem class to address the complex problem situations through a self-learning process. The cognitive computing of big data exploits the power of the several diversified technologies, such as mathematics, statistics, data science, computational science, etc., to build intelligent and insights for the intellectual e-BI applications. KDD (Knowledge discovery on data) feats the way to integrate the data mining with the data analytics that makes the use of data science in numerous e-BI applications, such as business intelligence e-BI (Chang et al, 2015). The machine learning becomes extremely important and useful in data science environment to deal not only objective with huge amounts of data and extract knowledge from it but also create trends in IoE big data analytics in increasing extensiveness with all levels of an organization. E-BI analysis is an important concern that helps to analyze the important problem scenarios of an application e-BI associated with physical world. The e-BI analysis integrates the data e-BI with intellectual e-BI applications, such as business, healthcare, and industrial. Knowledge reengineering, analytics, and inferences are the progressive concerns of the data science to re-engineer the superseded knowledge base into a renovated knowledge base system that may ensure higher operational efficiency through making the knowledge base useful and operative. The knowledge analytic is a major part of data science that studies the historical data to research potential trends, analyzes the effect of decisions and events, evaluates the performance of complex problem scenarios, and aims to improve values through gaining knowledge and insights (Chang et al, 2016). The knowledge analytic is the science of logical analysis that uses mathematics, statistics, computational intelligence, and other analytic tools to discover the potential knowledge and insights from large scale data science environment. Here the author highlights an ongoing evolution history of data science and knowledge analytics through its correlated operational functions and tasks. Peter Naur in 1960 uses data science as a substitute of computer science. In 1974, Naur uses data science as data processing methods for numerous applications. In 1977, Turkey suggests data science as exploratory data analysis (Tukey et al, 1980). In 1989-1996, more tasks/terms are included in data science, i.e. data classification, data mining, and knowledge discovery (Hayashi et al, 2013). In 1997-2001, statistical computing is included as a part of data science. In 2005, Thomas H. Davenport, et.al introduces the use of analytics and facts base decision making in data science (Davenport et al, 2004). In 2010, Hilary Mason and Chris Wiggins, introduce the term machine learning in data science. In 2011, Harlan Harris deliberates several data science techniques, such as; statistics and machine learning; data interpretation, classification, and visualization (Shron et al, 2014). In 2012 to till date, the data science progressively integrates with several new technologies, such as- IoE, big-data, clouds, deep learning, extreme learning machine (ELM), and many more emerging technologies.

The upcoming prospect of data science tends toward delivering both big-data processing and knowledge analytics, which are the most challenging aspects with the growing data dimension and diversity of numerous IoE driven intellectual e-BI applications. The data architecture of IoE relies on several NoSQL databases on Hadoop like platforms for batch processing of large scale data that consumes much more time; however the real-time or semi real-time data processing, management and knowledge analytics are much more thought-provoking tasks. Because, the current business intelligence platforms need the timely knowledge and insights to transform their business data into cognitive decisive goldmines in order to make huge revenues through minimizing the potential upcoming business risks. The NoSQL databases are not designed to execute the knowledge analytic tasks, which are the common minimal requirements for IoE driven intellectual e-BI applications.

Applications Analysis

In context to the knowledge analytics for industrial e-BI application, we consider a sensor environmental case, where different works are analyzed and implemented through diversified data science and knowledge analytic (data science and knowledge analytics) approaches, i.e. KDS-NN, KDS-GA, and KDS-DM (Mishra et al, 2018). Dinesh Kumar et al., propose the implementation of KDS-NN approach that uses the back propagation algorithm to execute the data filtration operations at gateway level for a sensor environment (Mishra et al, 2018). Khanna and liu, propose the data science and knowledge analytics implementation through KDS-GA approach that describes the genetic approach based pattern identification and activity monitoring application (Khanna et al, 2012). A number of other researches refer KDS-DM approach that involve in several data science and knowledge analytics operations, such as, data- calibration, cluster, replication, reduction, elicitation, and cleaning, pattern-identification, extraction, modelling, and mapping operations in and around the sensor environment (Mishra et al, 2018).. In those works, small data scale is considered to discover the big-values. However, for a large scale industrial automation application, we consider the prospective knowledge discovery and management of IoE big data, and study some relevant works that have the prospective over IoE big data platform. The work in (Boukerche et al, 2008) emphasizes to design an IoE data management reference framework that can perform following data science and knowledge analytic operations, i.e. data cleaning, storage, access analysis, and distribution operations. Furthermore, the work in (He et al, 2010) discusses some more data science and knowledge analytic operations at semantic level, such as, semantic analysis, semantic derivations for knowledge discovery and intelligent decision making.

In context to the knowledge analytics for elderly healthcare e-BI application, several systems and devices are studied to model an operationally feasible framework for elderly activity supervision (Defeng et al, 2010). In the works (Aggarwal et al, 2013; Ma et al, 2013; Ding et al, 2013), the data science and knowledge analytics functions of a cognitive IoE device or a cognitive sensor are analyzed that assist elderly to regulate the smart home appliances. Furthermore, the functional operations and implementations of several system and devices are analyzed that have the major roles towards data science and knowledge analytics operations for elderly, such as, abnormal activity detection, fall detection, online activity monitoring, and emergency situation detection (Wu et al, 2014; Kelly et al, 2013; Gaddam et al, 2011). Device cognition is a challenging matter for current researchers even the rapid advancement of medical engineering and instrumentation.

In context to the knowledge analytics and re-analytics for customer end and enterprise end business intelligence e-BI applications, the functions of several data science and knowledge analytics operations and BI applications are analyzed to design various intellectual BI frameworks (Tibor et al 2011; Andreoni et al, 2014). The work in (Anderoni et al, 2014), proposes a modern manufacturing service system that uses IoE and cloud computing technology for storage, analytics, and other data science and knowledge analytics operations. We also analyze the work of (Botia et al, 2012), which focuses an e-commerce service application for BI process monitoring system. In order to implement the analytics in credit card fraud detection service, the work in (Kiristisis eta l, 2011) emphasizes the implementation of Bayesian learning system as a mechanism to execute the data science and knowledge analytics operations for the said business intelligence service. A number of innovative data science and knowledge analytics operational analysis are considered for diversified BI service applications, such as, product life cycle management service that uses closed-loop PLM framework (Qu et al, 2014), transport logistic service that implements an IoE based ontology framework (Ciskosva et al, 2015), and a supply chain management service that uses a cognitive based smart logistic framework (Dagino et al, 2014).

In-context to the IoE driven e-BI applications, we may incorporate the important functions such as IoE big-data aggregation, IoE big-data classification, IoE big-data storage, and IoE big-data analysis. We mainly emphasize on IoE big-data analytics with a broad aim to transform the agile big-data into cognitive insights and actuations (Williams et al, 2019) In order to transform the IoE big-data into actionable insights, the machine learning features play a greater significant role. So, it is included in the process of IoE big-data analytic applications. However, the key research challenge is the real-time processing and transformation of large scale e-BI data through machine learning features. The cloud computing offers services at the infrastructure level that can scale to IoE data storage and analytics requirements. However, there are applications such time critical e-BI applications that require low latency, and delay caused by transferring data to the cloud and then back to the application can seriously impact their performances (Yassine et al, 2019). To overcome this limitation, Fog computing paradigm has been proposed, where cloud services are extended to the edge of the network to decrease the latency and network congestion. So, it will be more effective to configure a fog base IoE driven e-BI application, in which the fog devices are to be configured at the gateway level of service application and the computational analytic processes are to be ready to run in parallel among the pre-configured fog devices in order to obtain the real-time cognitions and cognitive actuations for the e-BI application. To realize the full potential of fog base IoE driven e-BI applications for real-time analytics, several challenges are addressed. The initial critical problem is designing resource management techniques that determine which modules of e-BI analytics applications are pushed to each fog device to minimize the latency and maximize the throughput (Tortonesi et al, 2019). IoE driven e-BI applications envision a new world of connected devices and humans in which quality of life is enhanced, because, management of smart city application and its infrastructure is less cumbrous, time critical health monitoring service applications are conveniently accessible, and other e-BI application's effectiveness are drastically improved. Fog computing extends cloud services to the edge of networks, which results in latency reduction through geographical distribution of IoE driven e-BI applications components, and provides support for better suppleness (Badii et al, 2019; Holland et al, 2019).

The extensive review on numerous diversified e-BI applications issues provide a vision to numerous data science and knowledge analytics operations that can be implemented on IoE driven data science and analytics environment.

IOE-DATA SCIENCE AND ANALYTIC FRAMEWORK

This is an integration of data science surroundings with evolutionary IoE network environment. IoE (Internet of Everything) is the network of physical objects or "things" embedded with electronics, software, sensors, and connectivity to enable it to achieve greater value and service. The

IoE objects may be any logical or physical thing associated with the real world entities. The Logical things comprise several process, frameworks, software, apps, etc., and the Physical things consist of people, places, devices, etc. Three main requirements to construct an IoE object. Those are physical IP system for unique object identity, Radio transceivers for communication (uses protocol stake), and Sensing unit for data sensing from physical environment. The main aim is to easily place into any real world entity associated with the IoE applications. IoE data science considers the data of everything's- place-process-device-people. IoE data science environment desires following connectivity among IoE objects: - any place connectivity, any process connectivity, any people connectivity, anything connectivity, any time connectivity, and constitutes a comprehensive IoE environment. Such connectivity leads to large heterogeneous data depository with incompatibilities among database frameworks. The incompatibilities, such as name, scale, structure, and level of abstraction, create exploration challenges to IoE data science environment to execute the analytic process. With the rapid increasing of IoE based intellectual applications, the networks of such billions of IoE objects constitute an IoE data science environment, from where huge structured, semi-structured, and unstructured IoE big-data are produced in a real time basis.

Several hazards are associated with the knowledge analytic contexts on IoE data. Those hazards are- managing heterogeneous knowledge, transforming the data into knowledge, transforming the knowledge into actions, transforming the actions into cognitive-decisions, and tuning IoE knowledge base to regulate numerous intellectual applications, such as industrial, healthcare, and Business.

ANALYTIC CONTEXTS FOR E-BI APPLICATIONS

In e-BI circumstance, the author considers several intellectual e-BI applications i.e. industrial, healthcare, etc., on business intelligence e-BIs. For the applications, some innovative problem requirements are identified, analyzed the problem requirements in term of proposed architectures, algorithms, functional explorations, structural analysis, mathematical analysis, implementation analysis, computational analysis, structural analysis, and modelled into operationally feasible application frameworks. The progressive evolution of IoE data science penetrates into each and every intellectual e-BI application, where the knowledge analytic plays major role. In IoE data science applications, the data sources are considered as disparate and agile, and it requires an effective management of several IoE data, such as, customer data, billing information, device data, web services data (e.g. weather and traffic data), sensor data, RFID data, place data, process data, and other data of things.

The figure 1 describes information frameworks for IoE data science and analytics operations. In this figure 1, we explore numerous data operations and analytics that are implemented on various data science frameworks engaged in different intellectual e-BI applications. The IoE data science regulates a large scale automated industry through generating real-time tactical and operational decisions and cognitive actuations, and thus, it can be effectively used in many industrial applications to regulate sensitive

Figure 1. Analytic contexts for e-BI applications

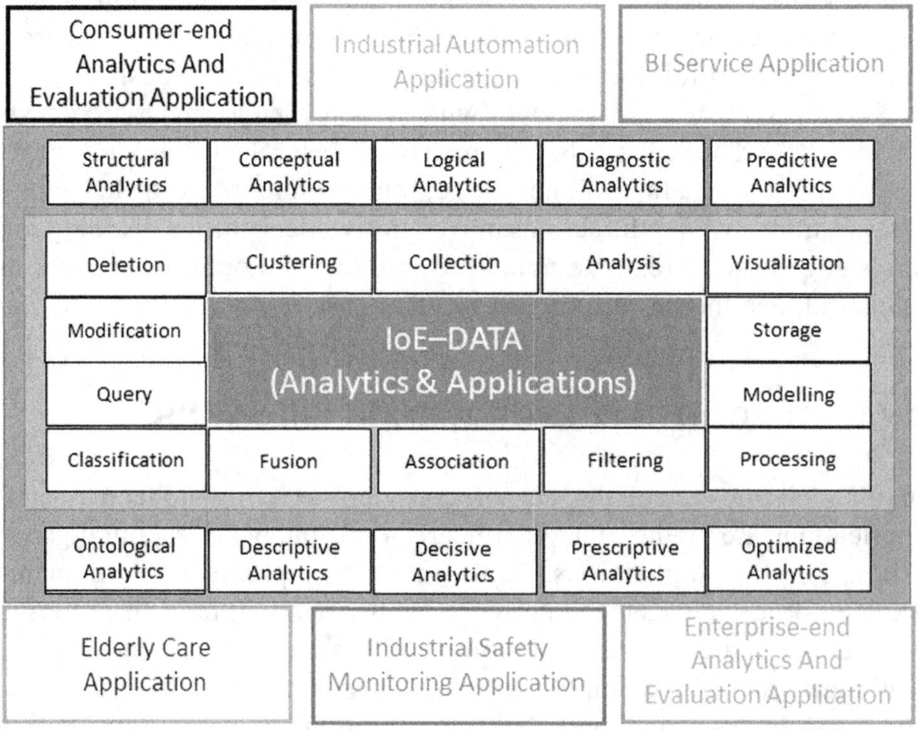

parameters, such as, machine load and distribution analysis, reliability analysis of machines, industrial safety analysis and monitoring, etc. With the advancement of industries and IoE data science, real-time knowledge analytic framework have been considered in many contexts to automate an industrial process that involves a high degree of risk.

The IoE data science regulates a large scale automated industry through generating real-time tactical and operational decisions and cognitive actuations, and thus, it can be effectively used in many industrial applications to regulate sensitive parameters, such as, machine load and distribution analysis, reliability analysis of machines, industrial safety analysis and monitoring, etc. With the advancement of industries and IoE data science, real-time knowledge analytic framework have been considered in many contexts to automate an industrial process that involves a high degree of risk. Therefore, based on risk quantification, we classify real-time data science applications into three different categories: business-critical applications, e.g., IoE applications in business intelligence monitoring, mission-critical application e.g., IoE applications in habitat monitoring, smart city monitoring, smart home monitoring, etc., and safety-critical sensor application e.g., IoE applications in industrial automations, healthcare automations, elderly activity supervisions, etc. Among the three applications, the highest degree of risk is measured in safety-critical IoE application. In business automation environment, IoE data science regulate several smart management tasks, such as, material logistic management, supplier chain management, product lifecycle management, compliance service work flow interoperations and management, proactive prediction of business security strategy, and much more.

The IoE data science also regulates the data of wearable and non-wearable computing devices and generate intelligence through analytic frameworks to transform into a smart environment in order to monitor several activities, such as human activity supervision; automated coordination of devices according to human activity in a smart home like environment; monitoring traffic congestions, social activities, environmental pollutions, water pollutions, citizen compliance tracking, wastage management, intelligent transportations, and other activity and services in a smart business environment.

IMPLEMETATION ANALYSIS

In a dynamic data driven environment, such as business intelligence (e-BI) environment, the data distribution and knowledge context scenarios are frequents changing along with the progressive evolutions of business requirements as well as technological requirements. So, we can use several e-BI heuristics to directly target the deep behavioral analytics, where we ensure that the IoE e-consumers are the intelligent nodes and have the capability to evaluate and assess the implicit BI parameters. The unstructured contents of IoE e-consumers create barrier to data science and knowledge analytics. For that, we can use a specific range and scale for each consumer centered query that allow them to assess the implicit BI parameters through scaled scoring. The data of IoE e-consumers can be potentially modelled as Data of Things or IoE edge point data. The IoE edge point data are the data that are generated from the IoE enabled devices or users, we also say this type of data as IoE touch point data. The consumer-end views can be collected from their registered IoE sensing devices that are exposed to the global cloud system for analytics using advanced machine learning algorithms. The consumer-end views are considered as the potential sources that need an effective cognitive analytics context to massively turn into the e-business goldmines.

As we know that, computational learning is a process of gaining knowledge and insights through computational process, so, we can integrate the statistical and machine learning mechanism into IoE-data science and knowledge analytics to generate the potential insights for the applications. We can explore several statistical and machine learning mechanisms that can be converged towards data science and knowledge analytics to work on the IoE-big data platform.

The IoE-data science and knowledge analytic frameworks can be considered as information frameworks that explore the basic structure of set of facts or ideas that can potentially support for various data science and knowledge analytics operations within the intellectual e-BI frame. The IoE-data science and knowledge analytics frameworks can also be explored as data driven frameworks. Based on the data distribution strategy we explore the information framework. The information frameworks are further synthesized with progressive convergence technologies with an aim to make the framework operational for application usage and to transform a dumb application into knowledgeable.

The error or deviant estimation is a way to analyze the data driven frameworks so as to as to estimate the functional accuracy, analytic accuracy, and operational precision of the data distribution for the framework. we can analyze several types of errors for the application framework based on the data distributions and rule re-analytics.

In-context to statistical machine learning implementation in the data distribution frameworks, we enhance a popular random forest process, in which random forest cluster prediction is done in unsupervised manner (without any class label). Random forest classification and regression are done in a supervised process (with defined class label). Classification creates the label of data points with number of classes (clusters). Regression targets a single value, whereas classification always targets a class. In a random forest classifier, large numbers of trees are constructed such that each tree represents a cluster class. Random forest regression is a liner regression model and here data fitting task is done by a linear least square estimator. For each cluster class, the center may be a Gaussian center. Random forest regression aids to detect percentage of error statistics due to outliers among data instances. Random forest classifier is used for cluster class prediction precision analysis. We can discover the fitness parameter estimation of set of knowledge cluster class with respect to percentage of outlier statistics among the data distribution sets of the BI application e-BI.

Several key technical analysis are done in-context to the neuro-fuzzy inference architecture for modelling BI context information, where we analyze data science and knowledge analytics operations, such as context and rule analytics, statistical analysis, data mapping and transformation, neurofuzzy inference. We analyze NFIS mechanisms for BI context information, where three operations are mainly analyzed to favor BI service analytics, i.e., Inputs fuzzification, put on fuzzy operations, and BI rules implications. From the analysis, we reveal that re-engineer both data and knowledge components can be a better way to minimize the framework errors and infer that knowledge re-engineering is better substitute for a dynamic data driven IoE environment, where knowledge context scenarios are frequently changing.

SYSTEM CONFIGURATION ANALYSIS

In this section, we highlight a detailed configuration of system for e-BI applications. In the system, we consider numbers of IoE e-consumer clusters that may be geo-demographic distribution centric over the e-business environment and each cluster corresponds to set of IoE objects that are possessed by the e-consumers as described in figure 2.

The geo-demographic clusters potentially preserve the integrated geographic and demographic IoE e-consumer's data into corresponding data set. That data set creates the big-data problem that analytic system tries to solve it. The IOEA mechanisms, such as data investigations, data wrangling, cleaning, sampling, etc. can be used to get good data; however it is important to know how to use those data to deal with real business problems to extract quick solutions. So in order to deal with the problem, an extensive analysis is performed on IoE e-consumer's data set that minimally includes an ETL (Extraction-transformation-load) operation to fetch the information details to the analytic engine. The analytic engine formulates mainly four types of problem queries, i.e. what happens, why did it happens, what will happen, and how can we make it happen? To solve those four different problem queries, four different analytic operations need to be performed by the analytic engine. As this analytic engine only deals with the e-BI problems, so we term it as e-BI analytic engine.

The functional assumptions of e-BI analytic engine are describes as follows.

1. Assume that ETL operational engine is always active to deliver the current information details and the e-BI engine gets desired information details through sending instant query to ETL operational engine.
2. Business queries Inception and problem solutions by the e-BI analytic engine meets the business critical application requirements.
3. e-BI analytic engine supports at least four different analytic operations, i.e. descriptive analytics, diagnostic analytics, predictive analytics, and prescriptive analytics.
4. The knowledge base consists of potential business problems, cases, and solutions to face the genuine business queries.

Figure 2. Frame for analytics and applications

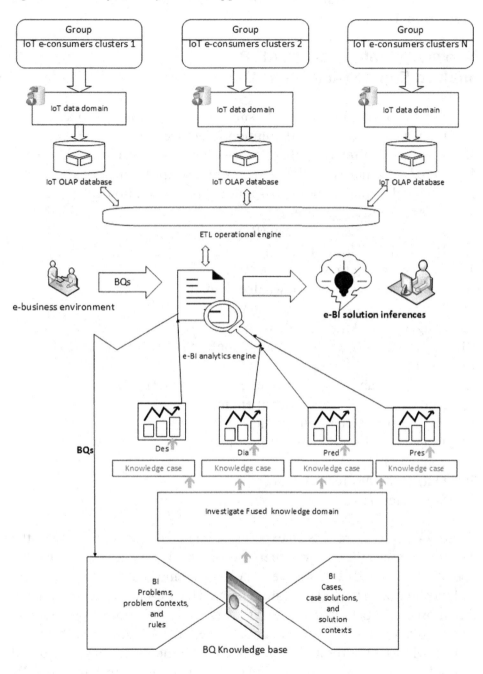

Now, the operational analysis of e-BI analytic engine is described in **Algorithm-1**.

Knowledge Inferences for E-BI analytic Engine (Algorithm-1)

1. Input- information details, business queries, knowledge base.
2. Output- prospective e-BI solution inferences.
3. // des← descriptive analytics; dia← diagnostic analytics;
4. //pred←predictive analytics; pres← prescriptive analytics;
5. AS = {des, dia, pred, pres}// four analytic operations;
6. KCs= {knowledge cases};
7. Receive the business query (BQ);
8. If BQ ∈ AS_i { for i=1,2,3,4}
9. Then send BQ to Knowledge Base;
10. Investigate the fused knowledge domain;
11. Invoke the analytic operation(AS_i);
12. Diagnose the knowledge cases;
13. Extract the knowledge case that meets the business query
14. end if
15. while(availability of knowledge case = 'true')
16. Activate the ETL operational engine;
17. Extract the current information details;
18. Diagnose KCs with current information;
19. end while
20. Output the desired inferences;
21. Go to step 7;

The BQ knowledge base is an expert system that dynamically models the data frames as per the business queries in order to invoke in specific analytic operations. The e-BI analytical engine has an important role in integrating and synchronizing the BQs that are generated from e-business environment, the information details that are extracted from ETL operational engine and the dynamic Meta data and data frames that are generated from the BQ knowledge base through invoking the analytic operations. The board vision behind this integration and synchronization are to mine the e-BI solution inferences for the BQs by which small scale e-business data depository generates potential business worth and transforms into a big data-value for the modernized e-BI applications.

DISCUSSIONS

This discussion explored the progressive data science and knowledge analytic operations. In this work, I discuss data science and knowledge analytic mechanisms for analyzing and exploring different operational tasks, such as-data transformation and analysis, data mining, knowledge discovery, semantic knowledge explorations, structural analysis, and many more tasks. The machine learning technics are implemented in many areas of knowledge discovery and semantic knowledge analytics to explore the application intelligence. The main aim is to get the insights from large scale IoE data that can be used to produce intelligence for an application.

In business automation environment, IoE data science regulate several smart management tasks, such as, material logistic management, supplier chain management, product lifecycle management, compliance service work flow interoperations and management, proactive prediction of business security strategy, and much more.

The IoE data science regulates a large scale automated industry through generating real-time tactical and operational decisions and cognitive actuations, and thus, it can be effectively used in many industrial applications to regulate sensitive parameters, such as, machine load and distribution analysis, reliability analysis of machines, industrial safety analysis and monitoring. With the advancement of industries and IoE data science, real-time knowledge analytic framework have been considered in many contexts to automate an industrial process that involves a high degree of risk.

Therefore, based on risk quantification, we classify real-time data science applications into three different categories: business-critical applications, e.g., IoE applications in business intelligence monitoring, mission-critical application e.g., IoE applications in habitat monitoring, smart city monitoring, smart home monitoring, etc., and safety-critical sensor application e.g., IoE applications in industrial automations, healthcare automations, elderly activity supervisions, etc. Among the three applications, the highest degree of risk is measured in safety-critical IoE application.

The IoE data science also regulates the data of wearable and non-wearable computing devices and generate intelligence through analytic frameworks to transform into a smart environment in order to monitor several activities, such as human activity supervision; automated coordination of devices according to human activity in a smart home like environment; monitoring traffic congestions, social activities, environmental pollutions, water pollutions, citizen compliance tracking, wastage management, intelligent transportations, and other activity and services in a smart city like environment.

In the convergence of IoE-DSA several emerging technologies are progressively integrated. In our work, we use data of everything for internet of everything to analyze case base problem scenarios to model in the Applications. If we diagnose the emerging Technologies, we observe that several emerging technologies are in the innovation trigger. Several convergence technologies, such as, Data Science and Analytics, cloud, IoT, IoE, computational learning, and Range base National Language Query are in the peak of inflated expectations.

CASE ANALYSIS

In this section, we briefly analyze an important e-business query, which processing needs the operational mechanisms of our proposed system to perform its knowledge analytic and inference operation. Enabling the IoE based product quality assessment in an advanced BI environment creates several research challenges. Here we take a small case example only to visualize the analytic functions of system.

Evaluating the consumer's end quality strategy of a product at any instance of time is a top business query for the e-business environment, in which the potential solution inferences can be studied though assessing an important e-BI parameter, i.e. product rating matrix assessment.

For a cluster of e-business products, let $Pk \leftarrow$ product id of the kth product, $QS \leftarrow$ quality strategy, $TQS \leftarrow$ target quality threshold, $\Phi \leftarrow$ quality threshold function, $N \leftarrow$ number of products that are rated, $NU_i \leftarrow$ number of users having i star rating, and $W_i \leftarrow$ fixed weights for value i=$\{1,2,3,4,5\}$.

Now if $\Phi(QS(Pk)) \geq TQS$ then quality assessment $(Y) = \Phi(QS(Pk))$ and product Pk has desired quality strategy;

Figure 3. Quality strategy vs. target quality analysis

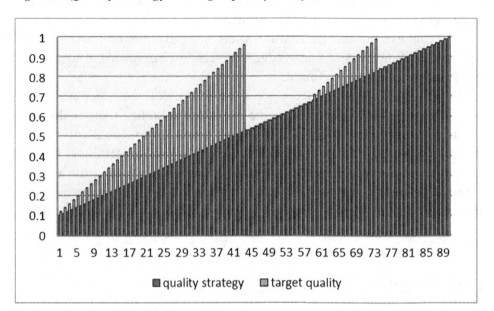

Else if Φ (QS (Pk)) < TQS then quality assessment (Y) = Φ (QS (Pk)) and product Pk has poor quality strategy.

In figure-3, an analysis is done by considering the case scenarios. In some instances, the quality strategy is mapped to the target strategy of the e-BI applications, but, in some instances many deviations are there in between them. Those deviations can be effectively minimized through the potential e-BI solution inferences.

Now for N number of rated products i.e. k=N, we obtain a list of Y values for the products and such values are normalized and transformed into a knowledge analysis and visualization tool for obtaining the e-BI solution inferences and accordingly the prospective e-BI strategy can be altered.

Hence based on BQ, the BQ knowledge base suggests the suitable knowledge analytic operation to the e-BI analytic engine that operates on the current information of registered IoE devices used by the e-consumers that are exposed to the global IoE network.

In this CASE, the author discusses an IoE environment, in which knowledge analytic and inference mechanism is implemented. To empower the knowledge analytic and inference from IoE enabled e-consumers, we propose a system that includes an e-BI analytic engine and a BQ knowledge base to execute the analytic operations.

We can extend the individual analytic operation and explore the operational functions of knowledge analytic and inference set-ups for an e-BI enabled IoE environment.

In e-business intelligence applications, the IoE and analytics play major role towards generating the business insights that enable the e-business to construct a global trends and strategy for the e-consumers. The e-consumers are the real back bone of the e-BI operations. So, the consumer-end analytics are the powerful tools to analyze the current e-business trends and strategy and such analytics deeply consider the e-consumer's feedbacks on several BI parameters that are strongly related to e-trading and other correlated operations.

CONCLUSION AND FUTURE WORK

This study explored the progressive data science and knowledge analytic frameworks, tasks, and operations for intellectual e-BI applications. In our works, Data science and knowledge analytic tools are used for analyzing and exploring different operational tasks, such as-data transformation and analysis, data mining, knowledge discovery, semantic knowledge explorations, structural analysis, and many more tasks. The machine learning technics are implemented in many areas of knowledge discovery and semantic knowledge analytics to explore the application intelligence. We consider the IoE data science and analytic frameworks for three application e-BIs i.e. industrial, healthcare, and business intelligence. The main aim is to get the insights from large scale IoE data that can be used to produce intelligence for the applications. The research methodologies encompass both theoretical and analytical research for various Intellectual e-BI applications. Some cognitive, conceptual, and logical frames are embedded into our research framework to enable the IoE data science applications and analytics. The different frameworks and algorithms are designed and explored for knowledge discovery, representation, semantic analytic, and inferences. The real world applications are modeled through smart architectures, algorithms, and frameworks to accomplish the data science and knowledge analytics tasks.

In this study, the author explores IoE–DSA framework as Information framework. The author also analyze the Major effort in DSA that consists of data e-BI analysis, Data munging for prepare data set for further analysis, data normalization, convergence technologies, and learning mechanisms, and reveal that IoE Creates big-data problems & DSA has the capability to solves those in an effective and efficient way.

In the study, the important discussions mainly encompass followings:-

- IoE edge devices of business consumers. {IoE edge data consider as Data of Things}.
- Analyze the intelligent e-BI considerations for e-BI applications.
- Data associated with the considerations are explored through advanced analytics.
- Leaning mechanisms and knowledge analytic tools support for data inspection, transformation, and error analysis, so that data can transformed into a representative form.

The Representative data set can be considered as a substitute of big-data for potential study and implications for intellectual e-BI applications.

The future work includes the further data science and knowledge analytic frameworks and applications that will have the potentiality to discover the big-value from disparate data sources irrespective of the data scales. Because managing and mining large scale disparate IoE data base is much more challenging along with its progressive data science and knowledge analytic operations.

REFERENCES

Aggarwal, C. C. (2013). An Introduction to Sensor Data Analytics. *Managing and Mining Sensor Data. Springer US, 2013*, 1–8.

Ahmed, M., Choudhury, S., & Al-Turjman, F. (2019). Big Data Analytics for Intelligent Internet of Things. In *Artificial Intelligence in IoT* (pp. 107–127). Cham: Springer.

Andreoni, G., Costa, F., Attanasio, A., Baroni, G., Muschiato, S., Nonini, P., . . . Perego, P. (2014). Design and Ergonomics of Monitoring System for Elderly. In Digital Human Modeling. Applications in Health, Safety, Ergonomics and Risk Management (pp. 499-507). Springer International Publishing. doi:10.1007/978-3-319-07725-3_49

Badii, C., Bellini, P., Difino, A., & Nesi, P. (2019). Sii-Mobility: An IoT/IoE architecture to enhance smart city mobility and transportation services. *Sensors (Basel), 19*(1), 1. doi:10.339019010001 PMID:30577434

Botia, J. A., Villa, A., & Palma, J. (2012). Ambient Assisted Living system for in-home monitoring of healthy independent elders. *Expert Systems with Applications, 39*(9), 8136–8148. doi:10.1016/j.eswa.2012.01.153

Boukerche, A., Samarah, S., & Harbi, H. (2008). *Knowledge discovery in wireless sensor networks for chronological patterns*. IEEE. doi:10.1109/LCN.2008.4664263

Chang, H. T., Li, Y-W., & Mishra, N. (2016). *mCAF: A Multi-dimensional Clustering Algorithm for Friends of Social Network Services*. Springer Plus.

Chang, H. T., Liu, S. W., & Mishra, N. (2015). A tracking and summarization system for online Chinese news topics. *Aslib Journal of Information Management, 67*(6), 687–699. doi:10.1108/AJIM-10-2014-0147

Chang, H.-T., Mishra, N., & Lin, C.-C. (2015). IoT Big-Data Centred Knowledge Granule Analytic and Cluster Framework for BI Applications: A Case Base Analysis. *PLoS One, 10*(11), e0141980. doi:10.1371/journal.pone.0141980 PMID:26600156

Csikósová, A., & Antošová, M. (2015, February). Supply Chain Management in Condition of Production Company. *Applied Mechanics and Materials, 718*, 168–172. doi:10.4028/www.scientific.net/AMM.718.168

Dagnino, A., & Cox, D. (2014). Industrial Analytics to Discover Knowledge from Instrumented Networked Machines. *Proceedings of the 26th International Conference on Software Engineering and Knowledge Engineering (SEKE'14).*

Davenport, T. H., Harris, J. G., & Cantrell, S. (2004). Enterprise systems and ongoing process change. *Business Process Management Journal, 10*(1), 16–26. doi:10.1108/14637150410518301

Defeng, T., Shixing, L., Wujun, X., & Yongming, Z. (2010). A Fire Monitoring System In ZigBee Wireless Network. *International Conference on Cyber-Enabled Distributed Computing and Knowledge Discovery 2010.*

Ding, Z. (2013). IOT-StatisticDB: A General Statistical Database Cluster Mechanism for Big Data Analysis in the Internet of Things. In *Green Computing and Communications (GreenCom), 2013 IEEE and Internet of Things (iThings/CPSCom), IEEE International Conference on and IEEE Cyber, Physical and Social Computing.* IEEE. 10.1109/GreenCom-iThings-CPSCom.2013.104

Gaddam, A., Mukhopadhyay, S. C., & Gupta, G. S. (2011). Elder care based on cognitive sensor network. *Sensors Journal, IEEE, 11*(3), 574–581. doi:10.1109/JSEN.2010.2051425

C. Hayashi, K. Yajima, H. H. Bock, N. Ohsumi, Y. Tanaka, & Y. Baba (Eds.). (2013). Data Science, Classification, and Related Methods. In *Proceedings of the Fifth Conference of the International Federation of Classification Societies (IFCS-96).* Kobe, Japan: Springer Science & Business Media.

He, Yang, & Yang. (2010). Real-time data mining methodology and emergency knowledge discovery in wireless sensor networks. *PGNet-2010.*

Holland, J. L., & Lee, S. (2019). Internet of everything (IoE): Eye tracking data analysis. In *Harnessing the Internet of Everything (IoE) for Accelerated Innovation Opportunities* (pp. 215–245). IGI Global. doi:10.4018/978-1-5225-7332-6.ch010

Kelly, S. D. T., Suryadevara, N., & Mukhopadhyay, S. C. (2013). *Towards the Implementation of IoT for Environmental Condition Monitoring in Homes.* Academic Press.

Khanna & Liu. (2012). Machine learning approach to data center monitoring using wireless sensor networks. *Globecom-2012*.

Kiritsis, D. (2011). Closed-loop PLM for intelligent products in the era of the Internet of things. *Computer Aided Design*, *43*(5), 479–501. doi:10.1016/j.cad.2010.03.002

Kumari, A., Tanwar, S., Tyagi, S., Kumar, N., Parizi, R. M., & Choo, K. K. R. (2019). Fog data analytics: A taxonomy and process model. *Journal of Network and Computer Applications*, *128*, 90–104. doi:10.1016/j.jnca.2018.12.013

Ma, M., Wang, P., & Chu, C.-H. (2013). Data Management for Internet of Things: Challenges, Approaches and Opportunities. In *Green Computing and Communications (GreenCom), 2013 IEEE and Internet of Things (iThings/CPSCom), IEEE International Conference on and IEEE Cyber, Physical and Social Computing*. IEEE. 10.1109/GreenCom-iThings-CPSCom.2013.199

Mehdipour, F., Javadi, B., Mahanti, A., & Ramirez-Prado, G. (2019). Fog Computing Realization for Big Data Analytics. *Fog and Edge Computing: Principles and Paradigms*, 259-290.

Mishra, N. (2017). In-network Distributed Analytics on Data-centric IoT Network for BI-service Applications. *International Journal of Scientific Research in Computer Science, Engineering and Information Technology*, *2*(5), 547-552.

Mishra, N. (2018). Internet of Everything Advancement Study in Data Science and Knowledge Analytic Streams. *International Journal of Scientific Research in Computer Science and Engineering*, *6*(1), 30–36. doi:10.26438/ijsrcse/v6i1.3036

Mishra, N., Alebachew, K., & Patnaik, B. C. (2018). Knowledge Analytics in Cloud Centric IoT Vicinities. *International Journal on Computer Science and Engineering*, *6*(1), 385–390. doi:10.26438/ijcse/v6i1.385390

Mishra, N., Alebachew, K., & Patnaik, B. C. (2018). Data Organization and Knowledge Inference from Sensor Database for Smart Wear. *International Journal of Scientific Research in Computer Science, Engineering and Information Technology*, *3*(1), 1039-1044.

Mishra, N., Chang, H. T., & Lin, C. C. (2014). Data-centric Knowledge Discovery Strategy for a Safety-critical Sensor Application. *International Journal of Antennas and Propagation.* doi:10.1155/2014/172186

Mishra, N., Chang, H. T., & Lin, C. C. (2015). An IoT Knowledge Reengineering Framework for Semantic Knowledge Analytics for BI-Services. *Mathematical Problems in Engineering.*

Mishra, N., Chang, H. T., & Lin, C. C. (2018). Sensor data distribution and knowledge inference framework for a cognitive-based distributed storage sink environment. *International Journal of Sensor Networks*, 26(1), 26–42. doi:10.1504/IJSNET.2018.088387

Mishra, N., Chang, H. T., & Lin, C. C. (2018). Sensor Data Distribution and Distributed Knowledge Inference Systems. LAP LAMBERT Academic Publishing.

Mishra, N., Lin, C. C., & Chang, H. T. (2014). A Cognitive Oriented Framework for IoT Big-data Management Perspective. In *High-Speed Intelligent Communication Forum (HSIC) with International Conference on Computational Problem-Solving (ICCP) China, 2014, 6th International* (pp. 1-4). IEEE.

Mishra, N., Lin, C. C., & Chang, H. T. (2014). Cognitive inference device for activity supervision in the elderly. *The Scientific World Journal.* PMID:25405211

Mishra, N., Lin, C. C., & Chang, H. T. (2014). A Cognitive Adopted Framework for IoT Big-Data Management and Knowledge Discovery Prospective. *International Journal of Distributed Sensor Networks.*

Mutlag, A. A., Ghani, M. K. A., Arunkumar, N., Mohamed, M. A., & Mohd, O. (2019). Enabling technologies for fog computing in healthcare IoT systems. *Future Generation Computer Systems*, 90, 62–78. doi:10.1016/j.future.2018.07.049

Qu, C., Liu, F., & Tao, M. (2014). Ontologies for the Transactions on IoT. *International Journal of Distributed Sensor Networks.*

Sarabia-Jácome, D., Gonzalez-Usach, R., & Palau, C. E. (2019). IoT Big Data Architectures, Approaches, and Challenges: A Fog-Cloud Approach. In *Handbook of Research on Big Data and the IoT* (pp. 125-148). IGI Global.

Shin, J. H., Lee, B., & Park, K. S. (2011). Detection of abnormal living patterns for elderly living alone using support vector data description. Information Technology in Biomedicine. *IEEE Transactions on, 15*(3), 438–448. PMID:21317086

Shron, M. (2014). *Thinking with Data: How to Turn Information Into Insights.* O'Reilly Media, Inc.

Tibor, B., Mark, H., Michel, C. A. K., & Jan, T. (2011). An ambient agent model for monitoring and analysing dynamics of complex human behavior. *Journal of Ambient Intelligence and Smart Environments, 3*(4), 283–303.

Tortonesi, M., Govoni, M., Morelli, A., Riberto, G., Stefanelli, C., & Suri, N. (2019). Taming the IoT data deluge: An innovative information-centric service model for fog computing applications. *Future Generation Computer Systems, 93*, 888–902. doi:10.1016/j.future.2018.06.009

Tukey, J. W. (1980). We need both exploratory and confirmatory. *The American Statistician, 34*(1), 23–25.

Williams, S., Hardy, C., & Nitschke, P. (2019, January). Configuring the Internet of Things (IoT): A Review and Implications for Big Data Analytics. *Proceedings of the 52nd Hawaii International Conference on System Sciences.* 10.24251/HICSS.2019.706

Wu, Q. (2014). Cognitive Internet of Things: A New Paradigm beyond Connection. *IEEE Internet of Things Journal, 1*(2).

Yassine, A., Singh, S., Hossain, M. S., & Muhammad, G. (2019). IoT big data analytics for smart homes with fog and cloud computing. *Future Generation Computer Systems, 91*, 563–573. doi:10.1016/j.future.2018.08.040

Chapter 8

IoT Interoperability on Top of SDN/NFV-Enabled Networks

Vaios Koumaras
INFOLYSIS P.C., Greece

Marianna Kapari
INFOLYSIS P.C., Greece

Angeliki Papaioannou
INFOLYSIS P.C., Greece

George Theodoropoulos
INFOLYSIS P.C., Greece

Ioannis Stergiou
INFOLYSIS P.C., Greece

Christos Sakkas
INFOLYSIS P.C., Greece

Harilaos Koumaras
NCSR "Demokritos", Greece

ABSTRACT

The ubiquity of the internet led to a diverse number of devices referred to as the "things" to have online access. The internet of things (IoT) framework's infrastructure is formed by sensors, actuators, computer servers, and the communication network. Within this framework, the chapter focuses on IoT interoperability challenges through virtualization agility. The use of SDN/NFVs aims to face the 5G interoperability challenge by allowing the automatic deployment and programming of network services. Consequently,

DOI: 10.4018/978-1-5225-8555-8.ch008

virtual gateways need to be used so that interoperability is ensured between various objects and technologies. As a result, experiments will be performed on various IoT platforms which consist of physical and virtual parts. In specific, the process will be on top of a testbed so that MQTT, CoAP, and UDP protocols will be instantiated and set up in order to provide an interoperable layer using a virtual gateway.

INTRODUCTION

Internet of Things (IoT) focuses on the interconnectivity amongst people, sensors, actuators and processes. This term aims on the connection of various devices in order to provide data analytics and automation (Haseeb, Hashim, Khalifa, & Ismail, (2017)). An important requirement of IoT is ubiquitous connectivity and in order to achieve it, applications are needed so as to support the various sets of devices that will be used as well as communication protocols (Buyya & Vahid Dastjerdi, (2016)). Devices as such can be for example a smartwatch, a fitness band (Ranger, 2018), a television, a car and so on (Rouse, 2018). There is the concept of a digital home in which various daily devices (for example appliances) go online, are connected and allow data exchange. Therefore, various sensing devices like Radio Frequency Identification Devices (RFID), scanners, GPS and so on are combined in order to form a wider network. The aim of that wider network is to have various devices connected and make possible the identification and management of them (Liu & Lu, (2012)). Due to the variety of devices being connected together in order to allow data exchange, interoperability issues are encountered, which limit the applicability of IoT-related services due to the variety of IoT data protocols utilized by different sensors and data nodes. This chapter discusses the problem of interoperability in IoT domains by introducing the most popular IoT data protocols that are commonly used today. In addition, virtual gateways will be needed in order to ensure interoperability amongst objects and technologies and experiments using the protocols MQTT, CoAP and UDP will be performed.

Background

During 1980s and 1990s, there was the concept of making objects smart, by integrating to them processing and connectivity capabilities, but it was slowed down due to the low progress in technological advancements (Ranger, 2018). Additionally, in the book "When Things Start to Think", professor Neil Gershenfeld used the term "Things" which shows that there was an initial vision of Internet of Things (IoT) concept, back in 1999 (Rouse, 2018)The term IoT was coined by Kevin Ashton in a presentation regarding supply-chain management in 1999 (Kramp, Kranenburg, & Lange, 2013). While he was part of the Auto-ID Center at MIT, he was involved in the Radio Frequency Identification Devices (RFID) applications extension in broader domains which is the basis of the Internet of Things (Buyya & Vahid Dastjerdi, (2016)). Kevin Ashton with the term IoT wanted to describe a system that the real world is being connected using a ubiquitous network of sensors (Corcoran, 2016).

In order to fully understand the concept of IoT is better to consider the Internet, which is the basic infrastructure for interconnecting remote networking nodes, such as the IoT objects. The Internet origins are dated back to 1960s. TCP /IP was introduced in 1974 and by 1984 a thousand nodes were switched over to it for data transmission and as a networking protocol. In the 1990s and early 2000s, this connectivity trend continued, which gradually resulted in numerous connected terminals and devices. In present-day, people use smartphones in order to perform their daily tasks, mobile network allows for ubiquitous connectivity and the internet allows device connection from anywhere (Corcoran, 2016).

Nowadays, IoT applications have been found in different sectors, such as to systems which are industrial and closed-loop to commercial ones (Kolias, Stavrou, Voas, Bojanova, & Kuhn, 2016). Examples of the devices are: cameras, lights, television, printers and so on. The number of devices which are currently connected to the internet is estimated to be around 5 billion and an increase is expected in 2020 to be around 25 billion. The future shows that IoT devices will be mainstream, increase technological advancements to areas such as healthcare by using monitoring wearables, to retail as well as transportation. There is a transition of the IoT devices and from monolithic boards are turning to modular devices so as to satisfy daily life's needs (Kolias, Stavrou, Voas, Bojanova, & Kuhn, 2016).

IoT devices can use a variety of networks such as LAN, WAN, PAN or cellular networks. In addition, due to device restriction requirements such as battery, high autonomy and low cost, wireless technologies, such as RFID, Bluetooth, NFC are used (DíazZayas, García Pérez, Recio Pérez & Merino, 2017). RFID takes an important role in IoT. The RFID system includes back-end network applications and data acquisition. Devices as such even though they play an important role in IoT, still face various problems like standards compatibility. Moreover, besides RFID, wireless networks play an important role, allowing users to connect via various devices, creating the basis for the wider deployment of IoT systems (Liu & Lu, (2012)).

IoT DATA PROTOCOLS

The devices, which are connected, have different protocols, which lead to interoperability issues (Blackstock& Lea, 2014). Examples of protocols that are usually utilized by sensors as data protocols are the MQTT, CoAP, HTTP and UDP. These protocols are briefly described in the following sections.

MQ Telemetry Transport Protocol (MQTT)

MQ Telemetry Transport (MQTT) is a lightweight messaging protocol, which is designed for constrained devices, networks which are not sufficiently reliable, namely utilizing low bandwidth with high latency (MQTT, 2014).According to (Rouse, What is MQTT?, 2018), it is a lightweight messaging protocol, since its messages consist of a fixed header which is 2 bytes, an optional variable header, a QoS (Quality of Service) level and a theoretically max message payload to 256Mb, but the max payload size supported by IoTF is 4Kb. MQTT's basic principles are to minimize the network bandwidth as well as the requirements of the device and ensure reliability and assurance of delivery. It is also ideal for machine to machine or IoT situations where various devices are connected as well as in cases where mobile applications are used and bandwidth and battery power are important. The term MQTT was coined in 1999 by Dr Andy Stanford-Clark from IBM and Arlen Nipper of Arcom(MQTT, 2014).MQTT has a diverse structure which can be a huge tree with no clear way to be able to divide it in smaller components that can be manageable. Therefore, this is a problem which in turn increases the complexity of the network. In addition, MQTT protocol has a problem with interoperability. A problem in terms of interoperability is due to the binary message payloads which contain no information of their encoding. Problems as such arise when applications from different manufacturers need to be connected and work together. Moreover, another problem is that the receiver is not able to know who the original message sender is. The only way to be able to know the sender is if it is mentioned in the message. The use of additional security features on top of the MQTT protocol causes a code increase which leads to difficulty handling the implementations (Rouse, What is MQTT?, 2018).

Constrained Application Protocol (CoAP)

Constrained Application Protocol (CoAP) is a web transfer protocol which is used with constrained nodes and networks. It is designed to be used with machine to machine applications like smart energy or building automation (Bormann, 2016). In addition, CoAP allows devices like low power sensors and actuators to be able to communicate via the Internet. This protocol runs on devices which support UDP (or else User Datagram Protocol) and is ideally suited for devices which are of low memory and power as it offers small message size, lightweight messages and message management (Johnson, 2016).

This protocol, like the HTTP protocol, is based on the REST model which allows servers to make resources available under a URL. The clients can access those resources by using methods like GET, POST, PUT and DELETE (Bormann, 2016). A description of the aforementioned methods can be found below (Shelby, Hartke, & Bormann, 2014).

- **GET:** This method allows the retrieval of a representation in relation to information of the resources identified by the URI. Get is a safe method to be used.
- **POST:** This method refers to the processing of the enclosed representation. POST is neither a safe method nor an idempotent one.
- **PUT:** This method refers to the update or creation of resources identified by URI. PUT is neither a safe nor an idempotent method like POST.
- **DELETE:** This method allows the deletion of information identified by the URI. It is not safe a safe method but is idempotent.

Hypertext Transfer Protocol (HTTP)

Hypertext Transfer Protocol (HTTP) is a network protocol that web browsers and servers use in order to communicate. The HTTP can be easily recognized in a web browser by looking at the URL as it has the signature of http in the beginning. This protocol is similar to other protocols like FTP (File Transfer Protocol) as it uses a program in order to request files from a server remotely. In the case of HTTP, the program that is used to request files is a web browser and requests HTML files which are displayed in the format of text, images, hyperlinks and so on. In addition, this protocol unlike other protocols is stateless, which refers to the ability that it has to stop the connection once a request has been made and executed. This protocol has been created by Tim Berners- Lee in the early 1990s (Mitchell, 2018).

HTTP offers three message types which are GET, POST and HEAD. The GET type refers to messages which are sent to a server and contain only a URL. The URL can have zero or more data parameters which can be added at the end of it (Mitchell, 2018).

The POST type refers to any additional data parameter which is placed in the body of the message and not in the end of the URL (as it happens in the case of the GET type). The HEAD type is similar to GET but instead of replying with full URL information, the server sends back only information in regards to the header (Mitchell, 2018).

As with the other protocols, the HTTP has its issues. Some of the issues in relation to this protocol relate to message transmission failure due to different reasons like:

- User error
- A problem with the web server or browser
- An error that exists in the web pages creation and
- Temporary problems in regards to the network

In case of an issue, the protocol captures the problem of failure and then reports an error code in order to point out what kind of error it is (Mitchell, 2018).

User Datagram Protocol (UDP)

User Datagram Protocol (UDP) is a transport layer protocol and is used with the IP network layer protocol. UDP is written by John Postel and defined by the RFC 768 and provides a datagram service to an end system (Fairhurst, 2018)The issue with this protocol is that it provides an unreliable service meaning that there is no guarantee that the message will be delivered and protected from duplication. It is an unreliable, minimal, message passing transport to applications as well as upper layer protocols. It offers an efficient communication transport but it does not have reliability or congestion control. Due to its unreliability, application designers often consider it as a transport. In cases of data duplication, the designers need to verify that the application can handle duplication and implement appropriate mechanisms in order to detect it. Moreover, this protocol has security issues. In cases of applications that have sensitive data, a separate security service needs to be provided in order to use additional protocol mechanisms (Fairhurst, 2018).

IoT ARCHITECTURE COUPLED WITH CLOUD COMPUTING SYSTEM

The architecture of a modern IoT system today is usually coupled with cloud computing systems, including both central and edge nodes, providing increased scalability and performance, as well as third party access to the IoT infrastructure. The first layer consists of sensors and actuators. The second layer (Internet Gateway) involves sensor data aggregation systems and a conversion of analog to digital data. The third layer (Edge IT and Fog computing systems) consists of IT systems which preprocess data prior to its transfer to a data center or a cloud. The last layer (Data Center/Cloud), layer four, is the stage where data can be analyzed, managed and stored. Below follows a description of each of these IoT stages.

Figure 1 depicts the four layers of an IoT architecture couple with cloud computing resources, which are briefly described hereby:

Figure 1. Architectural layers of a modern IoT system

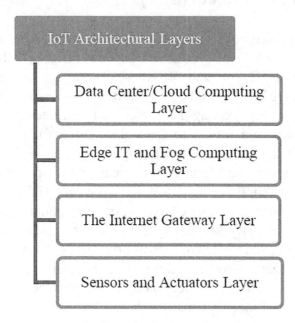

- **Sensors and Actuators:** The sensors have the ability to collect data from the environment and provide useful data. A different name of a sensor is transducer which is a physical device that is used so as to convert one energy form to another one. An example of a sensor is a microphone that can take the sound waves and convert them into electrical energy (Eller, 2017).

A transducer that can be found in different IoT systems is an actuator, which means that it operates in an opposite direction of a sensor. An actuator takes the electrical input and converts it to a physical (Eller, 2017). Examples of an actuator's process are: to shut off the power supply, to adjust the air flow valve and so on. The first stage of sensors/actuators involves different devices such as accelometers, air sensors, heart rate monitors and so on (Fuller, 2018).

- **The Internet Gateway Layer:** Data from sensors need to be agrregated to one node for further processing. Ccssioanlly and depending on the node type, the data may need to change before it enters the processing stage. Moreover, data need to change from its analog form to a digital one and the Internet Gateway Layer assists in achieving this. Sensors/ Actuators and the Internet Gateway Layer can be found close to each other and therefore, that is helpful in order to achieve real time preprocessing. Moreover, the internet gateways can be built and support analytics, malware protection and data management (Aher, 2018). A gateway is an edge device, it is located externally to the data center and it is important to know its location. Additionally, gateway devices can be found in various environments like factory floor to mobile field stations and they are built in order to be portable, durable to temperature changes, vibration and deployable (Fuller, 2018).

- **Edge IT and Fog Computing:** This is the third stage of the IoT architecture. In this stage, data enter in the IT systems so as to be further analyzed. This layer (Edge IT) is located in remote offices or in edge locations comparing to the two aforementioned layers (Sensors/ Actuators and the Internet Gateway Layer) which are located close to each other. The IoT data can be huge in size thus taking a big amount of network bandwidth and due to this reason, the edge systems via analytics allow data to be minimized in terms of its amount (Aher, 2018). In addition, while processing the data different issues can be encountered such as security issues, storage issues and data delay. By following a staged approach, the data can be preprocessed, meaningful results can be generated and only those will be passed on (Fuller, 2018)

- **Data Center/Cloud:** This is the fourth and last stage of the IoT architecture. Data can be forwarded to cloud-based systems or a physical data center when they need to be further processed. In this way, data will be analyzed, managed and stored by powerful IT systems (Fuller, 2018). Moreover, by exploiting the virtualization capabilities that cloud systems offer, additional functions may be also considered in the processing process in order to perform additionals tasks, such as big data analytics or business inteliigence tasks.

The generic architecture of IoT systems consists of systems which are complex and perform various tasks such as collecting information in relation to people, environment, psychological measurements, tracking things and so on. Information as such is stored in IoT back end with or without the aid of a gateway (Haseeb, Hashim, Khalifa, & Ismail, (2017)). A gateway stores, translates and forwards data to an IoT back–end system. There are also gateways which are more complex and allow the proprietary device management of IoT devices. In addition, there are IoT gateways which allow process automation prior to forwarding the processed data to a back- end cloud for storage and additional processing. The IoT back-end has a limit of the capabilities of a physical IoT device and does not have a mechanism in order to overcome this issue(Haseeb, Hashim, Khalifa, & Ismail, (2017)). The coupling of traditional IoT systems with cloud computing and virtualization infrastructure can contribute to overcome the aforementioned limitations by adding functions in an agile manner that are able to perform tasks on demand. Among the various functions, one of the main challenges that the modern gateways have to face is the interoperability provision over the various data protocols that the IoT sensors and nodes use.

IoT Interoperability: Vertical and Horizontal Deployments

An important requirement of IoT is interoperability as the "things" which are connected to the Internet need also to be found, accessed and managed in a unified way. Therefore, interoperability plays an important role in this case and is a feature that it should be appropriately supported by the IoT Gateway.

In an IoT architecture, the devices need to interoperate and communicate with a gateway which is cloud based. This though is not always true due to the various devices which are connected, many communication protocols which are used as well as many application layer interfaces. Thus, this diversity of devices leads to vertical solutions which are isolated. These vertical solutions don't allow systems to communicate in order to exchange valuable information and therefore do not follow the true nature of IoT (Haseeb, Hashim, Khalifa, & Ismail, (2017)).

Figure 2 depicts a graphic of the vertical isolated approach. Vertical solutions have dominated the IoT devices and systems. A company using a vertical model can control an IoT device, a gateway, an application and also a cloudbased service. Additionally, there is a clear control in terms of decision making from the entry stages and also the users deal with one provider in cases of technical difficulties. The vertical solutions have more drawbacks than benefits, specifically in terms of user perspective. An example is that there may be different companies offering different solutions to a building(one company can focus on remote control on

Figure 2. Vertical IoT approach

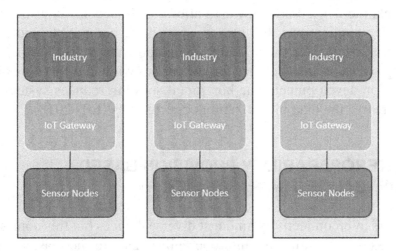

electric light usage and the other on the security system's IoT sensor) thus this is impossible to control the devices using a single application as each of the companies use their own platform (IoT, 2018).In addition, it is in a virtual manner impossible to be able to manage a diverse set of IoT devices (Haseeb, Hashim, Khalifa, & Ismail, (2017))

Besides the vertical solution, there is the horizontal approach. Figure 3 shows an example of an horizontal solution. A horizontal platform is

Figure 3. Horizontal IoT approach

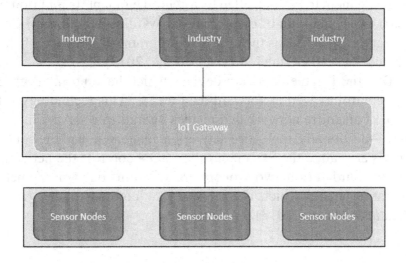

used so as to streamline the user control of IoT devices. In the horizontal approach, there is a platform which allows various companies to be able to develop applications, IoT devices, which are compatible and also to interact amongst each other using a common framework. Furthermore, this approach is an ideal choice for enterprises while it offers ease of use, application development. The horizontal solution reduces system costs and increases the data monetization opportunities (IoT, 2018).

IoT INTEROPERABILITY PROVISION BASED ON VIRTUALIZED INFRASTRUCTURE

IoT offers interconnectivity amongst diverse devices but this comes with a price as there is a lack of interoperability. Due to the reason that the companies offer solutions independently of each other, have different platforms and frameworks, there is a problem with integration with one another (Eastwood, 2017). In order to overcome the interoperability issue, a solution is by using virtualization and software-defined techniques. There are two technologies which promise a cost effective scale and versatility, which is necessary for IoT, namely the Software Defined Networking (SDN) and Network Functions Virtualization (NFV). (Bizanis & Kuipers, 2016).

Software Defined Networking

SDN come up with the idea of making network devices programmable and allowing them to be controlled by a central element. In addition, SDN allows: i) The separation of control and forwarding function, ii) Control centralization, and iii) Has the ability to program the network's behavior with the use of well-defined interfaces (Pate, 2013).

In SDN, the IoT elements are devices which have no intelligence in order to control as well as forward data traffic. This technology acts as the brain of an entire network and resides on multiple servers in a cloud network. Additionally, the entire network management and the control of operations are called the SDN controller. SDN controls the network and reduces the burden of network operators as it aims on avoiding network configuration errors which is an issue very common today (Alenezi, Almustafa, & Meerja, 2018).

Network Functions Virtualization

Network Functions Virtualization (NFV) was created by a service providers' working group. The service providers tried to speed up the network services so as to increase revenue and growth plans and found that hardware-based appliances had a limit in order to achieve that. So, NFV was a solution in order to accelerate service innovation and provisioning (Pate, 2013). In NFV, there is a software manager similar to SDN in order to allocate and release resources. In addition, NFV devices can be controlled by using a central SDN controller thus making it easier for SDN and NFV to coexist and function together. The NFV architecture is composed of three components: Physical Hardware, Virtual Hypervisor Layer and Virtual Machine (Alenezi, Almustafa, & Meerja, 2018). The Virtual Hypervisor Layer runs on hardware and manages resources like the power of CPU, memory and storage capacity. The Virtual Machine refers to software, which has the ability to emulate the architecture and functionalities of the physical platform by using hardware resources. A physical hardware is able to host more than one virtual machines. (Alenezi, Almustafa, & Meerja, 2018). NFV has been a popular choice amongst telecommunication companies or else Telcos as they are suffering from interoperability issues. NFV aimed at aiding on operational challenges, high costs, device heterogeneity and proprietary appliances. Issues regarding heterogeneous devices are the following (Haseeb, Hashim, Khalifa, & Ismail, (2017)):

1. **Fixed Configuration:** The Telco hardware has a fixed IP which does not change for a long period of time
2. **Manual Management:** The management and configuration of telco equipment requires moving physical staff and this can be achieved once at a time.
3. **Rapid Growth of IP End Points:** Many users are able to access the Internet thus this makes it difficult if a central provisioning is not established.
4. **Network Endpoint Mobility:** Due to the fixed nature of networks, the requirements for mobility take a longer time so as to reconfigure the network in regards to different scenarios.

5. **Elasticity:** Due to the reason that there is no mechanism in order to upgrade or even downgrade physical software, the networks need to be over provisioned.

Software Defined Network and Network Functions Virtualization

These two technologies are quite different but they share common principles. The use of SDN and NFV allows the networks to be driven by centralized software control capabilities which are able to program an entire network using a set of open APIs. Virtualization is also beneficial as the costs of deploying services around the network minimize (Vodafone, 2016). NFV is driven by dynamic requirements and is associated with the evolution of cloud. Nowadays, there is an evolution in terms of delivery service thus virtual technologies offer the same services as physical ones and they are also instantiated when they are needed. NFV offers a dynamic set of capabilities and requires a dynamic network in order to connect them. A challenge of SDN is that the network is controlled using open APIs without affecting the physical underlying connectivity. A customer will be able to see development in terms of self service capabilities which are not easily available in the current day in terms of WAN and security services. In addition, another positive aspect is to provide real-time visibility in terms of transport and application performance across the network. In order to decide whether to deploy SDN or not, an organization needs to understand several aspects such as the sites connected to the network, the application flows and the data type that these sites will traverse. When the previous aspects have been decided and understood, then it will be easier for the business to consider the dynamicity of its services, the criticality of data and the internet transport that the content needs to consume (Vodafone, 2016).

Furthermore, the use of these technologies (SDN and NFV) aims to face the 5G interoperability challenge by allowing the automatic deployment and programming of network services. These technologies are cost effective and provide the necessary versatility for the IoT services. Additionally, the 5G networks need to support software network technologies and the SDN and NFV are important as they are an ideal choice. As mentioned previously the SDN aims at basic connectivity services whereas the NFV provides orchestration, a virtualization framework and aims at a larger scope. In order to be able to implement these technologies a virtual gateway is needed as it ensures the interoperability amongst objects and technologies. Furthermore, additional KPIs metrics need to be evaluated in order to ensure the quality of QoS and QoE which is perceived by the end user. The IoT platform needs to be consisted of physical and virtual parts and be on top of a testbed so that the protocols MQTT, CoAP and UDP will be instantiated and set up in order to provide an interoperable layer by using a virtual gateway (INFOLYSiS, 2018).

The virtual gateway's aim is to provide the interoperability of IoT NFVs in different domains so as to unify the various and diverse smart objects which operate by using different IoT protocols. The ideal choice of protocols is MQTT and CoAP as they are open standards and they provide a more suitable solution to constrained environments in regards to HTTP.

In specific (see Fig. 4), the project envisages the testing/deployment of specific VNFs, which are mapping functions (i.e. proxies) of popular IoT data protocols (such as MQTT and CoAP) to generic data protocol (such as UDP or HTTP) in order to provide a common interoperable layer over the heterogeneous IoT nodes deployed at heterogeneous IoT domains and testbeds.

Figure 4. SDN/NFV-driven IoT interoperability on top of a virtual-based GW

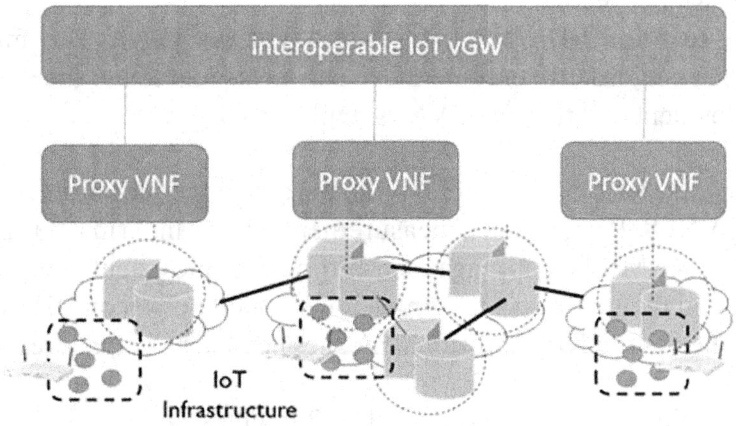

EXPERIMENTAL VALIDATION FOR THE PROPOSED IOT INTEROPERABILITY PROVISION PLATFORM

Three KPIs metrics are proposed for assessing IoT interoperability provision. The first KPI refers to the deployment of necessary VNFs and the testing of their functionality. In this KPI, all the necessary VNFs such as virtual gateways, mapping VNFs are on top of SDN/NFV testbeds. In addition, the deployment of the necessary VNFs and their functionality are based on quantitative metrics. In order to consider this KPI successful, additional metrics need to be considered such as:

- **Data Loss to be 0:** In this case mapping VNFs will be deployed so that one function receives the HTTP protocol and provides to the virtual gateway proprietary lightweight UDP data. A second function receives the MQTT protocol and provides to the virtual gateway proprietary lightweight UDP data and a third function receives the CoAP protocol and provides to the gateway UDP based data.
- **Real-time MONITORING at the GUI:** The virtual gateway is successfully deployed and runs and monitors in real-time the data sources which are received from the IoT nodes.
- **One IoT Message per Second per IoT Node:** In this case there will be equal IoT generators for each protocol (two CoAP generators, two MQTT generators and two HTTP generators) in order to generate one message per second.
- **Two to Four SDN/NFV Testbeds Will be Used:** The minimum testbeds, in order to execute the experiments and led to the successful deployment and testing of VNFs, will be two.

The second KPI metric refers to the performance measurement of the mapping VNFS. Performance measurement will be in terms of utilization of CPU and RAM and mapping (such as time of deployment, delay of VNF mapping and the IoT messages which are mapped per second). In order to measure the second KPI, additional metrics need to be considered such as:

- The deployment time to be less than 2 minutes
- The VNF mapping delay to be less than 2 seconds
- All IoT messages to be equal to the messages of the IoT virtual gateway
- CPU to use less than 3% and

- VNF RAM to use less than 5%.

The third KPI metric refers to the SDN-based IoT service isolation on top of testbeds. In this KPI, at least two IoT services will be isolated so as to achieve network slicing and multiletancy. In order to measure the third KPI, additional metrics are needed:

- Two isolated services
- The SDN setup to be less than two minutes
- The number of virtual IoT gateway instances to be equal to the number of services.

Experimental Setup

This experiment considers that a virtual gateway will deploy the necessary mapping VNFs like for example proxies and apply the appropriate commands through SDN manager. The SDN manager on top of each testbed is important as without it the IoT nodes' emulator will forward the data traffic to a respective gateway and to external domains.

Figure 5. Experiment on top of a testbed

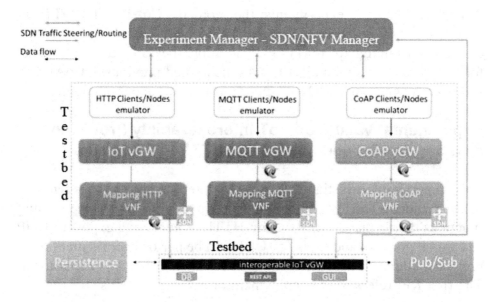

Figure 5 shows the experiment manager –SDN/NFV manager on top of a testbed. By using the SDN/NFV IoT system, the virtual gateway's data traffic will be routed to the SDN-node/switch and also will be routed, diverted and steered by the SDN switch of the testbed to a mapping VNF function. Moreover, it will be translated to a protocol which is interoperable like the UDP, then will be forwarded, routed back to the SDN and then will be led to an external domain (its original destination). The steps described above are based on the SDN programmability and are titled "SDN traffic steering and service chaining." (Cao, Kodialam, & Lakshman, 2014)

Moreover, at the MQTT and CoAP testbeds, the IoT traffic will be routed, steered from the respective nodes to a VNF proxy that maps a specific IoT protocol to a generic one and then to the virtual gateway so as to depict the mapped data which are received. A NFV and SDN manager is considered in order to achieve the deployment of VNFs and programming of SDN nodes at each of the testbeds.

Due to the mapping VNFs which are provided by an interoperable virtual gateway and also the support of SDN/NFV techniques, the virtual/softwarised IoT gateways are enhanced with mapping capabilities so as to aggregate the data of relevant sensors by utilizing an appropriate protocol like CoAP or MQTT and export data using common protocols like HTTP or UDP.

For this chapter's experiments, the protocols CoAP and MQTT are chosen so as to be tested as they are open standards and ideal for constrained environments in regards to HTTP. In addition, they provide mechanisms for asynchronous communication. As mentioned previously, CoAP is a state transfer model and MQTT supports a many-to-many communication.

Experimental Validation: IoT Interoperability Provision as a Service Between CoAP and HTTP IoT Domains

This experiment investigates the agile interoperability between two restful protocols and tests will be executed in order to assess the mapping functions' performance. Tests using HTTP protocol and export to UDP and CoAP protocol and export to UDP will be performed. As mentioned previously three KPI metrics will be used for this chapter's experiment. The first KPI refers to the deployment of necessary VNFs so as to test their functionality. In this metric, the data loss needs to be zero and the VNFs will be four and the following:

- HTTP protocol import and exports to UDP protocol
- CoAP protocol import and exports to UDP protocol.

Figure 6 shows the HTTP messages generator where four HTTP messages are captured. Moreover, this generator VNF has an internal counter and shows that a packet is produced per second and is sent to an interoperable virtual gateway. The packet will be diverted with the use of relevant SDN commands utilizing mapping functions so as to translate it in a format which is suitable for the gateway.

Figure 7 shows that HTTP is exported to UDP and incoming HTTP traffic packets and outgoing UDP packets are depicted. In order to be able to monitor the bandwidth and rate estimation, the bmon tool is used so as to monitor and debug, capture and prepare networking statistics. This tool offers a user interface and the ability to program.

Figure 8 shows the import of CoAP protocol and the export to UDP. The methodology followed in the case of the HTTP import and UDP export is followed in CoAP import and UDP export.

Figure 6. HTTP messages generator VNF

Figure 7. HTTP import and UDP export

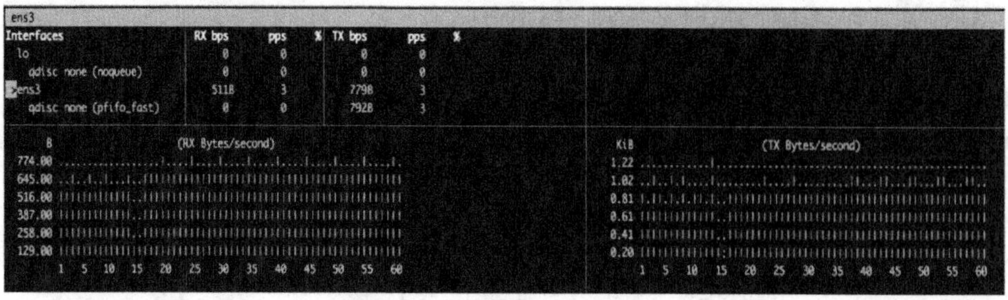

Figure 8. CoAP import and UDP export

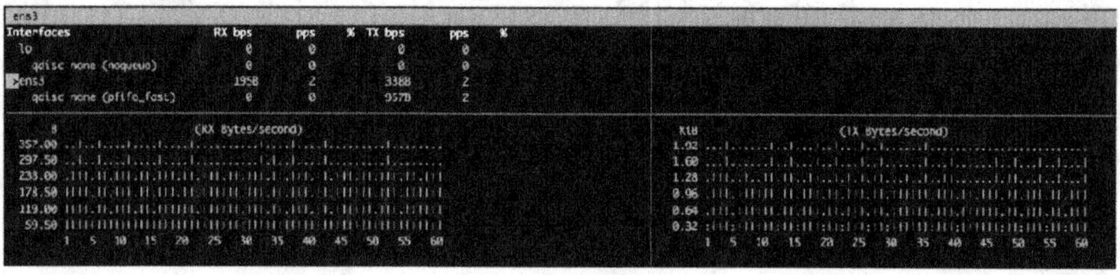

The second KPI metric focuses on the performance measurement of the mapping VNFs in terms of CPU and RAM utilization as well as the mapping performance (like throughput, latency and delay). This KPI, as mentioned previously, is based on 5 metrics:

- The deployment time to be less than 2 minutes
- The VNF mapping delay to be less than 2 seconds
- All IoT messages to be equal to the messages of the IoT virtual gateway
- CPU to use less than 3% and
- VNF RAM to use less than 5%.

This KPI metric was deployed using an experimenter tool, two testbeds and the experiment's deployment time was measured. Testbed one's deployment time was less than 2 minutes. In order to acquire an accurate deployment time estimation, the process was repeated five times and each time the deployment time was measured. Testbed two's deployment time was less than 7 minutes and this was in regards to the testbed's settings

Figure 9. HTTP-to-UDP mapping delay

```
Host: 10.44.57.8
Accept-Encoding: gzip, deflate
Accept: */*
User-Agent: python-requests/2.9.1
Via: 1.1 betermprx01.rm.eld.it.eu.ericsson.se (squid/3.5.17)
X-Forwarded-For: 10.44.57.20
Cache-Control: max-age=0
Connection: keep-alive

02:21:33.660374 IP (tos 0x0, ttl 64, id 59478, offset 0, flags [DF], proto UDP (17), length 56)
192.168.118.3.56811 > 172.20.30.113.53: [udp sum ok]
```

Figure 10. CoAP-to-UDP mapping delay

```
02:16:32.272095 IP (tos 0x0, ttl 64, id 45396, offset 0, flags [DF], proto UDP (17), length 62)
10.44.57.26.47913 > 192.168.118.14.5683: UDP, length 34
02:16:32.274650 IP (tos 0x0, ttl 64, id 63312, offset 0, flags [DF], proto UDP (17), length 56)
192.168.118.14.53176 > 172.20.30.113.53
```

which led to the delay of the process. The second metric part was the VNF mapping delay to be less than 2 minutes. The delay of the mapping functions of the experiment was estimated upon the experiment's deployment.

Figure 9 depicts the HTTP to UDP mapping delay and this is shown to be less than 1 sec.

Figure 10 shows the process of CoAP to UDP mapping delay. The delay time and in this process is shown to be less than 1 sec.

The third metric of this KPI is that all IoT messages to be equal to the messages of the IoT virtual gateway. All the messages derive from the two message generators HTTP and CoAP and each of them generates two messages. The virtual gateway receives the messages from these generators without having any loss. The experiment to provide interoperability is reliable and performs without any problem with one message per second.

The fourth metric is that the VNF CPU to utilize less than 3%. Figure 11 shows the CPU utilization for HTTP which is less than 1% (specifically 0.3%). These mapping functions are shown to be lightweight and efficient.

Figure 12 shows the CPU utilization for COAP which is 0.3% like in the HTTP example.

The last metric of the second KPI focuses on RAM utilization to be less than 5%. The experiment showed that RAM utilization in both message

Figure 11. CPU utilization for HTTP mapping function

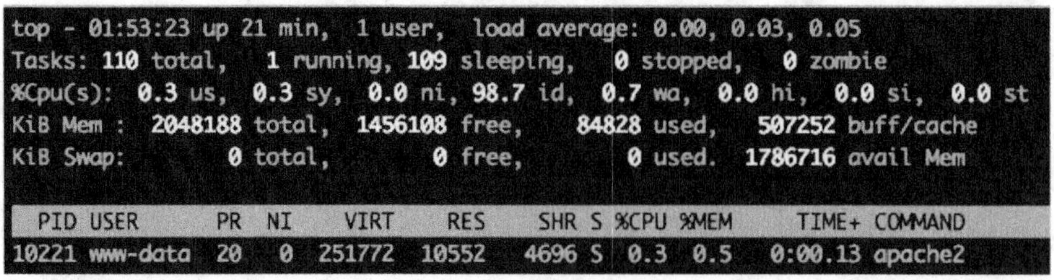

```
top - 01:53:23 up 21 min,  1 user,  load average: 0.00, 0.03, 0.05
Tasks: 110 total,   1 running, 109 sleeping,   0 stopped,   0 zombie
%Cpu(s):  0.3 us,  0.3 sy,  0.0 ni, 98.7 id,  0.7 wa,  0.0 hi,  0.0 si,  0.0 st
KiB Mem :  2048188 total,  1456108 free,     84828 used,    507252 buff/cache
KiB Swap:        0 total,        0 free,         0 used.  1786716 avail Mem

  PID USER      PR  NI    VIRT    RES    SHR S %CPU %MEM     TIME+ COMMAND
10221 www-data  20   0  251772  10552   4696 S  0.3  0.5   0:00.13 apache2
```

Figure 12. CPU utilization for CoAP mapping function

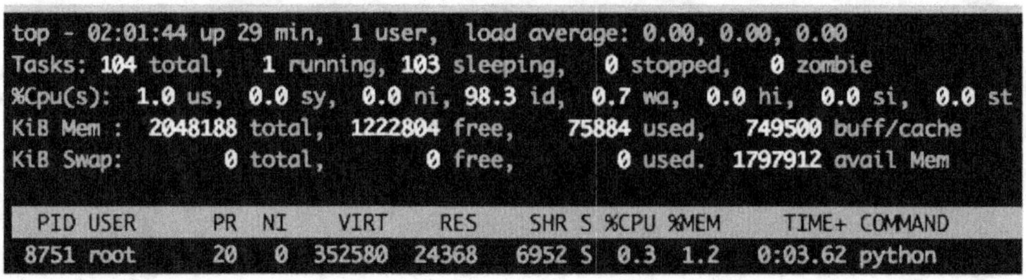

```
top - 02:01:44 up 29 min,  1 user,  load average: 0.00, 0.00, 0.00
Tasks: 104 total,   1 running, 103 sleeping,   0 stopped,   0 zombie
%Cpu(s):  1.0 us,  0.0 sy,  0.0 ni, 98.3 id,  0.7 wa,  0.0 hi,  0.0 si,  0.0 st
KiB Mem :  2048188 total,  1222804 free,     75884 used,    749500 buff/cache
KiB Swap:        0 total,        0 free,         0 used.  1797912 avail Mem

  PID USER      PR  NI    VIRT    RES    SHR S %CPU %MEM     TIME+ COMMAND
 8751 root      20   0  352580  24368   6952 S  0.3  1.2   0:03.62 python
```

generators (HTTP and CoAP) is between 0.5 to 1.2%. In this metric again is shown that the proposed functions are efficient and lightweight.

The third KPI metric refers to the SDN-based IoT service isolation on top of testbeds. In this KPI metric, two services will be isolated in order to achieve slicing and multiletancy of the network. This KPI metric is based on 3 metrics as mentioned previously therefore relevant experiments took place. The first metric of it is that there are two isolated services. Two descriptor files were prepared and used in order to deploy two of such services in parallel. For this metric, CoAP and HTTP generators were deployed, their respective mapping functions and two virtual gateways. The second metric refers to the setup time and service of SDN to be less than two minutes. Appropriate SDN rules were used so as to be able to steer traffic from each IoT node to the respective mapping function. The time that was measured was less than than 450 msec thus was less than the 2 minutes. The third metric of this KPI refers to an equal number of instances and services. The deployment of the generators, the mapping functions (HTTP to UPD and CoAP to UPD) and the applicability of the SDN rules, lead to interoperability and service isolation.

FUTURE RESEARCH DIRECTIONS

The VNF formulation of the software-based IoT mapping functions can facilitate further the SaaS business model of them, while the integration of SDN rules in the virtualization environment can further upgrade the provision of the interoperable services following the SaaS/PaaS model. A major factor towards this in the future is the provision and support of slicing, which will support that service isolation can be achieved and therefore multi-tenancy exploitation of the infrastructure.

CONCLUSION

Internet of Things aims at the interconnectivity between people, sensors, actuators and processes. Moreover, diverse devices from various vendors are being used and connected in order to provide data analytics and automation. IoT allows everyday objects to act like "smart" and being connected to the internet and allow the users to perform various tasks. Examples of IoT can be a smartwatch, a fridge, a car and so on. Due to the vast majority and diversity of devices which are being connected and share information, as well as the different protocols each of them uses, a problem of interoperability is being defined. This interoperability issue can be solved by using virtualization technologies such as SDN and NFV. These virtualization techniques allow the minimization of costs that existed in physical devices, share same services as the physical ones but they are instantiated when they are needed. In order to use these technologies at their best possible way, it is important to consider several aspects before proceeding on choosing them such as the sites that will be connected to the network, the application flows and the data type that these sites will traverse. Furthermore, the combination of SDN and NFV aims to face the interoperability challenge as these technologies are cost effective and provide versatility for the IoT services. In order to implement these technologies, a virtual gateway is needed so as to achieve the interoperability between the objects and technologies. The IoT platform consists of physical and virtual parts and is on top of a testbed so that the protocols MQTT, CoAP and UDP will be instantiated and set up in order to provide an interoperable layer using a virtual gateway.

REFERENCES

Aher, B. (2018). *A Look at the IoT Architecture*. Retrieved 8 24, 2018, from DZone: https://dzone.com/articles/iot-architecture-2

Alenezi, Almustafa, & Meerja. (2018). Cloud based SDN and NFV architectures for IoT infrastructure. *Egyptian Informatics Journal.*

Bizanis & Kuipers. (2016). SDN and Virtualization Solutions for the Internet of Things: A Survey. *IEEE Access*, 5591-5606.

Bormann. (2016). *CoAP- RFC 7252 Constrained Application Protocol*. Retrieved 8 7, 2018, from CoAP: http://coap.technology

Buyya, R., & Vahid Dastjerdi, A. (2016). *Internet of Things*. Cambridge, MA: Morgan Kaufmann.

Cao, Z., Kodialam, M., & Lakshman. (2014). *Traffic steering in software defined networks: planning and online routing*. ACM.

Corcoran, P. (2016). The Internet of Things: Why now, and what's next? *IEEE Consumer Electronics Magazine*, 5(1), 63–68. doi:10.1109/MCE.2015.2484659

Eastwood, G. (2017). *IoT's interoperability challenge*. Retrieved 8 11, 2018, from https://www.networkworld.com/article/3205207/internet-of-things/iots-interoperability-challenge.html

Eller, J. (2017). *IoT System | Sensors and Actuators*. Retrieved 8 24, 2018, from Bridgera: https://bridgera.com/iot-system-sensors-actuators/

Fairhurst, G. (2018). *The User Datagram Protocol (UDP)*. Retrieved 8 11, 2018, from https://www.erg.abdn.ac.uk/users/gorry/course/inet-pages/udp.html

Fuller, J. (2018). *The 4 stages of an IoT architecture*. Retrieved from TechBeacon: https://techbeacon.com/4-stages-iot-architecture

Haseeb, S., Hashim, A., Khalifa, O., & Ismail, A. (2017). Connectivity, interoperability and manageability challenges in internet of things. *AIP Conference Proceedings*, 020004. doi:10.1063/1.5002022

IoT. (2018). *Defining the IoT Ecosystem for Enterprises*. Retrieved from IoT Innovation: https://internet-of-things-innovation.com/insights/the-blog/defining-iot-ecosystem-enterprises/

Johnson, S. (2016). *Constrained Application Protocol: CoAP is IoT's 'modern' protocol*. Retrieved 8 9, 2018, from https://internetofthingsagenda. techtarget.com/feature/Constrained-Application-Protocol-CoAP-is-IoTs-modern-protocol

Kolias, S., & Voas, B. (2016). Learning Internet-of-Things Security "Hands-On". *IEEE Security and Privacy, 14*(1), 37–46. doi:10.1109/MSP.2016.4

Kramp, K. V., & Lange. (2013). Introduction to the Internet of Things. Berlin: Springer.

Liu, T., & Lu, D. ((2012)). The application and development of IOT. *International Symposium On Information Technologies In Medicine And Education*.

Mitchell, B. (2018). *What Does HTTP Mean?* Retrieved 8 8, 2018, from https://www.lifewire.com/hypertext-transfer-protocol-817944

MQTT. (2014). Retrieved from Oasis: http://docs.oasis-open.org/mqtt/mqtt/v3.1.1/os/mqtt-v3.1.1-os.html

Pate, P. (2013). *NFV and SDN: What's the Difference?* Retrieved 8 5, 2018, from https://www.sdxcentral.com/articles/contributed/nfv-and-sdn-whats-the-difference/2013/03/

Ranger, S. (2018). *What is the IoT? Everything you need to know about the Internet of Things right now*. Retrieved 7 29, 2018, from ZDNet.: https://www.zdnet.com/article/what-is-the-internet-of-things-everything-you-need-to-know-about-the-iot-right-now/

Rouse, M. (2018). *What is internet of things (IoT)?* Retrieved 8 1, 2018, from internetofthingsagenda.com: https://internetofthingsagenda. techtarget.com/definition/Internet-of-Things-IoT

Rouse, M. (2018). *What is MQTT?* Retrieved 8 1, 2018, from https://internetofthingsagenda.techtarget.com/definition/MQTT-MQ-Telemetry-Transport

Shelby, Hartke, & Bormann. (2014). *RFC 7252 - The Constrained Application Protocol (CoAP)*. Retrieved 8 9, 2018, from https://tools. ietf.org/html/rfc7252

Vodafone. (2016). *Software Defined Networking and Network Function Visualization*. Retrieved 7 25, 2018, from www.vodafone.com/business/ news-and-insights/blog/gigabit-thinking/software-defined-networking-and-network-function-virtualisation

Chapter 9
Modified Backward Chaining Algorithm Using Artificial Intelligence Planning IoT Applications

Pradheep Kumar K.
BITS Pilani, India

Srinivasan N.
Sathyabama Institute of Science and Technology, India

ABSTRACT

In this chapter, an automated planning algorithm has been proposed for IoT-based applications. A plan is a sequence of activities that leads to a goal or sub-goals. The sequence of sub-goals leads to a particular goal. The plans can be formulated using forward chaining where actions lead to goals or by backward chaining where goals lead to actions. Another method of planning is called partial order planning where all actions and sub-goals are not illustrated in the plan and left incomplete. When many IoT devices are interconnected, based on the tasks and activities involved resource allocation has to be optimized. An optimal plan is one where the total plan length is minimum, and all actions consume similar quantum of resources to achieve a goal. The scheduling cost incurred by way of resource allocation would be minimum. Compared to the existing algorithms L2-Plan (Learn to Plan) and API, the algorithm developed in this work improves optimality of resources by 14% and 36%, respectively.

DOI: 10.4018/978-1-5225-8555-8.ch009

INTRODUCTION

In today's world, automation of activities using artificial intelligence finds extensive applications in several areas. To ensure adequate quantum of resources for tasks, the wastage of resources should be avoided. When IoT devices are used the resource constraints become critical. This is mainly because when multiple IoT devices are integrated, each device would be having a separate goal. When multiple devices are integrated, sub-goals of each individual IoT device would be combined to get the final goal of the application.

Automated planning is used to schedule tasks and activities. A plan is a sequence of actions leading to sub-goals and goals. The actions, sub-goals and goals are decided based on the underlying functional behavior of the application.

A collection of actions leading to sub-goals and goals leads to a plan formulation. A number of such plans may be formulated based on the functionality of the application. The plan length is decided based on the number of actions and resource utilization by these actions.

The plans may be formulated by the following methods:

- Forward Chaining
- Backward Chaining
- Partial Order Plans

Forward Chaining

In Forward Chaining approach, a sequence of actions lead to sub-goals and goals. This approach is used in scenarios where the programmer has complete clarity on the actions involved in realizing sub-goals and goals. The information of the entire set of actions is presented in the plan. Plan length in many situations is minimum. It does not handle exceptional conditions and actions. If these need to be handled the programmer needs to address them.

Backward Chaining

In Backward Chaining approach, a sequence of goals or sub-goals lead to actions. In several applications, the outcome or ultimate goal is known, but knowledge of the actions and sub-goals involved in the process is unknown to the programmer. In such situations, the programmer has to work on all actions, tasks and activities associated. Exceptional tasks and actions are also handled as the programmer to explore all these actions. Plan length is always maximum as a number of hidden actions are explored and brought in the plan. This gives designer maximum information to create the application.

Partial Order Planning

In Partial Order Planning, not all actions and sub-goals are available in the plan. This is similar to Backward Chaining approach. Most of the actions are not illustrated and left as an open decision to the application. This is an advanced stage of planning and requires deep learning strategies for effective handling.

In this work, a modified Backward Chaining approach is used where the resource required by an action or sub-goal is computed by categorizing the nature of the action or sub-goal. Later, a priority factor is assigned to the action or sub-goal. The resource utilization is computed based on a proportion of the priority of the action or sub-goal to the sum of the priorities of the actions or sub-goals.

Based on these criteria a Linear Programming Model has been developed and the resource consumption is computed. Resource left unutilized is stored as slack and reused later. In this approach, optimality is guaranteed for the plan length. Compared to L2-Plan and API, the algorithm proposed in this work improves optimality of resource by 14% and 36% respectively.

LITERATURE SURVEY

Cyber OS as proposed by Akkermans et al in (2017) explains how resource sharing could be done in IoT devices. Here each IoT device is modelled as a node. Further a feature on resource security has also been included to ensure other IoT nodes do not access resource acquired by a particular IoT node. Here lightweight applications and restricted resource access has also been taken care.

Distributed QoS management as discussed by Samie et al in (2016) illustrates the QoS levels of resource constraints in ensuring adequate quantum of resource allocation.

Hierarchical goal based formalism as explained by Shivasankar et al in (2012) illustrates the hierarchical goal based formulation where multiple IoT devices have a sequence of goals.

AI planning strategies that would appreciate smart environments were discussed by Marquardt and Uhrmacher in (2008)

Existing algorithms for AI planning uses L2 Plan strategy as explained by Levine et al in (2009). This algorithm uses Knowledge representation strategies. It formulates a number of conjunction-based rules. The algorithm expects the goal to be known first and adds a pre-condition constraint to obtain the action. This strategy formulates a plan using several constraints imposed on achieving the goal. However, the success of this strategy depends on the pre-condition chosen on the goal. If the pre-condition handles exceptions, the goal formulation would be precise and accurate. Again, this strategy does not facilitate a large population.

Another policy is the briefcase domain policy or API policy as discussed by Machado et al (2016). In this strategy decision list is formulated. The decision list so formulated needs to contain all strategic actions in the plan, which involve the sub-goals to make the goal reachable. If the plan so developed does not contain all possible states, it would lead in failure to achieve the goal.

Another strategy of crowdsourcing in AI planning as discussed by Machado et al in [2]. Here complete information on the crowd population is needed. If there is any heterogeneity in the crowd, resource allocation constraints may also vary accordingly. The constraints needs to bring in all sub-factors associated to ensure the goals are achievable.

Soltani et al in (2012) explains the functional and non-functional aspects of the AI planning. They also highlight several features, which may have a positive or negative impact on the AI planning. SPLE (Software Product Line Engineering) show the software systems that have common features in AI planning.

Ferretti and Esquivel in (2005) explains how genetic algorithms which uses tardiness to incorporate knowledge for the AI planning strategy. When actions arrive online, this approach would need to have precise boundary constraints for resource assessment.

Desimone and Hollidge in (1990) explain fleet modelling using AI Scheduling. Scheduling Systems for fleet modelling use strategies like Capacity Planning, Representation of Constraint and resources and Constraint satisfaction. These strategies use decision support systems to handle resource allocation mechanisms. HERMES and DELVIS-0 are the two scheduling strategies that use the decision support systems.

Gil (2015) proposed self-adaptive systems with AI planning strategies by handling decision systems with adaptable resource constraints. Several Adaptive resource constraint-modelling strategies have been discussed by Salehie and Tahvildan (2009), Krammer and Maggie (2007). Garlan et al (2004) proposed a self adaptation model for Smart agents. Rosa et al (2013) for component based applications.

Figure 1. Block diagram architecture of IoT devices and clusters

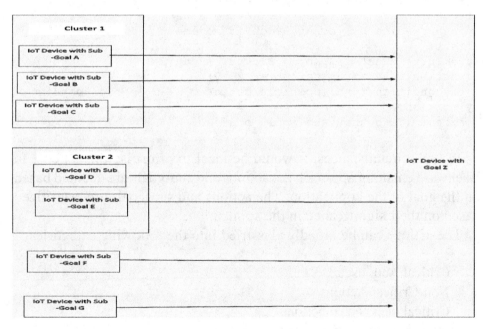

Proposed Work

In this work, we propose a modified approach for Backward Chaining by using a prioritizing technique. In several applications of robots using artificial intelligence, the backward chaining approach is used, as there are many unexpected actions. Robots are constructed with a number of IoT devices, each with sub-goal. Finally the sub-goals of these devices are integrated to have achieve a particular goal. A few IoT devices may also be paired to form a cluster which is also shown in Figure 1.

The block diagram architecture of the proposed model has been illustrated in Figure 1.

The approach has been simulated using PDDL (Planning Domain Definition Language)

A typical PDDL construct for robotic action would be

```
(: goal (and (at event 1, Take turn)
             (at event 2, apply brakes)
             (at event n, sub-goal n)))
Action / Operator:
Description: The robot drives a car
Precondition: (and (event 1? obstacle detected) (event 2?
person passing by (event 3? child movement)
Effect:
Take Turn (event 1), Apply Brakes (event 2)
(: action Take turn (parameter x, y)
: precondition (and (obstacle detected) and (person passing
by) or (child movement)
: effect (Take turn and Apply brakes)
```

In such circumstances, it would be ideal to prioritise the actions. In Backward chaining approach the actions and sub-goals are decided based on the goal of the application. The actions and sub-goals are prioritized based on their significance in the application.

The actions can be broadly classified into the following categories:

- Critical Actions
- Non-Critical Actions
- Critical unexpected actions
- Non-critical unexpected actions

Figure 2. Table action / sub-goal and priority weightage

Action / Sub-goal	Weight
Critical – Unexpected	Very High
Critical	High
Non-Critical –Unexpected	Low
Non-Critical	Very Low

The priorities assigned to these actions based on weights.

The resource constraints are modelled based on the rules formulated.

The rules are modelled as a premise. The resource quantum for each action and sub-goal has been formulated using Linear Programming constructs. The resource consumption of an action or sub-goal is computed as a ratio between the priority of the action of sub-goal to the sum of the priorities of a particular category of action or sub-goal.

Resource of Action / Sub-goal

$$R_i = \frac{P_i(ActionorSubgoal)}{\sum_{i=1}^{i=n} P_i(Actionorsubgoal)} \tag{1}$$

where P_i is the Priority of the Action or Sub-goal

Linear Programming Constraints

The constraints are formulated based on the goals, sub-goals and Actions. The Critical-Unexpected Actions have the highest priority. Based on the categories of actions as mentioned in table I. If the total quantum of resource is assumed to be Z, then we have n1 linear constraints. The resource requirement for each constraint would be Z/n1.

The procedure for resource assessment could be illustrated by an example given below:

Example

For a Goal G we may have sub-goals L, M, N, O, S,T and U. L,M,N are unexpected critical. O and S are critical. T is unexpected non-critical and U is non-critical.

N has the highest priority followed by M and then L. Similarly, S has highest Priority followed by O.

The priorities for unexpected Critical sub-goals N, M and L are 7, 6 and 5 respectively. The priorities of Critical sub-goals O and S are 4 and 3 respectively. The priorities and that for Unexpected Non-Critical sub-goal T is 2 and the priority of Non-Critical sub-goal U is 1.

If A,B,C,D,E,F,H are actions associated for sub-goals L,M,N,O,S,T and U. In this A, B, C are unexpected critical actions. D and E are critical actions. F is unexpected non-critical action and H is non-critical.

The LPP is modelled as follows:

Objective Function is Z

$$
\text{Max } z = (\frac{7}{7+6+5})N + (\frac{6}{7+6+5})M + (\frac{5}{7+6+5})L + \tag{2}
$$
$$
(\frac{4}{4+3})O + (\frac{3}{4+3})S + (\frac{2}{2+1})T + (\frac{1}{2+1})U
$$

$$
\text{Max } Z = (\frac{7}{18})N + (\frac{6}{18})M + (\frac{5}{18})L + (\frac{4}{7})O + (\frac{3}{7})S + (\frac{2}{3})T + (\frac{1}{3})U \tag{3}
$$

$$
126 \; Z = 49N + 42M + 35L + 72O + 54S + 84T + 42U \tag{4}
$$

If Z1,Z2,Z3,Z4,Z5,Z6 and Z7 are the resources required for each sub-goal N,M,L,O,S,T and U respectively.

Hence

$$
Z1 = (7/18)*Z \tag{5}
$$

$$
Z2 = ((6/18)*Z) \tag{6}
$$

$$Z3= ((5/18)*Z) \tag{7}$$

$$Z4= ((4/7)*Z) \tag{8}$$

$$Z5= ((3/7)*Z) \tag{9}$$

$$Z6= ((2/3)*Z) \tag{10}$$

and

$$Z7= ((1/3)*Z) \tag{11}$$

Now for actions A, B and C are unexpected critical actions leading to unexpected critical sub-goals. We need 3 constraints to evaluate resource for A, B and C

$$(\frac{9}{9+8+7})A + (\frac{8}{9+8+7})B + (\frac{7}{9+8+7})C \leq \frac{7}{18}Z \tag{12}$$

$$(\frac{6}{6+5+4})A + (\frac{5}{6+5+4})B + (\frac{4}{6+5+4})C \leq \frac{6}{18}Z \tag{13}$$

$$(\frac{3}{3+2+1})A + (\frac{2}{3+2+1})B + (\frac{1}{3+2+1})C \leq \frac{6}{18}Z \tag{14}$$

Which simplifies to

$$\frac{9}{24}A + \frac{8}{24}B + \frac{7}{24}C \leq \frac{7}{18}Z \tag{15}$$

$$\frac{6}{15}A + \frac{5}{15}B + \frac{4}{15}C \le \frac{6}{18}Z \tag{16}$$

$$\frac{3}{6}A + \frac{2}{6}B + \frac{1}{6}C \le \frac{5}{18}Z \tag{17}$$

On further simplification,

$$9A + 8B + 7C \le \frac{28}{3}Z \tag{18}$$

$$6A + 5B + 4C \le \frac{30}{6}Z \tag{19}$$

$$3A + 2B + C \le \frac{5}{3}Z \tag{20}$$

Hence,

$$27A + 24B + 21C \le 28Z \tag{21}$$

$$36A + 30B + 24C \le 30Z \tag{22}$$

$$9A + 6B + 3C \le 5Z \tag{23}$$

Similarly for sub-goals O and S resource required Z8 and Z9 are

Z8= (4/7)*Z and Z9= (3/7)*Z.

Sub-goals O and S which are Critical map onto Actions D and E. Hence the Constraints are

$$(\frac{4}{4+3})D + (\frac{3}{4+3})E \le \frac{4}{7}Z \tag{24}$$

$$(\frac{2}{2+1})D + (\frac{1}{2+1})E \le \frac{3}{7}Z \tag{25}$$

Which simplifies to

$$\frac{4}{7}D + \frac{3}{7}E \le \frac{4}{7}Z \tag{26}$$

$$\frac{2}{3}D + \frac{1}{3}E \le \frac{3}{7}Z \tag{27}$$

On Further Simplification,

$$4D + 3E \le 4Z \tag{28}$$

$$14D + 7E \le 9Z \tag{29}$$

For Sub-goals T and U which are unexpected non-critical and non-critical map on to Actions. Z10 and Z11 are the resource requirement, where

$$Z10 = ((2/3)*Z) \tag{30}$$

$$Z11 = ((1/3)*Z) \tag{31}$$

$$\frac{2}{3}F \le \frac{2}{3}Z \tag{32}$$

On Simplification

$$F \leq Z \tag{33}$$

Similarly

$$\frac{1}{3}G \leq \frac{1}{3}Z \tag{34}$$

On Simplification

$$G \leq Z \tag{35}$$

Based on the above LPP formulation, resource is allocated and additional resource available after utilisation is cumulated as Slack.

Algorithm

- For each goal in the plan

  - Formulate sub-goals and actions
  - If (Sub-goal | Action) is (Unexpected & Critical) Then
    - Assign Highest priority for resource required
    - Execute Procedure L1
  - If (Sub-goal | Action) is Critical Then
    - Assign a lower priority for resource required
    - Execute Procedure L1
  - If (Sub-goal | Action) is (Unexpected & Non-Critical) Then
    - Assign a lower priority for resource required
    - Execute Procedure L1
  - If (Sub-goal | Action) is (Non-Critical) Then
    - Assign a lower priority for resource required
    - Execute Procedure L1

L1: If Multiple sub-goals and actions exist in the plan for the above categories Then

- Assign different priorities and handle them by resolving ties.

  - If resource is left unused Then
    - Store the same as Slack
    - Check the status of next sub-goal and action

Else

- Check the status of next sub-goal and action
- End the Procedure

SIMULATION RESULTS

The algorithm has been simulated using PDDL. The algorithm has been tested by varying the problem size up to 400 to identify the number of optimal solutions obtained. Optimal solutions are based on exact assessment of resources for the tasks involved. The algorithm has been compared against L2 plan and API strategy. The simulation results are indicated in Figure 3.

Figure 3. Table on Effectiveness in terms of Optimality

S.No.	Problem size	No. of Optimal Solutions			Effectiveness (%)(Modified Backward Chaining Vs L2-Plan)	Effectiveness (%)(Modified Backward Chaining Vs API)
		L2-Plan	API	Modified Backward Chaining Approach		
1	1	83	70	98	18.07	40.00
2	17	80	66	95	18.38	43.94
3	33	78	60	81	4.52	35.00
4	49	74	56	79	6.40	41.07
5	65	72	52	73	2.10	40.38
6	81	69	48	71	3.27	47.92
7	97	66	55	75	14.50	36.36
8	113	62	47	63	1.20	34.04
9	129	60	49	61	2.09	24.49
10	145	57	48	63	11.50	31.25
11	161	53	44	60	12.68	36.36
12	177	52	41	59	14.01	43.90
13	193	49	34	49	1.03	44.12
14	209	46	37	49	7.69	32.43
15	225	42	34	45	6.26	32.35
16	241	40	31	41	3.80	32.26
17	257	36	33	45	24.14	36.36
18	273	34	31	43	26.47	38.71
19	289	35	32	43	22.86	34.38
20	305	41	38	49	19.51	28.95
21	321	45	41	53	17.78	29.27
22	337	48	42	62	29.17	47.62
23	353	49	46	61	24.49	32.61
24	369	51	49	67	31.37	36.73
25	385	52	47	65	25.00	38.30
26	401	56	56	71	26.79	26.79
	Average	55	46	62	14	36

Figure 4. Plot illustrating the number of Optimal Solutions

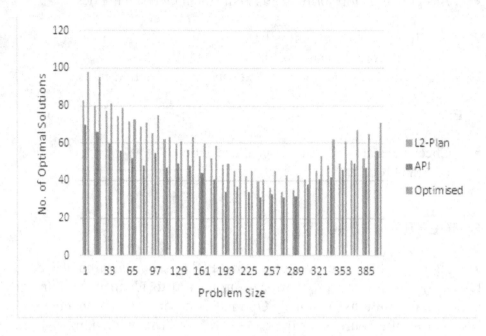

Figure 5. Plot Comparing the Effectiveness of Optimised Resource strategy

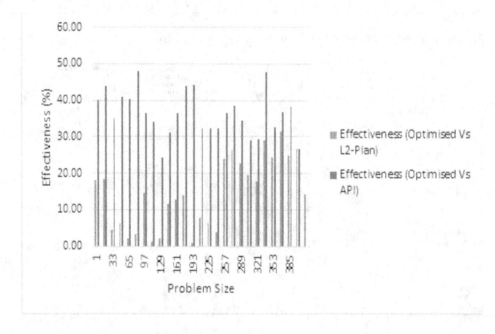

The number of optimal solutions obtained by varying the problem size is shown in Figure 4.

The effectiveness of the optimized resource strategy as compared to the L2 Plan and API strategy is illustrated in Figure 5.

The algorithm proposed improves optimality as compared to L2-Plan and API by 14% and 36% respectively.

CONCLUSION

In this work, an optimal resource assessment strategy for backward chaining approach has been proposed. The algorithm proposed improves optimality compared to L2-Plan and API by 14% and 36% respectively.

This approach attempts to store unutilized resource as slack for actions, which may arrive online. It handles unexpected critical actions in an effective manner to ensure that the application is reliable and has a high throughput.

FUTURE WORK

The work may be further extended by integrating applications to handle resource management globally in an IoT platform. The slack stored could be used as a shared resource across the applications. The overheads associated especially migration overhead could be either eliminated or kept as small as possible to prevent resource wastage.

REFERENCES

Akkermans, S., Daniels, W., Sankar, G. R., Crispo, B., & Hughes, D. (2017). Cerber OS: A resource-secure OS for sharing IoT Devices. *International Conference on Embedded Wireless Systems and Networks (EWSN)*, 96-108.

Desimone & Hollidge. (1990). *Case Studies in Fleet Operation Modelling: An application of AI scheduling techniques*. ACM.

Ferretti & Esquivel. (2005). *Knowledge Insertion: An Efficient Approach to Reduce Effort in Simple Genetic Algorithms for Unrestricted Parallel Equal Machines Scheduling*. ACM.

Garlan, D., Cheng, S. W., Huang, A. C., Schmerl, B., & Steenkiste, P. (2004). Rainbow: Architecture-based Self Adaptation with reusable Infrastructure. *Computer*, *37*(10), 46–54. doi:10.1109/MC.2004.175

Gil, R. (2015). *Automated Planning for Self-Adaptive Systems*. IEEE.

Krammer, J., & Magee, J. (2007). Self Managed Systems: an architectural challenge. In *Future of Software Engineering, 2007, FOSE'2007* (pp. 259–268). IEEE.

Levine, J., Westerberg, H., Galea, M., & Humphreys, D. (2009). *Evolutionary-Based Learning of Generalised Policies for AI Planning Domains*. ACM. doi:10.1145/1569901.1570062

Machado, L., Prikladnicki, R., Meneguzzi, F., Cleidson, R. B., & de Souza, E. C. (2016). Task Allocation for Crowdsourcing using AI Planning. ACM.

Marquardt & Uhramcher. (2008). *Evaluating AI Planning for Service Composition in Smart Environments*. ACM.

Rosa, L., Rodrigues, L., Lopes, A., Hiltunen, M. A., & Schlitching, R. D. (2013). Self-management of adaptable component-based applications. *IEEE Transactions on Software Engineering*, *39*(3), 403–421. doi:10.1109/TSE.2012.29

Salehie, M., & Tahvildan, L. (2009). Self-Adaptive Software: Landscape and research challenges. *ACM, TAAS*, *4*(2), 14.

Samie, F., Souras, V. T., Xydis, S., Bauer, L., Soudris, D., & Henkel, J. (2016). *Distributed QoS Management for Internet of Things under Resource Constraints*. ACM. doi:10.1145/2968456.2974005

Shivashankar, V., Kuter, U., Nau, D., & Alford, R. (2012). A Hierarchical Goal-Based Formalism and Algorithm for Single-Agent Planning. *Proceedings of the 11th Conference on Autonomous Agents and Multiagent Systems (AAMAS 2012)*, 981-989.

Soltani, S., Asadi, M., Gasevic, D., Hatala, M., & Bagheri, E. (2012). Automated Planning for Feature Model Configuration based on Functional and Non-Functional Requirements. In *SPLC* (pp. 201–214). ACM. doi:10.1145/2362536.2362548

Chapter 10
Data Security in WSN-Based Internet of Things Architecture Using LDS Algorithm:
WSN Architecture With Energy-Efficient Communication

Linoy A. Tharakan
Mar Thoma Institute of IT, India

Dhanasekaran R.
Syed Ammal Engineering College, India

Suresh A.
Syed Ammal Engineering College, India

ABSTRACT

The possibility of internet of things (IoT) was produced in parallel to WSNs. The term IoT was formulated by Kevin Ashton in 1999 and alludes to remarkably identifies items and their virtual portrayals in a "internet like" structure. While IoT does not accept a specific communication approach, wireless data transfer will assume a noteworthy part, and specifically, WSNs will multiply numerous applications. The small, cheap, and low-powered WSN sensors will bring the IoT to even the smallest items introduced in any sort of condition at sensible expenses. There are several methods and tactics for distributed IoT systems to prevent security attacks or contain the extent of damage of such attacks. Many of these deserve significant computational, communication,

DOI: 10.4018/978-1-5225-8555-8.ch010

and storage requirements, which often cannot be contented by resource-constrained sensor nodes. This chapter proposes a WSN architecture with energy-efficient communication with secure data packets with a proposed LDS (Lino-Dhanasekaran, Suresh) algorithm which is useful in IoT applications.

BACKGROUND

Internet of Things

There is a sweeping change in the daily life as well as in running environments of people with intrusion of the services of Internet and Internet enabled services. This is befitting a popular concept in industry, business and everyday life of the human being (Madakam et al, 2015). The expansion of the Internet to Internet of Things [IoT] has been chiefly obsessed by needs of large corporations. The IoT is a technological revolution that represents the future of computing and communications, and its development supports diverse dynamic technical innovations, from wireless sensors to nanotechnology. Naturally Wireless sensor network become the back bone of Internet of Things and its services. IoT is closely in contact with the sensors and actuators to communicate with the real world environment which can be manageable with the help of sensor network infrastructure. So data and information communicated via internet and sensors associated with the devices privacy, security as well as energy efficiency challenges. It is so difficult for developing energy aware software for WSN as they consist of small, tiny limited resource embedded devices that should communicate over low bandwidth wireless links (Linoy et al., 2014).

WIRELESS SENSOR NETWORK (WSN)

WSN has been identified as an important technology forming the back bone of many industries and services for the 21st century. A sensor network is an infrastructure consisting of monitoring a parameter, processing the sensor outputs and sending that processed data to higher hierarchical modules elements. WSN provides an infrastructure based service that couple between traditional computing and real-time environment. It is an emerging domain for ubiquitous computing paradigm and named as *motes*

Low cost, intelligent devices with a couple of onboard sensors, with radio waves connectivity and the internet, made to spread in a geographical area, provide incomparable opening for managing and monitoring homes, cities, and the environment. In addition, these micro-sensors connected in network provide immense roles in the defense by generating new capabilities for investigation and observation as well as other strategic roles. These sensors and actuators with local processing power can be deployed underground, in the air, underwater, on human bodies, in vehicles, habitat monitoring.

A given computing capacity becomes exponentially smaller and cheaper with each passing year. Technology advancement in various research centers use the semiconductor fabrication for the sensors helps in construct compatible and handheld communication devices with small tiny electromechanical components. These power regulated, low cost, communication nodes can be deployed throughout an area, helps to monitor physical phenomena and then local processing and communication centers or to the neighboring nodes and coordinating actions with other nodes. Intelligent WSNs has the ability to self-organizing and self-healing capability, illustrated in Figure 1. A wireless network connected to the internet may have a piece of networking hardware to interface with user and or other network called the gateway through which all the routing algorithms are implemented.

In an ad-hoc network, sensor nodes in a wireless module can be deployed in any manner and transferred to any location as needed. Scalability is almost hundred percentages possible in all the sensor network applications and nodes can be easily add on to the existing networks. All this is made possible through the use of robust, efficient network protocols developed specifically for WSNs. Wireless sensor nodes are characterized by being tiny intelligent, low in cost, battery-driven, and deployed randomly or in a deterministic pattern. Network nodes are equipped with wireless transmitters and receivers using antennas that may be unidirectional (isotropic radiation), highly directional (point-to-point), possibly steerable, or some combination thereof.

Challenges and Constraints

It is not like centralized wired network system but a sensor network which is subjected to a set of resource limitations such as restricted on board

Figure 1. WSN structure

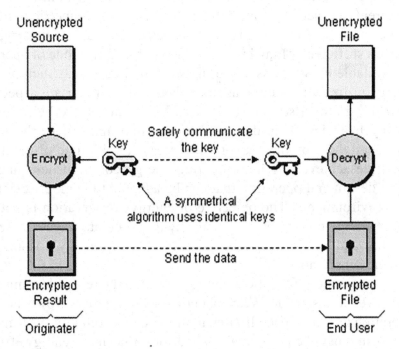

battery power and inadequate communication bandwidth. The constraints influence the design of a WSN, to take up new protocols and algorithms that differ from their counterparts in other distributed systems. These sensors and actuators with local processing power can be deployed underground, in the air, underwater, on human bodies, in vehicles, habitat monitoring.

Energy

Energy source of the sensor nodes (likely battery) are limited in capacity or short in life span with respect to the demands of the application. After the depletion of the battery power, the sensor will fail to communicate with each other or process internally. The energy insufficiency is a serious problem in the entire WSN network irrespective of applications. The efficiency of the network is determined by the ability to handle the number of requests in its energy budget. It is an important performance index of the network. So far, energy efficiency of the network has been not modeled or quantified. However lots of research has been carried out in this respect. Wireless network and a wireless network with infrastructure are different in aspects; because the later is highly asymmetric in nature. Even the energy of each node is limited because of draining battery; base station has sufficiently long lasting power supply. This mode of operation is not available for wireless sensor network with no infrastructure.

Energy utilization and management is the most important aspect that decides the life of a sensor network as sensor nodes are being mostly driven by batteries. This demands energy optimization in the sensor nodes to and there by the network to increase the lifetime of the nodes. This can be achieved by incorporating energy consciousness in every phase of design and operation that can be adapted to work efficiently in diverse environments. The objective of energy conservation is not only to reduce energy consumption during any intermediate stages of the data processing and manipulation but also to balance energy consumption among the sensor nodes.

The vast number of solutions that have driven the research community over the years has made WSN phenomenon a reality. However, their proliferation has so far been limited to the research community with just a minimum number of commercial applications. Enormous energy efficient solutions are required for each portion of WSN design to deliver the potential advantages of the WSN phenomenon. Therefore, in both existing and future researches for WSN, energy efficiency is the major challenge. From that, the problem of energy optimization in WSNs is important for modern researchers and it is being taken into considerations by all manufacturers and developers of such systems. Since energy conservation is the primary and key challenge for WSN, the research focuses on how to utilize the energy efficiently during the communication, data processing, security, and node deployment, so as to prolong network lifetime.

In WSNs, security is a crucial requirement for most of the applications. Perhaps, implementation of security in WSN differs from traditional networks due to the limited hardware and software resources and processing power constraints. It has been facing several security challenges due to the hardware limitations of the sensor nodes, wireless communication environment, real-time processing needs, heterogenic structure, and large number of nodes, mobility and cost. Privacy and confidentiality are the basic goal of security.

Energy Consumption: Factors in WSN

Energy is a narrow expedient within the sensor network architecture and has to be run conscientiously sequentially to raise the lifetime of the network. Many characteristics in the network which are also accountable for depletion of energy, shown in (Linoy et al, 2016; Madhumita et al, 2014; Ozturk et al, 2004; Raghunathan et al, 2002) are as follows:

1. Same data may be sensed by many sensor nodes manually scattered in a small geographical space.
2. Sending, similar values often to the base station also lowers channel effectiveness.
3. To send a data, keep on listening to the channel.
4. While not in use, keeping the node "on state" in periodic sensing,
5. Large volume of data transmission need supplemental energy
6. Processing complexity in sensor node devours more power.
7. Collision and retransmission (Liu et al, 2005).

There is a series of power devaluation practices has used each in the design of the circuits and in the design of protocols approaches. The major step against power desolation is a efficient design of circuits (Parool et al, 2013; Vieira et al, 2003; Zahra et al, 2012) picking the decisive circuits and using suitable design procedure to each case. When node even in idle-mode, it unusable listening to neighboring nodes, causes another reason of energy displace. Energy debt by reason of to packet collision is also a major issue, causes all data packets concerned are discarded and need to retransmit. Another reason is the offensive routing leads to the reception of packets to non addressed node (Muntz et al, 2001).

Ad-Hoc Deployment

Most of the network applications does not possess a predetermined deployment structure of all sensors other than center head or base station. For example, sensors serving the monitoring of battlefield or disaster areas could be dropped from air through helicopters or unmanned vehicles' over the areas of surveillance, But in some conditions some sensor nodes may not be able to start sensing and communication in such drops. However, the surviving modules must autonomously perform a series of setup and configuration procedure, including determining their positions, the establishment of communications with neighboring sensor nodes, and the initiation of their sensing responsibilities.

Unattended Operation

Nodes in the Sensor networks, once deployed, must operate without human intervention. Configuration, maintenance, adaptation and fault maintenance must be performed in a self-governing fashion. Automaticity can take place in a variety of forms. Self-optimization refers to a device's ability to monitor and optimize the use of its own system resources. Self-protection allows a device to recognize and protect itself from intrusions and attacks. Self-organization is the term frequently used to describe a network's ability to adapt configuration parameters based on system and environmental state. Most importantly the ability to fault tolerance gives the ability to discover, identify, and react to network disruptions.

While many WSNs operate on normal sensing modes, there are some applications that are, not able to collect the real time data due to communication limitations; refer to such networks as Unattended WSNs (UWSNs). For example, sensor networks deployed in hostile military environments might not have the luxury of an ever-present sink node. In some scenarios, to avoid the failure risk of the centralized fixed point sink node, sensor data might be collected by mobile sinks using robots or unmanned aerial vehicles. Access to the sensor network might be unpredictable and might occur at irregular intervals. As a result, sensors might be not capable to off-load their data in real time. Instead, they have to store and process data locally and wait for an explicit signal to upload it to the mobile sinks.

WSN SECURITY

Many WSNs collect crucial and critical information from the application area. Unattended operation of sensor hubs builds their introduction to noxious interruptions and assaults. Additionally, remote interchanges make it simple for an enemy to listen in on sensor transmissions. The results can be serious and rely upon the kind of sensor organize application.

There are a number of techniques yet strategies for disbursed systems to stop attacks or incorporate the sum on harm about such attacks. Many over these become considerable computational, communication, and storage requirements, as repeatedly cannot be contented through resource-constrained sensor nodes. From the dialogue consequently far, that becomes obvious that much design options into a WSN differ out of the design choices regarding other systems and networks. To summarize, the challenges we face of devising sensor network systems yet purposes include:

- **Hardware:** Each node has limited processing power, communication capabilities, and limited energy supply, bandwidth and internal memory.
- **Networking:** The topology and connectivity of network is commonly peer-to-peer approach, with a mesh topology and dynamic, mobile, and unreliable connectivity. Lack of universal routing protocols or central registry services is a considerable limitation. Each node acts both as a router and as an application host.
- **Software Development Support:** The node jobs are typically real-time and massively distributed that require dynamic collaboration among nodes in a network, and must deal with multiple competing events. Global properties can be specified only via local instructions. Because of the coupling between applications and system layers, the software architecture must be code signed with the information processing architecture.

Unreliable Communication

Certainly, another important threat to sensor network is the security issue due to unreliable network structure. The security of the network relies almost on a protocol, which, in turn, depends on communication. Unreliable transfer normally is based on packet routing of the sensor network. Packets may get damaged due to channel errors or due to the congestive nodes, they may drop. This results in packet loss or missing. The unreliable communication channel also results in scratched packets. Also, if the protocol lacks the error handling effectively there is a high possibility of losing critical security packets including even the cryptographic key.

There is another conflict is due to broadcast nature of the WSN. If the packets meet in the middle of a transfer, conflicts might occur and resulting in a failed transfer. In a high-density sensor network, this can be a major security issue. Major challenges in a network are

- Latency
- Unattended Operation
- Exposure to Physical Attacks
- Remote management

Congestion on network and node processing can cause more latency inside the multi-hop routing. sometimes, it is tough to achieve synchronization among sensors network. The synchronization problems are vital to sensor security in which the safety mechanism relies on cryptographic key distribution and many others.

Depending on the application of the sensor network, the sensor nodes may be left unattended for long period. The sensor may be deployed in an environment, which is open to adversaries, bad weather or may suffer a physical attack from the surroundings. Unattended Wireless Sensor Networks (UWSNs) refers to the category of WSNs that operate without an on-line data collection entity. In an UWSN the sink visits the network with irregular and even in unpredictable frequency. As a result, each sensor must retain its data (measurements) for a considerable time. Without the supervision and monitoring of an online sink, the disconnected network must be self-defensive against any adversary, which takes the advantage of the unattended nature of the network. Intervals between successive sink visits represent periods of vulnerability and incentive attacks.

The physical tampering may be difficult to detect in the case of remote management of a sensor network and physical maintenance issues (e.g., battery replacement). Perhaps, the most extreme example of this is a sensor node used for remote reconnaissance missions behind military operations lines. In such a case, the node may not have any physical contact with friendly forces once deployed.

Defensive Measures

Now that is between a role according to mark the measures because of satisfying protection necessities and defending the sensor network from attacks. Start together with key establishment in WSNs, which lays the foundation because protection between a WSN; followed by defending in opposition to Denial on Service attacks, invulnerable broadcasting yet multicasting; defending towards attacks on routing protocols, combating traffic analysis attacks; defending against attacks regarding sensor privacy, intrusion detection; secure data aggregation, defending towards physical attacks, then trust management.

The key establishment is certain important security factor so much receives a large bear regarding attention into WSNs is the area of key management. WSNs are special (among other embedded wi-fi networks) appropriate after theirs size, mobility, then computational government constraints. The operational constraints described previously, makes secure key management an utmost necessity in most WSN designs. Because encryption and key management/establishment are consequently vital in conformity with the defense regarding a WSN, with nearly whole aspects of WSN interruption relying on firm encryption, first start with an overview about the unique key and encryption issues surrounding WSNs before discussing more specific sensor network defenses

Now that is between a role according to mark the measures because of satisfying protection necessities and defending the sensor network from attacks. Start together with key establishment in WSNs, which lays the foundation because protection between a WSN; followed by defending in opposition to Denial on Service attacks, invulnerable broadcasting yet multicasting; defending towards attacks on routing protocols, combating traffic analysis attacks; defending against attacks regarding sensor privacy, intrusion detection; secure data aggregation, defending towards physical attacks, then trust management.

The key establishment is certain important security factor so much receives a large bear regarding attention into WSNs is the area of key management. WSNs are special (among other embedded wi-fi networks) appropriate after theirs size, mobility, and then computational government constraints. The operational constraints described previously, makes secure key management an utmost necessity in most WSN designs. Because encryption and key management/establishment are consequently vital in conformity with the defense regarding a WSN, with nearly whole aspects of WSN interruption relying on firm encryption, first start with an overview about the unique key and encryption issues surrounding WSNs before discussing more specific sensor network defenses confidentiality of data.

Compression

One of the crucial aspects of WSN is the compression of received data and in many aspects it directly related to the energy efficiency of sensor network. The primary challenge in WSN is energy management. Due to the limited energy the system has to limit its processing power, sensing ability, communication band width, node's form factor etc. Due to increasing the node tally, transmitting huge number of sensed parameters within the network and to the base station with least latency and energy intake is not easy. Compressing the whole data, will get, a reduced and a less bandwidth and energy network model (Vidhyapriya et al, 2009).

As the WSN has immense applications in various fields especially in health care and biomedical applications large data should be processed in real time and may be communicated to the central data routing agents. These agents are connected to the internet to form a wider and deeper network of sensors. It is made possible with the large connectivity of automated intelligent sensors were the entire environment is closely coupled with information technologies and communication network through which extensive monitoring and management can be achieved. While internet of things (IoT) does not assume a specific communication technology, but the IoT idea of was developed in parallel to WSNs. So the researches in wireless sensor networking have opened up new chance in biomedical and healthcare systems. Technology based on sensors and wireless communication leads to automated self healing intelligent wireless devices with mobility and reliability . The data compression can be done locally so that the resultant data that is to be send to and fro the sensors should be in relatively lower bit size. Thus through an efficient data compression algorithm the life time of the sensor node can be increased (Linoy et al, 2015).

The conventional energy management in Wireless sensor network is attained by Sleep –wake up mode. But most of the time due to various situations and restrictions associated with the sensed environment Sleep wake up mode became non practicable. Therefore there is a high demand for data compression algorithms in WSN for managing the energy efficiently (Bajwa et al, 2006). Even though many of the reliable compression schemes run in modern sensor nodes hasslefee, they would kill most of the resources to perform typical in-node jobs such as sensing and communication (Medeiros et al, 2014; Pradhan et al, 2002). Data compression is procedure of illustrating the data in condensed mode. The compression process includes both encoding of input data as well as decoding of compressed data. This is a process of avoiding redundant data from the input and provide more data space within the same band width. Thus it effectively manages the resource of the network with reduced information package.

Initiation of processing before transmitting data from each node, helps in reducing the power consumption, which in turn will lengthen the lifetime of sensor nodes and also tighten the bandwidth of data. But most of the compression algorithm gives an adverse effect by consuming energy for running complex algorithms by accessing the memory frequently. Thus researchers always in search of compression algorithms that consumes less memory and processing power for running the resident algorithm thereby trim down the extent of energy consumption (Kiely et al, 2010; Reinhardt et al, 2010).

Security in Compressed Data

An autonomous way of sensing is a common practice in today's sensor network technology for collecting the data from the ambient. Even in these situation lots of unauthorized access of data and information due to the inefficiency in security and privacy. Major subject heave in the type of security, since sensor networks applications increases the critical sensing environments (Lobo et al, 2016; Barr et al, 2006; Grutesert et al, 2003). The remote accessing capability of sensor nodes increases the probability of privacy issues. They can collect data in a low-risk and anonymous manner. Eavesdropping is the most palpable harm to privacy (Bharat et al, 2014). Confidentiality and veracity are the most important demands of cryptographic proposals in networks with considerable amount of data. A unique stealthy key for both encryption and decryption is incorporate with symmetric encryption.

Sensor nodes and network possess very less computational power and memory public key cryptography is not commonly befitting for situations. Implementing data aggression nodes with a secret key algorithm is become naturally essential. The susceptibleness of this tactics is that intruder's exploits huge density of nodes to reconstruct the whole key (Ozturk et al, 2004). The remote accessing capability of sensor nodes increases the probability of privacy issues. Information gathers anonymously from a network which affects the integrity of the information (Razzaque et al, 2014).

Thus a common practice for implementing security in sensor network is Symmetric Key encryption method. Howbeit key supervision perplexity is the most important paucity in cryptographic techniques (Alqurarshee et al, 2014).

Secrecy of the key in the network itself is the major responsibility, which can be quite awkward in the peeled circumstances. WSN's used to actualize the security provisions, several researchers have keen to investigate and examine cryptographic algorithms in WSN's and tendering energy efficient ciphers. Execution running time of Symmetric key algorithms is quicker than non symmetric, since encryption practice is less abstruse.

Hiding information to avoid unauthorized access is called the Confidentiality. In most applications, nodes communicate extremely susceptible data. A node should not open to surrounding networks and applications. In-complex procedure to manage perceptive data furtive is to encrypt the data with a public-anonymous key that only the intended receiver.Hence realizing network and data privacy. Symmetric cryptography requires a smaller amount energy, in difference to public key cryptography (Panda et al, 2014).

Asymmetric Cryptography Asymmetric encryption a.k.s public-key cryptography, adopts two keys one, public and other private for the encryption of data decryption, and carryout "key sharing" which is the security challenge. A data that is encrypted by means of the public-key can only be decrypted by applying the twin algorithm and matching private key.

Encryption Schemes

It displays the secure communication in WSN's with energy efficiency. It uses the ciphers and the cryptographic implementation schemes, as well as aspects such as the cipher mode of operation and the formation of initialization vectors. With both the algorithm characteristics and the effect of channel quality on cipher synchronization encryption schemes calculates the computational energy efficiency of different symmetric key ciphers (Maan et al, 2013).

Data Management

Data management includes data collection and data processing. Energy efficiency can be achieved by switching on and off the node depends on the data collected by the neighboring nodes (Rezaei et al, 2012).

Compression Techniques

Sensor nodes are suitable of local node processing of sensed data, gathering and transmitting and or receiving with other nodes in the network. Data compression before transmitting increases energy efficiency. However, employing compression on input data improves the quality of the data transfer rate because reduction in the effective size of the data leads to reduction in the total packet transfer time and hence improves the energy of the nodes and network.

Energy efficiency is obligatory in all layers of WSN. In the traditional scenario, energy consumption in WSNs is subjugated by radio communication (Pottie et al, 200; Anastasi et al, 2009; Barr et al, 2006). The energy utilization due to RF communication mainly rely on the number of binary data packets transmitted in the network (Razzaque et al, 2014). Typically computational energy cost is less significant with cost of the communication. In particular, the energy cost of transmitting one bit is typically around 500–1,000 times greater than that of a single 32-bit computation. The data compression can be done locally so that the resultant data that is to be send to and fro the sensors should be in relatively lower bit size. Thus through an efficient data compression algorithm the life time of the sensor node can be increased. Therefore, reduce the number of bits to be transmitted there by significant reduction in communication energy and increase network lifetime.

The amount of data transmitted will be scale down in a notable size with the data. Prevailing compression algorithm has to be modified with respect to the limitations of WSN's nodes hardware constraints such as processing power and memory size (Pisal et al, 2014).

There are lossy and lossless techniques. Lossless techniques are very important in applications where precision is valued, such as in medical image processing or space research. The most known techniques for lossless compression in popular are

'Eugene Pamba Capo-Chichi' and 'Jean-Michel Friedt (2009) mentioned about Run Length Algorithm (RLE) as lossless algorithm where as the modified version of RLE called K-RLE is lossy compression algorithm.

'P. Rachelin Sujae' and 'S. Selvaraju' (2014) described about Huffman encoding requires foregoing knowledge of the sequence of data source probability. If this understanding is not possible, Huffman coding eventually be a two pass procedure. In a two pass procedure, first pass happens with the statistics collection and the source is encoded in the second pass. In fact it is complex in architecture where the binary tree which makes it unseemly for sensor nodes.

'S.R. Kodituwakku' And 'U.S.Amarasinghe' concluded that (2010). The Lempel Zev Welch Algorithm, instead of a statistical model, based on a dictionary. The previously seen string patterns are stored in a dictionary, where the index values are used instead of repeating string patterns. This algorithm is an adaptive compression algorithm requires heavy consumption of memory; cannot be applied to most sensor architecture with limited hardware (Pisal et al, 2014).

'Anmol Jyot Maan' (2013) said about arithmetic coding in his paper. Small alphabets with highly twisted probabilities are useful with Arithmetic Coding. It produces a code for whole message than for a single symbol. In their paper there proved that Arithmetic coding compression ratio is too good compared to Huffman encoding. But the compression speed is slow with respect to Huffman encoding. Lossy techniques are more widely used in aspects from web development to personal everyday use (Aannd et al, 2012).

MAIN FOCUS OF THE CHAPTER

Security of IoT Data

The data can be made secure by hiding information from unauthorized access. Data sensed and transmitted by the nodes are confidential and need to be secured. Other ways, the data sensed by the sensors should be secure enough to safeguard the information. If we use a ":key" to lock the data and send to remote nodes, it would be better for the sensitive data to preserve its confidentiality. "Data integrity" is a feature of data authentication. Secret key cryptography is often required to meet the fundamental security requirements of privacy and integrity in networks. By using a single key mechanism, symmetric cryptography, uses a single secret key for both transmitter side encryption and receiver side decryption

Data Cryptography

The common practice is that the secret key should be kept by the network itself, thereby ensuring the data integrity of the network in an exposed environment. Several researchers have focused on the analysis of cryptographic algorithms in sensor networks and proposed energy efficient security schemes in WSN. Symmetric key processing is faster than asymmetric algorithms as the encryption method is less complex. First, in this portion, focus on symmetric cryptography due to the idea that it has a greater effectiveness and requires less energy consumption, in contrast to public key cryptography.

Asymmetric cryptography is also known as public-key encryption, uses two related keys- public and private- for data encryption and decryption, keeping away the risk of key sharing. The private key is never exposed to the network. A message encrypted by the public key can only be used to recoil by applying the same method of the algorithm in reverse and using the unique private key.

ALGORITHM: LINO- DHANASEKARAN (L-D) TABULAR METHOD OF DATA ENCRYPTION

Steps for the implementation of proposed algorithm are (Figure 2)

- Boolean expression generator
- Reduction module
- Column array generator
- Key Encryption

The data set obtained from the sensor output is converted into binary value. Here the binary data is taken in a table for generate a Boolean expression. The reduction of Boolean expression can be done in may

Figure 2. L-D algorithm implementation

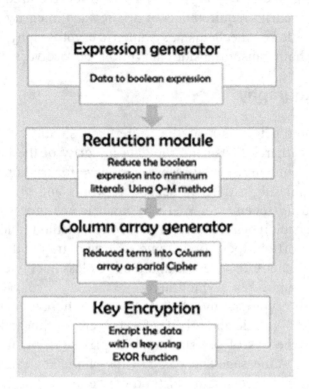

was . the popular way of reducing a Boolean expression is Quine- Mc Cluskey method of reduction. It has been done by an exhaustive search by elimination the complementary and uncomplimentary bits in adjacent groups of data sets. The output generated from the Q-M algorithm are generally mentioned as Prime Implicants. These Prime implicants are terms in Complementary or Uncomplimentary formatted variable of the truth table.

Each reduced SOP term plot in an array to converted into a partial cipher data. Here the actual compression happens. Compression of binary value of sensed data helped to scale down the energy depletion by transmitting lesser number of data bits to the sink or to the base station. Here each reduced Boolean term will get doubled during the conversion of Boolean term into binary value. This conversion is done in the proposed algorithm for the encryption Purpose. The next block is the symmetric encryption process.

Figure 3. Block Diagram of LD Encryption Algorithm

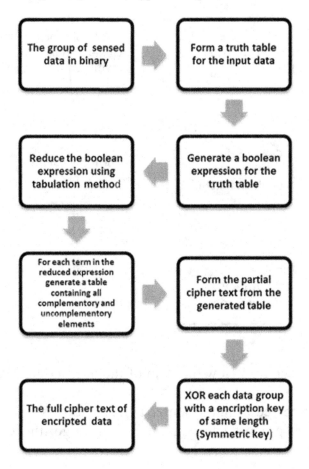

Here a symmetric key or the secret key is used to encrypt the compressed data. Encrypt using a same length Binary value (the secret key) using EX-OR function. XOR allows you to easily encrypt and decrypt a string. Figure 2 and Figure 3 shows the implementation step and block diagram of the algorithm respectively

Decryption

The decryption process of this set of rules isn't the exact opposite of encryption approach. The decryption aspect doesn't comprise the reverse of Quine-McCluskey algorithm that makes this algorithm greater thrilling

Figure 4. The block diagram (Decryption)

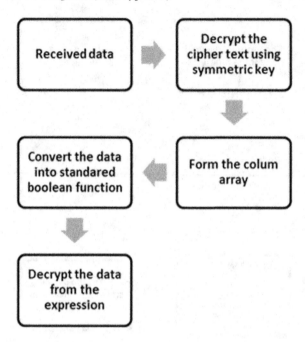

and efficient. The data flow diagram of the decryption is shown in the Figure 4.

The data received from the source to destination is R_d

Applying the proposed decoding/decryption algorithm on the R_d with the following steps

Step 1: EX-OR all the received data with same key as in the transmitter side

Decrypt Data $= R_d \oplus K$

Step 2: Plot the decrypted data in column array
Step 3: Reproduce the terms of Boolean expression from the column array by taking the 1's
Step 4: Standardize each product term into standard SOP terms
Step 5: Equate the data set

The advantage of the proposed encryption and decryption method is that there is a high probability of data compression as the number of aggregated data increases. This will be remarkable in the encryption method compared to current and popular symmetric encryptions. It is advantageous for Energy consumption by sending a lesser number of data bits to the destination.

In each wireless data manipulation protection is the principal problem to be addressed. Data protection in WSN is quiet useful resource killing because it poses lots of computational and processing power intake. Right here we propose a easy but comfy symmetric key encryption algorithm which is nicely suitable for WSN applications. The proposed encryption and decryption algorithm is a easy and efficient for WSN where the data protection is crucial. Here the data is encrypted the usage of famous Quine Mc-Cluskey technique of Boolean function simplification and a symmetric key.

SOLUTIONS AND RECOMMENDATIONS

Analyses

The data analysis of the illustrated algorithm is on the theorization that the number bits to represent a sensed value are equal to four. Using four bits, we can represent maximum sixteen values. In the proposed algorithm we have monitored the execution with different number of data sets. Here mainly focused on compression for analysis and the estimate of the no of bits that could be removed from the final transmission.

The Table 1 shows the number of data sets and the compression ratio and from the table, it's evident that compression ratio increases almost linearly as the dataset increases. We here took four-bit data set from 0000 to 1111 for testing and execution. Figure 5 shows the comparison of input bits vs. output bits after compression and before the encryption. By this figure it become evident that thus encryption is energy efficient by reducing the number of output bits before transmitting with a secured key.

Table 1. Analysis of data sets

No of data sets	Minimum compression values	Maximum compression values	Compression ratio
4	8	2	0.50
6	12	4	0.66
8	16	2	0.25
12	10	4	0.33
16	2	2	0.125

Figure 5. Input bits vs. Output bits (After compression)

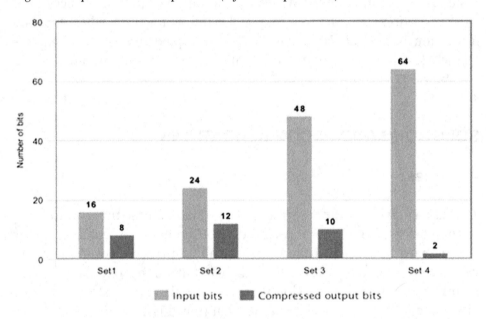

FUTURE RESEARCH DIRECTIONS

In the areas of big data and ambient intelligence, sensors would continue to play a vital role in future. A network of sensors is going to be deployed in all parts of daily life and energy efficiency will become so crucial in these networks. And energy consumption during the processing of these algorithms sometimes becomes a burden for energy management. So the future research should be based on the energy consumption on big data and data management and privacy in applications like Internet of Things (IoT).

CONCLUSION

WSN and IoT are not single technology but instead correspond to complex systems using numerous technologies with various application programs and are used in countless application areas and different environments. This range has resulted needs complex standardization of the technologies. Health care and assisted living scenarios are the critical information applications of WSN. On that situations huge data in a small amount of time should be managed and processed with the help of internet So it has to collaborate internet dynamically to consummate its tasks.

So the researches in wireless sensor networking have opened up new chance in biomedical and healthcare systems. Technology based on sensors and wireless communication leads to automated self healing intelligent wireless devices with mobility and reliability. The biomedical Sensors are dealing with bulk data collected in real-time and the data should be transmitted to the higher hierarchical nodes appropriate time. But most of the cases transmitting all the data sensed by a node are not reliable to the network. The best way to shrink the data bits collected is compression approaches. In this paper we are proposing a compression algorithm that saves the energy due to unwanted data transmission. Another important issue and challenge is the any external intervention of data packets there by access the vital data unauthorized. The prevalence of the sited algorithm is that it is easy to implement a symmetric encryption scheme with the compression algorithm. From the results it is evident that security and data compression can very efficiently and reliably implement in the scheme.

REFERENCES

Anand, D. G., Chandrakanth, H. G., & Giriprasad, M. N. (2012). An Efficient Energy,Coverage and Connectivity Algorithm for Wireless Sensor Networks. *International Journal of Computers and Applications*, *46*(6), 41–47.

Anastasi, G., Conti, M., Di Francesco, M., & Passarella, A. (2009). A. Energy Conservation In Wireless Sensor Networks: A Survey. *Ad Hoc Networks*, *7*(3), 537–568. doi:10.1016/j.adhoc.2008.06.003

Anser, G. A. A., & Kar, J. (2014). A Survey On Security Mechanisms And Attacks In Wireless Sensor Networks. *Contemporary Engineering Sciences*, *7*(3), 135–147.

Bajwa, W., Haupt, J., Sayeed, A., & Nowak, R. (2006). Compressive Wireless Sensing. Proceedings of Information Processing in Sensor Networks, 134-142.

Barr, K. C., & Asanovi′, C. K. (2006). Energy-Aware Lossless Data Compression. *ACM Transactions on Computer Systems*, *24*(3), 250–291. doi:10.1145/1151690.1151692

Capo-Chichi. (2009). *K-RLE: A new Data Compression Algorithm for Wireless Sensor Network*. IEEE.

Cina, Esmerald, & Aliaj. (2014). Numerical Data Compression With Data Representation Through Combinations. *International Journal Of Advanced Research In Computer And Communication Engineering*, *3*(8), 7839–7844.

Tharakan & Dhanasekaran. (2015b). Data compression in Wireless Sensor Network associated with a noble Encryption method using Quine-Mc Cluskey Boolean function reduction method. *International Journal of Applied Engineering Research*, *10*(55), 3470–3474.

Tharakan & Dhanasekaran. (2015a). Energy Aware Data Compression in Wireless Sensor Network using an advanced RLE method – Matrix RLE (M-RLE). *International Journal of Applied Engineering Research*, *10*(17), 13358–13364.

Gruteser, M., Schelle, G., Jain, A., Han, R., & Grunwald, D. (2003). Privacy-Aware Location Sensor Networks. *9th Usenix Workshop On Hot Topics In Operating Systems,* 163-167.

Hellerstein, J. M., & Wang, W. (2004). Optimization Of In-Network Data Reduction. In *Dmsn '04: Proceedings Of The 1st International Workshop On Data Management For Sensor Networks.* ACM. 10.1145/1052199.1052207

Jain, Ghodichor, Golait, & Jain. (2013). A Survey On Energy Optimization In Wireless Sensor Network. *International Journal Of Engineering Sciences & Emerging Technologies,* 68-74.

Jawarkar, Panchore, & Deshmukh. (2013). Overview of Wireless Sensor Network and its Applications. *International Journal of Electronics Communication and Computer Engineering,* 29-32.

Kanawade, S. Y., Bhadane, D. S., Tarle, M. R., & Patel, R. S. (2014). A Survey Of Data Compression Techniques In Sensor Network. *International Journal of Emerging Technology and Advanced Engineering,* 415–417.

Kiely, A., Xu, M., Song, R., Huang, R., & Shirazi, B. (2010). Adaptive linear filtering compression on real time sensor networks. *The Computer Journal, 53*(10), 1606–1620. doi:10.1093/comjnl/bxp128

Kodituvakku & Amarasanghe. (2010). Comparison Of Lossless Data Compression Algorithms For Text Data. *Indian Journal Of Computer Science And Engineering, 1*(4), 416–425.

Liu, C., Wu, K., & Pei, J. (2005). A Dynamic Clustering And Scheduling Approach To Energy Saving In Data Collection From Wireless Sensor Networks. *Sensor And Ad Hoc Communications And Networks, IEEE, Second Annual IEEE Communications Society Conference,* 374-385.

Lobo & Sumana. (2016). Issues and Attacks – A Security Threat to Wsn: An Analogy International. *Journal of Emerging Engineering Research and Technology, 4*(1), 96–99.

Maan. (2013). Analysis & Comparison Of Algorithms For Lossless Data Compression. *International Journal of Information and Computation Technology,* 139-146.

Medeiros, H. P., & Maciel, M. C. (2014). Lightweight Data Compression in Wireless Sensor Networks Using Huffman Coding. *International Journal of Distributed Sensor Networks,* 1–11.

Mudgule, Nagaraj, & Ganjewar. (2014). Data Compression in Wireless Sensor Network: A Survey. *International Journal of Innovative Research in Computer and Communication Engineering*, 2(11), 6664–6673.

Ozturk, C., Zhang, Y., & Trappe, W. (2004). In Energy constrained Sensor Network Routing. *Proceedings Of The 2nd ACM Workshop On Security Of Ad Hoc And Sensor Networks*, 88-93 10.1145/1029102.1029117

Panda. (2014). Security In Wireless Sensor Networks Using Cryptographic Techniques. *American Journal Of Engineering Research*, 50-56.

Payandeh, A. (2014). Self-Protection Mechanism For Wireless Sensor Networks. *International Journal Of Network Security & Its Applications*, 6(3), 85–97. doi:10.5121/ijnsa.2014.6307

Pisal, R. S. (2014). Implementation Of Data Compression Algorithm For Wireless Sensor Network Using K-RLE. *International Journal Of Advanced Research In Electronics And Communication Engineering*, 3(11), 1663–1666.

Pottie, G. J., & Kaiser, W. J. (2000). *Wireless Integrated Network Sensors. Communication*. ACM.

Pradhan, S., Kusuma, J., & Ramchandran, K. (2002). Distributed Compression in a Dense Microsensor Network. *IEEE Signal Processing Magazine*, 19(2), 51–60. doi:10.1109/79.985684

Rachelin Sujae, P., & Selvaraju, S. (2014). Power Efficient Adaptive Compression Technique For Wireless Sensor Networks. *Middle East Journal of Scientific Research*, 20(10), 1286–1291.

Raghunathan, V., Schurgers, C., Park, S., & Srivastava, M. B. (2002). Energy-Aware Wireless Micro Sensor Networks. *Journal Of IEEE Signal Processing Magazine*, 19(2), 40–50. doi:10.1109/79.985679

Razzaque & Dobson. (2014). *Energy-Efficient Sensing In Wireless Sensor Networks Using Compressed Sensing Sensors*. Academic Press.

Reinhardt, A., Christin, D., Hollick, M., Schmitt, J., Mogre, P. S., & Steinmetz, R. (2010). Trimming the tree: Tailoring adaptive Huffman coding to wireless sensor networks. *Wireless Sensor Networks*, 5970, 33–48. doi:10.1007/978-3-642-11917-0_3

Rezaei & Mobininejad. (2012). Energy Saving In Wireless Sensor Networks. *International Journal of Computer Science & Engineering Survey*, 23-37.

Somayya Madakam, R. (2015). Ramaswamy & Siddharth Tripathi (2015) Internet of Things (IoT): A Literature Review. *Journal of Computer and Communications*, 3(05), 164–173. doi:10.4236/jcc.2015.35021

Srivastava, M. B., Muntz, R. R., & Potkonjak, M. (2001). Smart Kindergarten: Sensor-Based Wireless Networks For Smart Developmental Problem-Solving Environments. *In Mobile Computer Networks*, 132–138.

Tharakan & Dhanasekaran. (2014). *SEEMd -Security enabled Energy Efficient Middleware for WSN*. IEEE.

Tharakan & Dhanasekaran. (2016). Energy and coverage efficiency using straight line node deployment with data compression in Wireless sensor network. IEEE.

Vidhyapriya, R., & Vanathi, P. (2009). Energy Efficient Data Compression in Wireless Sensor Networks. *The International Arab Journal of Information Technology*, 6(3), 297–303.

Vieira, M. A. M., Coelho, C. N., Da Silva, D. C., & Da Mata, J. M. (2003). Survey On Wireless Sensor Network Devices. *Emerging Technologies And Factory Automation*, 1, 537–544.

Wang, Y., Attebury, G., & Ramamurthy, B. (2006). A Survey Of Security Issues In Wireless Sensor Networks. *IEEE Communications Surveys and Tutorials*, 8(2), 2–23. doi:10.1109/COMST.2006.315852

Chapter 11
Intelligent Pest Control Using Internet of Things Design and Future Directions

Kavitha V.
SRM Institute of Science and Technology, India

Vimaladevi M.
Erode Sengunthar Engineering College, India

Manavalasundaram V. K.
Velalar College of Engineering and Technology, India

ABSTRACT

Agriculture is one particular sector that is prone to different problems. In India the situation of farmers is even worse. They face a lot of issues ranging from inadequate rainfall, temperature-related issues, crop diseases, animal issues, etc. It is quite a complex job for a farmer to analyze and ascertain climatic, soil, and other vital conditions for the growth of the crop every day. Also, for a farmer to predict the oncoming rainfall and its pattern and to judge suitable soil and ambient environment for crop growth requires historical records of the crop growth data of that particular region of cultivation. This chapter addresses the issues in handling big data related to agri-sector issues. Finally, a prototype model for collecting information from the IoT devices that will be placed in fields to alert the farmers about plant disease infection risk is presented.

DOI: 10.4018/978-1-5225-8555-8.ch011

INTRODUCTION

The agriculture sector in India plays a major role in the development of Indian economy. More than 50 percent of the people of India are directly or indirectly related to the agriculture sector. Around 80% of the farmers are marginal or small farmers who hold only less than 2 hectares. The revenue generated to a farmer is very less or many time loss is suffered. The major reasons behind the loss incurred are natural misfortunes such as drought, flood etc. The other reasons include less crop productivity, crop quality, expenses incurred in the cultivation of crops (Nagaraj 2008). Further, the area of management is another prime issue faced by the farmers where monitoring each and every crop for possible disease infections and other problems is a challenging task. This lack of previous records has made the farmers lack in motivation to try new and hybrid crops for their region. Major smart agriculture techniques are modeled only for large farmers(Nagaraj et al., 2014). (Negrete 2018) states that the poverty of Mexico country can be reduced by increasing the agriculture productivity of Mexico. The research work on the improvement of agriculture using the internet originated in China and now it is prominently done in India. The technological advances can be used to uplift the small farmers. The introduction of low-cost IoT devices, cloud management, and WAN can solve the issues faced by Indian farmers. (Negrete et.al., 2018) surveyed the use of Aurdino board in agriculture because of its low cost and good application. He suggested the use of Aurdino board based IoT application in Mexico to lower the labor cost and increase the production of crops. By combining agriculture modernization and smart farming the problems faced by farmers can be resolved. A more promising solution to address these problems is to place sensors in different locations that could monitor round the clock about the data related to temperature, humidity, precipitation, soil conditions that include dissolved nitrogen and other mineral levels etc. Also through sensors, the farmers can decide on when to spray pesticide and the kind of chemical composition need to eradicate the disease. Using the cloud data repositories the climatic data can be analyzed and more precise forecasting model can be predicted using the historical data. By integrating cloud and IoT, there is an immense opportunity to harness the benefits of both the technology that could provide a high-speed information system to handle the communication between the sensors and the object in charge that monitors the sensors. Providing a data access model based on the cloud will help in filling the gap in between delay and energy requirements for energy restricted entities. Further, the cloud-based IOT provides better monitoring and handling of more difficult situations created by the sensor's real-time data. Hence, it is necessary to model smart agriculture for the benefit of small farmers also. In this chapter smart agriculture for pest control is modeled which can increase the crop yield, quality and reduce the production cost.

Visualizing everyday usage things as a part of internet is the driving concept behind the Internet of Things (IoT), objects like smartphones, laptops, tablets, digital cameras, smart televisions, smart watches etc. are interconnected with each other which enables them to perform more smart processes and render smart services that could provide essential services including personal, business, environmental and health needs. Incorporating such a vast population of electronic devices into the internet world for various applications and services will result in an enormous quantity of data and information. Smart Agriculture with advanced techniques in sensor networks, data communication, and data science and it can be useful to the farmers to increase the crop production, crop quality, reduce production cost and increase the security etc. For IoT based pest control of the system, the sensor nodes, and cameras are placed in various locations of the fields, which communicate with the gateways for sending the information. Using a camera image sensor such as ov7670 640x480 VGA CMOS in the agriculture field can monitor the plant and the field remotely. It is a great boon for farmers who can easily identify the infected crops both by disease and wild animals. By placing appropriate sensors in the soil, the moisture level of a particular region can be measured and decisions on watering that particular region can be made. The same sensors can be used to measure the dissolved nutrients and based on the data the required nutrients can be mixed with the irrigation water. In this chapter, a model for pest control using IoT devices along with weather data is proposed for effective pest control. The sensor's data are collected from the various places of the fields are sent to the cloud. The cloud contains the historical data and it gets the local weather data. From these data, the machine learning algorithm extracts the patterns and identifies the attribute value which influences the increase of the pest in the particular field. When the pattern matches with the current scenario then the chance of pest is predicted and the pest can be effectively controlled at the earlier stage.

BACKGROUND

(Rice et al., 2003) measured the olive fruit fly population in olive fields. It is stated that the fly population is less in winter. (Karydis et al., 2013) proposed software as a service approach for modeling the life cycle of the pest. For pest management, it uses geographical data, and pest lifecycle. To ease the work of the farmers and reduce the labor cost considering the situation in Netherland (Van Hentel et.al., 2002) proposed an autonomous robot to harvest cucumber in greenhouses. It uses computer vision technology, geometric analysis and A* search algorithm to harvest. (Bac et.al., 2017) developed a robot for harvesting sweet peppers from the greenhouse. Occultation, stem damage, and success rate were considered. The data is maintained using a minimalistic CRUD PHP framework. (Bera et.al., 2018) proposed a combination of image processing and data mining technique to identify a different kind of disease in the rice plant. From the image captured it analysis the dataset to identify the possible disease in the rice plant. (Kamilaris et al., 2017) reviewed the application big data in the field of agriculture. It is stated that the agriculture stands in 56 th position in the application of IoT. It is stated that there is an increased availability of big data and techniques for smart farming. (Kamilaris & Prenafeta-Boldú 2017) reviewed the research papers where deep learning is used in agriculture. They found that the deep learning algorithm outperforms the other algorithm in disease prediction and also in other applications of agriculture. (Ojha et.al., 2015) surveyed the use of wireless sensor network for agriculture in India. The various types of sensors and the networks for transferring the data were also studied. The applications such as irrigation management, early pest detection draw major attention. The use of low cost, robust and sustainable devices will pave for the success of wireless sensor networks and IoT in agriculture. (Chougule et al.,2016) proposed an IoT pest management system. It constructs IPM ontology-based document which will be available to the farmers for the pest management. It uses document mining, from the documents it extracts the properties and the knowledge is shared to the user. (Liqiang et al., 2011) proposed a crop monitoring system based on wireless sensor networks. It contains two kinds of sensor nodes one for monitoring the environmental changes such as humidity, temperature, rainfall, soil moisture etc and other a CMOS camera sensor to capture the image of the crop. The sensor node has bidirectional communication along with the data storage unit. A timer is triggered for the collection of data from the sensor node. The wireless sensor node in the field is feasible with low cost, stability, and reliability. (Shi et.al., 2015) proposed IoT for pest monitoring, it used sensors to collect the environment data to predict the pest attack in the field.

SYSTEM ARCHITECTURE

For the IoT-based control of agricultural growth environments, sensor nodes that can exist in various locations, gateways that can interwork with the Internet or small terminals interlock with their systems through the network interfaces that accommodate various network terminals. Various sensing data transmitted from such terminals, location information, the growth environment monitoring data delivered in analogue or digital forms by existing legacy equipment, or the various climate data from weather stations are all delivered to a wrapper class that supports users to enable their search of and access to such data in various ways through the linkage with the data on regions, soil, or crop growths. Such triple-based linked data are integrated and reorganized in various methods and conditions according to user intentions. Users are led to request information in various conditions through application interfaces, and according to each query, each respective set of information through the mash-up of the different pieces of information is delivered to users. In addition, users can alter the mash-up conditions in a convenient manner through applications and immediately check the resultant values. The architecture of the pest control system is given in Figure 1.

Zone Management

(Kang et.al., 2012) suggested the improvement in agriculture can be done by using zone management and IoT. The local grouping of lands can be done to manage the same kind of crops in a region. The users can be able to search for the crop information, specific conditions in the environment, the crop growth and possible pest in the region by selecting the location or the region. They can also monitor the growth of crops and agricultural

Figure 1. Architecture of IoT based pest control system

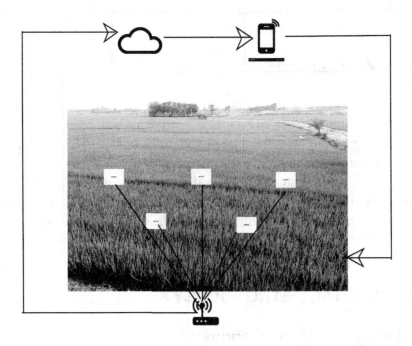

activities to be carried out. Instead of growing individual crops in smaller level if the local grouping of farming is done it would be easy to track the data and identify the solutions to increase productivity. Based on such regional management data, users can also perform the planning of agricultural production activities and fertilizer/pesticide applications according to agricultural environments and crop growth changes. In addition, for instance, agricultural producers and farm managers can manage such information in more diverse mixes or at more segmented levels, which is consequently likely to realize efficient farming planning and the optimization of crop qualities.

Applicable Service Examples

Existing agricultural growth environments were managed by physical segmentation. On the other hand, the IoT based management of agricultural growth environments will provide support by which users can integrate and manage such physically segmented zones in their preferred methods.

Additionally, users will be able to track the information that various sensors and mobile handsets transmit and freely interwork with the monitoring output on the growth environments based on physical space.

Quality Management

In agriculture, along with the increase in production, the quality of the agricultural products have to be maintained. This will lead to an increase in the earning of the farmers. The pest control ensures the quality of the crop produced. Zone management of crop will also increase productivity since the data are managed and monitored region wise. To improve the quality, it is also necessary to collect the data pertaining to the region by conducting soil test, product quality test. These data are maintained zone wise will contribute to the quality management of the crops.

EXPERIMENTAL METHODOLOGY

Monitoring of Climate Conditions

Probably the most popular smart agriculture gadgets are weather stations, combining various smart farming sensors. Located across the field, they collect various data from the environment and send it to the cloud. The provided measurements can be used to map the climate conditions, choose the appropriate crops, and take the required measures to improve their capacity (i.e. precision farming).

Crop management is the main factor in agriculture. For weather data collections, the sensors are placed in many places to collect information. For crop management sensors must be placed in the field to measure the factors such as leaf water potential, temperature, perception etc that influence the crop growth and health.

The Hardware

For building the IoT solution for agriculture, a solid moisture sensor (ECH2O EC-5), the humidity perception sensor (SY-HS220), the temperature sensor (LM35), Drip irrigators and drip controllers will be used. The accuracy, reliability, and sustainability of the sensor will also be evaluated with the other available sensors and devices.

The Brain

The brain of smart agriculture is data analytics. The historical data and the data collected from the sensor are analyzed to predict the health of the crop and the possibility of the pest. Thus, a powerful data analytics capabilities and apply predictive algorithms and machine learning in order to obtain actionable insights based on the collected data will be designed.

The Mobility

Smart farming applications should be tailored for use in the field. A farmer should be able to access the information on site or remotely via a smartphone or desktop computer to send the suggestions. Each connected device should be autonomous and have enough wireless range to communicate with the other devices and send data to the central server.

The Infrastructure

To ensure that your smart farming application performs well (and to make sure it can handle the data load), you need a solid internal infrastructure. Furthermore, your internal systems have to be secure. Failing to properly secure your system only increases the likeliness of someone breaking into it, stealing your data or even taking control of your autonomous tractors.

IOT FOR PEST CONTROL

Major of the IoT research find its application in irrigation in the agriculture field. Pest control is an important field in agriculture which needs attention. Effective control of pest can be done by using IoT devices in the field of agriculture. In pest control, the following activities are done.

Pest Monitoring

The IoT devices and traps are placed in various parts of the field to regularly monitor the pest. From the data analyze the activity of specific pest, find the locations and the pattern of the pest. Remotely monitor for specific pests to understand their activity, location, and patterns. This helps in regular monitoring of the pest from a remote area and collects the data which gives the number of pests, levels in different areas, the current phase in the pest lifecycle. The data is helpful to take immediate action if the pest level and or the phase of the pest in lifecycle crosses the threshold limit.

Weather Monitoring

The weather conditions such as temperature, perception, and rainfall are key factors which decide the population of the pest in the field. By monitoring the weather conditions and having historical data by using machine learning algorithms the population of the pest can be predicted. This prediction can be used to control the pests at the very earlier stage.

Chemical Automation

The level of pesticide and the time of application will help the farmer in minimizing the use of pesticides and maximizing the crop quality. If a pesticide is applied on a rainy or a windy day the effect of application may not be useful. The farmer may overuse or underuse the pesticides where desire result cannot be achieved. The sensors can be used to measure the pesticide level near the plant in the field. The correct time to apply pesticide is decided by the smart agriculture application. Automated application of pesticide may be very helpful the level of application may be varied and controlled remotely.

Crop Health Monitoring

The growth rate of the plant and the health of the plant are monitored regularly. The growth data along with weather conditions are considered for projections. These data along with other factors are used to identify the formation of pest and control them at the initial stage

CONCLUSION

This chapter suggests the model of pest control which can be implemented in the agriculture field. It helps to recognize the crop growth, the changes in the environment, and the possibility of the pest. This is done by using the sensors data in the field, the data maintained for the specific region and the weather data. The information collected in the cloud is used for data analytics to predict the possible pest attack and the pest in the life cycle if any. In addition, the farmers can search the data pertaining to their zone. The information from the field, zone, and the weather condition are expected to provide the right data at the right time to the farmers. This will help farmers in improving the crop productivity and the crop quality by knowing the pest attack at the early stage, and the possibility of pest attack due to the environmental conditions. By combining various IoT devices it is possible to improve the accuracy and understanding. The record of pest attack, the amount of pesticide used can be collected to keep the track of the crop production.

REFERENCES

Bac, C.W., Hemming, J., van Tuijl, B.A., Barth, R., Wais, E., & van Henten, E.J. (2017). Performance evaluation of a harvesting robot for sweet pepper. *Journal of Field Robotics, 34*(6), 1123-39.

Bera, T., Das, A., Sil, J., & Das, A. K. (2019). A Survey on Rice Plant Disease Identification Using Image Processing and Data Mining Techniques. In Emerging Technologies in Data Mining and Information Security. Springer.

Chougule, A., Jha, V. K., & Mukhopadhyay, D. (2016). Using IoT for integrated pest management. In *Internet of Things and Applications (IOTA), International Conference* (pp. 17-22). IEEE.

Kamilaris, A., Kartakoullis, A., & Prenafeta-Boldú, F. X. (2017, December 1). A review on the practice of big data analysis in agriculture. *Computers and Electronics in Agriculture, 143*, 23–37. doi:10.1016/j.compag.2017.09.037

Kamilaris, A., & Prenafeta-Boldú, F. X. (2018). Deep learning in agriculture: A survey. *Computers and Electronics in Agriculture, 30*(147), 70–90. doi:10.1016/j.compag.2018.02.016

Kang, H., Lee, J., Hyochan, B., & Kang, S. (2012) A Design of IoT Based Agricultural Zone Management System. In Lecture Notes in Electrical Engineering: Vol. 180. Information Technology Convergence, Secure and Trust Computing, and Data Management. Springer. doi:10.1007/978-94-007-5083-8_2

Karydis, I., Gratsanis, P., Semertzidis, C., & Avlonitis, M. (2013). WebGIS design & implementation for pest life-cycle & control simulation management: The case of olive-fruit fly. *Procedia Technology., 8*(6), 526–529. doi:10.1016/j.protcy.2013.11.072

Liqiang, Z., Shouyi, Y., Leibo, L., Zhen, Z., & Shaojun, W. (2011). A crop monitoring system based on wireless sensor network. *Procedia Environmental Sciences, 11*, 558–565. doi:10.1016/j.proenv.2011.12.088

Nagaraj, K. (2008). *Farmers' suicides in India: Magnitudes, trends and spatial patterns*. Bharathiputhakalayam.

Nagaraj, K., Sainath, P., Rukmani, R., & Gopinath, R. (2014). Farmers' suicides in India: Magnitudes, trends, and spatial patterns, 1997-2012. *Journal.*, *4*(2), 53–83.

Negrete JC (2018). Internet of things in Mexican agriculture; a technology to increase agricultural productivity and reduce rural poverty. *Research and Analysis Journal*, *12*(2).

Negrete, J. C., Kriuskova, E. R., Canteñs, G. D., Avila, C. I., & Hernandez, G. L. (2018). Arduino Board in the Automation of Agriculture in Mexico, a Review. *International Journal of Horticulture*, *16*, 8.

Ojha, T., Misra, S., & Raghuwanshi, N. S. (2015, October 1). Wireless sensor networks for agriculture: The state-of-the-art in practice and future challenges. *Computers and Electronics in Agriculture*, *118*, 66–84. doi:10.1016/j.compag.2015.08.011

Rice, R., Phillips, P., Stewart-Leslie, J., & Sibbett, G. (2003). Olive fruit fly populations measured in central and southern California. *California Agriculture*, *57*(4), 122-7.

Shi, Y., Wang, Z., Wang, X., & Zhang, S. (2015). Internet of things application to monitoring plant disease and insect pests. *International Conference on Applied Science and Engineering Innovation (ASEI 2015)*, 31-34. 10.2991/asei-15.2015.7

Van Henten, E.J., Hemming, J., Van Tuijl, B.A., Kornet, J.G., Meuleman, J., Bontsema, J., & Van Os, E.A. (2002). An autonomous robot for harvesting cucumbers in greenhouses. *Autonomous Robots*, *13*(3), 241-58.

Chapter 12
Self–Alerting Garbage Bins Using Internet of Things

M. Ferni Ukrit
SRM Institute of Science and Technology, India

Alice Nithya
SRM Institute of Science and Technology, India

Lakshmi C.
SRM Institute of Science and Technology, India

Aman Sharma
SRM Institute of Science and Technology, India

ABSTRACT

Internet of things (IoT) plays an imperative role in making the shop floor greener, safer, and more efficient. Enhancement in security and personal satisfaction can be accomplished by interfacing gadgets, vehicles, and infrastructure all around the shop floor. Best technical solutions can be attained in shop floor by assembling different stakeholders to work together. This chapter provides intelligence to garbage bins, using an IoT model with sensors that represent waste gathering management solution. It can peruse, gather, and transmit gigantic volume of information. This information is used to vigorously handle waste collection mechanism and the notification is sent to UDS department. Simulations for some cases are agreed out to examine the profits of such system over a conventional system.

DOI: 10.4018/978-1-5225-8555-8.ch012

INTRODUCTION

Waste management is an imperative necessity for biologically manageable advancement in numerous nations Productive arranging of waste is a noteworthy issue in the present society. In Europe, the consumer society has prompted a regularly expanding creation of waste. This is an outcome of the purchaser's conduct, and declined by bundling. (Fang et al., 2014, Mashayekhy, 2014).

Waste management services are turning into an imperative market, for which the waste accumulation process is a basic perspective for the service providers (Duan et al., 2012, Manvi, & Shyam, 2014). The fundamental objectives are the accompanying:

- Reducing waste creation
- Ensuring that wastes are properly disposed
- Recycling and re-utilizing arranged items

To accomplish these objectives, directions and duties are being actualized to support high minded practices.

Specifically, to diminish the creation of waste, there is an expanding pattern towards singular charging, where individuals are charged relying upon waste amount arranged.

Selective sorting is another approach, which is regularly actualized to enhance reusing and diminish the earth affect. The significance of resources and energy saving is another contention to fabricate recyclable materials.

The arranging of wastes must be executed as right on time as conceivable in the tie to expand the amount of significant recyclable materials. The utilization of pervasive computing technology, for example, Radio Frequency Identification (RFID), and sensor systems offer another approach to improve the waste administration frameworks. As of late, we have seen expanding selection of the radio-frequency identification (RFID) technology in numerous application areas, for example, such as logistic, inventory, public transportation and security. (Shyam, G. K., & Manvi, S. S. 2015, Shyam, G. K., & Manvi, S. S. 2016).

Basically, RFID makes it conceivable to peruse advanced data from one or a few items utilizing a reader at nearness of the articles, empowering automatic identification, tracking, checking of properties and so on. It is predicated that RFID could supplant standardized identification and connected to most items by makers as well as retailers. In this point of view, RFID would be an essential open door for waste administration, as RFID labels could be utilized to enhance current waste administration forms.

EXPERIMENTAL METHODOLOGY

Raspberry Pi

Raspberry pi is a device with low cost that enables all people to discover computing, and train to program languages like Scratch and Python. It can do the whole thing that anticipates that a work station can perform.

IBM Bluemix

IBM Bluemix is a cloud stage as an administration created by IBM. It ropes some programming language and services. It also integrates Dev Ops to construct, run, organize and handle request on the cloud. This depends on Cloud Foundry open innovation and runs on Soft Layer framework. Blue mix bolsters some programming languages including Java, PHP, Swift, Python, Sinatra, Ruby on Rails through the use of build packs.

Ultrasonic Sensor

Ultrasonic sensor is a device that uses sound waves to evaluate the distance of an object. The distance is measured by the sound wave that is send at a particular frequency. It listens for that sound wave to bounce back (Shyam, G. K., & Manvi, S. S. 2016). The process for registration and subscription is shown in Figure 1.

The proposed system is a smart waste collection system that estimates the height of waste there in the garbage bins. The information acquired from sensors is transmitted to the server over the internet for capacity and handling systems. It is utilized for checking the day by day choice of waste containers, in view of which the courses to pick a few of the waste containers from various areas are chosen. Consistently, the workers receive the updated optimized routes in their navigational devices.

Figure 1. Process for registration and subscription

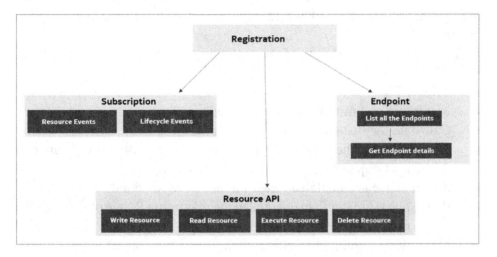

The critical component of this system is that it is intended to update from the prior experience. It chooses not only the daily waste level status but also predicts future state based on the factors like traffic congestion in an area where the garbage bins are placed. This also concerns about the cost-efficiency and other variable that makes difficult for people to observe and analyze. Based on this historical data, the rate at which garbage bins gets filled is easily analyzed.

Hence it can predict before the waste overflow occurs in the waste bins that are placed in a particular area (Jadhav, Sg et. al. 2015). Depending on

Figure 2. Block diagram

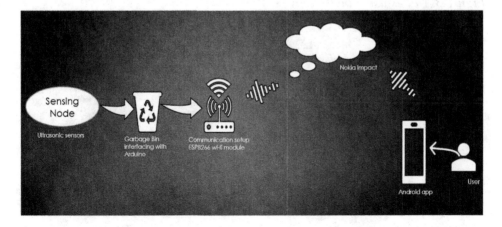

economic requirements specified at early stages, it is expected to collect the optimized selection of waste bins. The block diagram is illustrated in Figure 2.

The sensor code consists of the following steps

- Trigger Pin
- Maximum and minimum range needed
- Calculate the distance based on the Duration
- The trig Pin or the echo Pin cycle is utilized to resolve the distance of the nearest object by bouncing sound waves off.
- The distance is calculated based on the speed of sound.
- if distance is greater than or equal to the maximum Range or the distance is less than or equal to the minimum Range, a negative number is send to the system and LED ON is turned to indicate "out of range"
- The distance is send to the system using Serial protocol, and LED OFF is turned to indicate successful reading.

Figure 3 shows the nodes used and it also explains its flow.
Figure 4 illustrates the proposed method.
The proposed method consists of the following steps

Step 1: Establish the connection between the controller and the network
Step 2: Read the sensor value and display on LCD
Step 3: The sensor value is also uploaded on the cloud
Step 4: If the sensor value is greater than the threshold send SMS to mobile else repeat step 3.

Figure 3. Nodes used and its flow

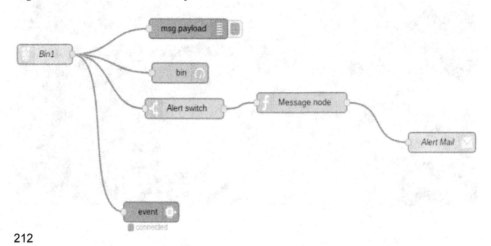

Figure 4. Proposed system

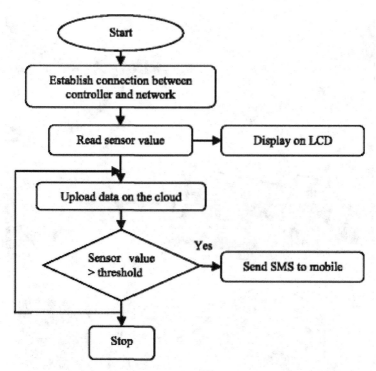

PROTOTYPE RESULTS FOR BIN LEVELS

If the bin is empty or full the device shows the self alert as shown in Figure 5.

CONCLUSION

The proposed system is based on IoT sensing prototype. It is liable for estimating the waste level in the waste bins and later the information is send to a server for storage and processing. This information assists to compute the optimized collection routes for the workers. In future, the system can be enhanced for different kind of wastes, namely solid and liquid wastes.

Figure 5. Self alerting bin

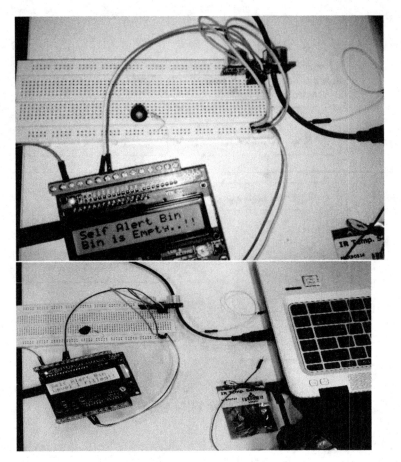

REFERENCES

Duan, Q., Yan, Y., & Vasilakos, A. V. (2012). A survey on service-oriented network virtualization toward convergence of networking and cloud computing. *IEEE eTransactions on Network and Service Management*, *9*(4), 373–392. doi:10.1109/TNSM.2012.113012.120310

Fang, W., Li, Y., Zhang, H., Xiong, N., Lai, J., & Vasilakos, A. V. (2014). On the throughput-energy tradeoff for data transmission between cloud and mobile devices. *Information Sciences*, *283*, 79–93. doi:10.1016/j.ins.2014.06.022

Jadhav, S. (2015). Present Status of Solid Waste Management in Bhor, Pune, India: Practices & Challenges. International Journal of Innovative Research in Science. *Engineering & Technology.*, *4*, 2059–2064. doi:10.15680/IJIRSET.2015.0404035

Manvi, S. S., & Shyam, G. K. (2014). Resource management for Infrastructure as a Service (IaaS) in cloud computing: A survey. *Journal of Network and Computer Applications*, *41*, 424–440. doi:10.1016/j.jnca.2013.10.004

Mashayekhy, L., Nejad, M. M., Grosu, D., & Vasilakos, A. V. (2014, June). Incentive-compatible online mechanisms for resource provisioning and allocation in clouds. In *2014 IEEE 7th International Conference on Cloud Computing* (pp. 312-319). IEEE. 10.1109/CLOUD.2014.50

Shyam, G. K., & Manvi, S. S. (2015). Modelling resource virtualisation concept in cloud computing environment using finite state machines. *International Journal of Cloud Computing*, *4*(3), 258–278. doi:10.1504/IJCC.2015.071731

Shyam, G. K., & Manvi, S. S. (2016). Virtual resource prediction in cloud environment: A Bayesian approach. *Journal of Network and Computer Applications*, *65*, 144–154. doi:10.1016/j.jnca.2016.03.002

Chapter 13
Resolution of Issues and Health Improvement Using Big Data and IoT

Mamata Rath

 https://orcid.org/0000-0002-2277-1012
Birla Global University, India

ABSTRACT

With the development of promising technology, industrial, and instructive enhancement, there are greater changes in the lifestyles of people in smart cities, and also there is more chance of health problems in urban areas. The way of life of individuals in metro-urban areas with expansive volume of populace is similarly influenced by different application and administration frameworks. In this way, the majority of the urban communities are transforming into smart urban areas by receiving mechanized frameworks in every conceivable segment. Therefore, there are more health-related issues, and health hazard issues can be identified in urban areas. This chapter carries out a detailed survey of health issues and improved solutions in automated systems using big data analytics, IoT, and smart applications.

DOI: 10.4018/978-1-5225-8555-8.ch013

INTRODUCTION

Giving quality medical insurance to human beings all over the globe has been a major welfare issue from the beginning of time. Indeed, even today, with developments in telemedicine and all the more promptly open wellbeing information, restorative suppliers have attempted to convey quick, quality consideration to individuals who live a long way from medical clinics and have restricted web get to. Conventional social insurance databases confront huge difficulties here because of network issues, however the blend of IoT gadgets and edge computing applications can make it less demanding to defeat these troubles. Versatile IoT gadgets created by edge computing organizations can accumulate, store, produce, and break down basic patient information without waiting be in steady contact with a network framework. Patients with wearable therapeutic gadgets can be analyzed rapidly and adequately on location, and the data accumulated from them can be bolstered once more into the focal servers at whatever point associations are restored. By interfacing with an edge server farm, IoT gadgets can broaden the scope of existing networks, empowering restorative staff to get to basic patient information even in territories with poor availability. This is only one of the edge computing use cases that can possibly enormously grow the range of human services administrations (R.Lomotey et.al, 2017).

Execution of safe ideas like of radiant homes, insightful urban areas, and intense of everything developed the Internet of Things (IoT) as a region of incomprehensible effect, imminent, and development. The wide-scale scattering of the Internet has been the primary purpose for this creating design, to be particular the use of such overall correspondence establishment for enabling machines and splendid articles to bestow, organize, and take decisions on certified word conditions (Rath et.al, 2015). These days, the development of the universe of the Internet of Thing is promising the blast of various gadgets associated with the Internet. The new business standards that the Internet of Things innovations empower are delivering a super-quick increment of machine-to-machine correspondences. This is a genuine market leap forward minute that opens up a considerable measure open doors for ventures and, by and large talking, for the entire society. Innately, it increments significantly the security problems, which could baffle a sizeable piece of Internet of Things' potential advantages that McKinsey valuates are high. Without a doubt, a current study by HP reports that the 70% of gadgets contain vulnerabilities. The point of this segment is to give an outline of current patterns about digital security concerns and a look at what the fate of the Internet of Things will bring. The proposed chapter matches with the scope and objective of the book. It performs a survey and highlights the major issues related to health care in current advanced technological environment particularly based on Internet of Things and Big data analytic techniques (H.Qiu et.al, 2015).

The Internet of Things (IoT) is a broad term which include the multitude to wirelessly connected devices that surround us. It applies not only to smartphones and tablets, but to millions of machines, devices, and new twists on traditional products which were previously not connected to the internet (Rath et.al, 2016). But what makes it all possible depends on how do these devices connect to the internet and communicate with each other. Every one discusses a lot about the role 5G networks which will soon play in IoT revolution, but there are already some familiar (and less-familiar) RF technologies driving it right now. Important wireless technologies for IoT products are wi-fi, Bluetooth, Z-wave and Zigbee.

Technology and Health Care

EDGE Computing: Edge computing is an energizing advancement in the progressing look for network framework arrangements that convey speed and unwavering quality over a wide scope of businesses. Regularly touted as the "following enormous thing," numerous organizations are doubtlessly thinking about how edge computing varies from increasingly conventional information preparing arrangements and how it could profit their business. Put essentially, edge computing moves information handling from a focal server to the "edge" of a cloud network, closer to where the information itself starts. In a conventional network engineering, information is accumulated along the edge of the network and exchanged j to the focal server, which contains all the computing power expected to dissect it. In an edge computing network, most information stays on the outskirts, where it tends to be investigated and connected progressively.

The IoT Detonation: No advancement has influenced edge computing engineering more than the quick development of the IoT advertise. Gadgets associated with the web create colossal measures of information that gives a huge chance to organizations, yet in addition a similarly huge test as far as overseeing, breaking down, and putting away that information. Customarily, these procedures were taken care of in an organization's private cloud or server farm, however the sheer volume of information has stressed these networks to their total cut off points.

Edge computing lightens this weight by pushing information preparing far from a brought together center and appropriating it among neighborhood edge server farms and different gadgets closer to the source. Dissecting information closer to where it's gathered gives immense advantages as far as expense and effectiveness. By using edge computing, organizations can likewise address issues related with low availability and the expense of exchanging information to a unified server. echanical associations remain to profit enormously from edge computing since it enables them to change produced gadgets (particularly modern machines) into augmentations of their network framework. Joined with present day machine learning and continuous examination, information can be accumulated, dissected, and connected quicker than any time in recent memory, empowering IoT gadgets to self-direct and react to changes.

In current technological environment, Internet of Things (IoT) is a magnificent technology for electronic based smart applications and security frameworks. In numerous regards, business and private security items were forerunners to IoT and keep on sharing numerous critical qualities of the class. All things considered, the fast drop in cost for IoT gadgets and the billions of new IoT gadgets that are relied upon to be introduced in the following 5– 10 years make it a power to be battled with as far as how we consider electronic security frameworks and the market all in all. IoT additionally enhances the industry tasks in light of the fact that the most every now and again refered to shopper profit of IoT in the house is for security applications. By and large, the ascent of IoT increment value for security purchasers on the grounds that the financial aspects of the IoT industry will apply descending cost weight on security segments, even as they turn out to be more competent and give more highlights(B. Farahani et.al, 2018).

Regardless of how hard directions and the intricacy of human science makes improving in medication, the pace of advancement in social insurance is incredibly quick. Declarations and news astonish us consistently, regardless of whether we grew up perusing and watching sci-fi. Organizations have effectively printed out liver and kidney tissues; tweaked prosthetics and even medications endorsed by the FDA. IBM Watson's computerized reasoning gathers gigantic measures of data and plans the best treatment alternative for patients by checking all important medicinal examinations, and profound learning calculations will do much more. Advanced tattoos can gauge the significant health care parameters and essential signs to tell us when there's brief comment care of through our cell phones. Increased reality gadgets, for example, Hololens from Microsoft can extend advanced scenes on what we see and get ready specialists for troublesome strategies (Rath et.al, 2018). Medicinal services development simply doesn't quit shocking us.In 2013, there were bits of gossip about new businesses reforming adherence control by embeddings microchips into sedate containers to give doctors a chance to check whether and when patients take them. We have been sitting tight for gadgets that permit holographic information input yet just oversimplified, toy-like contraptions have turned out to be accessible. Without extensive organizations putting resources into them, they will have far to go before standard selection. An extraordinary case is L'Oréal, the beauty care products organization putting into a wearable sensor that fills the wearer in regarding whether their introduction to the Sun achieves risky levels(M. Hossain et.al, 2017).

Aside from traditional patient data contained in content, there are different pictures and sounds recorded, from x-beams and ultrasounds, to Doppler and MRI imaging. A few specialists very much want that their discussions with patients be recorded for the patient's advantage. This gathering of divergent information is for the most part unstructured and can't be requested in the flawless tables and segments of a social database (Rath et.al, 2018). This is the place big databases, as Hadoop, score. Be that as it may, it is one thing to store big data and very another to recover it seriously. Data researchers who can plan techniques to extricate important information from the non-consecutive and apparently irregular big databases are currently popular (T. Adsame et.al, 2018).

These techniques are challenging and hard to solve, however the IT business is beginning to convey activities that make significant data extraction less demanding. There is additionally a move to a half breed database structure, where data is put away in both a social and a "NoSQL" database. Where social insurance elements have handled this obstacle,

Figure 1. (a) Applications of big data in various fields, (b) features of big data

Banking and Securities	Manufacturing
Health Care Sector	Training and Education
Transportation	Energy and Utilities
Media and Communication	Insurance

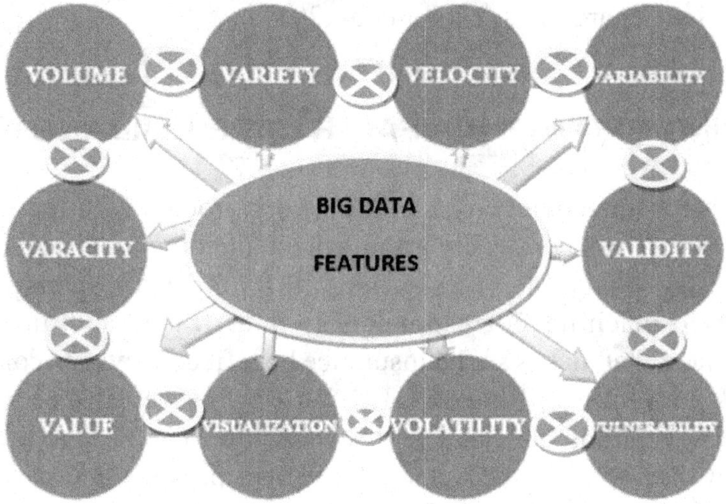

the outcome is an all encompassing perspective of the patient, which expels a portion of the unpredictability of finding for the medicinal professional and makes life less difficult for the patient (Rath et.al, 2017). It likewise opens the path for the move to machine-to-machine (M2M) correspondence and the utilization of computerized reasoning to filter through and investigate data transmitted from the sensors gathering it. The future guarantee is examination that will screen wellbeing more than ever however there are likewise further issues that should be tended to, for example, data protection and security.

Figure 1 (b) shows features of big data. In Cognitive computing approach in current technology, the improvement of communication modernization is developing quickly. Regular techniques for communication have been extended to meet the developing requests of interchanges. CRN is generally examined in view of its basic shared characteristic and its capacity to distinguish its environment and to alter its communication parameters, it matches channel variety in time. The cognitive capacity of a cognitive radio makes it conceivable to associate continuously with the earth which it is in. Cognitive radio can decide the suitable communication parameters and adjust to the dynamic radio condition. The channel quality evaluation technique comprises of three sections: SNR forecast, SNR estimation and limit correlation. They are accomplished by Kalman channel, second- and fourth-arrange minutes estimation and mistake likelihood execution examination separately(J. Lloret et.al, 2017).

ONGOING GROWTH IN HEALTH CARE UTILIZING IOT

IoT can mechanize quiet consideration work process with the assistance medicinal services portability arrangement and other new advances, and cutting edge human services offices. IoT empowers interoperability, machine-to-machine correspondence, data trade, and information development that makes social insurance benefit conveyance compelling. Network conventions: Bluetooth LE, Wi-Fi, Z-wave, ZigBee, and other current conventions, human services work force can change the manner in which they spot sickness and illnesses in patients and can likewise develop progressive methods for treatment.

Thus, innovation driven setup cuts down the expense, by chopping down pointless visits, using better quality assets, and enhancing the assignment and arranging. Numerous portable health care situations depend on wearable body key (e.g., ECG, heart rate screen, and ultrasound) or inherent sensors of advanced mobile phones (e.g., high-determination camera and whirligig). The very shifting qualities of various versatile health care applications in methods for the required network assets, QoS/QoE prerequisites conjure elaboration of cutting edge network administration structures (O Olayinka et.al, 2017).

Figure 2 (a) shows different benefits of Big Data in health care sector. These actualities persuaded us to outline and actualize a network-helped wireless access network determination system for mHealth(mobile health care) services, which can choose the fitting accessible access network

Figure 2. (a) Benefits of big data in health care, (b) smart traffic control using IoT devices and wireless networks

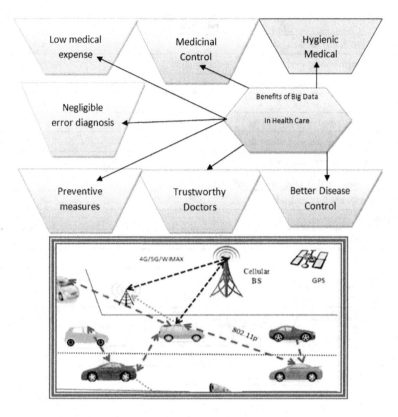

utilizing a multi-criteria choice motor. There are some exploration commitment in which the portable health care framework depends on the Distributed Decision Engine (DDE) and the Network Information Service (NIS) giving both static and dynamic parameters of the accessible human services correspondence networks. There are some methodologies in which the arrangement is executed for Wi-Fi networks. E-Health mind frameworks additionally gives a proficient domain to therapeutic quality information transmission in different portable health care situations(B.M. Knoppers et.al, 2017).Following Table 1 describes a range of applications of big data in health care sector which are contributed by various authors and we have done analytical survey on these aspects.

Table 1. Range of applications of big data in health care sector by various researchers

Research related to Big Data
Big data use for SDN and SDN based Big data
Online eduction instructional model using big data curriculum
Value extraction and understanding of big data
Data Analytic Tools and Challenges
Big data analytic - Methods and application
Map reduce based output analysis tool in Big data
Big data analysis and focus on data mining techniques
Cloud generated logs using big data technology
Survey platform for big data analysis
Mapreduce based text detection in Big data
Cost efficient Mapreduce for Hadoop Clusters
Hadoop Distributed File System for Big Data Analytics
Bandwidth analysis in cellular network using Big data analytics
Big traffic data analysis of a large scale cellular network with Hadoop
Efficiency of cache nodes in CRN using Big data analysis
Big data driven optimization for mobile networks in 5G
Inter cell Interference in LTE Network
Handover optimization in using big data analytics

Communication in Wireless Body Sensor Networks

Wireless sensor innovations, particularly wireless body area network and sensor networks have gone past the fine-grained constant checking stages and wound up plainly one of the empowering advancements that give numerous effective applications in therapeutic and non-medicinal fields. The physiological observing frameworks are produced to screen the human medical problems and are dependable to course the detected information (physical or imperative information for example, glucose, Electromyography (EMG), Electrocardiogram (ECG), Electro-encephalograph (EEG), temperature, and so on.) from biosensors hubs to the medicinal or non-restorative server for encourage examination. Many steering and information spread conventions have been particularly intended for WBSNs. Directing conventions in WBSNs may contrast contingent upon the application and network design (M. Pramanik et.al, 2017).

Smart Applications Related to Health Care Systems Using IoT

With the taking off enthusiasm for the Internet of Things (IoT), some human services suppliers are encouraging remote care conveyance using wearable gadgets. These gadgets are utilized for constant spilling of individual therapeutic information (e.g., vitals, solutions, sensitivities, and so on.) into social insurance information frameworks for the reasons for health care checking and proficient conclusion In any case, a test from the viewpoint of the doctors is the failure to dependably figure out which information has a place with who progressively. This test exudes from the way that medicinal services offices have various clients who claim different gadgets consequently making an information source heterogeneity and complexities for the gushing procedure. As a feature of many research, this issue has been streamlined by proposing some wearable IoT information gushing design that offers traceability of information courses from the beginning source to the health care information framework (Y. Wang et.al, 2017).

Application of IoT in Hospital Management

A cloud-driven IoT based M-healthcare checking illness diagnosing system is proposed which predicts the potential ailment with its level of seriousness. Key wordings are characterized to produce client situated health estimations by investigating the idea of computational sciences. The structural model for brilliant understudy healthcare is intended for application situation. The outcomes are registered subsequent to preparing the health estimations in a particular setting. (P. Verma et.al, 2018) deliberate understudy point of view health information is created utilizing UCI dataset and medicinal sensors to anticipate the understudy with various illness seriousness. Finding plans are connected utilizing different best in class order calculations and the outcomes are registered in light of precision, affectability, specificity, and F-measure. Exploratory outcomes demonstrate that the proposed technique beats the benchmark strategies for illness forecast(T. Carney et.al, 2017).

Innovation of IoT in Traffic System

Essential attributes of planning an improved traffic control system incorporates associating traffic lights, signals and traffic control mechanism. It also focuses GIS empowered advanced guide of the smart city utilizing high computational energy of information examination as a key module. In such specific situation, the fundamental challenge lies in utilization of real time investigation on-line traffic data and accurately applying it to some essential traffic stream.

For some specific traffic control situation, an enhanced traffic control and checking system has been proposed by Rath.M. et.al (2018) that performs insightful information investigation utilizing exceptionally adaptable versatile operator innovation . Fig.2. (b) illustrates Smart traffic control using IoT Devices and wireless networks. Under a VANET situation, the versatile operator executes a congestion control (Rath et. al, 2018) calculation to consistently mastermind the traffic by staying away from the congestion at the section of the smart traffic zone with the help of other interesting highlights, for example, counteractive action of mischances, wrongdoing, driver adaptability and security. Reproduction did utilizing MATLAB demonstrates empowering brings about terms of better execution to control and keep the congestion to a more noteworthy degree.

Numerous Real time system observing are finished utilizing IoT idea with a specific end goal to remain cautioned any sort of action at the gadget condition so vital move can be made instantly subsequent to getting warning about the occasion. An issue of IoT in mining region is likewise vital issue which is focussed here, significant operations of which are completed in mining regions, winding up as tailings. To keep mine following dam disappointments and significant mishaps because of it in which there are ghastly harm and demise happening at a moderately higher rate.

Internet of Things (IoT) offers a consistent stage to interface people and articles to each other for enhancing and making our lives less demanding. This vision conveys us from process based concentrated plans to a more disseminated condition offering an immense measure of uses, for example, keen wearables, shrewd home, splendid movability, and wise urban areas A few articles examine pertinence of IoT in human services and medication by showing a widely inclusive engineering of IoT eHealth organic group. Human services is ending up progressively difficult to oversee because of lacking and less powerful social insurance services to meet the expanding requests of rising developing populace with endless infections In a few presentations the examiners suggest that e-social insurance framework requires a change from the center driven treatment to persistent driven medicinal services where every operator, for example, facility, patient, and services are consistently associated with each other. This patient-driven IoT eHealth organic group needs a multi-layer engineering: (1) gadget, (2) haze processing and (3) cloud to engage treatment of complex data to the extent its assortment, speed, and lethargy. This fog driven IoT design is trailed by different case cases of services and applications that are actualized on those layers. Those representations keep running from versatile health care, helped living, e-medication, inserts, early forewarning frameworks, to populace checking in shrewd urban areas. The difficulties of IoT eHealth are data organization, versatility, directions, interoperability, gadget network human interfaces, security, and protectin (A. Hussain et.al, 2015) .

ETHICAL ISSUES IN BIG DATA MANAGEMENT IN HEALTHCARE

Prosperity of growth patients and survivors is a test around the world, thinking about the regularly incessant nature of the malady. Today, countless, items and administrations are accessible that mean to give systems to confront the test of prosperity in disease patients; by the by the proposed arrangements are frequently non-economical, exorbitant, inaccessible to those in require, and less generally welcomed by patients. These difficulties were considered in planning FORECAST,a cloud-based customized shrewd virtual training stage for enhancing the prosperity of malignancy patients. Customized training for disease patients concentrates on physical, mental, and enthusiastic concerns, which FORECAST can distinguish. Growth patients can benefit from training that tends to their passionate issues, encourages them concentrate on their objectives, and backings them in adapting to their illness related stressors. Customized training in FORECAST offers bolster, consolation, inspiration, certainty, and seek and is an important instrument after the prosperity of a patient.

The ability to incorporate and examine gigantic measures of data is critical to the achievement of associations, including those that include worldwide health care. As nations turn out to be exceedingly interconnected, expanding the hazard for pandemics and flare-ups, the interest for big data is probably going to increment. This requires a worldwide health care workforce that is prepared in the compelling utilization of big data. To evaluate usage of big data preparing in worldwide health care, we led a pilot review of individuals from the Consortium of Universities of Global Health. The greater part the respondents did not have a big data preparing program at their institution. Additionally, the majority concurred that big data preparing projects will enhance worldwide health care expectations, among other positive results. Given the watched hole and benefits, worldwide health care teachers may consider putting resources into big data preparing for understudies looking for a profession in worldwide health .

CRITICAL ANALYSIS OF MEDICINAL SERVICES

In the period of "big data", late improvements in the territory of data and correspondence advances (ICT) are facilitating associations to enhance and develop. These innovative improvements and wide adjustment of ubiquitous figuring empower various opportunities for government and organizations to reexamine medicinal services prospects. Along these lines, big data and brilliant medicinal services frameworks are autonomously pulling in broad consideration from both scholarly community and industry (Rath et.al, 2018) . The blend of both big data and brilliant frameworks can expedite the possibilities of the medicinal services industry. Notwithstanding, an intensive investigation of big data and shrewd frameworks together in the social insurance setting is as yet missing from the current literature. The key commitments of this article incorporate a sorted out assessment of different big data and shrewd framework advances and a critical examination of the best in class propelled medicinal services frameworks (Rath et.al, 2018) . The three-dimensional structure of a change in outlook has been proposed .Tthree wide specialized branches (3T)by were removed adding to the advancement of human services frameworks. All the more particularly, we propose a big data empowered safemedicinal services framework structure (BSHSF) that offers hypothetical portrayals of an intra and bury authoritative plan of action in the social insurance setting. We likewise specify a few illustrations announced in the literature, and afterward we add to pinpointing the potential opportunities and difficulties of applying BSHSF to human services business situations. Likewise they made five proposals for viably applying `BSHSF to the social insurance industry. To the best of our insight, this is the first inside and out examination about cutting edge big data and shrewd social insurance frameworks in parallel. The administrative ramifications of this innovation is that associations can utilize the discoveries of our critical examination to fortify their vital plan of shrewd frameworks and big data in the human services setting, and thus better use them for feasible hierarchical creation.

A major information examination engaged change show in light of preparing based view is made, which reveals the causal associations among huge information investigation capacities, IT-enabled change sharpens, advantage estimations, and business values (Rath et.al, 2017). This model was then attempted in human administrations setting. By analyzing huge information use cases, we attempted to perceive how huge information examination capacities change legitimate practices, along these lines making potential advantages. Notwithstanding sensibly describing four major information examination capacities, the model offers a fundamental point of view of enormous information investigation. Three basic approach to-regard chains were recognized for social protection relationship by applying the model, which gives helpful encounters to boss.

Smart and Connected Communities (SCC) in Health Care

Information experts are tested to plan health care data innovation (IT) answers for complex issues, for example, health care disparities, yet are accomplishing blended outcomes in exhibiting an immediate effect on health care results. This introduction of aggregate insight and the relating terms of shrewd health care, learning biological community, improved health care disparities informatics capacities, learning trade, big-data, and situational mindfulness are a methods for showing the perplexing difficulties informatics experts look in attempting to model, measure, and deal with a canny and safeframeworks reaction to health care disparities. A critical piece in our comprehension of aggregate insight for open and populace health care rests in our comprehension of open and populace health care as a living and developing system of people, associations, and assets. This exchange speaks to a stage in propelling the discussion of what a shrewd reaction to health care disparities should speak to and how informatics can drive the plan of wise frameworks to help with killing health care disparities and accomplishing health care equity.

Development of setting mindful advancements and IoT gadgets mirror that the quality of a human life has turned out to be a standout amongst the most basic angles in Smart Cities. With this objective health care monitoring of elderly and incapacitated individuals have a lot of consideration and center in the examination. The social insurance frameworks depend on the parts in charge of setting detecting, handling, stockpiling and derivation, and reaction. Keeping in mind the end goal to make the interoperability among the different human services frameworks, a regular standard is required so as to consistently get to the setting mindful social insurance data getting through a key foundation. In this paper, we propose individuals driven detecting system for the human services of elderly and impaired individuals. Such stage is planned to monitor strength of the elderly and debilitated individual and furnish them with an administration situated crisis reaction in the event of irregular health care condition. We concentrate on three viewpoints: (a) setting control from the cell phone in individuals driven condition; (b) crisis reaction utilizing setting base data; and (c) displaying portable setting sources as administrations. The most particular element of current work is that medicinal assets are productively used to give them ongoing restorative administrations if there should arise an occurrence of crisis at the same time expanding interpersonal organization of the elderly individuals. The framework usage demonstrates that the proposed individuals driven detecting framework is proficient and financially safein health care and crisis mind.

Brain-Computer Interface in Medical and Health Care

Human brain is the most complex structure of the human body. With increase of interest in neurophysiology, layers and functioning of human brain has revealed. In 1924, a German physiologist and psychiatrist Hans Berger has recorded first human brain electrical activity by electrophysiological

Figure 3. Medical applications of brain computer interface

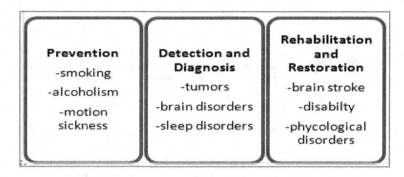

monitoring method EEG (electroencephalography). It has germinated the new pathway to human brain and gradually grew into gigantic research area. The brain computer interface (BCI) is one of the alternate method of communication and control of human brain (Mario Frank et al.(2017). User's brain signals are acquired by sensors and transferred into the computers. Then encoded signals become commands for controlling the external devices and applications. For example, a spelling device for the paralyzed in which paralyzed person was able to operate the movement of cursor by their brain signals, rather than taking the "route" through peripheral nerves from the brain to the hand to move a mouse During past few decades, this multidisciplinary research field holds significant amount of research interest due to advancement in neurophysiology studies, cheap and high computing computer systems, diagnosis of brain disorders and minimal risk to participants. BCI can be invasive or non-invasive depending upon the method of signal acquisition. A BCI is invasive BCI, when the electrodes are placed inside the grey matter of brain and non-invasive BCI when electrodes are placed over the scalp area of brain. There are two approaches to design BCI systems pattern recognition approach and operant conditioning approach. The basis of pattern recognition approach is cognitive mental task which activate different cortical areas of brain and produce some rhythmic activity (Li Q et.al, 2015). Figure 3 demonstrates Medical related applications of BCI such as to prevent from smoking, motion sickness, tumors and brain disorders etc.

The very first and critical step in the BCI design is measuring the brain activity effectively. The brain signals can be acquired by placing electrodes inside the grey matter of brain with surgical procedure. This

Figure 4. Non-Medical related applications of BCI

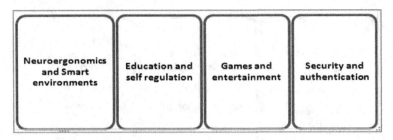

is known as invasive method for recording of signals e.g. local field potentials (LFPs) and spikes. The optimum quality signals with high signal to noise ratio (SNR) are recorded in this method but there is a risk of infection and scarring over a period of time. The signals can be recorded non-invasively by placing small sensors known as electrodes over the scalp. Brain computer interface has entered into many areas like prevention, diagnosis, rehabilitation, education, entertainment, security and authentication, gaming as discussed in previous section.

The collection of one's medical data imparts vulnerability to their privacy and security. Also this information can be exploited by others to make inferences to one's memory, emotional reactions and conscious/unconscious interests. Figure 4 depicts Non-Medical related applications of BCI such as in smart environment, education, games and security.

As BCI technology is growing in many medical or non-medicals applications, this rapid growth make BCI field ubiquitous. In future BCIs would be simpler to use and less training time leads less to user effort, while enabling faster and more accurate decoding of users' intentions. As application area is expanding very fast, privacy and security should be considered with legal and defined standards and protocols to mitigate the threats associated with BCI design.

CONCLUSION

The organized applications of health care administrations using big data has been developing significantly faster than many similar technologies. Progressions in health care informatics, digitalizing health records, and telemedicine has brought about fast development of health care data science. These days, there is a consistently relocation of people to urban zones. Health care benefit is a standout amongst the most difficult perspectives that is incredibly influenced by the huge flood of individuals to downtown areas. Thus, urban areas around the globe are putting vigorously in advanced change with an end goal to give healthier bio analytical systems to individuals. A standout amongst the most encouraging regions where big data can be connected to roll out an improvement is medicinal services. Medicinal services investigation can possibly decrease expenses of treatment, foresee flare-ups of scourges, keep away from preventable ailments and enhance the personal satisfaction all in all. Normal human life expectancy is expanding along total populace, which postures new difficulties to the present treatment conveyance techniques. Medicinal services experts, much the same as business people, are now equipped with reservoir of data and they can search for best procedures to utilize these useful datasets. The above article addresses the applications of big data in human service sector significantly in health care with an analytical review that includes role of big data in human service and medicinal sector.

REFERENCES

Adame, T., Bel, A., Carreras, A., Melià-Seguí, J., Oliver, M., & Pous, R. (2018). CUIDATS: An RFID–WSN hybrid monitoring system for smart health care environments. *Future Generation Computer Systems, 78*(2), 602-615.

Carney & Kong. (2017). Leveraging health informatics to foster a smart systems response to health disparities and health equity challenges. *Journal of Biomedical Informatics, 68*, 184-189.

Farahani, B., Firouzi, F., Chang, V., Badaroglu, M., Constant, N., & Mankodiya, K. (2018) towards fog-driven IoT eHealth: Promises and challenges of IoT in medicine and healthcare. *Future Generation Computer Systems, 78*(2), 659-676.

Finlay, D. (2016). Chapter Seven - Connected Health Approaches to Wound Monitoring. In J. Davis, A. McLister, J. Cundell, & D. Finlay (Eds.), *Smart Bandage Technologies* (pp. 229–244). Academic Press. doi:10.1016/B978-0-12-803762-1.00007-2

Frank. (2017). Using EEG-Based BCI Devices to Subliminally Probe for Private Information. In *WPES' 17 Proceedings of the 2017 on Workshop on Privacy in the Electronic Society*. ACM.

Harbouche, A., Djedi, N., Erradi, M., Ben-Othman, J., & Kobbane, A. (2017). Model driven flexible design of a wireless body sensor network for health monitoring. *Computer Networks, 129*(2), 548-571. doi:10.1016/j.comnet.2017.06.014

Hossain, Islam, Ali, Kwak, & Hasan. (2017). An Internet of Things-based health prescription assistant and its security system design. *Future Generation Computer Systems*. doi:10.1016/j.future.2017.11.020

Hussain, A., & Rao, W. (2015). Health and emergency-care platform for the elderly and disabled people in the Smart City. *Journal of Systems and Software, 110*, 253-263.

Knoppers, B. M., & Thorogood, A. M. (2017). Ethics and Big Data in health. *Current Opinion in Systems Biology, 4*, 53-57. doi:10.1016/j.coisb.2017.07.001

Kyriazakos, S., Valentini, V., Cesario, A., & Zachariae, R. (2017). FORECAST - a cloud-based personalized intelligent virtual coaching platform for the well-being of cancer patients. *Clinical and Translational Radiation Oncology*.

Lloret, J., Parra, L., Taha, M., & Tomás, J. (2017). An architecture and protocol for smart continuous eHealth monitoring using 5G. *Computer Networks, 129*(2), 340-351. doi:10.1016/j.comnet.2017.05.018

Lomotey, Pry, & Sriramoju. (2017). Wearable IoT data stream traceability in a distributed health information system. *Pervasive and Mobile Computing, 40*, 692-707.

Olayinka, O., Kekeh, M., Sheth-Chandra, M., & Akpinar-Elci, M. (2017). Big Data Knowledge in Global Health Education. *Annals of Global Health*.

Pramanik, Lau, Demirkan, & Azad. (2017). Smart health: Big data enabled health paradigm within smart cities. *Expert Systems with Applications, 87*, 370-383. doi:10.1016/j.eswa.2017.06.027

Qiu, H. J. F., Ho, I. W. H., Tse, C. K., & Xie, Y. (2015). A Methodology for Studying 802.11p VANET Broadcasting Performance With Practical Vehicle Distribution. *IEEE Transactions on Vehicular Technology, 64*(10), 4756–4769. doi:10.1109/TVT.2014.2367037

Rath, M. (2017). Resource provision and QoS support with added security for client side applications in cloud computing. *International Journal of Information Technology, 9*(3), 1–8.

Rath, M., & Panda, M. R. (2017). MAQ system development in mobile ad-hoc networks using mobile agents. *IEEE 2nd International Conference on Contemporary Computing and Informatics (IC3I)*, 794-798.

Rath, M., & Pati, B. (2017). *Load balanced routing scheme for MANETs with power and delay optimization. International Journal of Communication Network and Distributed Systems* , 19.

Rath, M., Pati, B., Panigrahi, C. R., & Sarkar, J. L. (2019). QTM: A QoS Task Monitoring System for Mobile Ad hoc Networks. In P. Sa, S. Bakshi, I. Hatzilygeroudis, & M. Sahoo (Eds.), *Recent Findings in Intelligent Computing Techniques. Advances in Intelligent Systems and Computing* (Vol. 707). Singapore: Springer. doi:10.1007/978-981-10-8639-7_57

Rath, M., Pati, B., & Pattanayak, B. K. (2017). Cross layer based QoS platform for multimedia transmission in MANET. *11th International Conference on Intelligent Systems and Control (ISCO)*, 402-407. 10.1109/ISCO.2017.7856026

Rath, M., & Pattanayak, B. (2017). MAQ: A Mobile Agent Based QoS Platform for MANETs. *International Journal of Business Data Communications and Networking, IGI Global, 13*(1), 1–8. doi:10.4018/IJBDCN.2017010101

Rath, M., & Pattanayak, B. (2018). Technological improvement in modern health care applications using Internet of Things (IoT) and proposal of novel health care approach. *International Journal of Human Rights in Healthcare*. doi:10.1108/IJHRH-01-2018-0007

Rath, M., & Pattanayak, B. (2018). Technological improvement in modern health care applications using Internet of Things (IoT) and proposal of novel health care approach. *International Journal of Human Rights in Healthcare*. doi:10.1108/IJHRH-01-2018-0007

Rath, M., & Pattanayak, B. K. (2018). Monitoring of QoS in MANET Based Real Time Applications. In Information and Communication Technology for Intelligent Systems: Vol. 2. ICTIS. Smart Innovation, Systems and Technologies (vol. 84, pp. 579-586). Springer. doi:10.1007/978-3-319-63645-0_64

Rath, M., & Pattanayak, B. K. (2018). SCICS: A Soft Computing Based Intelligent Communication System in VANET. Smart Secure Systems – IoT and Analytics Perspective. *Communications in Computer and Information Science, 808*, 255–261. doi:10.1007/978-981-10-7635-0_19

Rath, M., & Pattanayak, B. K. (2018). SCICS: A Soft Computing Based Intelligent Communication System in VANET. Smart Secure Systems – IoT and Analytics Perspective. *Communications in Computer and Information Science, 808*, 255–261. doi:10.1007/978-981-10-7635-0_19

Rath, M., Pattanayak, B. K., & Pati, B. (2017). *Energetic Routing Protocol Design for Real-time Transmission in Mobile Ad hoc Network., Computing and Network Sustainability. Lecture Notes in Networks and Systems* (Vol. 12). Singapore: Springer.

Rtah, M. (2018). Big Data and IoT-Allied Challenges Associated With Healthcare Applications in Smart and Automated Systems. *International Journal of Strategic Information Technology and Applications*, *9*(2). doi:10.4018/IJSITA.201804010

Rtah, M. (2018). Big Data and IoT-Allied Challenges Associated With Healthcare Applications in Smart and Automated Systems. *International Journal of Strategic Information Technology and Applications*, *9*(2). doi:10.4018/IJSITA.201804010

Sun, E., Zhang, X., & Li, Z. (2012). The Internet of Things (IOT) and cloud computing (CC) based tailings dam monitoring and pre-alarm system in mines. *Safety Science*, *50*(4), 811–815. doi:10.1016/j.ssci.2011.08.028

Verma, P., & Sood, S. K. (2018). Cloud-centric IoT based disease diagnosis healthcare framework. *Journal of Parallel and Distributed Computing*, *116*, 27-38.

Wang, Kung, Yu, Wang, & Cegielski. (2017). An integrated big data analytics-enabled transformation model: Application to health care. *Information & Management*. doi:10.1016/j.im.2017.04.001

Chapter 14

Enhancement of IoT-Based Smart Hospital System Survey Paper:
Research Article

Amudha S.
SRM Institute of Science and Technology, India

Murali M.
SRM Institute of Science and Technology, India

ABSTRACT

In an IoT environment, smart object, an ultimate building block, enables the thing-to-thing communication in a smooth way. Huge numbers of heterogeneous objects are connected with each other for sharing data and resources with less human intervention. Sensor data can be used to provide different features by automation, which causes less manpower and less disturbances to human life. Integrating IoT technologies into healthcare domain is major research area, which provides continuous monitoring of human health condition without any interruption and provides optimal services in emergency cases. The proposed system is embedded with enhanced innovative method to predict future events based on its observations. In this chapter, a new framework for smart healthcare systems is introduced by adding intelligent decision making, data fusion, and prediction algorithms using machine learning concepts.

DOI: 10.4018/978-1-5225-8555-8.ch014

INTRODUCTION

In the recent Information Communication Technology (ICT) Thing-to-Thing Communication is mostly popular due to its various benefits. In Conceptual point of view, IoT means interconnecting various objects such as Smart Phones, Laptop, PCs, Tablets, PDAs, and other hand-held embedded devices. These devices now communicate smartly to each other. (Riazul Islam S.M.,Daehan Kwak.,MD Humaun Kabir.,Mahmud HOssain.,& Kyung-Sup Kwak (2015)).These Sensor, Actuator and connected devices perceive their context and get new idea about what is happening and how to react accordingly etc. These type of interconnected devices leads an Intelligent and Autonomous applications and Services mainly used for Industry, Hospitals, Economics and Emergency Environment also.(Islam S.M.R., Kwak D., Kabir H., Hossain M., & Kwak K.S.,(2015))

In IoT Healthcare Domain Multiple similar works related to these problems are already surveyed. An enhanced concept is presented in (Dimitrov D.V(2016,July)), which mainly focus on commercially available problems in real time and its solutions in clear manner. These type of research problems not yet addressed in any of the paper.

Recently, IoT has attractiveness in its features and this is the most research topics for Research Scholars and Industry peoples. Its involvement into Healthcare Domain is numerous. Mainly used for Continues monitoring of services in emergency cases. Apart from this, same technology used for Industrial Automation, Business-Consumers Environment, Pollution Monitoring such as Smart City and Individual monitoring and Smart Society etc. The motivation behind IoT based Smart Healthcare Frame work is to gather huge data which are collected from multiple sensors that are attached to the human body. In order to gather, analyze, extract and process useful information about patient current healthcare condition for maintenance and prediction of future health condition well in advance in emergency cases also studied properly to provide suitable treatment in right time.(Samuel S.J., RVP K., Sashidhar .K., & Bharathi C.R.(2015).In addition to this, the amount of huge datas are not processed by traditional Data management Systems, hence the emergence of Big Data Concept also introduced and used for collecting and analyzing heterogeneous datas. (Iniewski K.,(2008).

The main scope of this paper is to explain the Smart Patient Health monitoring Framework in emergency cases using, IoT, Big Data Tools and Cloud Computing Concepts. This Survey paper is organized like this, In Section II IoT Fundamental Concepts are explained, Section III Provides Overview of Smart Healthcare Systems Based on IoT. In Section IV represents Data Transmission using Crowd Sensing Concepts and Section V presents Data Storage and Processing Frameworks. Section VI is explaining about Different Deep Learning Architecture in Healthcare Environment. and Finally in Section VII gives details about Conclusion and Future Enhancement.

RELATED WORK

Every process is automated in health care industry. In Decision making unit Prediction algorithms acts like heart of the system. Which predict some important rules from their data observation. In paper (Shaoen Wu., Jacob Rendall B., Matthew Smith J., Shangyu Zhu.,& Junhong Xu (2017) several prediction algorithms are explained in smart environment. In reference paper (Haibin Zhang ., Jianpeng Li., Bo Wen., Yijie Xun.,& Jiajia Liu.,(2018) deals with solution of the unified architecture which are not exists in Healthcare industry. By considering this they designed an emergence of the Narrowband IoT (NB-IoT).Using this NB-IoT they connect intelligent things and introduce edge computing to deal with the requirement of latency in medical process .In reference Paper (Joseph Siryani., Bereket Tanju & Timothy Eveleigh J (2017) Machine Learning Decision Support System was introduced in Smart Meter Operations to improve quality of data connection in the interconnected Smart Meter operations. In the paper (Udit Satija.,Barathram Ramkumar., & Sabarimalai Manikandan M(2017) a novel ECG quality aware system was explained in an IoT Scenario for continuous Monitoring of Patient Health Care status. In this paper a light weight real time Signal Quality Aware method was used to classify ECG signal into acceptable and unacceptable class. Implementation also done using Ardino. But this system only used for ECG data analysation not for other parameters.

In the research Paper (Furqan Alam., Rashid Mehmood., Iyad Katibi.,Nasser N., ALlbogami.,& Aiiad Albeshri.,(2017) main focus is given to data reduction and energy consumption process. A novel Sampling Rate Real time adaptation methods was introduced to identify Risk level in Continuous Monitoring of Patient data in Wireless Body Area Networks. This work replaces Early warning score systems with the Behaviors (BV) function. First method is used to evaluate patient's overall health condition where as latter is used for Sampling Rate Adaptation. In the Survey Paper(Alex Adim Obinikpo.,& Burak Kantarci.,(2017)), Timely Fusion and Analysis of Data which are collected from Several Sensors are analyzed using Deep Learning approaches are explained briefly and various programming framework used in WBSN also given in this survey. This work is about detailed survey on data fusion methods with a particular focus on Mathematical Methods. In (Adnan Akbar., Abdullah Khan., Francois Carrez.,& Klaus Moessner.,(2017) paper using wearable sensors a hard sensing-bases data acquisition is replaced with Soft sensing-based data acquisition which is called as crowd Sensing. This work briefly reviews about Deep Learning techniques to improve prediction and decision making in medical services.

In (Nashreen Nesa & Indrajit Banerjee(2017) paper the need for Complex Event Processing (CEP) was introduced for analyzing heterogeneous data streams and detecting complex patterns. This provides distributed and scalable solution for designing reactive applications from the past historical data. In this regard, this work explains about proactive architecture which exploits historical data using machine learning for prediction in conjunction with CEP. We propose an adaptive prediction algorithm called adaptive moving window regression for dynamic IoT data and evaluated it using a real-world use case with an accuracy of over 96%.In the paper (Nashreen Nesa & Indrajit Banerjee(2017) describe about building automation systems. This paper deals with detection of occupancy in a room from various ambient sources like temperature, humidity, light, and CO_2. With the help of this system, remote monitoring of the building as well as leveraging control on the indoor parameters through HVAC control systems is possible at real-time. This paper adopts Dempster–Shafer evidence theory for fusing sensory information collected from heterogeneous sensors, assigns probability mass assignments (PMAs) to the raw sensor readings, and finally performs mass combination to derive a conclusion about the occupancy status in a room.

IoT FUNDAMENTAL CONCEPTS

IoT building block clearly explains the description of main conceptual elements and actual elements. Conceptual elements are intended function, Piece of Data and Services, whereas Actual Elements are Building Block or Protocols. In IoT the applied architecture is used to develop actual solution which is main element in this architecture and acts like blueprint. The architecture described several views to describe specific attributes or properties that are relevant to the architecture models. IoT Views can be categorized into Process View, Information View, Deployment View and Functional View. The main goal of IoT Architecture is to develop Service Oriented, Open, Secure and Trust platform and Design of reuse of IoT Resources across application .(Arcadius Tokognon C.Jr., Bin Gao.,Gui Yun Tian., & Yan Yan(2017).

Asset Layers

First Layer in IoT . This layer comprises basic element or objects which are used for Monitoring and Controlling. This layer has various digital representation and Identifiers. Exp: Building, Utility Systems, Home and People.

Figure 1. IoT architecture outline

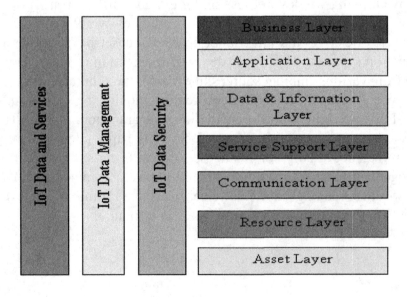

Resource Layer

Sensing, Actuation and Embedded Identities are main functionality of this layer. It has two types Primary Resources such as Sensors, Actuator and RFID Tags, Readers etc and Secondary Resources such as Gateways.

Communication Layer

This is Second Layer mainly used for communication among the interconnected different objects to provide specific services. Generally, the IoT nodes are operated using LLN(Low Power Lossy Network Communication) which are used for Resource Constraint applications. For example WiFi, Bluetooth, IEEE 802.15.4, Z-wave, and LTE-Advanced. Apart from this new identity technologies also used in IoT like RFID, Near Field Communication (NFC) and *ultra-wide bandwidth* (UWB). RFID –Radio Frequency Identification is new technology used to identify Object using unique identity in M2M technology. The RFID technology has Tags, Readers components. Tags are small chip, attached to provide object's identity which is normally assigned with Unique ID. The RFID reader is another component which is used to transmit a query signal to the tag and receives reflected signal from the tag. This signal is passed to the database for further processing (Khan R.,Khan S.U, R.,Zaheer.,&Khan S.,(2012)).

Service Support Layer

This layer typically executing in Data Center or Servers inside an Organization or Cloud Environment. This layer can provide numerous functions such as Remote Device Management, Remote Diagnostics or Recovery, Setting Event Filters and Communication related Functions such as LBS(Location Based Services) and GIS(Geographic Information Services).

Data and Information Layers

Abstract services are provided in this layer. Important goal is to capture knowledge and provide advanced Control Logic and Support

Application Layer

Customers request variety of services which are provided by this layer. It is present above the Data and Information Layer. This application layer can provide Blood Pressure, temperature and air humidity measurements of the patient who asks for analysization using machine learning concepts. The main aim of this layer is to provide High Quality Services to satisfy Customer requirements and their needs. Smart home, Smart building, Transportation, Industrial automation and Smart healthcare are numerous application field which are covered by Application Layer.(Sheng .Z *et al.*, (2013)

Business Layer

Last layer is business (management) layer which is mainly useful for different types of System activity and Services. They received data from this application layer which is used to build a business model, graphs, flowcharts, etc which is the unique Functions of this layer. This layer is responsible for Designing, analyzing, implementing, evaluation and Monitoring process. Based on Big Data Concepts an Intelligent Decision Making process is implemented in this layer. Security and Privacy enhancements are added advantages in this layer. (Khan et al.,(2012),((Sheng .Z *et al.*, (2013)).

Management, Security and Data Services

IoT Management Layer is responsible for Various Operations, Maintenance, Administration and Provisioning. IoT Security Layer is responsible for Communication and Information Security, Identity Management and Authentication, Authorization and used to protect from threats and Harms. Finally Data and Services layer is responsible for Event filtering, Data aggregation, Data Averaging and Contextual Meta Data.

DIFFERENT PROTOCOLS OVERVIEW IN IOT

In distributed communication this is main thing that everyone have to get knowledge about different types of protocols used in IoT environment .IoT can provide different types of communication. Type1.Device to Device Communication: In this Devices must communicate with each other and provide D2D services. Type2.Device to Server Communication: in this the server infrastructure collects Device data. (D2S). Type 3.Server to Server Communication in this server is responsible for devise data sharing (S2S), providing it back to devices for analysation.

MQTT

Main purpose of this protocol is Device to Server Communication. Data Collection takes place from different devices and those data are communicated to server(D2S) .Device data collection is targeted by the Message Queue Telemetry Transport protocol. As its name implies, Remote Monitoring is main of this protocol. Its further goal is to collect data from many devices and transport that data to the IT infrastructure. In a distributed computing environment the large type of data storage networks such as cloud data are monitored and controlled properly by this MQTT.

XMPP

It is abbreviated as Extensible Messaging and Presence protocol(XMPP) which is extension of XML(Extensible Markup Languages).This protocols if a special case of D2S pattern for providing communication between devices to people. In this D2S protocol, people are connected to the servers. It enables exchange of data between any two or more network entities. Via text messages peoples are connected to each other's and providing instant messaging (IM) services.

DDS

It is abbreviated as Data Distribution Service (DDS),which are mainly used to targets devices data directly. It is defined as fast bus for integrating intelligent machines and provide Device to Device Communications (D2D) in smooth manner. DDS main purpose is to connect devices to other devices and distributes it to other devices. It is a Data-Centric middleware standard used for high-performance defense, industrial, and

Table 1.

LAYERS	PROTOCOLS	
APPLICATION	CoAP	
TRANSPORT	UDP	ICMP
INTERNET	RPL	
	IPV6(6LoWPAN)	
DATA LINK	IEEE 802.15.4 MAC	
PHYSICAL	IEEE 802.15.4 PHY	

embedded applications. Millions of simultaneous messages are delivered by DDS per second.

AMQP

A queuing system designed to connect servers to each other (S2S). It sends transactional messages between servers. It can process thousands of reliable queued transactions. AMQP is focused on not losing messages. Publishers to subscribers message transfer used traditional TCP earlier, which provides strictly reliable point-to-point connection and for each transaction acknowledge are getting properly in this. But in AMQP describes an optional transaction mode with a formal multiphase commit sequence. This protocol mainly focuses on tracking all messages and ensuring each is delivered as intended, regardless of failures.

SMART AUTOMATION HEALTH MONITORING FRAMEWORK

Nowadays almost all the applications such as Manufacturing, Civil engineering, and Aerospace industries Smart Automation Health Monitoring Systems(SAHM) has been selected as a relevant subject of study. This smart automation is applied to Healthcare industries also for monitoring patient health condition always. The purpose of SAHM application is to collect real-time data related to the patients which are back bone of the health care industries and extract some useful information from the past historical data and then store this knowledgeable data to back end server for further processing. Since this work successfully allows multiple tasks in intelligent way for monitoring, performance identification, prediction, and report creation for the patient who are in emergency case (Tokognon et al.,). The main objective of SAHM application is to access a patient condition always and predict whether the patient health conditions are normal or abnormal. This prediction happened well in advance so that doctor's can provide appropriate treatment in emergency cases also. This framework is enhanced with various Technologies such as Decision Making, Prediction using machine learning algorithms. Hence this monitoring system tracks any changes on the patient body or environment in order to detect possible events or damage well in advances. This system should be maintained properly for giving maintenance, repair and safety details to other doctors.

All SAHM systems rely on the integration of four major sub-systems implemented to meet SAHM requirement and organize monitoring activities. These are sensing layer (data acquisition sub-system), Base Station Layer, Edge Server Layer and Cloud Center system for data accessing, Storage and retrieval process.

SAHM GENERAL COMPONENTS

Sensing Layer: This layer is the base which consists of various resources such as RFID, Sensors, Actuator and PDA devices for capturing patient data .This layer also called as perception layer. This layer observes and measure the data based on context or environment conditions also. Data from this acquisition layer are forwarded to the above layer through proper communication channel which is called as Wireless Medium. In this layer system performance metrics are considered as major factor to improve the performance of the system.

Base Station Layer: In order to provide an evaluation of the patient health condition this layer is used. In this layer all the collected data from Sensing layers are forwarded to above layer for further processing. Not all the collected data are forwarded directly to next layer called as Edge system layer. Some of the prediction process happened in this layer using innovative machine learning algorithms and these selective datas are further forwarded for next processing. It consists of various communication channels for data

Figure 2. WBSN architecture

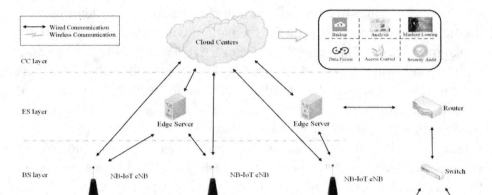

transformation. data collection techniques, data storage as well as data management. Preprocessing methods are included during the development of data management infrastructure which are used to organize raw data acquired from sensors and remove noise before processing. To extract feature that allows damage and undamaged identification in the system the data processing tasks is performed. To detect and localize damage in SAHM system several data processing techniques and analytical models have been developed. Based on machine learning or pattern recognition algorithms new innovative Techniques are used to process data from the sensor network. Novelty detection, classification and regression approaches are the specialty of this algorithms. Among them, based on Artificial Neural Networks novelty detection is done that has received growing attention in recent years for detecting damage in structures.

Data access and Retrieval Sub-System: This sub-system is based on online or offline data control and access; in this system to provide useful information for decision-making data analysis and interpretation are performed. An engineer can view the data analysis results remotely over the Internet.

Network Model

The following related entities exist in typical mobile WBSN scenarios:

Mobile Gateway (denoted as MG): This is usually mobile Smartphone with Internet connection. It uploads monitoring data that are collected from WBSN to cloud servers. Although it can conveniently upload body sensing data instantly, it imposes energy constraints.

Decision Measuring Unit (DMU)

A DMU is an automatic computing system which performs all major computing operations and is connected to the Internet. The role of the DMU is to collect, filter and analyze the information. . It is the main core of the solution where all important decisions are made. The aim of the DMU is to create a typical example of resident's environment that includes a comprehensive database of resident's medical profile. Subsequently, appropriate decisions are made automatically regarding the health status of inhabitant. The DMU is connected to a back-end medical institution such as a hospital in which physicians are able to consider people's health status

The DMU is able to recognize resident's conditions based on the information obtained from a number of sensors which are transformed into knowledge and a list of user-defined policy rules.

WBSN

Sensor nodes in this layer are designed such that they can be placed on the human body as very small patches (on-body sensors), sewed into fabric (wearable sensors), or implanted under the skin (in-body sensors The sink node in WBSN periodically uploads data into MG via a secure channel. Such sensors continuously capture and relay vital parameters. The collected data then may either initially be relayed to a central coordinator on the body or may be transmitted directly to the upper layers for further processing. However, depending on the functionalities and computation capabilities of nodes, data may require low-level on-tag processing prior to transmission. The required transmission power by a sensor node in an off-body communication is mainly dependent on a number of factors such as Body Path Loss (BPL), Receive Noise Figure (RNF) and Signal to Noise

Ratio (SNR) (Bhardwaj .A.,Bhattacherjee .S., Chavan A., Deshpande A., Elmore A.J.,Madden .S., Parameswaran S.G.,(2014)).

Accessor (Denoted as MA): This could be the mobile devices held by doctors, nurses, or guardians. They can usually access the data at BC in a pervasive manner. Layer 2 acts as an Access Point (AP). APs for residential monitoring are usually located within a room environment. Each room is equipped with an AP, where wireless devices are connected to a wired network, Wi-Fi or other relevant standards . Collected data from this layer is required to be transferred to an upper layer (layer 3) in order to be prepared for the final destination.

Cloud Servers (Denoted as BC): This is a back-end storage server with a very large capacity via virtualization of storage resources. The last layer (layer 4) of this architecture as shown in Figure 1 provides healthcare services to patients. In this layer, two different types of services may be provided by healthcare personnel: healthcare services and emergency services.(Bhardwaj .A.,Bhattacherjee .S., Chavan A., Deshpande A., Elmore A.J.,Madden .S., Parameswaran S.G.,(2014)) The analyzed data stored in the DMU is delivered to a remote server in a hospital, where medical professionals have access to it.

The type of sensors used to monitor structural health depends on the types of structures that are to be monitored. The number and placement of sensors to be used depends on the size of the structure but also the type of topology that is adopted for the sensor network deployment. The sensing technologies commonly used in aerospace, civil or mechanical engineering are summarized in Table 2.

Table 2.

Sensors	Measurements	Parameters
Fiber Bragg Grating Sensors (FBG), Strain Gauges, GPS Piezoelectric sensors, ...	Strain, displacement, rotations, curvature, distortions, forces, etc.	Mechanical
Fiber optical sensors, Phototube sensors...	Light, photon, etc.	Optical
RFID sensors, ...	pH value, Sulfate, chlorine, etc.	Chemical
Accelerometers, Temperature sensors, Anemometers, RFID sensors, seismometer, ...	Temperature, humidity, precipitation, wind speed and direction, solar irradiation, velocity, etc.	Environmental / Physical
Load cells	Cable Load, etc.	Loads

BIG DATA STORAGE AND PROCESSING PLATFORM

IoT Filed is heterogeneous collection of Sensor Data which are used for large application. To analyse and Extract useful data proper analytics platforms and Big Data tools are to be considered.(Ejaz Ahmed., Ibrar Yaqoob ., Ibrahim Abaker Targio Hashem., Imran Khan .,Abdelmuttlib Ibrahim Abdalla Ahmed., Muhammad Imran .,& Athanasios Vasilakos V(2017)

Apache Hadoop

One of the Big Data Open Source tool is Apache Hadoop which are used for storing and processing huge data in a cluster basis. Hadoop Distributed File System (HDFS) and the MapReduce programming model are important Components in the Hadoop architecture among several components. HDFS is used for storage purpose, where as MapReduce is used for processing those data in distributed way.(Ahmed et al.,).Even though HDFS has many advantages there are many problems yet to be addressed examples, this framework is lacking in encryption process at the storage and network levels. And has a limited flexibility which is not suitable for small data sets, and are having high I/O overhead also.

1010data

To deal Semi-Structured data in IoT environment 1010data (Daniele Ravi., Charence Wong., Benny Lo.,& Guang-Zhong Yang(2017) is used. Which acts like a columnar database.Large-scale infrastructure 1010data is also very supportive one. Optimization and statistical analysis are added further in this tool for providing Data reporting, visualization and Integration features. Through its recent innovative analytic features 1010data can satisfy customer demand. In this tool intelligent access control methods also included in centralized methods to interact effectively with back end storage networks. Even though this tool provide lots of advantages there are some problems yet to be addressed such as data loading, transformation and extraction process are inefficient one.

Cloudera Data Hub

A big data management model that uses a Hadoop platform as the central data repository are known as Enterprise Data Hub introduced by Cloudera. To manage huge amounts of IoT data from Cloudera a Hadoop based framework is used as central point for big IoT data processing and analytics. To achieve Secure data Access Control, reliability and backup process this Cloudera Data Hub combines with Manager, Navigator, and its backup and recovery components. Main issues in this tool is privacy and security concerns both in hardware and software level.(Jinwei Liu,, Xiang Zhang, Haiying Shen (2016,August)").

SAP-Hana

To perform large volume of data analytics by addressing transactional features SAP-Hana an in-memory platform is used. To accommodate big unstructured data, SAP supports various distributed solutions. Hana accesses big data through Hive, while SAP uses Sybase IQ to provide a columnar DBMS. Hana also has a built-in analytics library for containing, spatial processing, and supporting R language and text analytics libraries. Apart from its low latency, SAP-Hana can also analyze both text and unstructured data. However,in this tool, all data in a row must be read even though only the data from a few columns are required to be accessed. Moreover, the capabilities of SAP-Hana are not strong enough compared with those of other solutions.

4.5. HP-HAVEn

This is new innovative big data platform with enhanced architecture components built into that with improved security, where it is used in many applications. This tool acts like reference hardware configuration component provided by HP. For unstructured data search and exploration services provided by Autonomy's IDOL software. A new data base oriented platform for massive data processing called Vertica an analytical DBMS platform was introduced. Main goal for this is component is to analyze the structured datasets. To complement legacy enterprise data warehouses

HP HAVEn is currently mixed with large types of applications. HP also introduced "Flex-Zone" concepts for defining data into the database schema for exploration of large datasets. The main drawback of HP-HAVEn is scalability problem, when the number of tenants increases data management process also very high complicated and access control mechanism is very difficult to achieve successfully.

Horton Works

This is big data analytics and management platform based on Hadoop. This platform is free open source platform with lots of distributed computing features enhanced into this. If we consider cluster of data processing application, this tool is not suitable because it cannot reduce the number of node-groups in the generated cluster.

Info Bright

To solve information management and analytic problems Infobright tool specifically designed. 50 terabytes of data can be analyzed efficiently by this tool. With its popular high compression ratio and data skipping concepts this tool is considered best tool for machine-oriented system or applications.

MapR

To achieve security and high availability MapR replacing HDFS with Network File system approaches. To improve the performance of the system this tool mainly has enhanced big data analytical components with its own system recovery approach. MapR is linked with Lucid Works search and stream processing for enhancing its predictive capabilities and enable fast processing. Anyhow this tool increases the complexity of working modules compare to Hadoop.

CROWD SENSING IN WBSN

Mobile Crowd Sensing is new concept used in almost all field to obtain sensible data from the surroundings. In these ordinary citizens are acts

Figure 3. Some powerful big data analytics platform

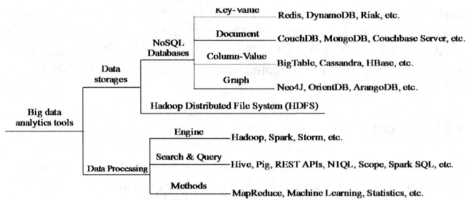

like main element for contributing data sensed from their mobile devices which acts like main data generating nodes, collects and filters those data in the back end server for intelligent crowd based extraction and people-centric service discovery.

Types

- **Human Intelligence:**
  - For Human beings the general abilities are Cognition, Knowledge, perception, and social interaction.
  - Further to understand knowledge based data handling strong contextual and Sensor processing activities are important to consider
- **Machine Intelligence:**
  - Automatic knowledge discovery and event/society understanding are achieved using advanced Machine Learning and data mining algorithms.

This type of Mobile crowd sensing used in Smart Cities various applications such as Road Transportation, Healthcare & Wellbeing and Marketing/Advertising .Different types of platforms introduced in this such as mCrowd - iPhone based platform, PEIR - for participatory sensing and Medusa - mobile crowd sensing framework .(Carol Habiba .B., Abdallah Makhoula., Rony Darazib.,& Raphaël Couturiera.,(2018).

DEEP LEARNING FOR HEALTH INFORMATICS

In an IoT domain Deep learning is a new innovative technological concept which is used in many applications. One of the application such as Health Informatics, this new evolution extracting important features with past historical data without human intervention has many benefits. (Daniele Rav., Charence Wong., Fani Deligianni., Melissa Berthelot., Javier Andreu-Perez., Benny Lo.,&Guang-Zhong Yang(2017)There are numerous challenges yet to be addressed in deep learning to health informatics applications. For example, an extensive amount of labeled data requires deep architecture training, This concept is very complicated to achieve in Healthcare industry. Extra Computational resources also need in Deep Learning which increases cost of the system model as well Special Training also needed which becomes Time consuming. New learning strategies are needed to address convergence issues as well as over fitting problem.

This concept is new approaches to train DNN(Deep Neural Networks) architectures. In this deep learning methodology two types of approaches are there, there can be trained different types of learning methods such as unsupervised and supervised learning methodologies. In unsupervised learning initial training data are combined with DNN in some applications,

Table 3. Multiple deep learning methods

Application Types	Deep Learning Methods	Applications	Input Data
Medical Imaging	Deep Auto encoders Convolutional Neural Network Deep Belief Networks	3D Brain reconstruction, Neural Cells Classification Brain Tissues Classifications	MRI /fMRI Fundu Image PET Scans
	Deep Autoencoder Deep Neural Networks	Tumour Detection Cell Clustering Organ Segmentation	Mincoscopy CT Image X-Ray image
Medical Informatics	Deep Autoencoders Convolutional Neural Network Deep Belief Networks	Prediction of disease Human behavior Monitoring	EHR Big Medical dataset Blood/Lab Test
Public Health	Deep Autoencoders Convolutional Neural Network Deep Belief Networks Deep Neural Networks	Predicting Demographic info Lifestyle diseases Infectious disease edidemics Air Pollutant prediction	Social Media data Mobile Phone Meta Data Geo-tagged images Text message

to extract the useful features. These extracted features are further used for classification by exploiting a new supervised learning. In supervised learning, labeled data are used to train the DNNs and learn the weights that minimize the error to predict a target value for classification or regression. In unsupervised learning, the training is performed without requiring labeled data which is mainly used for clustering, feature extraction or dimensionality reduction. The below table summarize different Deep Learning methods used in Medical Applications.

CHALLENGES AND FUTURE RESEARCH SCOPE

To connect intelligent things in Smart Hospitals using IoT concept there are many challenges not yet addressed, such as

Accuracy and Reliability of Data

In medical hospitals Accuracy and reliability of sensor datas are very important. Inaccurate rate due to external factor lead to insufficient treatment for the patients. The Mobility of patient leads to significant impact on devise data measurements and hence, intelligent devices cannot exclude this interference. Example for this is blood pressure data collection.

Due to environmental elements such as IoT attacks, device faults, IoT Data missing are inevitable. All these factors leads to incorrect treatment. Hence fault detection and reconstruction is another problem in building of smart hospitals.

Privacy and Security

IoT based Intelligent hospitals connect various IoT devices for collecting heterogeneous data from multiple resources. These data are more sensitive in human life. There may be lots of intruders involvement happened in the communication channel. As well as IoT devices and wireless communications are easily vulnerable to cyber attacks. IoT devices cannot be able to run complex algorithms since they are limited by size and poor processing ability. In addition, medical data may be related to the patient's life security, so security and privacy protection is a serious challenge to the smart hospitals. To ensure privacy and security in patient medical data a complex algorithm should be designed including proper data backup mechanism to restore data in time when unexpected situations occur.

Interference Problems in Channels

Interference problems in communication channels due to external noise, equipment's hardware, communication channel, and mutual interference between heterogeneous networks. Noise interference happened due to natural noise like lightning, sounding and manmade noise like medical equipment, which can affect electromagnetic wave of wireless communication. The signals transmitted by the BS can interact with each other, which is more likely to cause blockage of the signal or interference of the same frequency and the adjacent channel. The interference of wireless communication can result in data loss and faults. We must try to eliminate interference, by introducing fault detection and data reconstruction scheme in cloud server to minimize these faults.

Optimization of Energy Consume Process

IoT device uses their energy for data collection, Analysis, Storage and transmission. These data are collected with a high frequency and transmit data to the cloud platform using wireless links. Hence energy optimization is main issue in Smart Automation Hospital environment to continuously monitor patient data with minimal energy consumption and provide continuous work for a long time. To reduce the energy consumption of terminals, we can improve the design process of sensors to enable it to maintain low energy consumption without affecting its data collection accuracy. We can also use data fusion to reduce the amount of transmitted data and traffic also. In addition, a light weight low power protocol should be introduced to minimize the energy consumption of communication modules. Another way to reduce energy consumption is by introducing wireless charging technique. In the previous wired charging techniques introduces lots or practical difficulties such as charge down in emergency cases and unwanted data transfer. This insufficient charging greatly limits the patient's activities. So by introducing wireless charging technique without affecting the monitoring process of the devices is major challenges in today's world. Another important method is energy conversion technique. The energy conversion is sustainable for energy supply of IoT devices, which provides a new way to deal with the energy consumption issue.

CONCLUSION

This paper provides complete survey about current technologies in IoT and implements Patient Smart Health Monitoring Systems using Intelligent Machine Learning Concepts. The WSN application in Healthcare domain is huge, in this work a new concept for integrating IoT Concepts with Machine Learning and Data Analytics are included. As IoT is integration of numerous heterogeneous technologies with huge innovative development tools to meet the customer needs in ICT environment. In IoT Communication a number of research solutions for SAHM have been proposed in recent years. In all such research they explain about how integration happened using multiple devices having multiple processing tasks such as sensing, Acquisition, Collection, Analysis and extract useful information from the huge data.

This work completely explains about need for Big Data, Deep Learning Concept in IoT. Latest technology tools and its purpose also explained. Meanwhile this work also explains about various Deep Learning Concepts and Predictive Analysis Concept also. There are still lots of research problems have to be addressed further. Example such as virtualization and Externalization d on IoT. Apart from this, new innovative techniques have to be considering further for of sensors and IoT devices, interoperability, heterogeneity, scalability and security of systems-base IoT integration into SAHM in order to effectively achieve real-time Event-driven based data monitoring, Smart data collection and processing, and Smart decision-making to reduce Human interventions.

REFERENCES

Ahmed, Yaqoob, Hashem, Khan, Ahmed, Imran, & Vasilakos. (2017, June 15). The role of big data analytics in Internet of Things. *Elseiver Journal on Computer Netwroks*. DOI: doi:10.1016/j.comnet.2017.06.013

Akbar, Khan, Carrez, & Moessner. (2017 October). Predictive Analytics for Complex IoT Data Streams. *IEEE Internet of Things Journal, 4*(5).

Al-Fuqaha, Guizani, Mohammadi, Aledhari, & Ayyash. (2015). Internet of Things: A Survey on Enabling Technologies, Protocols, and Applications. IEEE Communication Surveys & Tutorials, 17(4).

Alam, Mehmood, Katib, Albogami, & Albeshri. (2017, April 25). Data Fusion and IoT for Smart Ubiquitous Environments: A Survey. *IEEE Journal on Special Section on Trends And Advances For Ambient Intelligence with Internet of Things (IOT) Systems, 5.*

Andreu-Perez, Poon, Merrifield, & Wong. (2015, July). Big Data for Health. *IEEE Journal of Biomedical and Health Informatics, 9*(4).

Baker. Xiang, & Atkinson. (2017, November 29). Internet of Things for Smart Healthcare: Technologies, Challenges, and Opportunities. *IEEE Open Access Journal, 5.*

Bhardwaj, A., Bhattacherjee, S., Chavan, A., Deshpande, A., Elmore, A. J., Madden, S., & Parameswaran, S. G. (2014). *Datahub: collaborative data science & dataset version management at scale*. +arXiv preprint arXiv:1409.0798.

Chatterjee, Chatterjee, Choudhury, Basak, Dey, Sain, ... Sircar. (2017). Internet of Things and Body Area Network-An Integrated Future. *IEEE Journal.*

Dimitrov. (2016, July). Medical Internet of Things and big data in healthcare,. *Healthcare Inform. Res., 22*(3), 156-163.

Ghamari, Janko, Sherratt, Harwin, Piechockic, & Soltanpur. (2016, June 7). *A Survey on Wireless Body Area Networks for eHealthcare Systems in Residential Environments*. Retrieved from www.mdpi.com/journal/sensors

Habiba, Makhoula, Darazib, & Couturiera. (2018, May). *Real-time Sampling Rate Adaptation based on Continuous Risk Level Evaluation in Wireless Body Sensor Networks*. IEEE Conference Paper.

Iniewski, K. (2008). VLSI Circuits for Biomedical Applications. Artech House.

Islam, Kwak, Kabir, Hossain, & Kwak. (2015). The Internet of Things for Health Care: A Comprehensive Survey. *IEEE Journal of Open Access Publishing, 3.*

Khan, R., Khan, S. U., Zaheer, R., &Khan, S. (2012). Future Internet: The Internet of Things architecture, possible applications and key challenges. *Proc. 10th Int. Conf. FIT*, 257–260. 10.1109/FIT.2012.53

Li, Zhang, Dong, Zhu, & Pavlovic. (2017, December). A Multisecret Value Access Control Framework for Airliner in Multinational Air Traffic Management. *IEEE Internet of Things Journal, 4*(6).

Liu, J., Zhang, X., & Shen, H. (2016, August). A Survey of Mobile Crowdsensing Techniques: A Critical Component for The Internet of Things. *IEEE Conference Paper*. 10.1109/ICCCN.2016.7568484

Nesa & Banerjee. (2017, October). IoT-Based Sensor Data Fusion for Occupancy Sensing Using Dempster–Shafer Evidence Theory for Smart Buildings. *IEEE Internet of Things Journal, 4*(5).

Obinikpo & Kantarci. (2017, November 20). Big Sensed Data Meets Deep Learning for Smarter Health Care in Smart Cities. *Journal of Sensor and Actuator Networks.*

Obinikpo & Kantarci. (2017, November). Big Sensed Data Meets Deep Learning for Smarter Health Care in Smart Cities. *Journal of Sensors and Actuator Networks.*

Park & Yen. (2018). Advanced algorithms and applications based on IoT for the smart Devices. *Journal of Ambient Intelligence and Humanized Computing*. doi:. doi:10.100712652-018-0715-5

Prasad & Bharat. (2017, April). Network Routing Protocols In IOT. *International Journal of Advances in Electronics and Computer Science, 4*(4).

Rav, Wong, Deligianni, Berthelot, Andreu-Perez, Lo, & Yang. (2017, January). Deep Learning for Health Informatics. *IEEE Journal of Biomedical and Health Informatics, 21*(1).

Samuel, S.J., Sashidhar, K., & Bharathi, C.R. (2015, May). A survey on big data and its research challenges. *ARPN J. Eng. Appl. Sci.*, *10*(8), 3343–3347.

Satija, Ramkumar, & Manikandan. (2017, June). Real-Time Signal Quality-Aware ECG Telemetry System for IoT-Based Health Care Monitoring. *IEEE Internet of Things Journal, 4*(3).

Sheng, Z., Yang, S., Yu, Y., Vasilakos, A., Mccann, J., & Leung, K. (2013, December). A survey on the IETF protocol suite for the Internet of Things: Standards, challenges, and opportunities. *IEEE Wireless Communications*, *20*(6), 91–98. doi:10.1109/MWC.2013.6704479

Siryani, Tanju, & Eveleigh. (2017). A Machine Learning Decision-Support System Improves the Internet of Things' Smart Meter Operations. *IEEE Internet of Things Journal, 4*(4).

Tokognon, Gao, Tian, & Yan. (2017, June). Structural Health Monitoring Framework Based on Internet of Things: A Survey. *IEEE Internet of Things Journal, 4*(3).

Webb, G. T., Vardanega, P. G., & Middleton, C. R. (2015, November). Categories of SHM deployments: Technologies and capabilities. *Journal of Bridge Engineering*, *20*(11), 04014118. doi:10.1061/(ASCE)BE.1943-5592.0000735

Wu, Rendall, Smith, Zhu, & Xu. (2017, June). Survey on Prediction Algorithms in Smart Homes. *IEEE Internet of Things Journal, 4*(3).

Xu, He, & Li. (2014, November). Internet of Things in Industries: A Survey. *IEEE Transactions on Industrial Informatics, 10*(4).

Zhang, Li, Wen, Xun, & Liu. (2018, June). Connecting Intelligent Things in Smart Hospitals Using NB-IoT. *IEEE Internet of Things Journal, 5*(3).

Chapter 15
Autonomous Crop Care System Using Internet of Things

Femilda Josephin J. S.
SRM Institute of Science and Technology, India

Ferni Ukrit M.
SRM Institute of Science and Technology, India

Alice Nithya A.
SRM Institute of Science and Technology, India

Arindam Gogoi
SRM Institute of Science and Technology, India

Vanshika Dewangan
SRM Institute of Science and Technology, India

ABSTRACT

In today's world, the quality of the crops is of utmost importance. Crops need to be effectively cared for, and steps are needed to ensure their healthy growth. Smart Irrigation is a major topic that has been implemented in certain regions, but the accumulation of various sensors is the key to the effective safety of crops. In the chapter, various sensors are being deployed and used in synchronization. The primary ones included in the system are the water level and moisture sensor, which works in correspondence with the water motor; the proximity (PIR) sensor, which works in accordance with the buzzer and the webcam; and finally, the light-dependent resistor (LDR), which works in relation with the artificial light. The analog data received from the sensors

DOI: 10.4018/978-1-5225-8555-8.ch015

are transmitted to the raspberry-pi and then sent over the network using a Wi-Fi module to Ubidots, where the data will be analyzed, and necessary actions will be taken. The components to be used in the system will guarantee overall prolific, scalable, and ardent implementation.

INTRODUCTION

IoT which stands for Internet of Things is a concept where things having a unique identity communicate with each other over different forms of mediums. In this scenario, with the help of the identity we can track the devices, control them and at the same time monitor them using remote systems that are connected over the network. The main idea here is to use internet that helps in supplying the communication and thus in a way results in a network of objects or 'Things'.

Physical Object + Controller, Sensor and Actuators + Internet = Internet of Things

Farming is irrefutably the biggest vocation supplier in India. With rising populace, there is a requirement for expanded farming generation. Keeping in mind the end goal to help more prominent creation in ranches, the necessity of the measure of new water utilized as a part of water system likewise rises. Right now, horticulture accounts 83% of the aggregate water utilization in India. Impromptu utilization of water unintentionally brings about wastage of water. This recommends there is a pressing need to develop systems that avoid water wastage without forcing weight on agriculturists.

At present, starvation is one of the main causes of deaths of people all around the world. One of the reasons for which is the spoiling of crops or unhealthy growth of crop which makes it unfit for consumption. Thus, there is a need to protect crops and ensure that crop growth is proper so that they are fit for consumption. Crops need protection from tramping by humans or animals or any unwanted intruder or obstacle. At the same time, they need proper light and heat for healthy growth. Also, appropriate quantity of water enhances the growth of crop. There is a need to provide just the right amount of water so that there is no lack of water or over flooding of crops with water. This would save a lot of hard-work of the farmers and their time and money as well which sometimes gets wasted due to unwanted factors that can easily be avoided through the proposed system.

In section 2 the paper discusses on the various techniques adopted by different researchers. Section 3 describes the architecture of the crop care system and in section 4 the results are discussed. Finally, section 5 discusses about the conclusion and the work that can be carried out in the future.

LITERATURE SURVEY

Crop irrigation has been a major concern always. The necessity to automate the irrigation was felt along with the use of smart techniques. Hence, this has been a target of study of many papers that were referenced.

In the recent years Sensor-Based irrigation system is the major research focus in many applications (Broeders et al., 2013). The sensors obtain the real-time data and send them to the microcontroller which in-turn will be send to Personal Computers (PC). IOT and cloud computing are incorporated ubiquitously to remove the inadequacy and lack of management which are the major concern in agriculture (Na, & Isaac, 2016).

Data mining concepts are used in (Ghosh et al., 2016) for the predicting the future outcomes. Data mining concepts generally examines the large pre-existing data and produces new information. The authors have used the concept of cloud computing to have a communication between the mobile phone and PC.

A GSM based smart farming was proposed (Dwarkani et al., 2015) which can do several farming tasks using automation. From the smart farm sensing system the GSM module receives signal for smart irrigation. The sensed data can then be transferred to the central database which can be analyzed and moved to irrigator system to do automatic actions.

Based on the moisture values collected by the sensor the motor turns on and off (Rajalakshmi, & Mahalakshmi, 2016, Wang et al., 2010) to keep the soil moisture. Added to it the based on the input given by the light sensor the light goes on and off in a green house environment. To increase the production of rice plants crop monitoring system is used in real time (Na, & Isaac, 2016) which used motes along with sensors to check the level of leaf wetness.

The information about the rainfall and temperature is gathered as early spatial data which is analyzed to reduce the crop damage and to increase the crop production (Tanaka et al., 2010). Also ultrasonic waves are used to predict the slope failure during heavy rainfall (Sakthipriya, 2014)

The proposed work concentrates on different aspects of crop care system like water level, moisture, light and also any intrusions in the green house.

CROP CARE SYSTEM

Figure 1 discusses the overall architecture of crop care system. Here, Raspberry pi is connected to six sensors- water level sensor, PIR sensor, LDR sensor, Ultrasonic sensor, Temperature and Humidity sensor and pH sensor. Relay connects the light and motor with the rest of the system. Motor is activated by the water level sensor and the light is handled by

Figure 1. Crop care system architecture

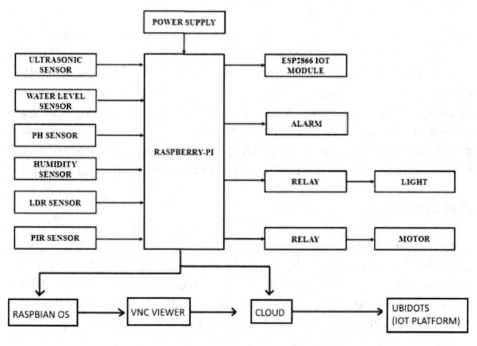

the LDR sensor. There is an alarm as well that buzzes when an intruder is detected by the PIR sensor. Additionally, ultrasonic sensor shows the growth of the plant and pH in the soil, humidity and room temperature is displayed by the remaining 2 sensors. Data from the micro-controller is sent to the cloud, directly or via Raspbian OS (where coding is being done) and that is accessible by the concept of Virtual Network Computing (VNC Viewer is the application that is being used). From the cloud, data is being accessed by the Ubidots (IOT Platform) where data is displayed and mined according to the user needs.

Moisture Module

Data from the moisture sensor is sent to the Raspberry-pi which in turn sends in to the Wi-Fi module to be sent to the IoT platform. Motor is connected with the board with the help of a relay connection. If water is present, then data will be sent to the motor via the micro-controller and it will be stopped. Also in other scenarios, if there is an absence of water then, data will be sent to the motor which will be turned on automatically.

LDR Module

Data from the LDR sensor is sent to the Raspberry-pi which in turn sends in to the Wi-Fi module to be sent to the IoT platform. Artificial light is connected with the board with the help of a relay connection. LDR is responsible for detecting the amount of natural light hence in the occurrence of irregular lighting conditions; signal will be sent to the artificial light via the micro-controller with the help of the relay connection which will automatically switch-on the light. This will ensure the providence of ample lighting conditions for the crop to grow in any environmental situations.

PIR Module

Data from the PIR sensor is sent to the Raspberry-pi which in turn sends in to the Wi-Fi module to be sent to the IoT platform. Micro-controller is in turn connected with the alarm or the buzzer and the webcam. PIR is responsible for detecting intruders in its vicinity. In the presence of any irrelevant object, alarm will be activated and the webcam will capture live images of that object (or intruder) and send it to the user's email address which will be configured from beforehand.

Ultrasonic Module

Data from the Ultrasonic sensor is sent to the Raspberry-pi which in turn sends in to the Wi-Fi module to be sent to the IoT platform. This sensor helps in approximating the height of the crop which will help the user for maintenance purposes.

pH Module

Data from the pH sensor is sent to the Raspberry-pi which in turn sends in to the Wi-Fi module to be sent to the IoT platform. pH helps in figuring the acidic or basic nature of the soil which is necessary to determine to ensure a healthy growth.

Temperature and Humidity Module

Data from the temperature and humidity sensor is sent to the Raspberry-pi which in turn sends in to the Wi-Fi module to be sent to the IoT platform. This sensor helps in determining the room temperature of the crop surroundings which helps the user to take effective steps to ensure a healthy growth of the crop.

Figure 2 shows the data flow from the user to Raspberry pi which is in the form of command that initiates the process of starting of sensors. Secondly, Raspberry pi sends inputs to the sensors that indicate them to start running; hence data flows to the different sensors. From water level sensor, the motor requires input to run. Same is the case for PIR sensor and alarm as well as LDR sensor and Artificial light.

RESULTS AND DISCUSSION

VNC is used here which is remote- control software that helps control another system through a network connection. Desktop, server or any other networked device can be managed due to the transmission of keystrokes

Figure 2. Data flow diagram

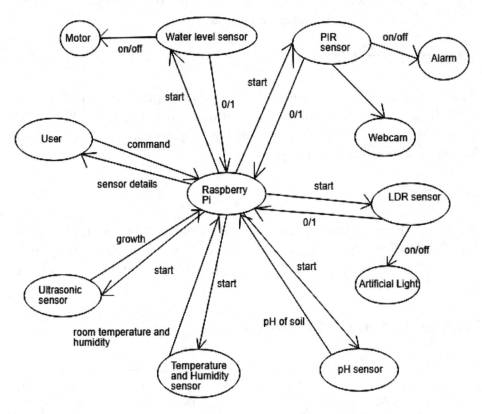

and mouse clicks irrespective of the geographical location. It mainly works on the client-server model. A VNC viewer is installed on the local computer which connects to the server installed in the remote computer. This server transmits a copy of remote computer's display screen to the viewer as well as interprets commands received from the viewer and carries them out on the remote computer.

VNC is not dependent on any platform and has high compatibility with any operating system. Computers must have TCP/IP networking and open ports that allows traffic from the IP addresses of devices wishing to connect. It is mainly used in home computer networks as well as by network administrators in business environments such as IT departments who may require to troubleshoot systems often. It uses a specialized network protocol called Remote Frame Buffer (RFB).Figure 3 shows the

Figure 3. Data display

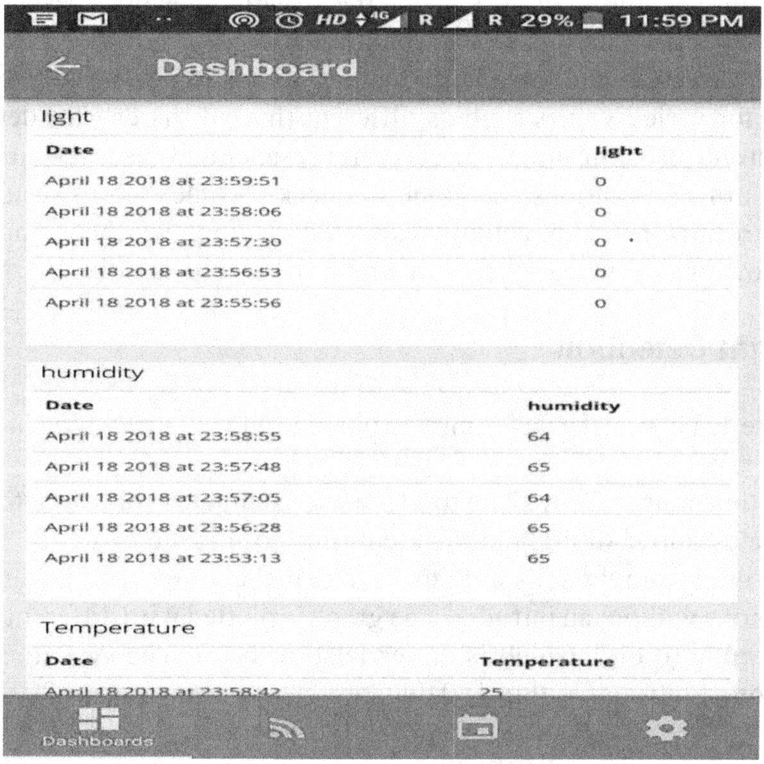

data display using a VNC viewer. Different measures like light, humidity, temperature and intruders can be monitored in its dashboard.

The aim of the project was to provide water or stop water supply depending on the level of water in the soil and at the same time detect any intruder nearby, also to provide artificial light at times when the sunlight is really low. We were successful in our approach and positive results were generated. Motor automatically was switched off when there was water in the soil and switched on when there was none. Any obstacle within 180-degree radius was successfully detected.

The alarm buzzed on intruder detection by the proximity sensor. Also, when LDR couldn't detect sunlight, the artificial light was automatically switched on to provide heat to the crop. The whole system worked successfully in recursion. In turn crop growth and safety was ensured.The additional features that were included such as the pH sensor, temperature and humidity sensor and ultrasonic sensor gave accurate pH, room temperature, humidity of the soil and the growth of the plant respectively.

We collected data for the two main functionalities of the system- i.e. sunlight detection and intruder detection. It was important to check the system for varied values such as different time of the day for detecting sunlight and different angles to detect the presence and absence of intruder. A series of observations was done to check for unexpected results and correct results that were actually expected. A graph was hence plotted.

Following are the categories in which the results are divided.

Sunlight Detection

In figure 4, Time of the day is plotted against value (0 or 1 which indicates false or true).

The time ranges from 12am to 11pm with an interval of 1 hour to check LDR detection of sunlight at different times of the day.

Two other comparisons were made, one in the presence of intruder and another one without an intruder. The graph is plotted with different angles vs the value (0 or 1 which is either false or true). The system ensures detection of intruder within 180 degrees. Hence every step of 20 degrees

Figure 4. Sunlight detection

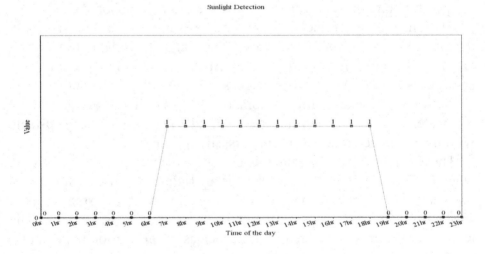

Figure 5. Intruder detection

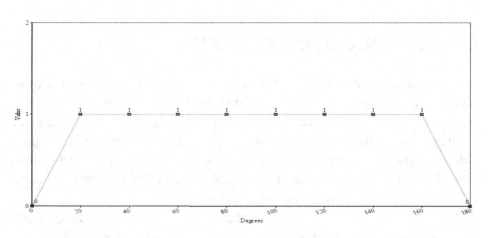

Figure 6. Absence of intruders

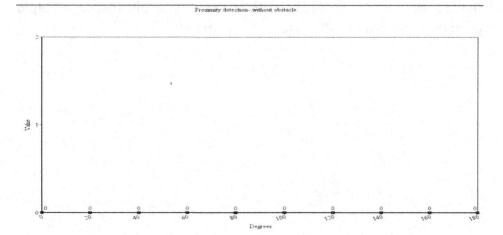

was considered to plot the graph. Figure 5 show the presence of intruder detection and figure 6 shows the absence of intruders.

CONCLUSION AND FUTURE WORK

Safe and healthy growth of crops is a major concern in the present world. IOT based Autonomous Crop Care System is an effective way to ensure crop protection from animals or tramping by humans as well as to ensure healthy crop growth by providing water and sunlight when needed. Additionally, the feature of a webcam makes it convenient for the user to see what threat is near to the crop so that he can take appropriate action immediately which helps him from loss of crops.

It behaves as a mini Greenhouse that guarantees all the benefits from the crop that are expected in a very easy and cost effective way reducing the farmer's effort and time. Further addition of more sensors can make it more efficient to get as much results as possible. Effective algorithms that can decide on the amount of water to be put in the soil comparing it with the threshold value of the soil would be of great use. Addition of fields such as recommended fertilizer and lack of nutrients can help a great deal to ensure healthy soil for crop growth.

REFERENCES

Broeders, J., Croux, D., Peeters, M., Beyens, T., Duchateau, S., Cleij, T. J., & De Ceuninck, W. (2013). Mobile application for impedance-based biomimetic sensor readout. *IEEE Sensors Journal*, *13*(7), 2659–2665. doi:10.1109/JSEN.2013.2256346

Dwarkani, M. C., Ram, R. G., Jagannathan, S., & Priyatharshini, R. (2015, July). Smart farming system using sensors for agricultural task automation. In *Proc. IEEE Technol. Innov. ICT Agricult. Rural Develop. (TIAR)* (pp. 49-53). IEEE.

Ghosh, S., Sayyed, S., Wani, K., Mhatre, M., & Hingoliwala, H. A. (2016, December). Smart irrigation: A smart drip irrigation system using cloud, android and data mining. In *2016 IEEE International Conference on Advances in Electronics, Communication and Computer Technology (ICAECCT)* (pp. 236-239). IEEE. 10.1109/ICAECCT.2016.7942589

Na, A., & Isaac, W. (2016, January). Developing a human-centric agricultural model in the IoT environment. In *2016 International Conference on Internet of Things and Applications (IOTA)* (pp. 292-297). IEEE. 10.1109/IOTA.2016.7562740

Rajalakshmi, P., & Mahalakshmi, S. D. (2016, January). IOT based crop-field monitoring and irrigation automation. In *2016 10th International Conference on Intelligent Systems and Control (ISCO)* (pp. 1-6). IEEE. 10.1109/ISCO.2016.7726900

Rajesh, D. (2011). Application of spatial data mining for agriculture. *International Journal of Computers and Applications*, *15*(2), 7–9. doi:10.5120/1922-2566

Sakthipriya, N. (2014). An effective method for crop monitoring using wireless sensor network. *Middle East Journal of Scientific Research*, *20*(9), 1127–1132.

Tanaka, K., Suda, T., Hirai, K., Sako, K., Fuakgawa, R., Shimamura, M., & Togari, A. (2009, October). Monitoring of soil moisture and groundwater levels using ultrasonic waves to predict slope failures. In SENSORS, 2009 IEEE (pp. 617-620). IEEE. doi:10.1109/ICSENS.2009.5398322

Wang, Q., Terzis, A., & Szalay, A. (2010, May). A novel soil measuring wireless sensor network. In *2010 IEEE Instrumentation & Measurement Technology Conference Proceedings* (pp. 412-415). IEEE. 10.1109/IMTC.2010.5488224

Compilation of References

Adame, T., Bel, A., Carreras, A., Melià-Seguí, J., Oliver, M., & Pous, R. (2018). CUIDATS: An RFID–WSN hybrid monitoring system for smart health care environments. *Future Generation Computer Systems, 78*(2), 602-615.

Aggarwal, C. C. (2013). An Introduction to Sensor Data Analytics. *Managing and Mining Sensor Data. Springer US, 2013*, 1–8.

Aher, B. (2018). *A Look at the IoT Architecture*. Retrieved 8 24, 2018, from DZone: https://dzone.com/articles/iot-architecture-2

Ahmed, Yaqoob, Hashem, Khan, Ahmed, Imran, & Vasilakos. (2017, June 15). The role of big data analytics in Internet of Things. *Elseiver Journal on Computer Netwroks*. Doi:10.1016/j.comnet.2017.06.013

Ahmed, M., Choudhury, S., & Al-Turjman, F. (2019). Big Data Analytics for Intelligent Internet of Things. In *Artificial Intelligence in IoT* (pp. 107–127). Cham: Springer.

Ai, Y., Peng, M., & Zhang, K. (2018). Edge computing technologies for Internet of Things: A primer. *Digital Communications and Networks, 4*(2), 77–86. doi:10.1016/j. dcan.2017.07.001

Akbar, Khan, Carrez, & Moessner. (2017 October). Predictive Analytics for Complex IoT Data Streams. *IEEE Internet of Things Journal, 4*(5).

Akkermans, S., Daniels, W., Sankar, G. R., Crispo, B., & Hughes, D. (2017). Cerber OS: A resource-secure OS for sharing IoT Devices. *International Conference on Embedded Wireless Systems and Networks (EWSN)*, 96-108.

Alam, Mehmood, Katib, Albogami, & Albeshri. (2017, April 25). Data Fusion and IoT for Smart Ubiquitous Environments: A Survey. *IEEE Journal on Special Section on Trends And Advances For Ambient Intelligence with Internet of Things (IOT) Systems, 5*.

Alenezi, Almustafa, & Meerja. (2018). Cloud based SDN and NFV architectures for IoT infrastructure. *Egyptian Informatics Journal*.

Al-Fuqaha, Guizani, Mohammadi, Aledhari, & Ayyash. (2015). Internet of Things: A Survey on Enabling Technologies, Protocols, and Applications. IEEE Communication Surveys & Tutorials, 17(4).

Ali, B., & Awad, A. (2018). Bako Ali 1 ID and Ali Ismail Awad(2018)."Cyber and Physical Security Vulnerability Assessment for IoT-Based Smart Homes. *Sensors (Basel)*, *18*(3), 817. doi:10.339018030817

Anand, D. G., Chandrakanth, H. G., & Giriprasad, M. N. (2012). An Efficient Energy,Coverage and Connectivity Algorithm for Wireless Sensor Networks. *International Journal of Computers and Applications*, *46*(6), 41–47.

Anastasi, G., Conti, M., Di Francesco, M., & Passarella, A. (2009). A. Energy Conservation In Wireless Sensor Networks: A Survey. *Ad Hoc Networks*, *7*(3), 537–568. doi:10.1016/j.adhoc.2008.06.003

Andreoni, G., Costa, F., Attanasio, A., Baroni, G., Muschiato, S., Nonini, P., . . . Perego, P. (2014). Design and Ergonomics of Monitoring System for Elderly. In Digital Human Modeling. Applications in Health, Safety, Ergonomics and Risk Management (pp. 499-507). Springer International Publishing. doi:10.1007/978-3-319-07725-3_49

Andreu-Perez, Poon, Merrifield, & Wong. (2015, July). Big Data for Health. *IEEE Journal of Biomedical and Health Informatics, 9*(4).

Anser, G. A. A., & Kar, J. (2014). A Survey On Security Mechanisms And Attacks In Wireless Sensor Networks. *Contemporary Engineering Sciences*, *7*(3), 135–147.

Atlam, H., Walters, R., & Wills, G. (2018). Fog Computing and the Internet of Things: A Review. *Big Data and Cognitive Computing*, *2*(2), 10.

Atzori, Iera, & Morabito. (2010). The Internet of Things: A survey. *Comput. Netw., 54*(15), 2787-2805.

Atzori, L., Iera, A., & Morabito, G. (2010). The Internet of Things: A survey. *Computer Networks*, *54*(15), 2787–2805. doi:10.1016/j.comnet.2010.05.010

Awada, U. (2018). CMS: Container Orchestration Across Multi-region Clouds.

Bac, C.W., Hemming, J., van Tuijl, B.A., Barth, R., Wais, E., & van Henten, E.J. (2017). Performance evaluation of a harvesting robot for sweet pepper. *Journal of Field Robotics*, *34*(6), 1123-39.

Badii, C., Bellini, P., Difino, A., & Nesi, P. (2019). Sii-Mobility: An IoT/IoE architecture to enhance smart city mobility and transportation services. *Sensors (Basel)*, *19*(1), 1. doi:10.339019010001 PMID:30577434

Bajwa, W., Haupt, J., Sayeed, A., & Nowak, R. (2006). Compressive Wireless Sensing. Proceedings of Information Processing in Sensor Networks, 134-142.

Baker. Xiang, & Atkinson. (2017, November 29). Internet of Things for Smart Healthcare: Technologies, Challenges, and Opportunities. *IEEE Open Access Journal, 5*.

Baldini, I., Castro, P., Chang, K., Cheng, P., Fink, S., Ishakian, V., & Suter, P. (2017). Serverless computing: Current trends and open problems. *Research Advances in Cloud Computing,* 1-20.

Barham, P., Dragovic, B., Fraser, K., Hand, S., Harris, T., Ho, A., & Warfield, A. (2003). Xen and the art of virtualization. *Operating Systems Review*, *37*(5), 164–177. doi:10.1145/1165389.945462

Barr, K. C., & Asanoviˊ, C. K. (2006). Energy-Aware Lossless Data Compression. *ACM Transactions on Computer Systems*, *24*(3), 250–291. doi:10.1145/1151690.1151692

Bera, T., Das, A., Sil, J., & Das, A. K. (2019). A Survey on Rice Plant Disease Identification Using Image Processing and Data Mining Techniques. In Emerging Technologies in Data Mining and Information Security. Springer.

Bettencourt, L. (2014). Impact of changing technology on the evolution of complex informational networks. *Proceedings of the IEEE*, *102*(12), 1878–1891. doi:10.1109/JPROC.2014.2367132

Bhanu Sravanthi, D., & Rekha, G. (2017). Fog Computing a Survey of Integrating Cloud and IOT. *International Journal of Innovative Research in Computer and Communication Engineering*, *5*(3).

Bhardwaj, A., Bhattacherjee, S., Chavan, A., Deshpande, A., Elmore, A. J., Madden, S., & Parameswaran, S. G. (2014). *Datahub: collaborative data science & dataset version management at scale.* +arXiv preprint arXiv:1409.0798.

Bizanis & Kuipers. (2016). SDN and Virtualization Solutions for the Internet of Things: A Survey. *IEEE Access*, 5591-5606.

Bonner, M. (2018). What is Industry 4.0 and What Does it Mean for My Manufacturing?

Bonomi, F., Milito, R., Natarajan, P., & Zhu, J. (2014). Fog Computing: A Platform for Internet of Things and Analytics. In *Big Data and Internet of Things: A Roadmap for Smart Environments* (pp. 169-186).

Bormann. (2016). *CoAP- RFC 7252 Constrained Application Protocol.* Retrieved 8 7, 2018, from CoAP: http://coap.technology

Botia, J. A., Villa, A., & Palma, J. (2012). Ambient Assisted Living system for in-home monitoring of healthy independent elders. *Expert Systems with Applications*, *39*(9), 8136–8148. doi:10.1016/j.eswa.2012.01.153

Boukerche, A., Samarah, S., & Harbi, H. (2008). *Knowledge discovery in wireless sensor networks for chronological patterns.* IEEE. doi:10.1109/LCN.2008.4664263

Bremler-Barr, A., Harchol, Y., Hay, D., & Koral, Y. (2014). Deep packet inspection as a service. In *Proceedings of the 10th ACM International on Conference on emerging Networking Experiments and Technologies* (pp. 271-282). New York: ACM.

Broeders, J., Croux, D., Peeters, M., Beyens, T., Duchateau, S., Cleij, T. J., & De Ceuninck, W. (2013). Mobile application for impedance-based biomimetic sensor readout. *IEEE Sensors Journal*, *13*(7), 2659–2665. doi:10.1109/JSEN.2013.2256346

Broido, A. (2001). Analysis of RouteViews BGP data: Policy atoms.

Brous, P. & Janssen, M. (2015). Effects of The Internet of Things (Iot): A Systematic Review of The Benefits and Risks. In *Proceedings of the 2015 International Conference on Electronic Business*, Taipei.

Buyya, R., & Vahid Dastjerdi, A. (2016). *Internet of Things.* Cambridge, MA: Morgan Kaufmann.

Cao, Z., Kodialam, M., & Lakshman. (2014). *Traffic steering in software defined networks: planning and online routing.* ACM.

Capo-Chichi. (2009). *K-RLE: A new Data Compression Algorithm for Wireless Sensor Network.* IEEE.

Carney & Kong. (2017). Leveraging health informatics to foster a smart systems response to health disparities and health equity challenges. *Journal of Biomedical Informatics, 68*, 184-189.

Catarinucci, L., Donno, D. D., Mainetti, L., Palano, L., Patrono, L., Stefanizzi, M. L., & Tarricone, L. (2015). An IoT-Aware Architecture for Smart Healthcare Systems. *IEEE Internet of Things Journal*, *2*(6), 515–526. doi:10.1109/JIOT.2015.2417684

Chang, H. T., Li, Y-W., & Mishra, N. (2016). *mCAF: A Multi-dimensional Clustering Algorithm for Friends of Social Network Services*. Springer Plus.

Chang, H. T., Liu, S. W., & Mishra, N. (2015). A tracking and summarization system for online Chinese news topics. *Aslib Journal of Information Management, 67*(6), 687–699. doi:10.1108/AJIM-10-2014-0147

Chang, H.-T., Mishra, N., & Lin, C.-C. (2015). IoT Big-Data Centred Knowledge Granule Analytic and Cluster Framework for BI Applications: A Case Base Analysis. *PLoS One, 10*(11), e0141980. doi:10.1371/journal.pone.0141980 PMID:26600156

Chan, H. C. Y. (2015). Internet of Things Business Models. *Journal of Service Science and Management, 8*(04), 552–568. doi:10.4236/jssm.2015.84056

Chatterjee, Chatterjee, Choudhury, Basak, Dey, Sain, … Sircar. (2017). Internet of Things and Body Area Network-An Integrated Future. *IEEE Journal*.

Chiang, M., & Zhang, T. (2016). Fog and IoT: An overview of research opportunities. *IEEE Internet Things J., 3*(6), 854–864. doi:10.1109/JIOT.2016.2584538

Chiosi, M., Clarke, D., Willis, P., Reid, A., Feger, J., Bugenhagen, M., & Benitez, J. (2012). Network functions virtualisation: An introduction, benefits, enablers, challenges and call for action. In *SDN and OpenFlow World Congress*.

Chougule, A., Jha, V. K., & Mukhopadhyay, D. (2016). Using IoT for integrated pest management. In *Internet of Things and Applications (IOTA), International Conference* (pp. 17-22). IEEE.

Cicirelli, F., Guerrieri, A., Spezzano, G., Vinci, A., Briante, O., Iera, A., & Ruggeri, G. (2018). Edge computing and social internet of things for large-scale smart environments development. *IEEE Internet of Things Journal, 5*(4), 2557–2571.

Cina, Esmerald, & Aliaj. (2014). Numerical Data Compression With Data Representation Through Combinations. *International Journal Of Advanced Research In Computer And Communication Engineering, 3*(8), 7839–7844.

Cisco Knowledge Network. (2014). Cisco global cloud index: Forecast and methodology 2014–2019 [Data file]. Retrieved from https://www.cisco.com/Cisco_GCI_Deck_2014-2019_for_CKN__10NOV2015_.pdf

Corcoran, P. (2016). The Internet of Things: Why now, and what's next? *IEEE Consumer Electronics Magazine, 5*(1), 63–68. doi:10.1109/MCE.2015.2484659

Csikósová, A., & Antošová, M. (2015, February). Supply Chain Management in Condition of Production Company. *Applied Mechanics and Materials, 718*, 168–172. doi:10.4028/www.scientific.net/AMM.718.168

Dagnino, A., & Cox, D. (2014). Industrial Analytics to Discover Knowledge from Instrumented Networked Machines. *Proceedings of the 26th International Conference on Software Engineering and Knowledge Engineering (SEKE'14)*.

Dasgupta, A., & Gill, A. Q. (2017). Fog Computing Challenges: A Systematic Review. In Proceedings of the *Australasian Conference on Information Systems*.

Davenport, T. H., Harris, J. G., & Cantrell, S. (2004). Enterprise systems and ongoing process change. *Business Process Management Journal, 10*(1), 16–26. doi:10.1108/14637150410518301

Defeng, T., Shixing, L., Wujun, X., & Yongming, Z. (2010). A Fire Monitoring System In ZigBee Wireless Network. *International Conference on Cyber-Enabled Distributed Computing and Knowledge Discovery 2010*.

Desimone & Hollidge. (1990). *Case Studies in Fleet Operation Modelling: An application of AI scheduling techniques*. ACM.

Dijkmana, R. M., Sprenkels, B., Peeters, T., & Janssenb, A. (2015). Business models for the Internet of Things. *International Journal of Information Management Elsevier, 35*(6), 672–678. doi:10.1016/j.ijinfomgt.2015.07.008

Dimitrov. (2016, July). Medical Internet of Things and big data in healthcare,. *Healthcare Inform. Res., 22*(3), 156-163.

Ding, Z. (2013). IOT-StatisticDB: A General Statistical Database Cluster Mechanism for Big Data Analysis in the Internet of Things. In *Green Computing and Communications (GreenCom), 2013 IEEE and Internet of Things (iThings/CPSCom), IEEE International Conference on and IEEE Cyber, Physical and Social Computing*. IEEE. 10.1109/GreenCom-iThings-CPSCom.2013.104

Domingo. (2012). An overview of the Internet of Things for people with disabilities. *J. Netw. Comput. Appl., 35*(2), 584-596.

Duan, Q., Yan, Y., & Vasilakos, A. V. (2012). A survey on service-oriented network virtualization toward convergence of networking and cloud computing. *IEEE eTransactions on Network and Service Management, 9*(4), 373–392. doi:10.1109/TNSM.2012.113012.120310

Dunn, R. (2018). *IoT Energy Applications: From Smart Vehicles to Smart Meters.* Retrieved from https://www.iotforall.com/iot-energy-applications/

Dwarkani, M. C., Ram, R. G., Jagannathan, S., & Priyatharshini, R. (2015, July). Smart farming system using sensors for agricultural task automation. In *Proc. IEEE Technol. Innov. ICT Agricult. Rural Develop. (TIAR)* (pp. 49-53). IEEE.

Eastwood, G. (2017). *IoT's interoperability challenge.* Retrieved 8 11, 2018, from https://www.networkworld.com/article/3205207/internet-of-things/iots-interoperability-challenge.html

Eller, J. (2017). *IoT System | Sensors and Actuators.* Retrieved 8 24, 2018, from Bridgera: https://bridgera.com/iot-system-sensors-actuators/

Elmangoush, A., Coskun, H., Wahle, S., & Magedanz, T. (2013, March). Design aspects for a reference M2M communication platform for Smart Cities. In *Proceedings of the 2013 9th International Conference on Innovations in Information Technology (IIT)* (pp. 204-209). IEEE.

Evans, D. (2011). The Internet of Things: How the next evolution of the Internet is changing everything. CISCO.

Fairhurst, G. (2018). *The User Datagram Protocol (UDP).* Retrieved 8 11, 2018, from https://www.erg.abdn.ac.uk/users/gorry/course/inet-pages/udp.html

Fang, W., Li, Y., Zhang, H., Xiong, N., Lai, J., & Vasilakos, A. V. (2014). On the throughput-energy tradeoff for data transmission between cloud and mobile devices. *Information Sciences, 283*, 79–93. doi:10.1016/j.ins.2014.06.022

Farahani, B., Firouzi, F., Chang, V., Badaroglu, M., Constant, N., & Mankodiya, K. (2018) towards fog-driven IoT eHealth: Promises and challenges of IoT in medicine and healthcare. *Future Generation Computer Systems, 78*(2), 659-676.

Ferretti & Esquivel. (2005). *Knowledge Insertion: An Efficient Approach to Reduce Effort in Simple Genetic Algorithms for Unrestricted Parallel Equal Machines Scheduling.* ACM.

Finlay, D. (2016). Chapter Seven - Connected Health Approaches to Wound Monitoring. In J. Davis, A. McLister, J. Cundell, & D. Finlay (Eds.), *Smart Bandage Technologies* (pp. 229–244). Academic Press. doi:10.1016/B978-0-12-803762-1.00007-2

Frank. (2017). Using EEG-Based BCI Devices to Subliminally Probe for Private Information. In *WPES' 17 Proceedings of the 2017 on Workshop on Privacy in the Electronic Society*. ACM.

Fuller, J. (2018). *The 4 stages of an IoT architecture*. Retrieved from TechBeacon: https://techbeacon.com/4-stages-iot-architecture

Gaddam, A., Mukhopadhyay, S. C., & Gupta, G. S. (2011). Elder care based on cognitive sensor network. *Sensors Journal, IEEE, 11*(3), 574–581. doi:10.1109/JSEN.2010.2051425

Galante, G., & Bona, L. C. E. D. (2012). A survey on cloud computing elasticity. In *Proceedings of the 2012 IEEE/ACM Fifth International Conference on Utility and Cloud Computing* (pp. 263-270). 10.1109/UCC.2012.30

Garlan, D., Cheng, S. W., Huang, A. C., Schmerl, B., & Steenkiste, P. (2004). Rainbow: Architecture-based Self Adaptation with reusable Infrastructure. *Computer, 37*(10), 46–54. doi:10.1109/MC.2004.175

Ghamari, Janko, Sherratt, Harwin, Piechockic, & Soltanpur. (2016, June 7). *A Survey on Wireless Body Area Networks for eHealthcare Systems in Residential Environments*. Retrieved from www.mdpi.com/journal/sensors

Ghosh, S., Sayyed, S., Wani, K., Mhatre, M., & Hingoliwala, H. A. (2016, December). Smart irrigation: A smart drip irrigation system using cloud, android and data mining. In *2016 IEEE International Conference on Advances in Electronics, Communication and Computer Technology (ICAECCT)* (pp. 236-239). IEEE. 10.1109/ICAECCT.2016.7942589

Gil, R. (2015). *Automated Planning for Self-Adaptive Systems*. IEEE.

Gruteser, M., Schelle, G., Jain, A., Han, R., & Grunwald, D. (2003). Privacy-Aware Location Sensor Networks. *9th Usenix Workshop On Hot Topics In Operating Systems*, 163-167.

Gubbi, J., Buyya, R., Marusic, S., & Palaniswam, M. (2013). IoT: A Vision, Architectural elements, and Future Directions. *Future Generation Computer Systems, 29*(7), 1645–1660. doi:10.1016/j.future.2013.01.010

Guo, L., Wei, S.-Y., Sharma, R., & Rong, K. (2017). Investigating e-business models' value retention for start-ups: The moderating role of venture capital investment intensity. *International Journal of Production Economics, 186*, 33–45. doi:10.1016/j.ijpe.2017.01.021

Habiba, Makhoula, Darazib, & Couturiera. (2018, May). *Real-time Sampling Rate Adaptation based on Continuous Risk Level Evaluation in Wireless Body Sensor Networks*. IEEE Conference Paper.

Haller, S., Karnouskos, S., & Schroth, C. (2008, September). The internet of things in an enterprise context. In Future Internet Symposium (pp. 14-28). Springer. doi:10.1007/978-3-642-00985-3_2

Harbouche, A., Djedi, N., Erradi, M., Ben-Othman, J., & Kobbane, A. (2017). Model driven flexible design of a wireless body sensor network for health monitoring. *Computer Networks, 129*(2), 548-571. doi:10.1016/j.comnet.2017.06.014

Haroon, A., Shah, M. A., Asim, Y., Naeem, W., Kamran, M., & Javaid, Q. (2016). Constraints in the IoT: The world in 2020 and beyond. *Constraints, 7*(11), 252–271.

Haseeb, S., Hashim, A., Khalifa, O., & Ismail, A. (2017). Connectivity, interoperability and manageability challenges in internet of things. *AIP Conference Proceedings*, 020004. doi:10.1063/1.5002022

Hassan & Lee. (2015). The paradox of the sustainable city: De_nitions and examples. *Environ. Develop. Sustainability, 17*(6), 1267-1285.

Hassan, N., Gillani, S., Ahmed, E., Yaqoob, I., & Imran, M. (2018). The Role of Edge Computing in Internet of Things. *IEEE Communications Magazine*, (99), 1–6.

C. Hayashi, K. Yajima, H. H. Bock, N. Ohsumi, Y. Tanaka, & Y. Baba (Eds.). (2013). Data Science, Classification, and Related Methods. In *Proceedings of the Fifth Conference of the International Federation of Classification Societies (IFCS-96)*. Kobe, Japan: Springer Science & Business Media.

He, Yang, & Yang. (2010). Real-time data mining methodology and emergency knowledge discovery in wireless sensor networks. *PGNet-2010*.

Hellerstein, J. M., & Wang, W. (2004). Optimization Of In-Network Data Reduction. In *Dmsn '04: Proceedings Of The 1st International Workshop On Data Management For Sensor Networks*. ACM. 10.1145/1052199.1052207

Hermann, M., Pentek, T., & Otto, B. (2016, January). Design principles for industrie 4.0 scenarios. In *Proceedings of the 2016 49th Hawaii international conference on system sciences (HICSS)* (pp. 3928-3937). IEEE.

Hognelid, P., & Kalling, T. (2015) Internet of things and business models. *Proceedings of the 9th international conference on standardization and innovation in information technology, IEEE SIIT 2015*, art. no. 7535598. 10.1109/SIIT.2015.7535598

Holland, J. L., & Lee, S. (2019). Internet of everything (IoE): Eye tracking data analysis. In *Harnessing the Internet of Everything (IoE) for Accelerated Innovation Opportunities* (pp. 215–245). IGI Global. doi:10.4018/978-1-5225-7332-6.ch010

Hossain, Islam, Ali, Kwak, & Hasan. (2017). An Internet of Things-based health prescription assistant and its security system design. *Future Generation Computer Systems*. doi:10.1016/j.future.2017.11.020

Hota, J., & Sinha, P. K. (2015). Scope and challenges of Internet of Things: An Emerging Technological Innovation. In *International Conference on Futuristic Trends in Computational analysis and Knowledge management*. IEEE.

Hui, G. (2014). How the internet of things changes business models. *Harvard Business Review*.

Hung, M. (2018). Control your IoT Destiny: Insights of IoT. *Gartner*. Retrieved from https://www.gartner.com/en/information-technology/insights/internet-of-things

Hussain, A., & Rao, W. (2015). Health and emergency-care platform for the elderly and disabled people in the Smart City. *Journal of Systems and Software, 110*, 253-263.

Iniewski, K. (2008). VLSI Circuits for Biomedical Applications. Artech House.

IoT. (2018). *Defining the IoT Ecosystem for Enterprises*. Retrieved from IoT Innovation: https://internet-of-things-innovation.com/insights/the-blog/defining-iot-ecosystem-enterprises/

Islam, Kwak, Kabir, Hossain, & Kwak. (2015). The Internet of Things for Health Care: A Comprehensive Survey. *IEEE Journal of Open Access Publishing, 3*.

Jadhav, S. (2015). Present Status of Solid Waste Management in Bhor, Pune, India: Practices & Challenges. International Journal of Innovative Research in Science. *Engineering & Technology.*, *4*, 2059–2064. doi:10.15680/IJIRSET.2015.0404035

Jain, Ghodichor, Golait, & Jain. (2013). A Survey On Energy Optimization In Wireless Sensor Network. *International Journal Of Engineering Sciences & Emerging Technologies*, 68-74.

Jawarkar, Panchore, & Deshmukh. (2013). Overview of Wireless Sensor Network and its Applications. *International Journal of Electronics Communication and Computer Engineering*, 29-32.

Johnson, S. (2016). *Constrained Application Protocol: CoAP is IoT's 'modern' protocol*. Retrieved 8 9, 2018, from https://internetofthingsagenda.techtarget.com/feature/Constrained-Application-Protocol-CoAP-is-IoTs-modern-protocol

Kamilaris, A., Kartakoullis, A., & Prenafeta-Boldú, F. X. (2017, December 1). A review on the practice of big data analysis in agriculture. *Computers and Electronics in Agriculture, 143*, 23–37. doi:10.1016/j.compag.2017.09.037

Kamilaris, A., & Prenafeta-Boldú, F. X. (2018). Deep learning in agriculture: A survey. *Computers and Electronics in Agriculture, 30*(147), 70–90. doi:10.1016/j.compag.2018.02.016

Kanawade, S. Y., Bhadane, D. S., Tarle, M. R., & Patel, R. S. (2014). A Survey Of Data Compression Techniques In Sensor Network. *International Journal of Emerging Technology and Advanced Engineering*, 415–417.

Kanda, W., Yumura, Y., Kinebuchi, Y., Makijima, K., & Nakajima, T. (2008). Spumone: Lightweight cpu virtualization layer for embedded systems. In *Proceedings of the IEEE/IFIP International Conference on Embedded and Ubiquitous Computing* (Vol. 1, pp. 144-151). IEEE. 10.1109/EUC.2008.157

Kang, H., Lee, J., Hyochan, B., & Kang, S. (2012) A Design of IoT Based Agricultural Zone Management System. In Lecture Notes in Electrical Engineering: Vol. 180. Information Technology Convergence, Secure and Trust Computing, and Data Management. Springer. doi:10.1007/978-94-007-5083-8_2

Karydis, I., Gratsanis, P., Semertzidis, C., & Avlonitis, M. (2013). WebGIS design & implementation for pest life-cycle & control simulation management: The case of olive-fruit fly. *Procedia Technology., 8*(6), 526–529. doi:10.1016/j.protcy.2013.11.072

Kelly, S. D. T., Suryadevara, N., & Mukhopadhyay, S. C. (2013). *Towards the Implementation of IoT for Environmental Condition Monitoring in Homes*. Academic Press.

Khan, R., Khan, S. U., Zaheer, R., &Khan, S. (2012). Future Internet: The Internet of Things architecture, possible applications and key challenges. *Proc. 10th Int. Conf. FIT*, 257–260. 10.1109/FIT.2012.53

Khanna & Liu. (2012). Machine learning approach to data center monitoring using wireless sensor networks. *Globecom-2012*.

Khorov, E., Lyakhov, A., Krotov, & Guschin, A (2015). A survey on IEEE 802.11 ah: An enabling networking technology for smart cities. *Computer Communications, 58*, 53–69.

Kiely, A., Xu, M., Song, R., Huang, R., & Shirazi, B. (2010). Adaptive linear filtering compression on real time sensor networks. *The Computer Journal, 53*(10), 1606–1620. doi:10.1093/comjnl/bxp128

Kiritsis, D. (2011). Closed-loop PLM for intelligent products in the era of the Internet of things. *Computer Aided Design, 43*(5), 479–501. doi:10.1016/j.cad.2010.03.002

Knoppers, B. M., & Thorogood, A. M. (2017). Ethics and Big Data in health. *Current Opinion in Systems Biology, 4*, 53-57. doi:10.1016/j.coisb.2017.07.001

Kodituvakku & Amarasanghe. (2010). Comparison Of Lossless Data Compression Algorithms For Text Data. *Indian Journal Of Computer Science And Engineering, 1*(4), 416–425.

Kolias, S., & Voas, B. (2016). Learning Internet-of-Things Security "Hands-On". *IEEE Security and Privacy, 14*(1), 37–46. doi:10.1109/MSP.2016.4

Kowatsch, T., & Maass, W. (2012). [Social Acceptance and Impact Evaluation.]. *IoT-I Deliverable, D2,* 4.

Krammer, J., & Magee, J. (2007). Self Managed Systems: an architectural challenge. In *Future of Software Engineering, 2007, FOSE'2007* (pp. 259–268). IEEE.

Kramp, K. V., & Lange. (2013). Introduction to the Internet of Things. Berlin: Springer.

Kuenzer, S., Ivanov, A., Manco, F., Mendes, J., Volchkov, Y., Schmidt, F., & Huici, F. (2017). Unikernels Everywhere: The Case for Elastic CDNs. *ACM SIGPLAN Notices, 52*(7), 15–29. doi:10.1145/3140607.3050757

Kumari, A., Tanwar, S., Tyagi, S., Kumar, N., Parizi, R. M., & Choo, K. K. R. (2019). Fog data analytics: A taxonomy and process model. *Journal of Network and Computer Applications, 128*, 90–104. doi:10.1016/j.jnca.2018.12.013

Kyriazakos, S., Valentini, V., Cesario, A., & Zachariae, R. (2017). FORECAST - a cloud-based personalized intelligent virtual coaching platform for the well-being of cancer patients. *Clinical and Translational Radiation Oncology.*

Lai, C. T. A., Jackson, P. R., & Jiang, W. (2018). Designing Service Business Models for the Internet of Things: Aspects from Manufacturing Firms. *American Journal of Management Science and Engineering, 3*(2), 7–22.

Leminen, S. (2012). Towards IOT Ecosystems and Business Models. *Internet of Things, Smart Spaces, and Next Generation Networking*, 15-26.

Levine, J., Westerberg, H., Galea, M., & Humphreys, D. (2009). *Evolutionary-Based Learning of Generalised Policies for AI Planning Domains*. ACM. doi:10.1145/1569901.1570062

Li, Zhang, Dong, Zhu, & Pavlovic. (2017, December). A Multisecret Value Access Control Framework for Airliner in Multinational Air Traffic Management. *IEEE Internet of Things Journal, 4*(6).

Liqiang, Z., Shouyi, Y., Leibo, L., Zhen, Z., & Shaojun, W. (2011). A crop monitoring system based on wireless sensor network. *Procedia Environmental Sciences, 11*, 558–565. doi:10.1016/j.proenv.2011.12.088

Liu, C., Wu, K., & Pei, J. (2005). A Dynamic Clustering And Scheduling Approach To Energy Saving In Data Collection From Wireless Sensor Networks. *Sensor And Ad Hoc Communications And Networks, IEEE, Second Annual IEEE Communications Society Conference*, 374-385.

Liu, L., & Jia, W. (2010). Business model for drug supply chain based on the internet of things. *IEEE International Conference on Network Infrastructure and Digital Content*, 982-986.

Liu, J., Zhang, X., & Shen, H. (2016, August). A Survey of Mobile Crowdsensing Techniques: A Critical Component for The Internet of Things. *IEEE Conference Paper*. 10.1109/ICCCN.2016.7568484

Liu, T., & Lu, D. ((2012)). The application and development of IOT. *International Symposium On Information Technologies In Medicine And Education*.

Liu, T., & Lu, D. (2012). The application and development of IoT. *Int. Symp. Inf. Technol. Med. Educ. (ITME), 2*, 991–994.

Lloret, J., Parra, L., Taha, M., & Tomás, J. (2017). An architecture and protocol for smart continuous eHealth monitoring using 5G. *Computer Networks, 129*(2), 340-351. doi:10.1016/j.comnet.2017.05.018

Lobo & Sumana. (2016). Issues and Attacks – A Security Threat to Wsn: An Analogy International. *Journal of Emerging Engineering Research and Technology, 4*(1), 96–99.

Lomotey, Pry, & Sriramoju. (2017). Wearable IoT data stream traceability in a distributed health information system. *Pervasive and Mobile Computing, 40*, 692-707.

Ma, M., Wang, P., & Chu, C.-H. (2013). Data Management for Internet of Things: Challenges, Approaches and Opportunities. In *Green Computing and Communications (GreenCom), 2013 IEEE and Internet of Things (iThings/CPSCom), IEEE International Conference on and IEEE Cyber, Physical and Social Computing.* IEEE. 10.1109/GreenCom-iThings-CPSCom.2013.199

Maan. (2013). Analysis & Comparison Of Algorithms For Lossless Data Compression. *International Journal of Information and Computation Technology*, 139-146.

Mach, P., & Becvar, Z. (2017). Mobile Edge Computing: A Survey on Architecture and Computation Offloading. IEEE Communications Surveys & Tutorials, 19(3), 1628-1656.

Machado, L., Prikladnicki, R., Meneguzzi, F., Cleidson, R. B., & de Souza, E. C. (2016). Task Allocation for Crowdsourcing using AI Planning. ACM.

Mach, P., & Becvar, Z. (2017). Mobile edge computing: A survey on architecture and computation offloading. *IEEE Communications Surveys and Tutorials*, *19*(3), 1628–1656. doi:10.1109/COMST.2017.2682318

Manvi, S. S., & Shyam, G. K. (2014). Resource management for Infrastructure as a Service (IaaS) in cloud computing: A survey. *Journal of Network and Computer Applications*, *41*, 424–440. doi:10.1016/j.jnca.2013.10.004

Mao, Y., You, C., Zhang, J., Huang, K., & Letaief, K. B. (2017). A survey on mobile edge computing: The communication perspective. *IEEE Communications Surveys and Tutorials*, *19*(4), 2322–2358. doi:10.1109/COMST.2017.2745201

Marquardt & Uhramcher. (2008). *Evaluating AI Planning for Service Composition in Smart Environments*. ACM.

Marr, B. (2018). Why Everyone Must Get Ready For The 4th Industrial Revolution.

Mashayekhy, L., Nejad, M. M., Grosu, D., & Vasilakos, A. V. (2014, June). Incentive-compatible online mechanisms for resource provisioning and allocation in clouds. In *2014 IEEE 7th International Conference on Cloud Computing* (pp. 312-319). IEEE. 10.1109/CLOUD.2014.50

Masmano, M., Ripoll, I., Crespo, A., & Metge, J. (2009). Xtratum: a hypervisor for safety critical embedded systems. In *Proceedings of the 11th Real-Time Linux Workshop* (pp. 263-272).

Medaglia, C. M., & Serbanati, A. (2010). An overview of privacy and security issues in the Internet of Things. In The Internet of Things. New York, NY: Springer. doi:10.1007/978-1-4419-1674-7_38

Medeiros, H. P., & Maciel, M. C. (2014). Lightweight Data Compression in Wireless Sensor Networks Using Huffman Coding. *International Journal of Distributed Sensor Networks,* 1–11.

Mehdipour, F., Javadi, B., Mahanti, A., & Ramirez-Prado, G. (2019). Fog Computing Realization for Big Data Analytics. *Fog and Edge Computing: Principles and Paradigms*, 259-290.

Minerva, R., Biru, A., & Rotondi, D. (2015). Towards a definition of the Internet of Things (IoT). *IEEE Internet of Things Journal, 1*(1).

Mishra, N. (2017). In-network Distributed Analytics on Data-centric IoT Network for BI-service Applications. *International Journal of Scientific Research in Computer Science, Engineering and Information Technology, 2*(5), 547-552.

Mishra, N., Alebachew, K., & Patnaik, B. C. (2018). Data Organization and Knowledge Inference from Sensor Database for Smart Wear. *International Journal of Scientific Research in Computer Science, Engineering and Information Technology, 3*(1), 1039-1044.

Mishra, N., Chang, H. T., & Lin, C. C. (2014). Data-centric Knowledge Discovery Strategy for a Safety-critical Sensor Application. *International Journal of Antennas and Propagation*. doi:10.1155/2014/172186

Mishra, N., Chang, H. T., & Lin, C. C. (2015). An IoT Knowledge Reengineering Framework for Semantic Knowledge Analytics for BI-Services. *Mathematical Problems in Engineering*.

Mishra, N., Chang, H. T., & Lin, C. C. (2018). Sensor Data Distribution and Distributed Knowledge Inference Systems. LAP LAMBERT Academic Publishing.

Mishra, N., Lin, C. C., & Chang, H. T. (2014). A Cognitive Oriented Framework for IoT Big-data Management Perspective. In *High-Speed Intelligent Communication Forum (HSIC) with International Conference on Computational Problem-Solving (ICCP) China, 2014, 6th International* (pp. 1-4). IEEE.

Mishra, N. (2018). Internet of Everything Advancement Study in Data Science and Knowledge Analytic Streams. *International Journal of Scientific Research in Computer Science and Engineering, 6*(1), 30–36. doi:10.26438/ijsrcse/v6i1.3036

Mishra, N., Alebachew, K., & Patnaik, B. C. (2018). Knowledge Analytics in Cloud Centric IoT Vicinities. *International Journal on Computer Science and Engineering*, *6*(1), 385–390. doi:10.26438/ijcse/v6i1.385390

Mishra, N., Chang, H. T., & Lin, C. C. (2018). Sensor data distribution and knowledge inference framework for a cognitive-based distributed storage sink environment. *International Journal of Sensor Networks*, *26*(1), 26–42. doi:10.1504/IJSNET.2018.088387

Mishra, N., Lin, C. C., & Chang, H. T. (2014). A Cognitive Adopted Framework for IoT Big-Data Management and Knowledge Discovery Prospective. *International Journal of Distributed Sensor Networks*.

Mishra, N., Lin, C. C., & Chang, H. T. (2014). Cognitive inference device for activity supervision in the elderly. *The Scientific World Journal*. PMID:25405211

Mitake, H., Kinebuchi, Y., Courbot, A., & Nakajima, T. (2011). Coexisting real-time OS and general purpose OS on an embedded virtualization layer for a multicore processor. In *Proceedings of the 2011 ACM Symposium on Applied Computing* (pp. 629-630). New York: ACM. 10.1145/1982185.1982322

Mitchell, B. (2018). *What Does HTTP Mean?* Retrieved 8 8, 2018, from https://www.lifewire.com/hypertext-transfer-protocol-817944

Mobile-edge Computing Industry Initiative-ETSI. (2015),Mobile-edge Computing Introductory Technical White Paper [Data Sheet]. Retrieved from, https://portal.etsi.org/

Morabito, R. (2017). Virtualization on internet of things edge devices with container technologies: A performance evaluation. *IEEE Access*, *5*, 8835–8850. doi:10.1109/ACCESS.2017.2704444

Morabito, R., Cozzolino, V., Ding, A. Y., Beijar, N., & Ott, J. (2018). Consolidate IoT edge computing with lightweight virtualization. *IEEE Network*, *32*(1), 102–111. doi:10.1109/MNET.2018.1700175

Morabito, R., Petrolo, R., Loscrì, V., & Mitton, N. (2018). LEGIoT: A Lightweight Edge Gateway for the Internet of Things. *Future Generation Computer Systems*, *81*, 1–15. doi:10.1016/j.future.2017.10.011

Morris, M., Schindehutte, M., & Allen, J. (2005). The entrepreneur's business model: Toward a unified perspective. *Journal of Business Research*, *58*(6), 726–735. doi:10.1016/j.jbusres.2003.11.001

MQTT. (2014). Retrieved from Oasis: http://docs.oasis-open.org/mqtt/mqtt/v3.1.1/os/mqtt-v3.1.1-os.html

Mudgule, Nagaraj, & Ganjewar. (2014). Data Compression in Wireless Sensor Network: A Survey. *International Journal of Innovative Research in Computer and Communication Engineering*, *2*(11), 6664–6673.

Mutlag, A. A., Ghani, M. K. A., Arunkumar, N., Mohamed, M. A., & Mohd, O. (2019). Enabling technologies for fog computing in healthcare IoT systems. *Future Generation Computer Systems*, *90*, 62–78. doi:10.1016/j.future.2018.07.049

Na, A., & Isaac, W. (2016, January). Developing a human-centric agricultural model in the IoT environment. In *2016 International Conference on Internet of Things and Applications (IOTA)* (pp. 292-297). IEEE. 10.1109/IOTA.2016.7562740

Nagarajan, G., & Minu, R. I. (2018). Wireless soil monitoring sensor for sprinkler irrigation automation system. *Wireless Personal Communications*, *98*(2), 1835–1851. doi:10.100711277-017-4948-y

Nagaraj, K. (2008). *Farmers' suicides in India: Magnitudes, trends and spatial patterns*. Bharathiputhakalayam.

Nagaraj, K., Sainath, P., Rukmani, R., & Gopinath, R. (2014). Farmers' suicides in India: Magnitudes, trends, and spatial patterns, 1997-2012. *Journal.*, *4*(2), 53–83.

Negrete JC (2018). Internet of things in Mexican agriculture; a technology to increase agricultural productivity and reduce rural poverty. *Research and Analysis Journal*, *12*(2).

Negrete, J. C., Kriuskova, E. R., Canteñs, G. D., Avila, C. I., & Hernandez, G. L. (2018). Arduino Board in the Automation of Agriculture in Mexico, a Review. *International Journal of Horticulture*, *16*, 8.

Nesa & Banerjee. (2017, October). IoT-Based Sensor Data Fusion for Occupancy Sensing Using Dempster–Shafer Evidence Theory for Smart Buildings. *IEEE Internet of Things Journal*, *4*(5).

Obinikpo & Kantarci. (2017, November 20). Big Sensed Data Meets Deep Learning for Smarter Health Care in Smart Cities. *Journal of Sensor and Actuator Networks*.

Obinikpo & Kantarci. (2017, November). Big Sensed Data Meets Deep Learning for Smarter Health Care in Smart Cities. *Journal of Sensors and Actuator Networks*.

Odusote, A., Naik, S., Tiwari, A., & Arora, G. (2016). *Turning value into revenue: What IoT players can learn from software monetization.* Academic Press.

Ojha, T., Misra, S., & Raghuwanshi, N. S. (2015, October 1). Wireless sensor networks for agriculture: The state-of-the-art in practice and future challenges. *Computers and Electronics in Agriculture, 118,* 66–84. doi:10.1016/j.compag.2015.08.011

Olayinka, O., Kekeh, M., Sheth-Chandra, M., & Akpinar-Elci, M. (2017). Big Data Knowledge in Global Health Education. *Annals of Global Health.*

OpenFog Consortium. (2016). OpenFog Reference Architecture for Fog Computing [Data Sheet]. Retrieved from https://www.openfogconsortium.org

Osterwalder, A., & Pigneur, Y. (2010). *Business model generation: a handbook for visionaries, game changers, and challengers.* Hoboken, NJ: John Wiley & Sons.

Ozturk, C., Zhang, Y., & Trappe, W. (2004). In Energy constrained Sensor Network Routing. *Proceedings Of The 2nd ACM Workshop On Security Of Ad Hoc And Sensor Networks,* 88-93 10.1145/1029102.1029117

Panda. (2014). Security In Wireless Sensor Networks Using Cryptographic Techniques. *American Journal Of Engineering Research,* 50-56.

Park & Yen. (2018). Advanced algorithms and applications based on IoT for the smart Devices. *Journal of Ambient Intelligence and Humanized Computing.* doi:. doi:10.100712652-018-0715-5

Pate, P. (2013). *NFV and SDN: What's the Difference?* Retrieved 8 5, 2018, from https://www.sdxcentral.com/articles/contributed/nfv-and-sdn-whats-the-difference/2013/03/

Payandeh, A. (2014). Self-Protection Mechanism For Wireless Sensor Networks. *International Journal Of Network Security & Its Applications, 6*(3), 85–97. doi:10.5121/ijnsa.2014.6307

Perera, C., Qin, Y., Estrella, J. C., Reiff-Marganiec, S., & Vasilakos, A. V. (2017). Fog computing for sustainable smart cities: A survey. *ACM Computing Surveys, 50*(3), 32.

Pisal, R. S. (2014). Implementation Of Data Compression Algorithm For Wireless Sensor Network Using K-RLE. *International Journal Of Advanced Research In Electronics And Communication Engineering, 3*(11), 1663–1666.

Plauth, M., Feinbube, L., & Polze, A. (2017, September). A performance survey of lightweight virtualization techniques. In *Proceedings of the European Conference on Service-Oriented and Cloud Computing* (pp. 34-48). Cham: Springer.

Porambage, P., Okwuibe, J., Liyanage, M., Ylianttila, M., & Taleb, T. (2018). Survey on Multi-Access Edge Computing for Internet of Things Realization. IEEE Communications Surveys & Tutorials, 20(4), 2961-2991. doi:10.1109/COMST.2018.2849509

Pottie, G. J., & Kaiser, W. J. (2000). *Wireless Integrated Network Sensors. Communication*. ACM.

Pradhan, S., Kusuma, J., & Ramchandran, K. (2002). Distributed Compression in a Dense Microsensor Network. *IEEE Signal Processing Magazine, 19*(2), 51–60. doi:10.1109/79.985684

Pramanik, Lau, Demirkan, & Azad. (2017). Smart health: Big data enabled health paradigm within smart cities. *Expert Systems with Applications, 87*, 370-383. doi:10.1016/j.eswa.2017.06.027

Prasad & Bharat. (2017, April). Network Routing Protocols In IOT. *International Journal of Advances in Electronics and Computer Science, 4*(4).

Premsankar, G., Di Francesco, M., & Taleb, T. (2018). Edge computing for the Internet of Things: A case study. *IEEE Internet of Things Journal, 5*(2), 1275–1284. doi:10.1109/JIOT.2018.2805263

Qiu, H. J. F., Ho, I. W. H., Tse, C. K., & Xie, Y. (2015). A Methodology for Studying 802.11p VANET Broadcasting Performance With Practical Vehicle Distribution. *IEEE Transactions on Vehicular Technology, 64*(10), 4756–4769. doi:10.1109/TVT.2014.2367037

Qu, C., Liu, F., & Tao, M. (2014). Ontologies for the Transactions on IoT. *International Journal of Distributed Sensor Networks*.

Quilici-Gonzalez, J. A., Broens, M. A., Gonzalez, M. E. Q., & Kobayashi, G. (2014). Complexity and information technologies: an ethical inquiry into human autonomous action. Scientiae Studia, 12.

Rachelin Sujae, P., & Selvaraju, S. (2014). Power Efficient Adaptive Compression Technique For Wireless Sensor Networks. *Middle East Journal of Scientific Research, 20*(10), 1286–1291.

Raghunathan, V., Schurgers, C., Park, S., & Srivastava, M. B. (2002). Energy-Aware Wireless Micro Sensor Networks. *Journal Of IEEE Signal Processing Magazine, 19*(2), 40–50. doi:10.1109/79.985679

Rajalakshmi, P., & Mahalakshmi, S. D. (2016, January). IOT based crop-field monitoring and irrigation automation. In *2016 10th International Conference on Intelligent Systems and Control (ISCO)* (pp. 1-6). IEEE. 10.1109/ISCO.2016.7726900

Rajesh, D. (2011). Application of spatial data mining for agriculture. *International Journal of Computers and Applications, 15*(2), 7–9. doi:10.5120/1922-2566

Ranger, S. (2018). *What is the IoT? Everything you need to know about the Internet of Things right now.* Retrieved 7 29, 2018, from ZDNet.: https://www.zdnet.com/article/what-is-the-internet-of-things-everything-you-need-to-know-about-the-iot-right-now/

Rath, M., & Panda, M. R. (2017). MAQ system development in mobile ad-hoc networks using mobile agents. *IEEE 2nd International Conference on Contemporary Computing and Informatics (IC3I)*, 794-798.

Rath, M., & Pattanayak, B. (2018). Technological improvement in modern health care applications using Internet of Things (IoT) and proposal of novel health care approach. *International Journal of Human Rights in Healthcare.* doi:10.1108/IJHRH-01-2018-0007

Rath, M., & Pattanayak, B. K. (2018). Monitoring of QoS in MANET Based Real Time Applications. In Information and Communication Technology for Intelligent Systems: Vol. 2. ICTIS. Smart Innovation, Systems and Technologies (vol. 84, pp. 579-586). Springer. doi:10.1007/978-3-319-63645-0_64

Rath, M. (2017). Resource provision and QoS support with added security for client side applications in cloud computing. *International Journal of Information Technology, 9*(3), 1–8.

Rath, M., & Pati, B. (2017). *Load balanced routing scheme for MANETs with power and delay optimization. International Journal of Communication Network and Distributed Systems* , 19.

Rath, M., Pati, B., Panigrahi, C. R., & Sarkar, J. L. (2019). QTM: A QoS Task Monitoring System for Mobile Ad hoc Networks. In P. Sa, S. Bakshi, I. Hatzilygeroudis, & M. Sahoo (Eds.), *Recent Findings in Intelligent Computing Techniques. Advances in Intelligent Systems and Computing* (Vol. 707). Singapore: Springer. doi:10.1007/978-981-10-8639-7_57

Rath, M., Pati, B., & Pattanayak, B. K. (2017). Cross layer based QoS platform for multimedia transmission in MANET. *11th International Conference on Intelligent Systems and Control (ISCO)*, 402-407. 10.1109/ISCO.2017.7856026

Rath, M., & Pattanayak, B. (2017). MAQ: A Mobile Agent Based QoS Platform for MANETs. *International Journal of Business Data Communications and Networking, IGI Global, 13*(1), 1–8. doi:10.4018/IJBDCN.2017010101

Rath, M., & Pattanayak, B. K. (2018). SCICS: A Soft Computing Based Intelligent Communication System in VANET. Smart Secure Systems – IoT and Analytics Perspective. *Communications in Computer and Information Science, 808*, 255–261. doi:10.1007/978-981-10-7635-0_19

Rath, M., Pattanayak, B. K., & Pati, B. (2017). *Energetic Routing Protocol Design for Real-time Transmission in Mobile Ad hoc Network., Computing and Network Sustainability. Lecture Notes in Networks and Systems* (Vol. 12). Singapore: Springer.

Rav, Wong, Deligianni, Berthelot, Andreu-Perez, Lo, & Yang. (2017, January). Deep Learning for Health Informatics. *IEEE Journal of Biomedical and Health Informatics, 21*(1).

Razzaque & Dobson. (2014). *Energy-Efficient Sensing In Wireless Sensor Networks Using Compressed Sensing Sensors.* Academic Press.

Rebbeck, T., Mackenzie, M., & Afonso, Z. (2014). *Low-powered wireless solutions have the potential to increase the m2m market by over 3 billion connections.* Academic Press.

Reinhardt, A., Christin, D., Hollick, M., Schmitt, J., Mogre, P. S., & Steinmetz, R. (2010). Trimming the tree: Tailoring adaptive Huffman coding to wireless sensor networks. *Wireless Sensor Networks, 5970*, 33–48. doi:10.1007/978-3-642-11917-0_3

Rezaei & Mobininejad. (2012). Energy Saving In Wireless Sensor Networks. *International Journal of Computer Science & Engineering Survey*, 23-37.

Rice, R., Phillips, P., Stewart-Leslie, J., & Sibbett, G. (2003). Olive fruit fly populations measured in central and southern California. *California Agriculture, 57*(4), 122-7.

Rosa, L., Rodrigues, L., Lopes, A., Hiltunen, M. A., & Schlitching, R. D. (2013). Self-management of adaptable component-based applications. *IEEE Transactions on Software Engineering, 39*(3), 403–421. doi:10.1109/TSE.2012.29

Rouse, M. (2018). *What is internet of things (IoT)?* Retrieved 8 1, 2018, from internetofthingsagenda.com: https://internetofthingsagenda.techtarget.com/definition/Internet-of-Things-IoT

Rouse, M. (2018). *What is MQTT?* Retrieved 8 1, 2018, from https://internetofthingsagenda.techtarget.com/definition/MQTT-MQ-Telemetry-Transport

Rtah, M. (2018). Big Data and IoT-Allied Challenges Associated With Healthcare Applications in Smart and Automated Systems. *International Journal of Strategic Information Technology and Applications*, 9(2). doi:10.4018/IJSITA.201804010

Sakthipriya, N. (2014). An effective method for crop monitoring using wireless sensor network. *Middle East Journal of Scientific Research*, 20(9), 1127–1132.

Salehie, M., & Tahvildan, L. (2009). Self-Adaptive Software: Landscape and research challenges. *ACM, TAAS, 4*(2), 14.

Samie, F., Souras, V. T., Xydis, S., Bauer, L., Soudris, D., & Henkel, J. (2016). *Distributed QoS Management for Internet of Things under Resource Constraints.* ACM. doi:10.1145/2968456.2974005

Samuel, S.J., Sashidhar, K., & Bharathi, C.R. (2015, May). A survey on big data and its research challenges. *ARPN J. Eng. Appl. Sci., 10*(8), 3343–3347.

Sarabia-Jácome, D., Gonzalez-Usach, R., & Palau, C. E. (2019). IoT Big Data Architectures, Approaches, and Challenges: A Fog-Cloud Approach. In Handbook of Research on Big Data and the IoT (pp. 125-148). IGI Global.

Satija, Ramkumar, & Manikandan. (2017, June). Real-Time Signal Quality-Aware ECG Telemetry System for IoT-Based Health Care Monitoring. *IEEE Internet of Things Journal, 4*(3).

Satyanarayanan, M. (2017). The emergence of edge computing. *Computer, 50*(1), 30–39. doi:10.1109/MC.2017.9

Satyanarayanan, M., Bahl, P., Caceres, R., & Davies, N. (2009). The case for VM-base cloudlets in mobile computing. *Pervasive Comput., 8*(4), 14–23. doi:10.1109/MPRV.2009.82

Satyanarayanan, M., Lewis, G., Morris, E., Simanta, S., Boleng, J., & Ha, K. (2013). The Role of Cloudlets in Hostile Environments. *IEEE Pervasive Computing, 12*(4), 40–49. doi:10.1109/MPRV.2013.77

Satyanarayanan, M., Schuster, R., Ebling, M., Fettweis, G., Flinck, H., Joshi, K., & Sabnani, K. (2015). An open ecosystem for mobile-cloud convergence. *IEEE Communications Magazine, 53*(3), 63–70. doi:10.1109/MCOM.2015.7060484

Server., B.R.A. (2004). Technical Report DSL Forum TR-092.

Shahzadi, S., Iqbal, M., Dagiuklas, T., & Qayyum, Z. U. (2017). Multi-access edge computing: Open issues, challenges and future perspectives. *Journal of Cloud Computing*, *6*(1), 30.

Shelby, Hartke, & Bormann. (2014). *RFC 7252 - The Constrained Application Protocol (CoAP)*. Retrieved 8 9, 2018, from https://tools.ietf.org/html/rfc7252

Sheng, Z., Yang, S., Yu, Y., Vasilakos, A., Mccann, J., & Leung, K. (2013, December). A survey on the IETF protocol suite for the Internet of Things: Standards, challenges, and opportunities. *IEEE Wireless Communications*, *20*(6), 91–98. doi:10.1109/MWC.2013.6704479

Shen, S., & Carug, M. (2014). An Evolutionary Way to Standardize the Internet of Things. *J. ICT Stand.*, *2*(2), 87–108. doi:10.13052/jicts2245-800X.222

Shin, J. H., Lee, B., & Park, K. S. (2011). Detection of abnormal living patterns for elderly living alone using support vector data description. Information Technology in Biomedicine. *IEEE Transactions on*, *15*(3), 438–448. PMID:21317086

Shivashankar, V., Kuter, U., Nau, D., & Alford, R. (2012). A Hierarchical Goal-Based Formalism and Algorithm for Single-Agent Planning. *Proceedings of the 11th Conference on Autonomous Agents and Multiagent Systems (AAMAS 2012)*, 981-989.

Shi, W., Cao, J., Zhang, Q., Li, Y., & Xu, L. (2016). Edge computing: Vision and challenges. *IEEE Internet of Things Journal*, *3*(5), 637–646. doi:10.1109/JIOT.2016.2579198

Shi, W., & Dustdar, S. (2016). The Promise of Edge Computing. *Computer*, *49*(5), 78–81. doi:10.1109/MC.2016.145

Shi, Y., Wang, Z., Wang, X., & Zhang, S. (2015). Internet of things application to monitoring plant disease and insect pests. *International Conference on Applied Science and Engineering Innovation (ASEI 2015)*, 31-34. 10.2991/asei-15.2015.7

Shron, M. (2014). *Thinking with Data: How to Turn Information Into Insights*. O'Reilly Media, Inc.

Shyam, G. K., & Manvi, S. S. (2015). Modelling resource virtualisation concept in cloud computing environment using finite state machines. *International Journal of Cloud Computing*, *4*(3), 258–278. doi:10.1504/IJCC.2015.071731

Shyam, G. K., & Manvi, S. S. (2016). Virtual resource prediction in cloud environment: A Bayesian approach. *Journal of Network and Computer Applications, 65*, 144–154. doi:10.1016/j.jnca.2016.03.002

Singh, V., Mani, A., & Pentland, A. (2014). Social persuasion in online and physical networks. *Proceedings of the IEEE, 102*(12), 1903–1910. doi:10.1109/JPROC.2014.2363986

Siponen, M. T., & Willison, R. (2009). Information Security Management Standards: Problems and Solutions. *Information & Management, 46*(5), 267–270. doi:10.1016/j.im.2008.12.007

Siryani, Tanju, & Eveleigh. (2017). A Machine Learning Decision-Support System Improves the Internet of Things' Smart Meter Operations. *IEEE Internet of Things Journal, 4*(4).

Soltani, S., Asadi, M., Gasevic, D., Hatala, M., & Bagheri, E. (2012). Automated Planning for Feature Model Configuration based on Functional and Non-Functional Requirements. In *SPLC* (pp. 201–214). ACM. doi:10.1145/2362536.2362548

Somayya Madakam, R. (2015). Ramaswamy & Siddharth Tripathi (2015) Internet of Things (IoT): A Literature Review. *Journal of Computer and Communications, 3*(05), 164–173. doi:10.4236/jcc.2015.35021

Srivastava, M. B., Muntz, R. R., & Potkonjak, M. (2001). Smart Kindergarten: Sensor-Based Wireless Networks For Smart Developmental Problem-Solving Environments. *In Mobile Computer Networks*, 132–138.

Stankovic, J. A. (2014). Research directions for the Internet of Things. *IEEE Internet of Things Journal, 1*(1), 3–9. doi:10.1109/JIOT.2014.2312291

Sun, E., Zhang, X., & Li, Z. (2012). The Internet of Things (IOT) and cloud computing (CC) based tailings dam monitoring and pre-alarm system in mines. *Safety Science, 50*(4), 811–815. doi:10.1016/j.ssci.2011.08.028

Sun, Y., Yan, H., Lu, C., Bie, R., & Thomas, P. (2012). A holistic approach to visualizing business models for the internet of things. *Communications in Mobile Computing, 1*(1), 1–7. doi:10.1186/2192-1121-1-4

Tanaka, K., Suda, T., Hirai, K., Sako, K., Fuakgawa, R., Shimamura, M., & Togari, A. (2009, October). Monitoring of soil moisture and groundwater levels using ultrasonic waves to predict slope failures. In SENSORS, 2009 IEEE (pp. 617-620). IEEE. doi:10.1109/ICSENS.2009.5398322

Tharakan & Dhanasekaran. (2014). *SEEMd -Security enabled Energy Efficient Middleware for WSN*. IEEE.

Tharakan & Dhanasekaran. (2015a). Energy Aware Data Compression in Wireless Sensor Network using an advanced RLE method – Matrix RLE (M-RLE). *International Journal of Applied Engineering Research, 10*(17), 13358–13364.

Tharakan & Dhanasekaran. (2015b). Data compression in Wireless Sensor Network associated with a noble Encryption method using Quine-Mc Cluskey Boolean function reduction method. *International Journal of Applied Engineering Research, 10*(55), 3470–3474.

Tharakan & Dhanasekaran. (2016). Energy and coverage efficiency using straight line node deployment with data compression in Wireless sensor network. IEEE.

Tibor, B., Mark, H., Michel, C. A. K., & Jan, T. (2011). An ambient agent model for monitoring and analysing dynamics of complex human behavior. *Journal of Ambient Intelligence and Smart Environments, 3*(4), 283–303.

Tokognon, Gao, Tian, & Yan. (2017, June). Structural Health Monitoring Framework Based on Internet of Things: A Survey. *IEEE Internet of Things Journal, 4*(3).

Tortonesi, M., Govoni, M., Morelli, A., Riberto, G., Stefanelli, C., & Suri, N. (2019). Taming the IoT data deluge: An innovative information-centric service model for fog computing applications. *Future Generation Computer Systems, 93*, 888–902. doi:10.1016/j.future.2018.06.009

Tukey, J. W. (1980). We need both exploratory and confirmatory. *The American Statistician, 34*(1), 23–25.

Ustundag, A., & Cevikcan, E. (2018). *Industry 4.0: Managing The Digital Transformation*. Springer Series in Advanced Manufacturing; doi:10.1007/978-3-319-57870-5

Vakulenko, M. (2016). *What can a toothbrush teach us about IoT business models?* Academic Press.

Van Henten, E.J., Hemming, J., Van Tuijl, B.A., Kornet, J.G., Meuleman, J., Bontsema, J., & Van Os, E.A. (2002). An autonomous robot for harvesting cucumbers in greenhouses. *Autonomous Robots, 13*(3), 241-58.

Vaquero, L. M., & Rodero-Merino, L. (2014). Finding your way in the fog: Towards a comprehensive definition of fog computing. *Computer Communication Review*, *44*(5), 27–32. doi:10.1145/2677046.2677052

Vashi, S., Ram, J., Modi, J., Verma, S., & Prakash, C. (2017). Internet of Things (IoT): A vision, architectural elements, and security issues. In *Proceedings of the International Conference on I-SMAC (IoT in Social, Mobile, Analytics and Cloud)*. 10.1109/I-SMAC.2017.8058399

Verma, P., & Sood, S. K. (2018). Cloud-centric IoT based disease diagnosis healthcare framework. *Journal of Parallel and Distributed Computing, 116*, 27-38.

Vermesan, O. (2013). Internet of Things strategic research and innovation agenda. In Internet of Things: Converging Technologies for Smart Environments and Integrated Ecosystems. River Publishers.

Vidhyapriya, R., & Vanathi, P. (2009). Energy Efficient Data Compression in Wireless Sensor Networks. *The International Arab Journal of Information Technology*, *6*(3), 297–303.

Vieira, M. A. M., Coelho, C. N., Da Silva, D. C., & Da Mata, J. M. (2003). Survey On Wireless Sensor Network Devices. *Emerging Technologies And Factory Automation*, *1*, 537–544.

Villamizar, M., Garcés, O., Ochoa, L., Castro, H., Salamanca, L., Verano, M., ... Lang, M. (2017). Cost comparison of running web applications in the cloud using monolithic, microservice, and aws lambda architectures. *Service Oriented Computing and Applications*, *11*(2), 233–247. doi:10.100711761-017-0208-y

Vippalapalli, V., & Ananthula, S. (2017). Internet of things (IoT) based smart health care system. In *International Conference on Signal Processing, Communication, Power and Embedded System (SCOPES)*. IEEE.

Vodafone. (2016). *Software Defined Networking and Network Function Visualization*. Retrieved 7 25, 2018, from www.vodafone.com/business/news-and-insights/blog/gigabit-thinking/software-defined-networking-and-network-function-virtualisation

Wang, Kung, Yu, Wang, & Cegielski. (2017). An integrated big data analytics-enabled transformation model: Application to health care. *Information & Management*. doi:10.1016/j.im.2017.04.001

Wang, Q., Terzis, A., & Szalay, A. (2010, May). A novel soil measuring wireless sensor network. In *2010 IEEE Instrumentation & Measurement Technology Conference Proceedings* (pp. 412-415). IEEE. 10.1109/IMTC.2010.5488224

Wang, Y., Attebury, G., & Ramamurthy, B. (2006). A Survey Of Security Issues In Wireless Sensor Networks. *IEEE Communications Surveys and Tutorials*, *8*(2), 2–23. doi:10.1109/COMST.2006.315852

Want, R. (2015). The physical web. *Workshop on IoT Challenges in Mobile and Industrial Systems, 1*(1).

Webb, G. T., Vardanega, P. G., & Middleton, C. R. (2015, November). Categories of SHM deployments: Technologies and capabilities. *Journal of Bridge Engineering*, *20*(11), 04014118. doi:10.1061/(ASCE)BE.1943-5592.0000735

Weber, R. (2010). Internet of Things - New security and privacy challenges. *Computer Law & Security Review*, *26*(1), 23–30. doi:10.1016/j.clsr.2009.11.008

Weinberger, M., Bilgeri, D., & Fleisch, E. (2016). IoT business models in an industrial context. *Automatisierungstechnik*, *64*(9), 699–706. doi:10.1515/auto-2016-0054

Westerlund, M., Leminen, S., & Rajahonka, M. (2014). Designing Business Models for the Internet of Things. *Technology Innovation Management Review*, 345-389.

Wigmore, I. (2014). Internet of Things (IoT). *TechTarget*. Available: http://whatis.techtarget.comldefinition/Internet-of-Things

Williams, S., Hardy, C., & Nitschke, P. (2019, January). Configuring the Internet of Things (IoT): A Review and Implications for Big Data Analytics. *Proceedings of the 52nd Hawaii International Conference on System Sciences*. 10.24251/HICSS.2019.706

Wirtz, B. W., Pistoia, A., Ullrich, S., & Göttel, V. (2016). Business models: Origin, development and future research perspectives. *Long Range Planning*, *49*(1), 36–54. doi:10.1016/j.lrp.2015.04.001

Wu, Q. (2014). Cognitive Internet of Things: A New Paradigm beyond Connection. *IEEE Internet of Things Journal, 1*(2).

Wu, Rendall, Smith, Zhu, & Xu. (2017, June). Survey on Prediction Algorithms in Smart Homes. *IEEE Internet of Things Journal, 4*(3).

Xavier, M. G., Neves, M. V., Rossi, F. D., Ferreto, T. C., Lange, T., & De Rose, C. A. (2013). Performance evaluation of container-based virtualization for high performance computing environments. In *Proceedings of the 21st Euromicro International Conference* on *Parallel, Distributed and Network-Based Processing (PDP)* (pp. 233-240). 10.1109/PDP.2013.41

Xu, He, & Li. (2014, November). Internet of Things in Industries: A Survey. *IEEE Transactions on Industrial Informatics, 10*(4).

Yassine, A., Singh, S., Hossain, M. S., & Muhammad, G. (2019). IoT big data analytics for smart homes with fog and cloud computing. *Future Generation Computer Systems*, *91*, 563–573. doi:10.1016/j.future.2018.08.040

Yi, S., Qin, Z., & Li, Q. (2015). Security and privacy issues of fog computing: A survey. In *Proceedings of the International conference on wireless algorithms, systems, and applications*. Cham: Springer. 10.1007/978-3-319-21837-3_67

Yu, W., Liang, F., He, X., Hatcher, W., Lu, C., Lin, J., & Yang, X. (2018). A Survey on the Edge Computing for the Internet of Things. *IEEE Access*, *6*, 6900–6919. doi:10.1109/ACCESS.2017.2778504

Zanella, A., Bui, N., Castellani, A., Vangelista, L., & Zorz, M. (2014). Internet of Things for Smart Cities. *IEEE Internet Things J*, *1*(1), 22–32. doi:10.1109/JIOT.2014.2306328

Zhang, Li, Wen, Xun, & Liu. (2018, June). Connecting Intelligent Things in Smart Hospitals Using NB-IoT. *IEEE Internet of Things Journal, 5*(3).

Zhao, Z., Min, G., Gao, W., Wu, Y., Duan, H., & Ni, Q. (2018). Deploying edge computing nodes for large-scale IoT: A diversity aware approach. *IEEE Internet of Things Journal*, *5*(5), 3606–3614.

Related References

To continue our tradition of advancing information science and technology research, we have compiled a list of recommended IGI Global readings. These references will provide additional information and guidance to further enrich your knowledge and assist you with your own research and future publications.

Aasi, P., Rusu, L., & Vieru, D. (2017). The Role of Culture in IT Governance Five Focus Areas: A Literature Review. *International Journal of IT/Business Alignment and Governance, 8*(2), 42-61. doi:10.4018/IJITBAG.2017070103

Abdrabo, A. A. (2018). Egypt's Knowledge-Based Development: Opportunities, Challenges, and Future Possibilities. In A. Alraouf (Ed.), *Knowledge-Based Urban Development in the Middle East* (pp. 80–101). Hershey, PA: IGI Global. doi:10.4018/978-1-5225-3734-2.ch005

Abu Doush, I., & Alhami, I. (2018). Evaluating the Accessibility of Computer Laboratories, Libraries, and Websites in Jordanian Universities and Colleges. *International Journal of Information Systems and Social Change, 9*(2), 44–60. doi:10.4018/IJISSC.2018040104

Adeboye, A. (2016). Perceived Use and Acceptance of Cloud Enterprise Resource Planning (ERP) Implementation in the Manufacturing Industries. *International Journal of Strategic Information Technology and Applications, 7*(3), 24–40. doi:10.4018/IJSITA.2016070102

Adegbore, A. M., Quadri, M. O., & Oyewo, O. R. (2018). A Theoretical Approach to the Adoption of Electronic Resource Management Systems (ERMS) in Nigerian University Libraries. In A. Tella & T. Kwanya (Eds.), *Handbook of Research on Managing Intellectual Property in Digital Libraries* (pp. 292–311). Hershey, PA: IGI Global. doi:10.4018/978-1-5225-3093-0. ch015

Adhikari, M., & Roy, D. (2016). Green Computing. In G. Deka, G. Siddesh, K. Srinivasa, & L. Patnaik (Eds.), *Emerging Research Surrounding Power Consumption and Performance Issues in Utility Computing* (pp. 84–108). Hershey, PA: IGI Global. doi:10.4018/978-1-4666-8853-7.ch005

Afolabi, O. A. (2018). Myths and Challenges of Building an Effective Digital Library in Developing Nations: An African Perspective. In A. Tella & T. Kwanya (Eds.), *Handbook of Research on Managing Intellectual Property in Digital Libraries* (pp. 51–79). Hershey, PA: IGI Global. doi:10.4018/978-1-5225-3093-0.ch004

Agarwal, R., Singh, A., & Sen, S. (2016). Role of Molecular Docking in Computer-Aided Drug Design and Development. In S. Dastmalchi, M. Hamzeh-Mivehroud, & B. Sokouti (Eds.), *Applied Case Studies and Solutions in Molecular Docking-Based Drug Design* (pp. 1–28). Hershey, PA: IGI Global. doi:10.4018/978-1-5225-0362-0.ch001

Ali, O., & Soar, J. (2016). Technology Innovation Adoption Theories. In L. Al-Hakim, X. Wu, A. Koronios, & Y. Shou (Eds.), *Handbook of Research on Driving Competitive Advantage through Sustainable, Lean, and Disruptive Innovation* (pp. 1–38). Hershey, PA: IGI Global. doi:10.4018/978-1-5225-0135-0.ch001

Alsharo, M. (2017). Attitudes Towards Cloud Computing Adoption in Emerging Economies. *International Journal of Cloud Applications and Computing, 7*(3), 44–58. doi:10.4018/IJCAC.2017070102

Amer, T. S., & Johnson, T. L. (2016). Information Technology Progress Indicators: Temporal Expectancy, User Preference, and the Perception of Process Duration. *International Journal of Technology and Human Interaction, 12*(4), 1–14. doi:10.4018/IJTHI.2016100101

Amer, T. S., & Johnson, T. L. (2017). Information Technology Progress Indicators: Research Employing Psychological Frameworks. In A. Mesquita (Ed.), *Research Paradigms and Contemporary Perspectives on Human-Technology Interaction* (pp. 168–186). Hershey, PA: IGI Global. doi:10.4018/978-1-5225-1868-6.ch008

Anchugam, C. V., & Thangadurai, K. (2016). Introduction to Network Security. In D. G., M. Singh, & M. Jayanthi (Eds.), Network Security Attacks and Countermeasures (pp. 1-48). Hershey, PA: IGI Global. doi:10.4018/978-1-4666-8761-5.ch001

Anchugam, C. V., & Thangadurai, K. (2016). Classification of Network Attacks and Countermeasures of Different Attacks. In D. G., M. Singh, & M. Jayanthi (Eds.), Network Security Attacks and Countermeasures (pp. 115-156). Hershey, PA: IGI Global. doi:10.4018/978-1-4666-8761-5.ch004

Anohah, E. (2016). Pedagogy and Design of Online Learning Environment in Computer Science Education for High Schools. *International Journal of Online Pedagogy and Course Design*, *6*(3), 39–51. doi:10.4018/IJOPCD.2016070104

Anohah, E. (2017). Paradigm and Architecture of Computing Augmented Learning Management System for Computer Science Education. *International Journal of Online Pedagogy and Course Design*, *7*(2), 60–70. doi:10.4018/IJOPCD.2017040105

Anohah, E., & Suhonen, J. (2017). Trends of Mobile Learning in Computing Education from 2006 to 2014: A Systematic Review of Research Publications. *International Journal of Mobile and Blended Learning*, *9*(1), 16–33. doi:10.4018/IJMBL.2017010102

Assis-Hassid, S., Heart, T., Reychav, I., & Pliskin, J. S. (2016). Modelling Factors Affecting Patient-Doctor-Computer Communication in Primary Care. *International Journal of Reliable and Quality E-Healthcare*, *5*(1), 1–17. doi:10.4018/IJRQEH.2016010101

Bailey, E. K. (2017). Applying Learning Theories to Computer Technology Supported Instruction. In M. Grassetti & S. Brookby (Eds.), *Advancing Next-Generation Teacher Education through Digital Tools and Applications* (pp. 61–81). Hershey, PA: IGI Global. doi:10.4018/978-1-5225-0965-3.ch004

Balasubramanian, K. (2016). Attacks on Online Banking and Commerce. In K. Balasubramanian, K. Mala, & M. Rajakani (Eds.), *Cryptographic Solutions for Secure Online Banking and Commerce* (pp. 1–19). Hershey, PA: IGI Global. doi:10.4018/978-1-5225-0273-9.ch001

Baldwin, S., Opoku-Agyemang, K., & Roy, D. (2016). Games People Play: A Trilateral Collaboration Researching Computer Gaming across Cultures. In K. Valentine & L. Jensen (Eds.), *Examining the Evolution of Gaming and Its Impact on Social, Cultural, and Political Perspectives* (pp. 364–376). Hershey, PA: IGI Global. doi:10.4018/978-1-5225-0261-6.ch017

Banerjee, S., Sing, T. Y., Chowdhury, A. R., & Anwar, H. (2018). Let's Go Green: Towards a Taxonomy of Green Computing Enablers for Business Sustainability. In M. Khosrow-Pour (Ed.), *Green Computing Strategies for Competitive Advantage and Business Sustainability* (pp. 89–109). Hershey, PA: IGI Global. doi:10.4018/978-1-5225-5017-4.ch005

Basham, R. (2018). Information Science and Technology in Crisis Response and Management. In M. Khosrow-Pour, D.B.A. (Ed.), Encyclopedia of Information Science and Technology, Fourth Edition (pp. 1407-1418). Hershey, PA: IGI Global. doi:10.4018/978-1-5225-2255-3.ch121

Batyashe, T., & Iyamu, T. (2018). Architectural Framework for the Implementation of Information Technology Governance in Organisations. In M. Khosrow-Pour, D.B.A. (Ed.), Encyclopedia of Information Science and Technology, Fourth Edition (pp. 810-819). Hershey, PA: IGI Global. doi:10.4018/978-1-5225-2255-3.ch070

Bekleyen, N., & Çelik, S. (2017). Attitudes of Adult EFL Learners towards Preparing for a Language Test via CALL. In D. Tafazoli & M. Romero (Eds.), *Multiculturalism and Technology-Enhanced Language Learning* (pp. 214–229). Hershey, PA: IGI Global. doi:10.4018/978-1-5225-1882-2.ch013

Bennett, A., Eglash, R., Lachney, M., & Babbitt, W. (2016). Design Agency: Diversifying Computer Science at the Intersections of Creativity and Culture. In M. Raisinghani (Ed.), *Revolutionizing Education through Web-Based Instruction* (pp. 35–56). Hershey, PA: IGI Global. doi:10.4018/978-1-4666-9932-8.ch003

Bergeron, F., Croteau, A., Uwizeyemungu, S., & Raymond, L. (2017). A Framework for Research on Information Technology Governance in SMEs. In S. De Haes & W. Van Grembergen (Eds.), *Strategic IT Governance and Alignment in Business Settings* (pp. 53–81). Hershey, PA: IGI Global. doi:10.4018/978-1-5225-0861-8.ch003

Bhatt, G. D., Wang, Z., & Rodger, J. A. (2017). Information Systems Capabilities and Their Effects on Competitive Advantages: A Study of Chinese Companies. *Information Resources Management Journal, 30*(3), 41–57. doi:10.4018/IRMJ.2017070103

Bogdanoski, M., Stoilkovski, M., & Risteski, A. (2016). Novel First Responder Digital Forensics Tool as a Support to Law Enforcement. In M. Hadji-Janev & M. Bogdanoski (Eds.), *Handbook of Research on Civil Society and National Security in the Era of Cyber Warfare* (pp. 352–376). Hershey, PA: IGI Global. doi:10.4018/978-1-4666-8793-6.ch016

Boontarig, W., Papasratorn, B., & Chutimaskul, W. (2016). The Unified Model for Acceptance and Use of Health Information on Online Social Networks: Evidence from Thailand. *International Journal of E-Health and Medical Communications, 7*(1), 31–47. doi:10.4018/IJEHMC.2016010102

Brown, S., & Yuan, X. (2016). Techniques for Retaining Computer Science Students at Historical Black Colleges and Universities. In C. Prince & R. Ford (Eds.), *Setting a New Agenda for Student Engagement and Retention in Historically Black Colleges and Universities* (pp. 251–268). Hershey, PA: IGI Global. doi:10.4018/978-1-5225-0308-8.ch014

Burcoff, A., & Shamir, L. (2017). Computer Analysis of Pablo Picasso's Artistic Style. *International Journal of Art, Culture and Design Technologies, 6*(1), 1–18. doi:10.4018/IJACDT.2017010101

Byker, E. J. (2017). I Play I Learn: Introducing Technological Play Theory. In C. Martin & D. Polly (Eds.), *Handbook of Research on Teacher Education and Professional Development* (pp. 297–306). Hershey, PA: IGI Global. doi:10.4018/978-1-5225-1067-3.ch016

Calongne, C. M., Stricker, A. G., Truman, B., & Arenas, F. J. (2017). Cognitive Apprenticeship and Computer Science Education in Cyberspace: Reimagining the Past. In A. Stricker, C. Calongne, B. Truman, & F. Arenas (Eds.), *Integrating an Awareness of Selfhood and Society into Virtual Learning* (pp. 180–197). Hershey, PA: IGI Global. doi:10.4018/978-1-5225-2182-2.ch013

Carlton, E. L., Holsinger, J. W. Jr, & Anunobi, N. (2016). Physician Engagement with Health Information Technology: Implications for Practice and Professionalism. *International Journal of Computers in Clinical Practice*, *1*(2), 51–73. doi:10.4018/IJCCP.2016070103

Carneiro, A. D. (2017). Defending Information Networks in Cyberspace: Some Notes on Security Needs. In M. Dawson, D. Kisku, P. Gupta, J. Sing, & W. Li (Eds.), Developing Next-Generation Countermeasures for Homeland Security Threat Prevention (pp. 354-375). Hershey, PA: IGI Global. doi:10.4018/978-1-5225-0703-1.ch016

Cavalcanti, J. C. (2016). The New "ABC" of ICTs (Analytics + Big Data + Cloud Computing): A Complex Trade-Off between IT and CT Costs. In J. Martins & A. Molnar (Eds.), *Handbook of Research on Innovations in Information Retrieval, Analysis, and Management* (pp. 152–186). Hershey, PA: IGI Global. doi:10.4018/978-1-4666-8833-9.ch006

Chase, J. P., & Yan, Z. (2017). Affect in Statistics Cognition. In *Assessing and Measuring Statistics Cognition in Higher Education Online Environments: Emerging Research and Opportunities* (pp. 144–187). Hershey, PA: IGI Global. doi:10.4018/978-1-5225-2420-5.ch005

Chen, C. (2016). Effective Learning Strategies for the 21st Century: Implications for the E-Learning. In M. Anderson & C. Gavan (Eds.), *Developing Effective Educational Experiences through Learning Analytics* (pp. 143–169). Hershey, PA: IGI Global. doi:10.4018/978-1-4666-9983-0.ch006

Chen, E. T. (2016). Examining the Influence of Information Technology on Modern Health Care. In P. Manolitzas, E. Grigoroudis, N. Matsatsinis, & D. Yannacopoulos (Eds.), *Effective Methods for Modern Healthcare Service Quality and Evaluation* (pp. 110–136). Hershey, PA: IGI Global. doi:10.4018/978-1-4666-9961-8.ch006

Cimermanova, I. (2017). Computer-Assisted Learning in Slovakia. In D. Tafazoli & M. Romero (Eds.), *Multiculturalism and Technology-Enhanced Language Learning* (pp. 252–270). Hershey, PA: IGI Global. doi:10.4018/978-1-5225-1882-2.ch015

Cipolla-Ficarra, F. V., & Cipolla-Ficarra, M. (2018). Computer Animation for Ingenious Revival. In F. Cipolla-Ficarra, M. Ficarra, M. Cipolla-Ficarra, A. Quiroga, J. Alma, & J. Carré (Eds.), *Technology-Enhanced Human Interaction in Modern Society* (pp. 159–181). Hershey, PA: IGI Global. doi:10.4018/978-1-5225-3437-2.ch008

Cockrell, S., Damron, T. S., Melton, A. M., & Smith, A. D. (2018). Offshoring IT. In M. Khosrow-Pour, D.B.A. (Ed.), Encyclopedia of Information Science and Technology, Fourth Edition (pp. 5476-5489). Hershey, PA: IGI Global. doi:10.4018/978-1-5225-2255-3.ch476

Coffey, J. W. (2018). Logic and Proof in Computer Science: Categories and Limits of Proof Techniques. In J. Horne (Ed.), *Philosophical Perceptions on Logic and Order* (pp. 218–240). Hershey, PA: IGI Global. doi:10.4018/978-1-5225-2443-4.ch007

Dale, M. (2017). Re-Thinking the Challenges of Enterprise Architecture Implementation. In M. Tavana (Ed.), *Enterprise Information Systems and the Digitalization of Business Functions* (pp. 205–221). Hershey, PA: IGI Global. doi:10.4018/978-1-5225-2382-6.ch009

Das, A., Dasgupta, R., & Bagchi, A. (2016). Overview of Cellular Computing-Basic Principles and Applications. In J. Mandal, S. Mukhopadhyay, & T. Pal (Eds.), *Handbook of Research on Natural Computing for Optimization Problems* (pp. 637–662). Hershey, PA: IGI Global. doi:10.4018/978-1-5225-0058-2.ch026

De Maere, K., De Haes, S., & von Kutzschenbach, M. (2017). CIO Perspectives on Organizational Learning within the Context of IT Governance. *International Journal of IT/Business Alignment and Governance, 8*(1), 32-47. doi:10.4018/IJITBAG.2017010103

Demir, K., Çaka, C., Yaman, N. D., İslamoğlu, H., & Kuzu, A. (2018). Examining the Current Definitions of Computational Thinking. In H. Ozcinar, G. Wong, & H. Ozturk (Eds.), *Teaching Computational Thinking in Primary Education* (pp. 36–64). Hershey, PA: IGI Global. doi:10.4018/978-1-5225-3200-2.ch003

Deng, X., Hung, Y., & Lin, C. D. (2017). Design and Analysis of Computer Experiments. In S. Saha, A. Mandal, A. Narasimhamurthy, S. V, & S. Sangam (Eds.), Handbook of Research on Applied Cybernetics and Systems Science (pp. 264-279). Hershey, PA: IGI Global. doi:10.4018/978-1-5225-2498-4. ch013

Denner, J., Martinez, J., & Thiry, H. (2017). Strategies for Engaging Hispanic/ Latino Youth in the US in Computer Science. In Y. Rankin & J. Thomas (Eds.), *Moving Students of Color from Consumers to Producers of Technology* (pp. 24–48). Hershey, PA: IGI Global. doi:10.4018/978-1-5225-2005-4.ch002

Devi, A. (2017). Cyber Crime and Cyber Security: A Quick Glance. In R. Kumar, P. Pattnaik, & P. Pandey (Eds.), *Detecting and Mitigating Robotic Cyber Security Risks* (pp. 160–171). Hershey, PA: IGI Global. doi:10.4018/978-1-5225-2154-9.ch011

Dores, A. R., Barbosa, F., Guerreiro, S., Almeida, I., & Carvalho, I. P. (2016). Computer-Based Neuropsychological Rehabilitation: Virtual Reality and Serious Games. In M. Cruz-Cunha, I. Miranda, R. Martinho, & R. Rijo (Eds.), *Encyclopedia of E-Health and Telemedicine* (pp. 473–485). Hershey, PA: IGI Global. doi:10.4018/978-1-4666-9978-6.ch037

Doshi, N., & Schaefer, G. (2016). Computer-Aided Analysis of Nailfold Capillaroscopy Images. In D. Fotiadis (Ed.), *Handbook of Research on Trends in the Diagnosis and Treatment of Chronic Conditions* (pp. 146–158). Hershey, PA: IGI Global. doi:10.4018/978-1-4666-8828-5.ch007

Doyle, D. J., & Fahy, P. J. (2018). Interactivity in Distance Education and Computer-Aided Learning, With Medical Education Examples. In M. Khosrow-Pour, D.B.A. (Ed.), Encyclopedia of Information Science and Technology, Fourth Edition (pp. 5829-5840). Hershey, PA: IGI Global. doi:10.4018/978-1-5225-2255-3.ch507

Elias, N. I., & Walker, T. W. (2017). Factors that Contribute to Continued Use of E-Training among Healthcare Professionals. In F. Topor (Ed.), *Handbook of Research on Individualism and Identity in the Globalized Digital Age* (pp. 403–429). Hershey, PA: IGI Global. doi:10.4018/978-1-5225-0522-8.ch018

Eloy, S., Dias, M. S., Lopes, P. F., & Vilar, E. (2016). Digital Technologies in Architecture and Engineering: Exploring an Engaged Interaction within Curricula. In D. Fonseca & E. Redondo (Eds.), *Handbook of Research on Applied E-Learning in Engineering and Architecture Education* (pp. 368–402). Hershey, PA: IGI Global. doi:10.4018/978-1-4666-8803-2.ch017

Estrela, V. V., Magalhães, H. A., & Saotome, O. (2016). Total Variation Applications in Computer Vision. In N. Kamila (Ed.), *Handbook of Research on Emerging Perspectives in Intelligent Pattern Recognition, Analysis, and Image Processing* (pp. 41–64). Hershey, PA: IGI Global. doi:10.4018/978-1-4666-8654-0.ch002

Filipovic, N., Radovic, M., Nikolic, D. D., Saveljic, I., Milosevic, Z., Exarchos, T. P., ... Parodi, O. (2016). Computer Predictive Model for Plaque Formation and Progression in the Artery. In D. Fotiadis (Ed.), *Handbook of Research on Trends in the Diagnosis and Treatment of Chronic Conditions* (pp. 279–300). Hershey, PA: IGI Global. doi:10.4018/978-1-4666-8828-5.ch013

Fisher, R. L. (2018). Computer-Assisted Indian Matrimonial Services. In M. Khosrow-Pour, D.B.A. (Ed.), Encyclopedia of Information Science and Technology, Fourth Edition (pp. 4136-4145). Hershey, PA: IGI Global. doi:10.4018/978-1-5225-2255-3.ch358

Fleenor, H. G., & Hodhod, R. (2016). Assessment of Learning and Technology: Computer Science Education. In V. Wang (Ed.), *Handbook of Research on Learning Outcomes and Opportunities in the Digital Age* (pp. 51–78). Hershey, PA: IGI Global. doi:10.4018/978-1-4666-9577-1.ch003

García-Valcárcel, A., & Mena, J. (2016). Information Technology as a Way To Support Collaborative Learning: What In-Service Teachers Think, Know and Do. *Journal of Information Technology Research*, 9(1), 1–17. doi:10.4018/JITR.2016010101

Gardner-McCune, C., & Jimenez, Y. (2017). Historical App Developers: Integrating CS into K-12 through Cross-Disciplinary Projects. In Y. Rankin & J. Thomas (Eds.), *Moving Students of Color from Consumers to Producers of Technology* (pp. 85–112). Hershey, PA: IGI Global. doi:10.4018/978-1-5225-2005-4.ch005

Garvey, G. P. (2016). Exploring Perception, Cognition, and Neural Pathways of Stereo Vision and the Split–Brain Human Computer Interface. In A. Ursyn (Ed.), *Knowledge Visualization and Visual Literacy in Science Education* (pp. 28–76). Hershey, PA: IGI Global. doi:10.4018/978-1-5225-0480-1.ch002

Ghafele, R., & Gibert, B. (2018). Open Growth: The Economic Impact of Open Source Software in the USA. In M. Khosrow-Pour (Ed.), *Optimizing Contemporary Application and Processes in Open Source Software* (pp. 164–197). Hershey, PA: IGI Global. doi:10.4018/978-1-5225-5314-4.ch007

Ghobakhloo, M., & Azar, A. (2018). Information Technology Resources, the Organizational Capability of Lean-Agile Manufacturing, and Business Performance. *Information Resources Management Journal, 31*(2), 47–74. doi:10.4018/IRMJ.2018040103

Gianni, M., & Gotzamani, K. (2016). Integrated Management Systems and Information Management Systems: Common Threads. In P. Papajorgji, F. Pinet, A. Guimarães, & J. Papathanasiou (Eds.), *Automated Enterprise Systems for Maximizing Business Performance* (pp. 195–214). Hershey, PA: IGI Global. doi:10.4018/978-1-4666-8841-4.ch011

Gikandi, J. W. (2017). Computer-Supported Collaborative Learning and Assessment: A Strategy for Developing Online Learning Communities in Continuing Education. In J. Keengwe & G. Onchwari (Eds.), *Handbook of Research on Learner-Centered Pedagogy in Teacher Education and Professional Development* (pp. 309–333). Hershey, PA: IGI Global. doi:10.4018/978-1-5225-0892-2.ch017

Gokhale, A. A., & Machina, K. F. (2017). Development of a Scale to Measure Attitudes toward Information Technology. In L. Tomei (Ed.), *Exploring the New Era of Technology-Infused Education* (pp. 49–64). Hershey, PA: IGI Global. doi:10.4018/978-1-5225-1709-2.ch004

Grace, A., O'Donoghue, J., Mahony, C., Heffernan, T., Molony, D., & Carroll, T. (2016). Computerized Decision Support Systems for Multimorbidity Care: An Urgent Call for Research and Development. In M. Cruz-Cunha, I. Miranda, R. Martinho, & R. Rijo (Eds.), *Encyclopedia of E-Health and Telemedicine* (pp. 486–494). Hershey, PA: IGI Global. doi:10.4018/978-1-4666-9978-6.ch038

Gupta, A., & Singh, O. (2016). Computer Aided Modeling and Finite Element Analysis of Human Elbow. *International Journal of Biomedical and Clinical Engineering*, *5*(1), 31–38. doi:10.4018/IJBCE.2016010104

H., S. K. (2016). Classification of Cybercrimes and Punishments under the Information Technology Act, 2000. In S. Geetha, & A. Phamila (Eds.), *Combating Security Breaches and Criminal Activity in the Digital Sphere* (pp. 57-66). Hershey, PA: IGI Global. doi:10.4018/978-1-5225-0193-0.ch004

Hafeez-Baig, A., Gururajan, R., & Wickramasinghe, N. (2017). Readiness as a Novel Construct of Readiness Acceptance Model (RAM) for the Wireless Handheld Technology. In N. Wickramasinghe (Ed.), *Handbook of Research on Healthcare Administration and Management* (pp. 578–595). Hershey, PA: IGI Global. doi:10.4018/978-1-5225-0920-2.ch035

Hanafizadeh, P., Ghandchi, S., & Asgarimehr, M. (2017). Impact of Information Technology on Lifestyle: A Literature Review and Classification. *International Journal of Virtual Communities and Social Networking*, *9*(2), 1–23. doi:10.4018/IJVCSN.2017040101

Harlow, D. B., Dwyer, H., Hansen, A. K., Hill, C., Iveland, A., Leak, A. E., & Franklin, D. M. (2016). Computer Programming in Elementary and Middle School: Connections across Content. In M. Urban & D. Falvo (Eds.), *Improving K-12 STEM Education Outcomes through Technological Integration* (pp. 337–361). Hershey, PA: IGI Global. doi:10.4018/978-1-4666-9616-7.ch015

Haseski, H. İ., Ilic, U., & Tuğtekin, U. (2018). Computational Thinking in Educational Digital Games: An Assessment Tool Proposal. In H. Ozcinar, G. Wong, & H. Ozturk (Eds.), *Teaching Computational Thinking in Primary Education* (pp. 256–287). Hershey, PA: IGI Global. doi:10.4018/978-1-5225-3200-2.ch013

Hee, W. J., Jalleh, G., Lai, H., & Lin, C. (2017). E-Commerce and IT Projects: Evaluation and Management Issues in Australian and Taiwanese Hospitals. *International Journal of Public Health Management and Ethics*, *2*(1), 69–90. doi:10.4018/IJPHME.2017010104

Hernandez, A. A. (2017). Green Information Technology Usage: Awareness and Practices of Philippine IT Professionals. *International Journal of Enterprise Information Systems*, *13*(4), 90–103. doi:10.4018/IJEIS.2017100106

Hernandez, A. A., & Ona, S. E. (2016). Green IT Adoption: Lessons from the Philippines Business Process Outsourcing Industry. *International Journal of Social Ecology and Sustainable Development*, 7(1), 1–34. doi:10.4018/IJSESD.2016010101

Hernandez, M. A., Marin, E. C., Garcia-Rodriguez, J., Azorin-Lopez, J., & Cazorla, M. (2017). Automatic Learning Improves Human-Robot Interaction in Productive Environments: A Review. *International Journal of Computer Vision and Image Processing*, 7(3), 65–75. doi:10.4018/IJCVIP.2017070106

Horne-Popp, L. M., Tessone, E. B., & Welker, J. (2018). If You Build It, They Will Come: Creating a Library Statistics Dashboard for Decision-Making. In L. Costello & M. Powers (Eds.), *Developing In-House Digital Tools in Library Spaces* (pp. 177–203). Hershey, PA: IGI Global. doi:10.4018/978-1-5225-2676-6.ch009

Hossan, C. G., & Ryan, J. C. (2016). Factors Affecting e-Government Technology Adoption Behaviour in a Voluntary Environment. *International Journal of Electronic Government Research*, 12(1), 24–49. doi:10.4018/IJEGR.2016010102

Hu, H., Hu, P. J., & Al-Gahtani, S. S. (2017). User Acceptance of Computer Technology at Work in Arabian Culture: A Model Comparison Approach. In M. Khosrow-Pour (Ed.), *Handbook of Research on Technology Adoption, Social Policy, and Global Integration* (pp. 205–228). Hershey, PA: IGI Global. doi:10.4018/978-1-5225-2668-1.ch011

Huie, C. P. (2016). Perceptions of Business Intelligence Professionals about Factors Related to Business Intelligence input in Decision Making. *International Journal of Business Analytics*, 3(3), 1–24. doi:10.4018/IJBAN.2016070101

Hung, S., Huang, W., Yen, D. C., Chang, S., & Lu, C. (2016). Effect of Information Service Competence and Contextual Factors on the Effectiveness of Strategic Information Systems Planning in Hospitals. *Journal of Global Information Management*, 24(1), 14–36. doi:10.4018/JGIM.2016010102

Ifinedo, P. (2017). Using an Extended Theory of Planned Behavior to Study Nurses' Adoption of Healthcare Information Systems in Nova Scotia. *International Journal of Technology Diffusion*, 8(1), 1–17. doi:10.4018/IJTD.2017010101

Ilie, V., & Sneha, S. (2018). A Three Country Study for Understanding Physicians' Engagement With Electronic Information Resources Pre and Post System Implementation. *Journal of Global Information Management, 26*(2), 48–73. doi:10.4018/JGIM.2018040103

Inoue-Smith, Y. (2017). Perceived Ease in Using Technology Predicts Teacher Candidates' Preferences for Online Resources. *International Journal of Online Pedagogy and Course Design, 7*(3), 17–28. doi:10.4018/IJOPCD.2017070102

Islam, A. A. (2016). Development and Validation of the Technology Adoption and Gratification (TAG) Model in Higher Education: A Cross-Cultural Study Between Malaysia and China. *International Journal of Technology and Human Interaction, 12*(3), 78–105. doi:10.4018/IJTHI.2016070106

Islam, A. Y. (2017). Technology Satisfaction in an Academic Context: Moderating Effect of Gender. In A. Mesquita (Ed.), *Research Paradigms and Contemporary Perspectives on Human-Technology Interaction* (pp. 187–211). Hershey, PA: IGI Global. doi:10.4018/978-1-5225-1868-6.ch009

Jamil, G. L., & Jamil, C. C. (2017). Information and Knowledge Management Perspective Contributions for Fashion Studies: Observing Logistics and Supply Chain Management Processes. In G. Jamil, A. Soares, & C. Pessoa (Eds.), *Handbook of Research on Information Management for Effective Logistics and Supply Chains* (pp. 199–221). Hershey, PA: IGI Global. doi:10.4018/978-1-5225-0973-8.ch011

Jamil, G. L., Jamil, L. C., Vieira, A. A., & Xavier, A. J. (2016). Challenges in Modelling Healthcare Services: A Study Case of Information Architecture Perspectives. In G. Jamil, J. Poças Rascão, F. Ribeiro, & A. Malheiro da Silva (Eds.), *Handbook of Research on Information Architecture and Management in Modern Organizations* (pp. 1–23). Hershey, PA: IGI Global. doi:10.4018/978-1-4666-8637-3.ch001

Janakova, M. (2018). Big Data and Simulations for the Solution of Controversies in Small Businesses. In M. Khosrow-Pour, D.B.A. (Ed.), Encyclopedia of Information Science and Technology, Fourth Edition (pp. 6907-6915). Hershey, PA: IGI Global. doi:10.4018/978-1-5225-2255-3.ch598

Jha, D. G. (2016). Preparing for Information Technology Driven Changes. In S. Tiwari & L. Nafees (Eds.), *Innovative Management Education Pedagogies for Preparing Next-Generation Leaders* (pp. 258–274). Hershey, PA: IGI Global. doi:10.4018/978-1-4666-9691-4.ch015

Jhawar, A., & Garg, S. K. (2018). Logistics Improvement by Investment in Information Technology Using System Dynamics. In A. Azar & S. Vaidyanathan (Eds.), *Advances in System Dynamics and Control* (pp. 528–567). Hershey, PA: IGI Global. doi:10.4018/978-1-5225-4077-9.ch017

Kalelioğlu, F., Gülbahar, Y., & Doğan, D. (2018). Teaching How to Think Like a Programmer: Emerging Insights. In H. Ozcinar, G. Wong, & H. Ozturk (Eds.), *Teaching Computational Thinking in Primary Education* (pp. 18–35). Hershey, PA: IGI Global. doi:10.4018/978-1-5225-3200-2.ch002

Kamberi, S. (2017). A Girls-Only Online Virtual World Environment and its Implications for Game-Based Learning. In A. Stricker, C. Calongne, B. Truman, & F. Arenas (Eds.), *Integrating an Awareness of Selfhood and Society into Virtual Learning* (pp. 74–95). Hershey, PA: IGI Global. doi:10.4018/978-1-5225-2182-2.ch006

Kamel, S., & Rizk, N. (2017). ICT Strategy Development: From Design to Implementation – Case of Egypt. In C. Howard & K. Hargiss (Eds.), *Strategic Information Systems and Technologies in Modern Organizations* (pp. 239–257). Hershey, PA: IGI Global. doi:10.4018/978-1-5225-1680-4.ch010

Kamel, S. H. (2018). The Potential Role of the Software Industry in Supporting Economic Development. In M. Khosrow-Pour, D.B.A. (Ed.), Encyclopedia of Information Science and Technology, Fourth Edition (pp. 7259-7269). Hershey, PA: IGI Global. doi:10.4018/978-1-5225-2255-3.ch631

Karon, R. (2016). Utilisation of Health Information Systems for Service Delivery in the Namibian Environment. In T. Iyamu & A. Tatnall (Eds.), *Maximizing Healthcare Delivery and Management through Technology Integration* (pp. 169–183). Hershey, PA: IGI Global. doi:10.4018/978-1-4666-9446-0.ch011

Kawata, S. (2018). Computer-Assisted Parallel Program Generation. In M. Khosrow-Pour, D.B.A. (Ed.), Encyclopedia of Information Science and Technology, Fourth Edition (pp. 4583-4593). Hershey, PA: IGI Global. doi:10.4018/978-1-5225-2255-3.ch398

Khanam, S., Siddiqui, J., & Talib, F. (2016). A DEMATEL Approach for Prioritizing the TQM Enablers and IT Resources in the Indian ICT Industry. *International Journal of Applied Management Sciences and Engineering, 3*(1), 11–29. doi:10.4018/IJAMSE.2016010102

Khari, M., Shrivastava, G., Gupta, S., & Gupta, R. (2017). Role of Cyber Security in Today's Scenario. In R. Kumar, P. Pattnaik, & P. Pandey (Eds.), *Detecting and Mitigating Robotic Cyber Security Risks* (pp. 177–191). Hershey, PA: IGI Global. doi:10.4018/978-1-5225-2154-9.ch013

Khouja, M., Rodriguez, I. B., Ben Halima, Y., & Moalla, S. (2018). IT Governance in Higher Education Institutions: A Systematic Literature Review. *International Journal of Human Capital and Information Technology Professionals*, 9(2), 52–67. doi:10.4018/IJHCITP.2018040104

Kim, S., Chang, M., Choi, N., Park, J., & Kim, H. (2016). The Direct and Indirect Effects of Computer Uses on Student Success in Math. *International Journal of Cyber Behavior, Psychology and Learning*, 6(3), 48–64. doi:10.4018/IJCBPL.2016070104

Kiourt, C., Pavlidis, G., Koutsoudis, A., & Kalles, D. (2017). Realistic Simulation of Cultural Heritage. *International Journal of Computational Methods in Heritage Science*, 1(1), 10–40. doi:10.4018/IJCMHS.2017010102

Korikov, A., & Krivtsov, O. (2016). System of People-Computer: On the Way of Creation of Human-Oriented Interface. In V. Mkrttchian, A. Bershadsky, A. Bozhday, M. Kataev, & S. Kataev (Eds.), *Handbook of Research on Estimation and Control Techniques in E-Learning Systems* (pp. 458–470). Hershey, PA: IGI Global. doi:10.4018/978-1-4666-9489-7.ch032

Köse, U. (2017). An Augmented-Reality-Based Intelligent Mobile Application for Open Computer Education. In G. Kurubacak & H. Altinpulluk (Eds.), *Mobile Technologies and Augmented Reality in Open Education* (pp. 154–174). Hershey, PA: IGI Global. doi:10.4018/978-1-5225-2110-5.ch008

Lahmiri, S. (2018). Information Technology Outsourcing Risk Factors and Provider Selection. In M. Gupta, R. Sharman, J. Walp, & P. Mulgund (Eds.), *Information Technology Risk Management and Compliance in Modern Organizations* (pp. 214–228). Hershey, PA: IGI Global. doi:10.4018/978-1-5225-2604-9.ch008

Landriscina, F. (2017). Computer-Supported Imagination: The Interplay Between Computer and Mental Simulation in Understanding Scientific Concepts. In I. Levin & D. Tsybulsky (Eds.), *Digital Tools and Solutions for Inquiry-Based STEM Learning* (pp. 33–60). Hershey, PA: IGI Global. doi:10.4018/978-1-5225-2525-7.ch002

Lau, S. K., Winley, G. K., Leung, N. K., Tsang, N., & Lau, S. Y. (2016). An Exploratory Study of Expectation in IT Skills in a Developing Nation: Vietnam. *Journal of Global Information Management*, *24*(1), 1–13. doi:10.4018/JGIM.2016010101

Lavranos, C., Kostagiolas, P., & Papadatos, J. (2016). Information Retrieval Technologies and the "Realities" of Music Information Seeking. In I. Deliyannis, P. Kostagiolas, & C. Banou (Eds.), *Experimental Multimedia Systems for Interactivity and Strategic Innovation* (pp. 102–121). Hershey, PA: IGI Global. doi:10.4018/978-1-4666-8659-5.ch005

Lee, W. W. (2018). Ethical Computing Continues From Problem to Solution. In M. Khosrow-Pour, D.B.A. (Ed.), Encyclopedia of Information Science and Technology, Fourth Edition (pp. 4884-4897). Hershey, PA: IGI Global. doi:10.4018/978-1-5225-2255-3.ch423

Lehto, M. (2016). Cyber Security Education and Research in the Finland's Universities and Universities of Applied Sciences. *International Journal of Cyber Warfare & Terrorism*, *6*(2), 15–31. doi:10.4018/IJCWT.2016040102

Lin, C., Jalleh, G., & Huang, Y. (2016). Evaluating and Managing Electronic Commerce and Outsourcing Projects in Hospitals. In A. Dwivedi (Ed.), *Reshaping Medical Practice and Care with Health Information Systems* (pp. 132–172). Hershey, PA: IGI Global. doi:10.4018/978-1-4666-9870-3.ch005

Lin, S., Chen, S., & Chuang, S. (2017). Perceived Innovation and Quick Response Codes in an Online-to-Offline E-Commerce Service Model. *International Journal of E-Adoption*, *9*(2), 1–16. doi:10.4018/IJEA.2017070101

Liu, M., Wang, Y., Xu, W., & Liu, L. (2017). Automated Scoring of Chinese Engineering Students' English Essays. *International Journal of Distance Education Technologies*, *15*(1), 52–68. doi:10.4018/IJDET.2017010104

Luciano, E. M., Wiedenhöft, G. C., Macadar, M. A., & Pinheiro dos Santos, F. (2016). Information Technology Governance Adoption: Understanding its Expectations Through the Lens of Organizational Citizenship. *International Journal of IT/Business Alignment and Governance, 7*(2), 22-32. doi:10.4018/IJITBAG.2016070102

Mabe, L. K., & Oladele, O. I. (2017). Application of Information Communication Technologies for Agricultural Development through Extension Services: A Review. In T. Tossy (Ed.), *Information Technology Integration for Socio-Economic Development* (pp. 52–101). Hershey, PA: IGI Global. doi:10.4018/978-1-5225-0539-6.ch003

Manogaran, G., Thota, C., & Lopez, D. (2018). Human-Computer Interaction With Big Data Analytics. In D. Lopez & M. Durai (Eds.), *HCI Challenges and Privacy Preservation in Big Data Security* (pp. 1–22). Hershey, PA: IGI Global. doi:10.4018/978-1-5225-2863-0.ch001

Margolis, J., Goode, J., & Flapan, J. (2017). A Critical Crossroads for Computer Science for All: "Identifying Talent" or "Building Talent," and What Difference Does It Make? In Y. Rankin & J. Thomas (Eds.), *Moving Students of Color from Consumers to Producers of Technology* (pp. 1–23). Hershey, PA: IGI Global. doi:10.4018/978-1-5225-2005-4.ch001

Mbale, J. (2018). Computer Centres Resource Cloud Elasticity-Scalability (CRECES): Copperbelt University Case Study. In S. Aljawarneh & M. Malhotra (Eds.), *Critical Research on Scalability and Security Issues in Virtual Cloud Environments* (pp. 48–70). Hershey, PA: IGI Global. doi:10.4018/978-1-5225-3029-9.ch003

McKee, J. (2018). The Right Information: The Key to Effective Business Planning. In *Business Architectures for Risk Assessment and Strategic Planning: Emerging Research and Opportunities* (pp. 38–52). Hershey, PA: IGI Global. doi:10.4018/978-1-5225-3392-4.ch003

Mensah, I. K., & Mi, J. (2018). Determinants of Intention to Use Local E-Government Services in Ghana: The Perspective of Local Government Workers. *International Journal of Technology Diffusion*, 9(2), 41–60. doi:10.4018/IJTD.2018040103

Mohamed, J. H. (2018). Scientograph-Based Visualization of Computer Forensics Research Literature. In J. Jeyasekar & P. Saravanan (Eds.), *Innovations in Measuring and Evaluating Scientific Information* (pp. 148–162). Hershey, PA: IGI Global. doi:10.4018/978-1-5225-3457-0.ch010

Moore, R. L., & Johnson, N. (2017). Earning a Seat at the Table: How IT Departments Can Partner in Organizational Change and Innovation. *International Journal of Knowledge-Based Organizations*, *7*(2), 1–12. doi:10.4018/IJKBO.2017040101

Mtebe, J. S., & Kissaka, M. M. (2016). Enhancing the Quality of Computer Science Education with MOOCs in Sub-Saharan Africa. In J. Keengwe & G. Onchwari (Eds.), *Handbook of Research on Active Learning and the Flipped Classroom Model in the Digital Age* (pp. 366–377). Hershey, PA: IGI Global. doi:10.4018/978-1-4666-9680-8.ch019

Mukul, M. K., & Bhattaharyya, S. (2017). Brain-Machine Interface: Human-Computer Interaction. In E. Noughabi, B. Raahemi, A. Albadvi, & B. Far (Eds.), *Handbook of Research on Data Science for Effective Healthcare Practice and Administration* (pp. 417–443). Hershey, PA: IGI Global. doi:10.4018/978-1-5225-2515-8.ch018

Na, L. (2017). Library and Information Science Education and Graduate Programs in Academic Libraries. In L. Ruan, Q. Zhu, & Y. Ye (Eds.), *Academic Library Development and Administration in China* (pp. 218–229). Hershey, PA: IGI Global. doi:10.4018/978-1-5225-0550-1.ch013

Nabavi, A., Taghavi-Fard, M. T., Hanafizadeh, P., & Taghva, M. R. (2016). Information Technology Continuance Intention: A Systematic Literature Review. *International Journal of E-Business Research*, *12*(1), 58–95. doi:10.4018/IJEBR.2016010104

Nath, R., & Murthy, V. N. (2018). What Accounts for the Differences in Internet Diffusion Rates Around the World? In M. Khosrow-Pour, D.B.A. (Ed.), Encyclopedia of Information Science and Technology, Fourth Edition (pp. 8095-8104). Hershey, PA: IGI Global. doi:10.4018/978-1-5225-2255-3.ch705

Nedelko, Z., & Potocan, V. (2018). The Role of Emerging Information Technologies for Supporting Supply Chain Management. In M. Khosrow-Pour, D.B.A. (Ed.), Encyclopedia of Information Science and Technology, Fourth Edition (pp. 5559-5569). Hershey, PA: IGI Global. doi:10.4018/978-1-5225-2255-3.ch483

Ngafeeson, M. N. (2018). User Resistance to Health Information Technology. In M. Khosrow-Pour, D.B.A. (Ed.), Encyclopedia of Information Science and Technology, Fourth Edition (pp. 3816-3825). Hershey, PA: IGI Global. doi:10.4018/978-1-5225-2255-3.ch331

Nozari, H., Najafi, S. E., Jafari-Eskandari, M., & Aliahmadi, A. (2016). Providing a Model for Virtual Project Management with an Emphasis on IT Projects. In C. Graham (Ed.), *Strategic Management and Leadership for Systems Development in Virtual Spaces* (pp. 43–63). Hershey, PA: IGI Global. doi:10.4018/978-1-4666-9688-4.ch003

Nurdin, N., Stockdale, R., & Scheepers, H. (2016). Influence of Organizational Factors in the Sustainability of E-Government: A Case Study of Local E-Government in Indonesia. In I. Sodhi (Ed.), *Trends, Prospects, and Challenges in Asian E-Governance* (pp. 281–323). Hershey, PA: IGI Global. doi:10.4018/978-1-4666-9536-8.ch014

Odagiri, K. (2017). Introduction of Individual Technology to Constitute the Current Internet. In *Strategic Policy-Based Network Management in Contemporary Organizations* (pp. 20–96). Hershey, PA: IGI Global. doi:10.4018/978-1-68318-003-6.ch003

Okike, E. U. (2018). Computer Science and Prison Education. In I. Biao (Ed.), *Strategic Learning Ideologies in Prison Education Programs* (pp. 246–264). Hershey, PA: IGI Global. doi:10.4018/978-1-5225-2909-5.ch012

Olelewe, C. J., & Nwafor, I. P. (2017). Level of Computer Appreciation Skills Acquired for Sustainable Development by Secondary School Students in Nsukka LGA of Enugu State, Nigeria. In C. Ayo & V. Mbarika (Eds.), *Sustainable ICT Adoption and Integration for Socio-Economic Development* (pp. 214–233). Hershey, PA: IGI Global. doi:10.4018/978-1-5225-2565-3.ch010

Oliveira, M., Maçada, A. C., Curado, C., & Nodari, F. (2017). Infrastructure Profiles and Knowledge Sharing. *International Journal of Technology and Human Interaction*, *13*(3), 1–12. doi:10.4018/IJTHI.2017070101

Otarkhani, A., Shokouhyar, S., & Pour, S. S. (2017). Analyzing the Impact of Governance of Enterprise IT on Hospital Performance: Tehran's (Iran) Hospitals – A Case Study. *International Journal of Healthcare Information Systems and Informatics*, *12*(3), 1–20. doi:10.4018/IJHISI.2017070101

Otunla, A. O., & Amuda, C. O. (2018). Nigerian Undergraduate Students' Computer Competencies and Use of Information Technology Tools and Resources for Study Skills and Habits' Enhancement. In M. Khosrow-Pour, D.B.A. (Ed.), Encyclopedia of Information Science and Technology, Fourth Edition (pp. 2303-2313). Hershey, PA: IGI Global. doi:10.4018/978-1-5225-2255-3.ch200

Özçınar, H. (2018). A Brief Discussion on Incentives and Barriers to Computational Thinking Education. In H. Ozcinar, G. Wong, & H. Ozturk (Eds.), *Teaching Computational Thinking in Primary Education* (pp. 1–17). Hershey, PA: IGI Global. doi:10.4018/978-1-5225-3200-2.ch001

Pandey, J. M., Garg, S., Mishra, P., & Mishra, B. P. (2017). Computer Based Psychological Interventions: Subject to the Efficacy of Psychological Services. *International Journal of Computers in Clinical Practice*, 2(1), 25–33. doi:10.4018/IJCCP.2017010102

Parry, V. K., & Lind, M. L. (2016). Alignment of Business Strategy and Information Technology Considering Information Technology Governance, Project Portfolio Control, and Risk Management. *International Journal of Information Technology Project Management*, 7(4), 21–37. doi:10.4018/IJITPM.2016100102

Patro, C. (2017). Impulsion of Information Technology on Human Resource Practices. In P. Ordóñez de Pablos (Ed.), *Managerial Strategies and Solutions for Business Success in Asia* (pp. 231–254). Hershey, PA: IGI Global. doi:10.4018/978-1-5225-1886-0.ch013

Patro, C. S., & Raghunath, K. M. (2017). Information Technology Paraphernalia for Supply Chain Management Decisions. In M. Tavana (Ed.), *Enterprise Information Systems and the Digitalization of Business Functions* (pp. 294–320). Hershey, PA: IGI Global. doi:10.4018/978-1-5225-2382-6.ch014

Paul, P. K. (2016). Cloud Computing: An Agent of Promoting Interdisciplinary Sciences, Especially Information Science and I-Schools – Emerging Techno-Educational Scenario. In L. Chao (Ed.), *Handbook of Research on Cloud-Based STEM Education for Improved Learning Outcomes* (pp. 247–258). Hershey, PA: IGI Global. doi:10.4018/978-1-4666-9924-3.ch016

Paul, P. K. (2018). The Context of IST for Solid Information Retrieval and Infrastructure Building: Study of Developing Country. *International Journal of Information Retrieval Research*, *8*(1), 86–100. doi:10.4018/IJIRR.2018010106

Paul, P. K., & Chatterjee, D. (2018). iSchools Promoting "Information Science and Technology" (IST) Domain Towards Community, Business, and Society With Contemporary Worldwide Trend and Emerging Potentialities in India. In M. Khosrow-Pour, D.B.A. (Ed.), Encyclopedia of Information Science and Technology, Fourth Edition (pp. 4723-4735). Hershey, PA: IGI Global. doi:10.4018/978-1-5225-2255-3.ch410

Pessoa, C. R., & Marques, M. E. (2017). Information Technology and Communication Management in Supply Chain Management. In G. Jamil, A. Soares, & C. Pessoa (Eds.), *Handbook of Research on Information Management for Effective Logistics and Supply Chains* (pp. 23–33). Hershey, PA: IGI Global. doi:10.4018/978-1-5225-0973-8.ch002

Pineda, R. G. (2016). Where the Interaction Is Not: Reflections on the Philosophy of Human-Computer Interaction. *International Journal of Art, Culture and Design Technologies*, *5*(1), 1–12. doi:10.4018/IJACDT.2016010101

Pineda, R. G. (2018). Remediating Interaction: Towards a Philosophy of Human-Computer Relationship. In M. Khosrow-Pour (Ed.), *Enhancing Art, Culture, and Design With Technological Integration* (pp. 75–98). Hershey, PA: IGI Global. doi:10.4018/978-1-5225-5023-5.ch004

Poikela, P., & Vuojärvi, H. (2016). Learning ICT-Mediated Communication through Computer-Based Simulations. In M. Cruz-Cunha, I. Miranda, R. Martinho, & R. Rijo (Eds.), *Encyclopedia of E-Health and Telemedicine* (pp. 674–687). Hershey, PA: IGI Global. doi:10.4018/978-1-4666-9978-6.ch052

Qian, Y. (2017). Computer Simulation in Higher Education: Affordances, Opportunities, and Outcomes. In P. Vu, S. Fredrickson, & C. Moore (Eds.), *Handbook of Research on Innovative Pedagogies and Technologies for Online Learning in Higher Education* (pp. 236–262). Hershey, PA: IGI Global. doi:10.4018/978-1-5225-1851-8.ch011

Radant, O., Colomo-Palacios, R., & Stantchev, V. (2016). Factors for the Management of Scarce Human Resources and Highly Skilled Employees in IT-Departments: A Systematic Review. *Journal of Information Technology Research*, *9*(1), 65–82. doi:10.4018/JITR.2016010105

Rahman, N. (2016). Toward Achieving Environmental Sustainability in the Computer Industry. *International Journal of Green Computing*, 7(1), 37–54. doi:10.4018/IJGC.2016010103

Rahman, N. (2017). Lessons from a Successful Data Warehousing Project Management. *International Journal of Information Technology Project Management*, 8(4), 30–45. doi:10.4018/IJITPM.2017100103

Rahman, N. (2018). Environmental Sustainability in the Computer Industry for Competitive Advantage. In M. Khosrow-Pour (Ed.), *Green Computing Strategies for Competitive Advantage and Business Sustainability* (pp. 110–130). Hershey, PA: IGI Global. doi:10.4018/978-1-5225-5017-4.ch006

Rajh, A., & Pavetic, T. (2017). Computer Generated Description as the Required Digital Competence in Archival Profession. *International Journal of Digital Literacy and Digital Competence*, 8(1), 36–49. doi:10.4018/IJDLDC.2017010103

Raman, A., & Goyal, D. P. (2017). Extending IMPLEMENT Framework for Enterprise Information Systems Implementation to Information System Innovation. In M. Tavana (Ed.), *Enterprise Information Systems and the Digitalization of Business Functions* (pp. 137–177). Hershey, PA: IGI Global. doi:10.4018/978-1-5225-2382-6.ch007

Rao, Y. S., Rauta, A. K., Saini, H., & Panda, T. C. (2017). Mathematical Model for Cyber Attack in Computer Network. *International Journal of Business Data Communications and Networking*, 13(1), 58–65. doi:10.4018/IJBDCN.2017010105

Rapaport, W. J. (2018). Syntactic Semantics and the Proper Treatment of Computationalism. In M. Danesi (Ed.), *Empirical Research on Semiotics and Visual Rhetoric* (pp. 128–176). Hershey, PA: IGI Global. doi:10.4018/978-1-5225-5622-0.ch007

Raut, R., Priyadarshinee, P., & Jha, M. (2017). Understanding the Mediation Effect of Cloud Computing Adoption in Indian Organization: Integrating TAM-TOE- Risk Model. *International Journal of Service Science, Management, Engineering, and Technology*, 8(3), 40–59. doi:10.4018/IJSSMET.2017070103

Regan, E. A., & Wang, J. (2016). Realizing the Value of EHR Systems Critical Success Factors. *International Journal of Healthcare Information Systems and Informatics*, 11(3), 1–18. doi:10.4018/IJHISI.2016070101

Rezaie, S., Mirabedini, S. J., & Abtahi, A. (2018). Designing a Model for Implementation of Business Intelligence in the Banking Industry. *International Journal of Enterprise Information Systems, 14*(1), 77–103. doi:10.4018/IJEIS.2018010105

Rezende, D. A. (2016). Digital City Projects: Information and Public Services Offered by Chicago (USA) and Curitiba (Brazil). *International Journal of Knowledge Society Research, 7*(3), 16–30. doi:10.4018/IJKSR.2016070102

Rezende, D. A. (2018). Strategic Digital City Projects: Innovative Information and Public Services Offered by Chicago (USA) and Curitiba (Brazil). In M. Lytras, L. Daniela, & A. Visvizi (Eds.), *Enhancing Knowledge Discovery and Innovation in the Digital Era* (pp. 204–223). Hershey, PA: IGI Global. doi:10.4018/978-1-5225-4191-2.ch012

Riabov, V. V. (2016). Teaching Online Computer-Science Courses in LMS and Cloud Environment. *International Journal of Quality Assurance in Engineering and Technology Education, 5*(4), 12–41. doi:10.4018/IJQAETE.2016100102

Ricordel, V., Wang, J., Da Silva, M. P., & Le Callet, P. (2016). 2D and 3D Visual Attention for Computer Vision: Concepts, Measurement, and Modeling. In R. Pal (Ed.), *Innovative Research in Attention Modeling and Computer Vision Applications* (pp. 1–44). Hershey, PA: IGI Global. doi:10.4018/978-1-4666-8723-3.ch001

Rodriguez, A., Rico-Diaz, A. J., Rabuñal, J. R., & Gestal, M. (2017). Fish Tracking with Computer Vision Techniques: An Application to Vertical Slot Fishways. In M. S., & V. V. (Eds.), Multi-Core Computer Vision and Image Processing for Intelligent Applications (pp. 74-104). Hershey, PA: IGI Global. doi:10.4018/978-1-5225-0889-2.ch003

Romero, J. A. (2018). Sustainable Advantages of Business Value of Information Technology. In M. Khosrow-Pour, D.B.A. (Ed.), Encyclopedia of Information Science and Technology, Fourth Edition (pp. 923-929). Hershey, PA: IGI Global. doi:10.4018/978-1-5225-2255-3.ch079

Romero, J. A. (2018). The Always-On Business Model and Competitive Advantage. In N. Bajgoric (Ed.), *Always-On Enterprise Information Systems for Modern Organizations* (pp. 23–40). Hershey, PA: IGI Global. doi:10.4018/978-1-5225-3704-5.ch002

Rosen, Y. (2018). Computer Agent Technologies in Collaborative Learning and Assessment. In M. Khosrow-Pour, D.B.A. (Ed.), Encyclopedia of Information Science and Technology, Fourth Edition (pp. 2402-2410). Hershey, PA: IGI Global. doi:10.4018/978-1-5225-2255-3.ch209

Rosen, Y., & Mosharraf, M. (2016). Computer Agent Technologies in Collaborative Assessments. In Y. Rosen, S. Ferrara, & M. Mosharraf (Eds.), *Handbook of Research on Technology Tools for Real-World Skill Development* (pp. 319–343). Hershey, PA: IGI Global. doi:10.4018/978-1-4666-9441-5. ch012

Roy, D. (2018). Success Factors of Adoption of Mobile Applications in Rural India: Effect of Service Characteristics on Conceptual Model. In M. Khosrow-Pour (Ed.), *Green Computing Strategies for Competitive Advantage and Business Sustainability* (pp. 211–238). Hershey, PA: IGI Global. doi:10.4018/978-1-5225-5017-4.ch010

Ruffin, T. R. (2016). Health Information Technology and Change. In V. Wang (Ed.), *Handbook of Research on Advancing Health Education through Technology* (pp. 259–285). Hershey, PA: IGI Global. doi:10.4018/978-1-4666-9494-1.ch012

Ruffin, T. R. (2016). Health Information Technology and Quality Management. *International Journal of Information Communication Technologies and Human Development*, 8(4), 56–72. doi:10.4018/IJICTHD.2016100105

Ruffin, T. R., & Hawkins, D. P. (2018). Trends in Health Care Information Technology and Informatics. In M. Khosrow-Pour, D.B.A. (Ed.), Encyclopedia of Information Science and Technology, Fourth Edition (pp. 3805-3815). Hershey, PA: IGI Global. doi:10.4018/978-1-5225-2255-3.ch330

Safari, M. R., & Jiang, Q. (2018). The Theory and Practice of IT Governance Maturity and Strategies Alignment: Evidence From Banking Industry. *Journal of Global Information Management*, 26(2), 127–146. doi:10.4018/JGIM.2018040106

Sahin, H. B., & Anagun, S. S. (2018). Educational Computer Games in Math Teaching: A Learning Culture. In E. Toprak & E. Kumtepe (Eds.), *Supporting Multiculturalism in Open and Distance Learning Spaces* (pp. 249–280). Hershey, PA: IGI Global. doi:10.4018/978-1-5225-3076-3.ch013

Sanna, A., & Valpreda, F. (2017). An Assessment of the Impact of a Collaborative Didactic Approach and Students' Background in Teaching Computer Animation. *International Journal of Information and Communication Technology Education*, *13*(4), 1–16. doi:10.4018/IJICTE.2017100101

Savita, K., Dominic, P., & Ramayah, T. (2016). The Drivers, Practices and Outcomes of Green Supply Chain Management: Insights from ISO14001 Manufacturing Firms in Malaysia. *International Journal of Information Systems and Supply Chain Management*, *9*(2), 35–60. doi:10.4018/IJISSCM.2016040103

Scott, A., Martin, A., & McAlear, F. (2017). Enhancing Participation in Computer Science among Girls of Color: An Examination of a Preparatory AP Computer Science Intervention. In Y. Rankin & J. Thomas (Eds.), *Moving Students of Color from Consumers to Producers of Technology* (pp. 62–84). Hershey, PA: IGI Global. doi:10.4018/978-1-5225-2005-4.ch004

Shahsavandi, E., Mayah, G., & Rahbari, H. (2016). Impact of E-Government on Transparency and Corruption in Iran. In I. Sodhi (Ed.), *Trends, Prospects, and Challenges in Asian E-Governance* (pp. 75–94). Hershey, PA: IGI Global. doi:10.4018/978-1-4666-9536-8.ch004

Siddoo, V., & Wongsai, N. (2017). Factors Influencing the Adoption of ISO/IEC 29110 in Thai Government Projects: A Case Study. *International Journal of Information Technologies and Systems Approach*, *10*(1), 22–44. doi:10.4018/IJITSA.2017010102

Sidorkina, I., & Rybakov, A. (2016). Computer-Aided Design as Carrier of Set Development Changes System in E-Course Engineering. In V. Mkrttchian, A. Bershadsky, A. Bozhday, M. Kataev, & S. Kataev (Eds.), *Handbook of Research on Estimation and Control Techniques in E-Learning Systems* (pp. 500–515). Hershey, PA: IGI Global. doi:10.4018/978-1-4666-9489-7.ch035

Sidorkina, I., & Rybakov, A. (2016). Creating Model of E-Course: As an Object of Computer-Aided Design. In V. Mkrttchian, A. Bershadsky, A. Bozhday, M. Kataev, & S. Kataev (Eds.), *Handbook of Research on Estimation and Control Techniques in E-Learning Systems* (pp. 286–297). Hershey, PA: IGI Global. doi:10.4018/978-1-4666-9489-7.ch019

Simões, A. (2017). Using Game Frameworks to Teach Computer Programming. In R. Alexandre Peixoto de Queirós & M. Pinto (Eds.), *Gamification-Based E-Learning Strategies for Computer Programming Education* (pp. 221–236). Hershey, PA: IGI Global. doi:10.4018/978-1-5225-1034-5.ch010

Sllame, A. M. (2017). Integrating LAB Work With Classes in Computer Network Courses. In H. Alphin Jr, R. Chan, & J. Lavine (Eds.), *The Future of Accessibility in International Higher Education* (pp. 253–275). Hershey, PA: IGI Global. doi:10.4018/978-1-5225-2560-8.ch015

Smirnov, A., Ponomarev, A., Shilov, N., Kashevnik, A., & Teslya, N. (2018). Ontology-Based Human-Computer Cloud for Decision Support: Architecture and Applications in Tourism. *International Journal of Embedded and Real-Time Communication Systems*, 9(1), 1–19. doi:10.4018/IJERTCS.2018010101

Smith-Ditizio, A. A., & Smith, A. D. (2018). Computer Fraud Challenges and Its Legal Implications. In M. Khosrow-Pour, D.B.A. (Ed.), Encyclopedia of Information Science and Technology, Fourth Edition (pp. 4837-4848). Hershey, PA: IGI Global. doi:10.4018/978-1-5225-2255-3.ch419

Sohani, S. S. (2016). Job Shadowing in Information Technology Projects: A Source of Competitive Advantage. *International Journal of Information Technology Project Management*, 7(1), 47–57. doi:10.4018/IJITPM.2016010104

Sosnin, P. (2018). Figuratively Semantic Support of Human-Computer Interactions. In *Experience-Based Human-Computer Interactions: Emerging Research and Opportunities* (pp. 244–272). Hershey, PA: IGI Global. doi:10.4018/978-1-5225-2987-3.ch008

Spinelli, R., & Benevolo, C. (2016). From Healthcare Services to E-Health Applications: A Delivery System-Based Taxonomy. In A. Dwivedi (Ed.), *Reshaping Medical Practice and Care with Health Information Systems* (pp. 205–245). Hershey, PA: IGI Global. doi:10.4018/978-1-4666-9870-3.ch007

Srinivasan, S. (2016). Overview of Clinical Trial and Pharmacovigilance Process and Areas of Application of Computer System. In P. Chakraborty & A. Nagal (Eds.), *Software Innovations in Clinical Drug Development and Safety* (pp. 1–13). Hershey, PA: IGI Global. doi:10.4018/978-1-4666-8726-4.ch001

Srisawasdi, N. (2016). Motivating Inquiry-Based Learning Through a Combination of Physical and Virtual Computer-Based Laboratory Experiments in High School Science. In M. Urban & D. Falvo (Eds.), *Improving K-12 STEM Education Outcomes through Technological Integration* (pp. 108–134). Hershey, PA: IGI Global. doi:10.4018/978-1-4666-9616-7.ch006

Stavridi, S. V., & Hamada, D. R. (2016). Children and Youth Librarians: Competencies Required in Technology-Based Environment. In J. Yap, M. Perez, M. Ayson, & G. Entico (Eds.), *Special Library Administration, Standardization and Technological Integration* (pp. 25–50). Hershey, PA: IGI Global. doi:10.4018/978-1-4666-9542-9.ch002

Sung, W., Ahn, J., Kai, S. M., Choi, A., & Black, J. B. (2016). Incorporating Touch-Based Tablets into Classroom Activities: Fostering Children's Computational Thinking through iPad Integrated Instruction. In D. Mentor (Ed.), *Handbook of Research on Mobile Learning in Contemporary Classrooms* (pp. 378–406). Hershey, PA: IGI Global. doi:10.4018/978-1-5225-0251-7.ch019

Syväjärvi, A., Leinonen, J., Kivivirta, V., & Kesti, M. (2017). The Latitude of Information Management in Local Government: Views of Local Government Managers. *International Journal of Electronic Government Research*, *13*(1), 69–85. doi:10.4018/IJEGR.2017010105

Tanque, M., & Foxwell, H. J. (2018). Big Data and Cloud Computing: A Review of Supply Chain Capabilities and Challenges. In A. Prasad (Ed.), *Exploring the Convergence of Big Data and the Internet of Things* (pp. 1–28). Hershey, PA: IGI Global. doi:10.4018/978-1-5225-2947-7.ch001

Teixeira, A., Gomes, A., & Orvalho, J. G. (2017). Auditory Feedback in a Computer Game for Blind People. In T. Issa, P. Kommers, T. Issa, P. Isaías, & T. Issa (Eds.), *Smart Technology Applications in Business Environments* (pp. 134–158). Hershey, PA: IGI Global. doi:10.4018/978-1-5225-2492-2.ch007

Thompson, N., McGill, T., & Murray, D. (2018). Affect-Sensitive Computer Systems. In M. Khosrow-Pour, D.B.A. (Ed.), Encyclopedia of Information Science and Technology, Fourth Edition (pp. 4124-4135). Hershey, PA: IGI Global. doi:10.4018/978-1-5225-2255-3.ch357

Trad, A., & Kalpić, D. (2016). The E-Business Transformation Framework for E-Commerce Control and Monitoring Pattern. In I. Lee (Ed.), *Encyclopedia of E-Commerce Development, Implementation, and Management* (pp. 754–777). Hershey, PA: IGI Global. doi:10.4018/978-1-4666-9787-4.ch053

Triberti, S., Brivio, E., & Galimberti, C. (2018). On Social Presence: Theories, Methodologies, and Guidelines for the Innovative Contexts of Computer-Mediated Learning. In M. Marmon (Ed.), *Enhancing Social Presence in Online Learning Environments* (pp. 20–41). Hershey, PA: IGI Global. doi:10.4018/978-1-5225-3229-3.ch002

Tripathy, B. K. T. R., S., & Mohanty, R. K. (2018). Memetic Algorithms and Their Applications in Computer Science. In S. Dash, B. Tripathy, & A. Rahman (Eds.), Handbook of Research on Modeling, Analysis, and Application of Nature-Inspired Metaheuristic Algorithms (pp. 73-93). Hershey, PA: IGI Global. doi:10.4018/978-1-5225-2857-9.ch004

Turulja, L., & Bajgoric, N. (2017). Human Resource Management IT and Global Economy Perspective: Global Human Resource Information Systems. In M. Khosrow-Pour (Ed.), *Handbook of Research on Technology Adoption, Social Policy, and Global Integration* (pp. 377–394). Hershey, PA: IGI Global. doi:10.4018/978-1-5225-2668-1.ch018

Unwin, D. W., Sanzogni, L., & Sandhu, K. (2017). Developing and Measuring the Business Case for Health Information Technology. In K. Moahi, K. Bwalya, & P. Sebina (Eds.), *Health Information Systems and the Advancement of Medical Practice in Developing Countries* (pp. 262–290). Hershey, PA: IGI Global. doi:10.4018/978-1-5225-2262-1.ch015

Vadhanam, B. R. S., M., Sugumaran, V., V., V., & Ramalingam, V. V. (2017). Computer Vision Based Classification on Commercial Videos. In M. S., & V. V. (Eds.), Multi-Core Computer Vision and Image Processing for Intelligent Applications (pp. 105-135). Hershey, PA: IGI Global. doi:10.4018/978-1-5225-0889-2.ch004

Valverde, R., Torres, B., & Motaghi, H. (2018). A Quantum NeuroIS Data Analytics Architecture for the Usability Evaluation of Learning Management Systems. In S. Bhattacharyya (Ed.), *Quantum-Inspired Intelligent Systems for Multimedia Data Analysis* (pp. 277–299). Hershey, PA: IGI Global. doi:10.4018/978-1-5225-5219-2.ch009

Vassilis, E. (2018). Learning and Teaching Methodology: "1:1 Educational Computing. In K. Koutsopoulos, K. Doukas, & Y. Kotsanis (Eds.), *Handbook of Research on Educational Design and Cloud Computing in Modern Classroom Settings* (pp. 122–155). Hershey, PA: IGI Global. doi:10.4018/978-1-5225-3053-4.ch007

Wadhwani, A. K., Wadhwani, S., & Singh, T. (2016). Computer Aided Diagnosis System for Breast Cancer Detection. In Y. Morsi, A. Shukla, & C. Rathore (Eds.), *Optimizing Assistive Technologies for Aging Populations* (pp. 378–395). Hershey, PA: IGI Global. doi:10.4018/978-1-4666-9530-6.ch015

Wang, L., Wu, Y., & Hu, C. (2016). English Teachers' Practice and Perspectives on Using Educational Computer Games in EIL Context. *International Journal of Technology and Human Interaction, 12*(3), 33–46. doi:10.4018/IJTHI.2016070103

Watfa, M. K., Majeed, H., & Salahuddin, T. (2016). Computer Based E-Healthcare Clinical Systems: A Comprehensive Survey. *International Journal of Privacy and Health Information Management, 4*(1), 50–69. doi:10.4018/IJPHIM.2016010104

Weeger, A., & Haase, U. (2016). Taking up Three Challenges to Business-IT Alignment Research by the Use of Activity Theory. *International Journal of IT/Business Alignment and Governance, 7*(2), 1-21. doi:10.4018/IJITBAG.2016070101

Wexler, B. E. (2017). Computer-Presented and Physical Brain-Training Exercises for School Children: Improving Executive Functions and Learning. In B. Dubbels (Ed.), *Transforming Gaming and Computer Simulation Technologies across Industries* (pp. 206–224). Hershey, PA: IGI Global. doi:10.4018/978-1-5225-1817-4.ch012

Williams, D. M., Gani, M. O., Addo, I. D., Majumder, A. J., Tamma, C. P., Wang, M., ... Chu, C. (2016). Challenges in Developing Applications for Aging Populations. In Y. Morsi, A. Shukla, & C. Rathore (Eds.), *Optimizing Assistive Technologies for Aging Populations* (pp. 1–21). Hershey, PA: IGI Global. doi:10.4018/978-1-4666-9530-6.ch001

Wimble, M., Singh, H., & Phillips, B. (2018). Understanding Cross-Level Interactions of Firm-Level Information Technology and Industry Environment: A Multilevel Model of Business Value. *Information Resources Management Journal, 31*(1), 1–20. doi:10.4018/IRMJ.2018010101

Wimmer, H., Powell, L., Kilgus, L., & Force, C. (2017). Improving Course Assessment via Web-based Homework. *International Journal of Online Pedagogy and Course Design, 7*(2), 1–19. doi:10.4018/IJOPCD.2017040101

Wong, Y. L., & Siu, K. W. (2018). Assessing Computer-Aided Design Skills. In M. Khosrow-Pour, D.B.A. (Ed.), Encyclopedia of Information Science and Technology, Fourth Edition (pp. 7382-7391). Hershey, PA: IGI Global. doi:10.4018/978-1-5225-2255-3.ch642

Wongsurawat, W., & Shrestha, V. (2018). Information Technology, Globalization, and Local Conditions: Implications for Entrepreneurs in Southeast Asia. In P. Ordóñez de Pablos (Ed.), *Management Strategies and Technology Fluidity in the Asian Business Sector* (pp. 163–176). Hershey, PA: IGI Global. doi:10.4018/978-1-5225-4056-4.ch010

Yang, Y., Zhu, X., Jin, C., & Li, J. J. (2018). Reforming Classroom Education Through a QQ Group: A Pilot Experiment at a Primary School in Shanghai. In H. Spires (Ed.), *Digital Transformation and Innovation in Chinese Education* (pp. 211–231). Hershey, PA: IGI Global. doi:10.4018/978-1-5225-2924-8.ch012

Yilmaz, R., Sezgin, A., Kurnaz, S., & Arslan, Y. Z. (2018). Object-Oriented Programming in Computer Science. In M. Khosrow-Pour, D.B.A. (Ed.), Encyclopedia of Information Science and Technology, Fourth Edition (pp. 7470-7480). Hershey, PA: IGI Global. doi:10.4018/978-1-5225-2255-3.ch650

Yu, L. (2018). From Teaching Software Engineering Locally and Globally to Devising an Internationalized Computer Science Curriculum. In S. Dikli, B. Etheridge, & R. Rawls (Eds.), *Curriculum Internationalization and the Future of Education* (pp. 293–320). Hershey, PA: IGI Global. doi:10.4018/978-1-5225-2791-6.ch016

Yuhua, F. (2018). Computer Information Library Clusters. In M. Khosrow-Pour, D.B.A. (Ed.), Encyclopedia of Information Science and Technology, Fourth Edition (pp. 4399-4403). Hershey, PA: IGI Global. doi:10.4018/978-1-5225-2255-3.ch382

Zare, M. A., Taghavi Fard, M. T., & Hanafizadeh, P. (2016). The Assessment of Outsourcing IT Services using DEA Technique: A Study of Application Outsourcing in Research Centers. *International Journal of Operations Research and Information Systems, 7*(1), 45–57. doi:10.4018/IJORIS.2016010104

Zhao, J., Wang, Q., Guo, J., Gao, L., & Yang, F. (2016). An Overview on Passive Image Forensics Technology for Automatic Computer Forgery. *International Journal of Digital Crime and Forensics*, 8(4), 14–25. doi:10.4018/IJDCF.2016100102

Zimeras, S. (2016). Computer Virus Models and Analysis in M-Health IT Systems: Computer Virus Models. In A. Moumtzoglou (Ed.), *M-Health Innovations for Patient-Centered Care* (pp. 284–297). Hershey, PA: IGI Global. doi:10.4018/978-1-4666-9861-1.ch014

Zlatanovska, K. (2016). Hacking and Hacktivism as an Information Communication System Threat. In M. Hadji-Janev & M. Bogdanoski (Eds.), *Handbook of Research on Civil Society and National Security in the Era of Cyber Warfare* (pp. 68–101). Hershey, PA: IGI Global. doi:10.4018/978-1-4666-8793-6.ch004

About the Contributors

G. Nagarajan is presently working as Professor - School of EEE, Sathyabama Institute of Science and Technology, Chennai. He had received his BE degree in EEE from MS University 2000. He received his ME degree in Applied Electronic Engg. from Anna University 2005. He also received his ME degree in CSE from Sathyabama University in 2007. He obtained his Ph.D. degree in CSE from Sathyabama University2015. He has 15 years of teaching experience. He is a member of IAENG, IACSIT, IACSE. He has been reviewer of Elsevier Journal on International Journal of Electrical Power and Energy Systems, Springer Wireless Personal Communications, Taylor & Francis International Journal of Computers and Applications, IGI-Global -International Journal of Grid and High Performance Computing, Inderscience International Journal of Enterprise Network Management, World Review of Science, Technology and Sustainable Development. He has published more than 50 papers in refereed International Journals as well. His interests focus on Smart Grid, Internet of Things, Artificial Intelligent, Ontology Learning, Machine Leaning, NLP, Wireless Sensor Network and Computer Vision.

R. I. Minu is presently working as Associate Professor, Department of Computer Science and Engineering, SRM Institute of Science and Technology, Kattankulathur. She had received her BE degree in Electronic and Communication Engineering from Bharadhidasan University. She received her ME degree in Computer Science Engineering from Anna University. She obtained her Ph.D. degree in Computer Science Engineering from Anna University, her thesis titled "Ontology Enhanced Image retrieval for Semantic Web". She has 13 years of teaching experience. She is an active participant of IIT-Bombay e-Yantra project initiative (Robotic), also she received the funding from MHRD for setup robotics lab. Some of her projects are funded by TNSCST student Projects Scheme and CSI students chapter had recognized her project. She is a life time member of ISTE,CSI,ACM, IAENG, IACSIT, IACSE She is on Editorial Board Member of International Journal on Integrating Technology in Education and The International Journal of Chaos, Control, Modeling and Simulation. She is a reviewer of journals such as Elsevier's Data & Knowledge Engineering Journal, Springer Wireless Personal Communications, Taylor & Francis International Journal of Computers and Applications, IGI-Global -International Journal of Grid and High Performance Computing, Inderscience International Journal of Enterprise Network Management and so on She has published more than 50 research papers in refereed International Journals and International Conferences as well. Her thirst areas are Internet of Things, Smart Grid, Edge Computing, Artificial Intelligent, Ontology Learning, Machine Leaning, Wireless Sensor Network and Computer Vision.

* * *

Alice Nithya A. holds a Ph.D. degree in Computer Science and Engineering from SRM IST and is currently working in the Department of Computer Science & Engineering, SRM IST. Her main area of interest includes pattern recognition, image processing, machine learning, IOT and Big data analytics. She has published several papers in well-known peer-reviewed journals.

Pravin A. received the B.E degree in Computer Science & Engineering from Bharath Niketan Engineering College, Madurai Kamaraj University, Madurai, India in 2003, M.E degree in Computer Science & Engineering from Sathyabama University, Chennai, India in 2005 and Ph.D degree in Computer Science & Engineering at Sathyabama University, Chennai, India in 2014. He works currently as an Assistant Professor for the Department of Computer Science and Engineering at Sathyabama Institute of Science and Technology, Chennai and he has 14 Years of teaching experience. He has participated and presented many Research Papers in International and National Conferences and also published many papers in International and National Journals. His area of interests includes Software Engineering, Image Processing, Data mining, Internet of Things and Big data.

Suresh A. obtained his M.E degree from Sathyabama University, Chennai in 2005 and Ph.D. degree from Sathyabama University in the year 2012. His area of interest is Induction Heating. He has 16 years of teaching experience in Engineering College and a member in various social bodies like IET, ISTE and GEPRA. He has published more than 100 papers in the area of Power Electronics, Power Systems, Network Security and Data Mining. He has received Indira Gandhi Sadbavana Gold Medal award in 2014.He is currently working as a Professor at SA Engineering College, Chennai, India.

Vinothini Arumugam is working as an Assistant Professor in Rajalakshmi Engineering College, Chennai. She Completed M.Tech (IT)in Anna University, Coimbatore and B.Tech (IT) in Karpagam College of Engineering, Coimbatore. She is currently pursuing PhD in Anna University, Chennai. She is a university third rank holder in PG. Her area of interest embraces Data Mining, Machine Learning, Big Data Analytics etc. She has published papers in reputed journals in those areas.

Lakshmi C. holds a Ph.D. in Computer Science and Engineering from SRM University and is professor in the Department of Software Engineering, SRM IST. Her main area of interest includes pattern recognition, image processing, machine learning and web services. She is a Life Member of the Indian Society for Technical Education (ISTE), International Association of Computer Science and Information Technology, Singapore and International Association of Engineers-IAENG, Hong Kong. She has published several papers in well known peer reviewed journals.

R. Dhanasekaran is a Professor in Electrical and Electronics Engineering Department and Director - Research at Syed Ammal Engineering College, Ramanathapuram, Tamilnadu, India. He has published 160 papers in International Journals, 80 Papers in International Conferences and 70 papers in National Conferences. His areas of interest are EMI, EMC, Image Processing and Control Systems. He is a Fellow member of IETE and Senior Member of IEEE.

Matheus Breno dos Santos is an Internet Systems' undergraduate student in Federal Institute of Education, Science, and Technology of Brasilia. Web development, RAD, Python, Java and R skills. Scientific research covers Data Science, Machine Learning, and Cloud Computing.

Geetha G. is a professor and head of the department with 15 yrs. of teaching experience. her research interest includes mobile ad hoc networks and data management.

Arindam Gogoi holds his bachelors degree in Software Engineering from SRM Institute of Science and Technology. His area of interest is Internet of Things.

Sundari Govindarajan is a professor in Department of Electronics and Communication Engineering, Sathyabama Institute of Science and Technology where her research and teaching focusses on image processing and wireless sensor networks. She is a author/co-author over 50 publications. She is a member of IEEE, IETE and ISTE.

T. Prem Jacob received the B.E degree in Computer Science and Engineering from C.S.I Institute of Technology, Manonmaniam Sundaranar University, Nagercoil, India in 2004, M.E degree in Computer Science and Engineering from Sathyabama University, Chennai, Indiain 2006 and Ph.D. degree from Sathyabama University, Chennai, India. He works currently as an Associate Professor of Computer Science and Engineering in Sathyabama Institute of Science and Technology Chennai. He has participated and presented many Research Papers in International and National Conferences. The area of interests includes Software Engineering, Data mining and Data warehouse, Networks, Machine Learning, Deep Learning, and Cloud computing. Published more than 40 research articles in reputed journals.

Femilda Josephin holds a PhD in Information and Communication Engineering from Anna University, Chennai, India during 2015. Currently she is working as an Associate Professor in SRM Institute of Science and Technology India. She has 8 years of research and 14 years of teaching experience. Her area of research includes network routing, security in networks and IOT. At present she is working on prediction and classification using machine learning. She has published 12 research papers at International level. She is the reviewer for more than 4 International journals. She has guided more than 20 batches of students at both undergraduate and post graduate level.

Pradheep Kumar K. is working as Assistant Professor in BITS Pilani. His areas of interest include Artificial Intelligence, Machine Learning, IoT, Data Analytics, Multicore Programming, Edge Computing. He has worked as a database administrator in Oracle. He was a recipient of CSIR SRF award. He has 2 patents to his credit.

Marianna Kapari holds a MSc in Human Computer Interaction from Uppsala University, Sweden, a BSc degree in Computer Science from London Metropolitan University, UK, and a BA in Communication from the American College of Greece. Marianna joined INFOLYSiS as Frontend and digital media developer with experience in web technologies (HTML, CSS, PHP, Javascript, MySQL), prototyping tools (InVision, Balsamiq Mockups, Axure, WireframeSketcher), video editing (Adobe Premier, Ulead VideoStudio, Cyberlink Power Director) and software design tools with UML. Her research interests include IoT interoperability and IoT GW frontends with emphasis on novel HCI technologies, such as Chatbots with Machine Learning techniques.

Ramgopal Kashyap's areas of interest are image processing, pattern recognition, and machine learning. He has published many research papers in international journals and conferences like Springer, Inderscience, Elsevier, ACM, and IGI-Global indexed by Science Citation Index (SCI) and Scopus (Elsevier) and many book chapters. He has Reviewed Research Papers in the Science Citation Index Expanded, Springer Journals and Editorial Board Member and conferences programme committee member of the IEEE, Springer international conferences and journals held in countries: Czech Republic, Switzerland, UAE, Australia, Hungary, Poland, Taiwan, Denmark, India, USA, UK, Austria, and Turkey. He has written many book chapters published by IGI Global, USA.

Harilaos Koumaras is a research assistant professor at NCSR De-mokritos. Dr. Koumaras in an active researcher in the field of 5G, Mobile Communications, including video and picture quality assessment, quality of experience (QoE), video traffic modeling, digital terrestrial television and video compression techniques. Within this framework, Dr. Koumaras is an active member of the Interest Group (IG) on QoE for Multimedia Communications of IEEE Multimedia Communication Technical Com-mittee. During the last years Dr. Koumaras has developed consulting and project management activities by participating in research and industry projects.

Vaios Koumaras received his BSc degree in Business Administration with major in Computer Information Systems from the American College of Greece and his MBA in IT Project Management from the City University, USA. Since 1997, he has worked in several positions as Computer Analyst and Software Developer, participating in major IT projects. Currently, he is the managing director of INFOLYSIS P.C., with participation and collaboration in R&D IT projects of numerous companies worldwide, mainly in the applicability of IoT on top of virtualized infrastructures mainly in the shipping sector for optimizing the cargo containers embark-ing process and choosing the optimal route, subject to the load and the weather/sea factors. Moreover, Mr. Koumaras is specialized in the IoT interoperability provision, researching also the applicability with novel SDN/NFV techniques.

Murali M. has completed his M.Tech degree from M.S. University, Tamilnadu on 2004. Further he has completed Ph.D degree in SRM Uni-versity. His area of interest is Data Mining, Machine Learning, Cloud Computing and Internet of Things. He has published more than 20 papers in refereed journals. Currently he is guiding six research scholars. He has registered a patent on Internet of Things.

Vimaladevi M. completed UG in Computer Science and PG in Computer Science and Engineering at Velalar College of Engineering and Technol-ogy, Doctorate in Information and Communication Engineering at Anna University, Chennai. Published research papers on various international journals and presented papers in various conferences.

Nilamadhab Mishra is an Assistant Professor in Post Graduate Teaching & Research Dept., at School of Computing, Debre Berhan University, Ministry of Education, Government of Ethiopia (Africa). He has 16+ years of International Involvement in Academic Teaching & Research across recognized Indian, Taiwan, and African Universities. He Publishes over twenty researches in SCI/SCIE & SCOPUS indexed Journals; other peer-reviewed Journals; ISBN Book; IEEE Conference proceedings; and Serves as the Reviewer and Editorial Member in peer-reviewed Journals and Conferences. He receives his, Master degree in Computer Applications (MCA) from Utkal University, Orissa, India in 2002; Master of Technology (M. Tech) in Computer Science & Engineering from Biju Patnaik University of Technology, Orissa, India in 2011; Doctor of Philosophy (PhD) in Computer Science & Information Engineering from Chang Gung University (CGU), Taiwan in June 2016. {[CGU is under QS World University Ranking - 429 (2019)]; [Times Higher Education World University Ranking - 601-800 (2019)]}. Dr. Mishra is the recipient of multiple research fellowships from the Ministry of Education (MOE), Taiwan, Ministry of Science and Technology (MOST), Taiwan, and CGU, Taiwan during his Ph.D. He has also worked on multiple funded research projects from the MOST, NSC, and CGU Memorial Hospital, Taiwan. He has significant research contributions in the field of IoT network centric big-data analytics integrates with Cognitive Apps Policy & Explorations. The works have been published in reputed SCI journals. He is associated with Academic Teaching & Research by functioning as a Research Committee Member; Master Thesis Examiner; University Curriculum Revision Committee Member; Course Instructor; University Question Setter; Master Program Evaluator; Journal Editor; SCIE & Scopus indexed Journals Referee; ISBN Book Author; and IEEE Conference Referee. He has been pro-involved with several professional bodies: Life Member of "CSI"; Member of "ORCID"; Member of "IAENG"; Fellow Member of "ISROSET"; Fellow Member of "ISRD"; Senior Member of "ASR" (Hong Kong); Senior Member of "IEDRC" (Hong Kong); and Member of "IEEE Collabratec". He has qualified Test of English as International Communication (TOEIC); Listed in Marquis who's who Publications Biography; Featured as a Top Author in PubFacts.com; and recorded in World Book of Researchers 2018, published at Oxford, United Kingdom. His Research areas incorporate Network Centric Data Analytics & Exploration, Data Science: Analytics and Applications, IoT Big-Data Applications, and Cognitive Apps Policy & Explorations.

Bruno Neves de Castro is an Internet Systems' undergraduate student in Federal Institute of Education, Science, and Technology of Brasilia. Web development, RAD, Python, Java and R skills. Scientific research covers Data Science, Machine Learning, and Cloud Computing.

Angeliki Papaioannou studied Physics and Computer Science at the National and Kapodistrian University of Athens and received her B.Sc. in Physics in 2003 and her M.Sc. in Electronics and Automation with specialization in Informatics and Information Systems in 2010. Angeliki has worked for LogicDIS as Software Engineer and later as Product Manager of Securities ERP. In 2017, she joined as an associate software engineer INFOLYSiS, developing various IoT applications of INFOLYSiS portofolio, using Arduino nodes, Zigbee, web, mobile and Java tools. Her current research interests include interoperability IoT mapping functions for heterogeneous IoT platforms, SDN, NFV, Cloud Computing, IoT infrastructures, Monitoring systems and web/mobile applications.

Iman Raeesi Vanani is a PhD Graduate in Systems Management, School of Management, University of Tehran. He is currently an assistant professor in Allameh Tabataba'i University. He received his MSc in Information Technology Management from School of Management, University of Tehran and his BA in Public Administration from Allameh Tabataba'i University. His research interests include Data Science, Advanced Analytics, Business Intelligence, Data Mining, Enterprise Resource Planning, and Big Data Management. He has published many conceptual and practical research papers in various international journals, conference proceedings, and books including International Journal of Hospitality Management, Neural Computing and Applications, The IUP Journal of Knowledge Management, Intelligent Engineering Informatics, Iranian Management Vision Journal, Iranian Journal of Science and Technology Policy, Journal of Information Technology and Sciences, Information Science Reference Publications, and other international and Iranian journals, Books and conferences.

Mamata Rath, M.Tech, Ph.D (Comp.Sc), has twelve years of experience in teaching as well as in research and her research interests include Mobile Adhoc Networks, Internet of Things, Ubiquitous Computing, VANET and Computer Security.

Mehrzad Rezaei Nayeri is a D.A student of information Technology Management in Allameh Tabataba'i University. He received his MS in Information Technology Management from Payame noor university of Tehran. He received his B.E in Electronic Engineering from Islamic Azad University, South Tehran Branch. His research interests include Data Science, Internet of Things (IOT), and Big Data Management. He is currently an IT Expert in Telecommunication Infrastructure Company. He is familiar with telecommunication equipment. He is also involved in data transmission and switching systems, IPv6 and data center maintenance.

Fabio Rossi has a PhD in Computer Science from the Pontifical Catholic University of Rio Grande do Sul (2016) with a sandwich period at the University of Melbourne, Australia (2014-2015). He received his Master's degree in Computer Science from the same University in 2008. He holds a Bachelor's Degree in Computer Science (2000) and a Specialist in Educational Management (2002) from the University of the Region of Campaign. Professor at the Farroupilha Federal Institute - Alegrete Campus, his research interests include cloud computing, computing resource management, virtualization, and energy-saving techniques. Cisco Certified Network Associate (CCNA) Instructor.

Baghavathi Priya S. is a Professor of Information Technology at Rajalakshmi Engineering College since 2008. She graduated B.E Computer Science & Engineering from Manonmaniam Sundranar University,M. Tech Computer Science & Engineering from Dr.M.G.R Educational and Research Institute. She received Ph.D. from Jawaharlal Nehru Technological University Hyderabad. She has guided many U.G and P.G projects. She has published over 40 peer reviewed research articles. Her research is focused on Grid Computing, Network Security, Machine learning and Big Data Analytics. She received gold medal in M.Tech degree. She received best paper award in ICTIS 2015 at Ahmedabad and in CAASR International conference 2017 at Dubai. She visited several countries for presenting papers and chairing sessions. She is a Life time member in CSI and IAENG.

Thilagamani S. received the B.E. degree in Computer Science and Engineering from Periyar University, Salem, Tamil Nadu, India in 2002, M.E. degree in Computer Science and Engineering from Anna University, Chennai, Tamil Nadu, India in 2007 and secured university second rank, Ph.D. degree in Information and Communication Engineering from Anna University, Chennai, Tamil Nadu, India in 2014. She has teaching experience of about 15years. Presently working as Dean - Department of Computer Science & Engineering in M.Kumarasamy College of Engineering, Karur. She has published 14 papers in the reputed international journals, 13 papers in the International conferences and 02 papers in the National conferences. She has published 1 Copy Right and 3 books. She has received many awards for teaching and education Excellence. Few of the outstanding awards are teaching awards in Engineering from Staffordshire University, UK and Education Matters & Excellence Teaching in Higher Education- Award from AIRF –Arunai International Women researchers Connect and Awards in 2018. She is an active member of CSI and coordinator of CSI student branch. She is well connected with industries like Infosys, TCS etc as a SPOC. Her area of interest is Data Mining and Image Processing. She is a Research supervisor under Anna University Chennai and guiding 8 Research Scholars at present.

Christos Sakkas received his BSc degree in Informatics and his MSc degree in Computer Science from Department of Informatics of Athens University of Economics and Business (AUEB). Mr. Sakkas has been an active research associate of Media Net Lab at the NCSR "Demokritos" from 2013 until 2018. Since 2018 he has joined the R&D team of INFOLYSiS P.C. He has participated in many EU-funded projects, collaborating with various universities and enterprises with presentations and publications at international conferences. His current research interests include IoT, SDN, NFV, Cloud Computing, Monitoring systems and web/mobile applications.

Aman Sharma completed his B.tech in the Department of Software Engineering in SRM Institute of Science and Technology.

343

V. J. K. Kishor Sonti has done research in MicroElectronics. He is a teacher by profession, writer, poet and motivational speaker. He has written many international and naitonal journals and Co-authored a book on Mechatronics and hand book on Electronics. He has delivered numerous lectures on Vedic Engineering, Perception Listening, Artificial Intelligence and Motivational Talks. He is a life member of IETE, ISNT, and ISOI. He is the reviewer for reputed international and national journals.

Ioannis Stergiou holds a BSc degree in Agriculture Engineering from the Aristotle University of Thessaloniki, Greece and a MSc degree in Agriculture and Environmental Sciences from the University of the Aegean, Greece. Since 2010, Ioannis has worked as agronomist and technical support IT officer at various agricultural commerce trade and IT related companies with focus on GIS and IoT smart farming through the use of IT systems for monitoring crop fields with the help of IoT sensors (light, humidity, temperature, soil moisture, etc.) and automating the irrigation systems and methodologies.

George Theodoropoulos holds a BSc degree in Mathematics from the University of Athens, Greece. George has more than thirty years professional experience as computer analyst and programmer in the shipping sector participating in various research and development IT projects related to maritime software, vessel communications as well as vessel data transfer and data synchronization with offshore offices. Currently, he is a senior research and development engineer dealing with the applicability of IoT in the shipping sector.

M. Ferni Ukrit holds a Ph.D in Computer Science and Engineering from Sathyabama Institute of Science and Technology Chennai, India. She is working as Assistant Professor in SRM Institute of Science and Technology. She received her M.E (CSE) from Sathyabama University in 2006 and B.E (CSE) from M.S University, Nagercoil, India in 2002. Her current research interests include Medical Image Compression, Image Processing, Machine Learning and IOT. She has published several papers in well-known peer-reviewed journals.

Kavitha V. has completed her Doctoral degree in the year 2018 in Anna University, Chennai and she has completed her ME degree in 2009 in Anna University, Coimbatore. Her research area includes Data science, Data Mining, and IoT.

Srini Vasan is working as a Professor in the Department of Computer Science and Engineering, Sathyabama Institute of Science and Technology. His areas of interests are web search personalisation, data mining, software reliability, software architecture, medical image processing, IoT, edge computing, artificial intelligence.

Index

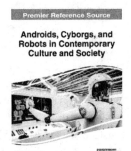

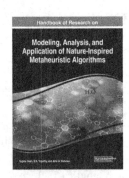

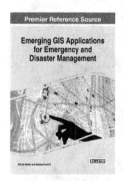
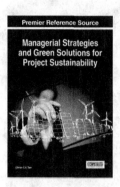

Printed in the United States
By Bookmasters